KORNGOLD AND HIS WORLD

KORNGOLD
AND HIS WORLD

EDITED BY
DANIEL GOLDMARK AND
KEVIN C. KARNES

PRINCETON UNIVERSITY PRESS
PRINCETON AND OXFORD

Copyright © 2019 by Princeton University Press

Published by Princeton University Press, 41 William Street,
Princeton, New Jersey 08540
In the United Kingdom: Princeton University Press,
6 Oxford Street, Woodstock, Oxfordshire OX20 1TW
press.princeton.edu

All Rights Reserved

For permissions/credits, see page xv

Library of Congress Control Number: 2019939962

Cloth ISBN: 978-0-691-19828-6
Paper ISBN: 978-0-691-19829-3

British Library Cataloging-in-Publication Data is available

This publication has been produced by the Bard College Publications Office:
Mary Smith, Director
Irene Zedlacher, Project Director
Karen Walker Spencer, Designer
Text edited by Paul De Angelis and Erin Clermont
Music typeset by Christopher Deschene
Indexed by Scott Smiley

This publication has been underwritten in part by a grant from Roger and Helen Alcaly

1 3 5 7 9 10 8 6 4 2

Contents

Preface and Acknowledgments	ix
Permissions and Credits	xv

ESSAYS

Korngold Father and Son in Vienna's Prewar Public Eye DAVID BRODBECK	3
"You must return to life": Notes on the Reception of *Das Wunder der Heliane* and *Jonny spielt auf* CHARLES YOUMANS	37
Acoustic Space, Modern Interiority, and Korngold's Cities SHERRY LEE AND SADIE MENICANIN	67
Korngold and Jewish Identity in Concert LILY E. HIRSCH	89
New Opportunities in Film: Korngold and Warner Bros. BEN WINTERS	111
"The caverns of the human mind are full of strange shadows": Disability Representation, Henry Bellamann, and Korngold's Musical Subtexts in the Score for *Kings Row* NEIL LERNER	131
American and Austrian Ruins in Korngold's Symphony in F-sharp AMY LYNN WLODARSKI	167

DOCUMENTS

Recollections of Zemlinsky from My Years of Study   193
ERICH WOLFGANG KORNGOLD
TRANSLATED BY ELISABETH STAAK AND DAVID BRODBECK
INTRODUCED AND ANNOTATED BY DAVID BRODBECK

Notes for an Interview   201
ERICH WOLFGANG KORNGOLD
TRANSLATED BY ELISABETH STAAK
EDITED AND INTRODUCED BY KEVIN C. KARNES

A Farewell to Vienna   207
LUZI KORNGOLD
TRANSLATED BY ELISABETH STAAK
INTRODUCED BY KEVIN C. KARNES

Composing for the Pictures: An Interview   223
INTRODUCED BY DANIEL GOLDMARK

"Give up your plans of coming home":   233
Letters of a Viennese Father to His Son
JULIUS KORNGOLD
TRANSLATED BY ELISABETH STAAK
INTRODUCED BY BRYAN GILLIAM
EDITED AND ANNOTATED BY KEVIN C. KARNES

Some Experiences in Film Music   247
ERICH WOLFGANG KORNGOLD
EDITED AND INTRODUCED BY DANIEL GOLDMARK

Faith in Music!   255
ERICH WOLFGANG KORNGOLD
INTRODUCED BY KEVIN C. KARNES

CODA

Before and After Auschwitz: 263
Korngold and the Art and Politics of the Twentieth Century
LEON BOTSTEIN

Index   315

Notes on Contributors   327

Preface and Acknowledgments

The life of the composer Erich Wolfgang Korngold (1897–1957) is often described as having unfolded in two distinct, even melodramatic acts. The first stars a wunderkind whose prodigious and unusually mature works brought him, in nearly equal measure, international acclaim and disdain, the latter on account of the outsized reputation and overbearing nature of his father Julius, then widely regarded as Vienna's most powerful music critic. This first act came to an abrupt end with the Anschluss of 1938, which prompted the permanent resettlement of the extended Korngold family in California, where the second act is said to have commenced. In fact, it had already begun there a few years earlier: a one-time experiment with writing music for a Hollywood film in 1935 had laid the groundwork to score other films, most notably the blockbuster *The Adventures of Robin Hood* (1938), which brought the composer back to the States in January of the fateful year. The composer's parents, eldest son, and in-laws would join him, his wife Luzi, and their younger son in Hollywood shortly thereafter.

Looking back, one can clearly see the many links that bind the two acts. In the 1920s and 1930s, momentous changes were taking place in both the European and the American markets for classical music. In Vienna and Berlin, as in New York and Los Angeles, American popular music, and the sounds of jazz in particular, were on the rise in concert halls and on operatic stages. Ernst Krenek's *Jonny spielt auf* (1927) is perhaps the most famous example, but Korngold himself brought echoes of the dance hall into the reorchestrations of operettas by Johann Strauss that he prepared for the Vienna theater in the 1920s. These same years also saw an explosion of interest in cinema on both sides of the Atlantic, as the production of soundtracks mixing classical and popular idioms brought both to center stage together.

Korngold's career in film was anything but typical. While the vanguard of music composition in today's media-rich environment resides in music written for film, television, video games, and other formats, only a handful of well-known composers in the early twentieth century—Prokofiev, Saint-Saëns, and Vaughan Williams, among others—had ventured into the new technology of film. Korngold thus arrived in Hollywood as a double anomaly: not only was he a wunderkind, but his continued success—long outlasting the novelty of his precocious youth—made him the only film composer in Hollywood who could be considered both a legitimate talent by music critics and also popular enough to be familiar to mainstream audiences.

From 1938 until the end of his life, Korngold lived in Hollywood, but he held out hope that he and his family might someday return to Europe, where he dreamed of reconnecting with his earlier life as a composer for the stage and concert hall. The Korngolds did in fact return, but the composer's dream eluded him. Simply put, too much had changed while they were away. Audiences and critics had moved on from the style of his concert music, which had remained largely unchanged since the 1920s. And his success in Hollywood had tarred him for many as a commercial composer, and therefore not one to be taken seriously. His early death, just a few months after his sixtieth birthday, was an all-too-apt end to the disillusionment that had come to shadow his life.

Over the next half-century, Korngold's works largely disappeared from the concert repertoire, and his film scores, while critically lauded, were only heard during the occasional revival of the films themselves. It was not until 1972 that a rise of interest in classic Hollywood film scores led to what would turn out to be the momentous issue of an LP, *The Classic Film Scores of Erich Wolfgang Korngold*, conducted by Charles Gerhardt and produced by Korngold's younger son, George, who had followed his father into the film industry as a music editor. The success of that recording, along with the contemporaneous rise of the instrumentally fecund, "neo-classical" style of film scoring epitomized by John Williams's work in *Jaws* (1975), *Close Encounters of the Third Kind* (1977), and *Star Wars* (1977), focused new light on Korngold's music. Soon, an authorized biography was underway, compiled by Brendan G. Carroll with cooperation from the Korngold family. Korngold's works gradually began to reappear on concert programs and opera stages. Old recordings were remastered and reissued. New recording projects were underway.

And yet, as all of us who have contributed to this book hope emphatically to show, there is still a tremendous amount that we do not understand or appreciate about Korngold's story, and just as much that his story can still teach us about the times he lived in and the spaces he knew. It is only now, more than twenty years after the publication of Carroll's biography, that musicians and scholars are returning broadly to the mass of documents in the composer's estate, most of which are held at the Library of Congress in Washington. Many of these remain largely unexamined, and the questions we are accustomed to asking about the music we perform and the composers we admire have changed as well. Studies of migration, diaspora, and refugee experience now shape our thinking about wartime culture, and we have amassed a bookshelf full of publications on émigré musicians and artists in Los Angeles. Jewish studies has emerged as a central concern of musicology; prewar Vienna is now widely appreciated as a deeply contested, multicultural space; and studying film music has become not only respectable but mainstream. As we approach the 125th anniversary of Korngold's birth, the time feels right for a reassessment of his experience and his contributions. The essays, translations, and archival documents in this book are presented with this goal in mind.

We find some expected themes that emerge throughout the essays in *Korngold and His World*. Not only does the old vs. new world narrative play a central role, but the fine line between artistic endeavor and popular pleasures also surfaces, especially when considering how often his work straddled the impossibly wavy line between high and low art. The first three essays address the struggle Korngold faced with critics, the public, and his family—especially his father—as he tried to establish himself as a composer, just as the musical terrain around him was undergoing seismic shifts of taste and technique. His travels between Vienna and Hollywood in 1934–38 and the rising threat of war only added to the instability in Korngold's life, and yet his output remained constant, even as he began work in the new (to him) field of film music. Korngold's more atypical qualities as a composer for film tend to be overlooked in favor of the romantic, adrenalin-infused scenes of sword and storm that dominated the films with which he made his name in Hollywood: *Captain Blood*, *The Adventures of Robin Hood*, and *The Sea Hawk*. Two essays look at different elements of Korngold's compositional palette that made his scores innovative both in the 1940s and today, while another addresses some of the ways in which Korngold's Jewish parentage shaped his identity as a composer. The coda brings all of these themes together, assessing Korngold's experience and contributions against the broader social and cultural currents through which he lived and traveled.

These essays are complemented by a selection of documents that provide glimpses of Korngold's experiences and views as recorded by family or the composer himself over the course of his life. Some of these appear here for the first time in English translation, and one has never before been published. Others are brought together from the now obscure and hard-to-find journals and books in which they first appeared. From Korngold himself we learn about his studies with his teacher Alexander von Zemlinsky around 1910, and his thoughts, probably recorded around

1930, about the music of Schoenberg, Stravinsky, and other contemporary composers. We also include two of his statements about composing music for films made just after he settled in California, as well as his last published words, on music and faith, penned shortly before his death. From a selection of letters Julius sent his son from Vienna just before and after the Anschluss, we may begin to fathom the trauma and uncertainty the family experienced on both sides of the Atlantic in the terrible year. Finally, selections from the memoirs of Erich's wife Luzi remind us of the strength of the bonds that tied the family together through the experience of displacement and emigration.

All books come together only with the help of a significant cast of characters, and collaborations like this one depend even more strongly on the efforts of many. The editors would like to thank the authors who contributed essays and introductions to this book, and also Elisabeth Staak for her translations of documents originally in German. Paul De Angelis provided expert guidance through the process of compiling and editing the volume. The research assistance of James Aldridge was indispensable, as was the help of many libraries, librarians, archivists, and scholars: Jessica Duchen, Kate Rivers at the Library of Congress, Brett Service at the Warner Bros. Archives, and Warren Sherk at the Margaret Herrick Library of the Academy of Motion Picture Arts and Sciences. Katy Korngold Hubbard provided invaluable information and assistance at just the right moments. And, as always, working with the Bard Music Festival crew—Byron Adams, Leon Botstein, Christopher Gibbs, and Irene Zedlacher—was a dream. Thank you.

Daniel Goldmark and Kevin C. Karnes
Cleveland and Atlanta

Permissions and Credits

The following copyright holders, institutions, and individuals have graciously granted permission to reprint or reproduce the following materials:

Bildarchiv und Graphiksammlung. Österreichische Nationalbibliothek (Austrian National Library) for Figures 1, 2, and 3 in David Brodbeck, "Korngold Father and Son in Vienna's Prewar Public Eye"; Lebrecht Music Arts / Bridgeman Images for Figure 4 in the same essay.

Bildarchiv und Graphiksammlung. Österreichische Nationalbibliothek (Austrian National Library) for Figures 1 and 2 in Charles Youmans, "You must return to life"; KHM-Museumsverband, Theatermuseum Vienna for Figure 4, program of *Das Wunder der Heliane* as well as Figure 7, program of *Jonny spielt auf;* photo in Figure 3 is by Anny Breer (1891–1969), courtesy Schott Music GmbH & Co. KG.; private collection for Figure 5; also, in the same essay, Schott Music GmbH & Co. KG, Mainz, Germany for Examples 1–4 from Korngold's *Das Wunder der Heliane*, copyright © 1926 (renewed). All rights reserved. Used by permission of European American Music Distributors Company, sole U.S. and Canadian agent for Schott Music.

KHM-Museumsverband, Theatermuseum Vienna for Figure 2 in Sherry Lee & Sadie Menicanin, "Acoustic Space, Modern Interiority, and Korngold's Cities."

Library of Congress, with permission of the Korngold family, for Figures 1 and 4 in Ben Winters, "New Opportunities in Film"; Warner Bros. Archives, USC School of Cinematic Arts for Figure 2; the Korngold family for Figure 3; and, in the same essay, WB Music Corp for Example 1 from Korngold's piano-conductor score to *Devotion*, copyright © 1946 (renewed); used by permission of Alfred Music.

Warner-Olive Music LLC (ASCAP) for Examples 1 and 3–8 from Korngold's score to *Kings Row* in Neil Lerner's "The caverns of the human mind are full of strange shadows," copyright © 1940 (renewed); all rights administered by Universal Music Group (ASCAP); exclusive worldwide print rights administered by Alfred Music; all print rights reserved; used by permission of Alfred Music; and in the same essay, Warner-Tamerlane Publishing Corp. and Bantha Music (75%) for Example 2 from John Williams's score to *Star Wars*, copyright © 1977 (renewed); all rights reserved; used by permission of Alfred Music; and Disney Music Group (25%) for the same music example, copyright © 1977 (renewed); print rights administered by Hal Leonard; used by permission of Hal Leonard. In the same essay, Figure 1 is courtesy the South Caroliniana Library, University of South Carolina, Columbia, S.C.; Figure 2 is from Photofest, Inc.

Schott Music GmbH & Co. KG, Mainz, Germany for Examples 1, 3, and 4 in Amy Lynn Wlodarski, "American and Austrian Ruins in Korngold's Symphony in F-sharp" from Korngold's Symphony in F-sharp; copyright © 1952 (renewed); all rights reserved;

used by permission of European American Music Distributors Company, sole U.S. and Canadian agent for Schott Music; Belmont Music Publishers, Los Angeles, for Example 2 in the same essay from Arnold Schoenberg's *Verklärte Nacht*, used by permission; and The Aaron Copland Fund for Music, Inc. for Example 5 from Aaron Copland's *Appalachian Spring*, © copyright 1945 (renewed), Boosey & Hawkes, Inc., sole publisher & licensee. Figure 1 in the same essay is courtesy the Vienna State Opera.

Brendan G. Carroll Collection for Figure 1 in "Recollections of Zemlinsky from My Years of Study."

Courtesy the Korngold family for Figure 1 in "A Farewell to Vienna."

Akg-images Ltd. for Figure 1 in "Composing for the Pictures: An Interview."

Courtesy the Korngold family for Figure 1 in "'Give up your plans of coming home': Letters of a Viennese Father to His Son."

Courtesy Michael Haas for Figure 1 in "Some Experiences in Film Music."

Library of Congress, with permission of the Korngold family, for Figure I in "Faith in Music!"

Essays

Korngold Father and Son in Vienna's Prewar Public Eye

DAVID BRODBECK

> In what year did I meet your late husband? Unfortunately, I can't say with certainty. I only know that he had come with his parents and that he was a boy. He was probably around eleven, at most thirteen. We all had the impression that he was *a great talent*!
> —Paul Wittgenstein to Luzi Korngold, February 1958

In a feuilleton published in the *Neues Wiener Tagblatt* on 24 April 1910, Max Kalbeck, the paper's longtime music critic, wrote in celebration and appreciation of the Vienna Philharmonic, which was then completing its fiftieth season of subscription concerts. Although most of the essay was concerned with the orchestra's glorious past, toward the end Kalbeck looked into its future: "We can wish for nothing better for the members of the Philharmonic on their Golden Jubilee than that, in this latest, so grandly inaugurated era, there might ripen a young, truly creative genius worthy of being introduced by them to the musical world."[1] We cannot be certain, but Kalbeck may well have been thinking here of the twelve-year-old son of his friend and colleague Julius Korngold, music critic of the city's *Neue freie Presse*. After all, Vienna was at this very moment in the grip of reports telling of "the astounding talent of little Erich Wolfgang Korngold," a wunderkind who had recently "caused quite a stir."[2]

It is not difficult to see why. The boy was a prodigy the likes of which had scarcely been encountered before. He was not only an accomplished pianist but also a composer of preternaturally mature and astonishingly modern-sounding music.[3] Eduard Hanslick, who heard Erich perform at the piano at least once before his death in 1904, declared him "the little Mozart."[4] In 1907, at the age of ten, the boy began contrapuntal studies with Robert Fuchs, a venerable teacher at the Vienna Conservatory. In June of that year Julius arranged for Erich to show Gustav Mahler one of his original compositions, a cantata entitled *Gold*. (To avoid confusion, hereafter I will generally refer to the father and son by their given names.) Such was Mahler's astonishment that he reportedly exclaimed, "Send the boy to Zemlinsky. No Conservatory, no drill!! Zemlinsky will give him everything he needs in a free way!"[5]

That Julius sought Mahler's opinion is no surprise; he was among the composer's staunchest supporters in Vienna and had very much regretted Mahler's recent decision to resign his position as director of the Court Opera.[6] As Mahler had hoped, the counterpoint lessons with Fuchs were supplemented in due course by instruction with Alexander Zemlinsky, beginning in 1908 and continuing until Zemlinsky's departure for Prague in 1911 to become First Kapellmeister at that city's German Provincial Theater. During these years, Erich composed, albeit for the most part without Zemlinsky's knowledge, the compositions for piano by which he would first become known to the public—the Piano Sonata No. 1 in D Minor, a set of six characteristic pieces after Cervantes's *Don Quixote*, and *Der Schneemann* (The Snowman), a ballet-pantomime based on figures from commedia dell'arte.[7]

Not only Mahler, but also the composer Carl Goldmark and other leading musicians in Vienna came to know some of these early compositional efforts through domestic performances by Erich at the piano. One such occasion took place in mid-1909, when Felix Weingartner, Mahler's successor at the Court Opera, heard the boy perform *Der Schneemann* and a recently composed passacaglia with twenty variations. Duly impressed, Weingartner went so far as offer to perform *Der Schneemann* at the Court Opera were it to be orchestrated. Citing the boy's unreadiness to make such a grand debut, Julius refused this offer in no uncertain terms.[8] In fact, he took pains at first to keep his son's extraordinary musical gifts out of the public eye in Vienna. As Hanslick's handpicked successor at the music desk of the city's only newspaper of international repute, and as a critic of strong and often acerbic opinions, Julius Korngold was both a powerful and polarizing figure in Vienna's musical scene. He thus had good reason to worry about how his many adversaries would respond to the presentation of Erich's music in his own bailiwick. Would the boy, because of the father's position, be thought to be the beneficiary of undeserved favored treatment? Would the spite opponents felt toward the father be taken out unfairly on the son?

In December 1909 Julius hit upon the idea of seeking expert opinion on Erich's abilities from persons living outside Vienna, neutral parties who would presumably have no reason to take a biased position one way or the other. He quietly arranged for the piano sonata, *Don Quixote* pieces,

Figure 1. Erich in 1910.

and *Der Schneemann* to be printed and distributed to a select number of musicians and musical experts in cities ranging from Berlin and Leipzig in the German Reich to Budapest and Graz in Austria-Hungary, with each being asked to reply with a written evaluation. The reviews soon began to pour in, perhaps as many as forty altogether, from the likes of the composers Richard Strauss and Engelbert Humperdinck, the conductors Artur Nikisch and Anton Seidl, the historical musicologists Hermann Kretzschmar and Hugo Leichtentritt, the systematic musicologists Erich von Hornbostel and Carl Stumpf, and the critics Ferdinand Pfohl and Paul Marsop. From within Vienna came at least one evaluation, by family friend Goldmark, who seems to have asked to see the scores himself.[9]

Not surprisingly, Erich's remarkable story did not remain off the record for long. On 16 February 1910, the Budapest music critic August Beer broke the news in an effusive article entitled "Ein musikalisches Phänomen":

> You have to go back far in the history of music, to the young Mozart, to encounter a similar musical phenomenon. Equally inconceivable in the piano music of the little composer are the mature and imaginative design, the mastery of the form, the extraordinary rhythmic variety and, what is probably most notable of all, the complete familiarity with the latest possibilities in harmony. How rapidly must this twelve-year-old have made the monstrous journey in order to arrive already at the ultramoderns, mixing it up—well past Brahms and Wagner—in the dissonant domains of a Richard Strauss, a Max Reger, a Debussy![10]

Nine days later, on 25 February, came a report by Richard Specht published in *Der Merker*, a new Viennese journal for music and theater.[11] Finally, on 29 February, there appeared an article, written in the form of an extended anecdote, in Julius's *Neue freie Presse*. This was not written by the composer's father, of course, but by Ernst Decsey, a music writer from Graz and one of the experts to whom the scores had originally been sent. It was probably this colorful account, more than anything else, that was responsible for setting off the Korngold sensation that swept through the city's educated classes.[12]

Things now moved quickly—and largely out of Julius Korngold's control. With Erich at his side, Zemlinsky undertook to teach his student the basics of orchestration by transcribing *Der Schneemann* for orchestra: the cover page of an incomplete manuscript full score carries the initials "A.v.Z./E.W.K," and is dated "Mitte März" (middle of March).[13] Around the same time, Ludwig Winter, the secretary to the General Intendant of the Court Theaters, arranged for the work to be performed in a benefit concert in the Palais Modena, the residence of the Austrian prime minister. In the event, two private performances took place there, both hosted by the prime minister's wife, Baroness Anka von Bienerth. The first, on April 14, was given during a soirée to which members of both the first society of the old established aristocracy and the second society of "movers and shakers," disproportionately Jewish and Protestant, "from the world of officialdom, finance, and industry" were invited; the second, on April 26, was the benefit concert itself. On both occasions, Erich was joined by Richard Pahlen, Mahler's favorite pianist, in playing a hastily made two-piano arrangement. Fritz Brunner of the Vienna Philharmonic played the violin solos, and dancers and sets were brought in from the Court Ballet.[14]

Meanwhile Emil Hertzka, head of Universal Edition, made a bid to publish the sonata and ballet-pantomime. Julius agreed on the condition that the latter would not be released to any theater without his express permission. Ignoring this stipulation, Herztka immediately offered *Der Schneemann* to Weingartner, who readily accepted, confident that Zemlinsky's orchestration would be effective. All this put Julius in a difficult spot. He had long targeted Weingartner with barbed reviews, not, as the conductor saw things, primarily on account of artistic differences, but merely for having been the person appointed to replace the critic's beloved Mahler at the head of the institution that lay at the center of Viennese musical culture.[15] Julius reasonably assumed that people would think Weingartner had agreed to perform Erich's work only as a way of making peace with his father and therefore of securing better notices from him in the future. Accordingly, he tried, to no avail, to put a stop to things then and there.

As Weingartner later recalled the matter:

> I had already heard of the great talent of the eleven-year-old Erich. Perusal of the ballet confirmed the rumors and led me to conclude the performance contract with Universal Edition. I later reassured Dr. Julius Korngold that he had had no influence on this decision. He even appeared in my office and asked me not to perform the work because it would put him in an awkward position. I could only tell him what I already had told Director Hertzka, namely, that the father and son are completely separate persons for me. The publisher offered me *Der Schneemann*, along with other

> new works, and I accepted it only after objective examination. Dr. Korngold did not change his attitude toward me; he was and remained the opponent of the successor of Gustav Mahler. If attentive observers nevertheless wanted to see the halfhearted appearance of a benevolent glimmer in his critiques of me, it would only have been human to understand things this way, for I was well disposed toward his talented, precocious, and thoroughly pleasant boy, which, by the way, I considered a duty, not a credit to me.[16]

That Julius had correctly anticipated the public reaction is seen in contemporary press reports such as this one from 23 May: "You see, that's how people are. They get all worked up because the Court Opera Director has made peace with Herr Korngold at the price of a performance of his little child prodigy's *Schneemann*. . . . How was the director of the Court Opera supposed to find the courage to be hostile to the critic of a newspaper of international renown?"[17] This suspicion gained credence when, in the prospectus of the 1910–11 season made public a month later, the premiere of *Der Schneemann* was announced for October 4, the emperor's name day, along with Ermanno Wolf-Ferrari's intermezzo *Susannens Geheimnis (Il secreto di Susanna)*, on a double bill of short new works under the direction of Kapellmeister Franz Schalk.[18]

The premiere was by every measure a resounding success with the public, no doubt in part because of the composer's tender age and all the buildup preceding it. The critical response, however, was mixed. Very much in Erich's corner was Max Kalbeck, who began his review of the concert by attempting to inoculate his friend Julius Korngold from charges that he had used his influence to bring it about:

> We are reminded of the young Mozart by another child prodigy who goes by the name of Wolfgang. Erich Wolfgang, the brilliant son of our highly esteemed colleague Dr. Julius Korngold, is the author of the pantomime that appeared on the boards together with *Susannens Geheiminis* to unanimous cheers by old and young alike. Erich Wolfgang was eleven years old when he breezily composed *Der Schneemann* out of the Nicolomarkt and into the piano studio. And he only had to wait two years until the work, endowed by his teacher Alexander v. Zemlinsky with magical orchestral splendor, was acquired by the Vienna Court Opera on the basis of a conspiracy of influential friends and colleagues who were

Figure 2. Alexander von Zemlinsky.

enthusiastic about the unusual talent of the boy. The surprised Herr Papa had nothing to do but say yes and Amen.[19]

Kalbeck then goes on to note how "everything came together in the wonderfully disciplined imagination of the imaginative child's head to form an indivisible whole, albeit with so many details." Indeed, he declares that "anybody who wishes to pursue the motivic and thematic relationships of the work will be amazed by the spirit of strict objectivity and systematic order that governs it." No less worthy of admiration, in Kalbeck's view, was Erich's ability to find apt musical depictions of his characters and the dramatic situations in which they find themselves, as well as his rhythmic and harmonic sensibilities, "unusually rich and powerful, though often raw and unbalanced." This last observation leads to the expression of some skepticism—widely shared among the critics—regarding the boy's adoption of the most modern tonal styles found in the works of contemporary French and Italian composers, not to speak of "the truly childish character of Secessionist-musical nonsense." Nevertheless, Kalbeck concludes, "For these poster children [of ultramodernism], let us be just as grateful to the composer as he approaches his teenage years as for the highly gratifying revelations of his talent; they promise a great future for the young composer and make us glad of his presence."

Very different was the reaction of Max Graf, music critic for the *Neues Wiener Journal*.[20] Graf gave Erich's work its due as a successful proving ground (*Talentprobe*) of the boy's remarkable musical gifts. But he scarcely judged it worthy of making its way from the private, intimate salon into the broad public space of the Court Opera Theater. On the contrary, because the pantomime did not, in his view, amount to a fully worked-out piece of theater, the Court Opera had no business staging it. As to why the performance was allowed to take place, Graf pulls no punches in pointing to what he calls "the incessant blowing on the trumpet of familial promotion." Were it not for Julius's assumed lobbying, he pointedly suggests, the work "would never have been dragged from the boy's study and playroom into a great opera house."

This last, dismissive remark leads to some cutting advice in conclusion:

> The fact that the little work was performed under the external signs of lively success, and that the young composer was called forth several times at the end with thunderous applause by a section of the audience, cannot change this opinion. Who would not want to treat the gifted boy with joyous approval? Who would not be interested in applauding the boy's appearance?

> But it would have been wise to usher the young musician into the Court Opera for the second and third performances. He would have then learned the difference between the artificial coaxed applause of relatives, friends, and the fashionable crowd and the chill of an unbiased audience, and perhaps would not be a little affected by it. This embarrassing surprise would be more conducive to his artistic education than pleasing praise. In his pantomime, out of one snowman come two, three, four, five snowmen . . . until the room is full of snowmen. It will certainly be the other way around in the opera house, and one hundred applauding people will dwindle away into twenty, ten, five, one.[21]

When, on the day following the premiere, Julius wrote to thank Schalk for the successful performance, there can be little question that he was steaming over Graf's brutal review:

> Heartfelt thanks to you *yourself* and *your artists* for leading my little one's little work to victory! The act of revenge that an unscrupulous *enemy* has committed against me in a *local newspaper* (!) will leave you cold. *Der Schneemann* has proved its theatricality [*Hofopermäßigkeit*], and its composer, as you know from his latest works, is stronger than any malice [*Niedertracht*].[22]

In Julius's view, Graf's unfounded charge that he had effectively forced the performance on Weingartner had poisoned the well for a handful of other Viennese music critics, who likewise would soon come to think that he was willing to abuse his power to further Erich's career. The bitterness engendered by this episode would linger for years to come.[23]

Maliciousness of a different kind could be found in the pages of Vienna's anti-Semitic press. Karl Schreder began his review for the *Deutsches Volksblatt*, Vienna's most widely read political daily of this type, by seemingly admiring Erich's ability at so young an age to find his stride alongside Richard Strauss and other modernist composers. This is immediately shown to be a backhanded compliment, however, when Schreder dismisses modernism using coded anti-Semitic language that dates back to Wagner's *Das Judenthum in der Musik*, in particular, the suggestions of Jewish cunning and shallowness:

> In the composition of the young Korngold, who, with the early maturity of Semitic youth, has effortlessly learned the secrets

and tricks of modern music, it can be seen how the creation of modern tonal works is absolutely child's play [*kinderleicht*]. The rummaging about in harmonies, the unraveling of the motives, the overripe changes in meter and key, all this can be learned and utilized. Composing becomes mechanical work. . . . Heart and mind no longer need to be taken into consideration.[24]

This was mild stuff by comparison to the over-the-top rhetoric at work in the review of *Der Schneemann* published in the *Ostdeutsche Rundschau*, a political daily given to full-blown *völkisch* cultural critique.[25] Here Julius Korngold is the primary target, not merely on the basis of an alleged misuse of his powerful position, as was the case with Graf and certain other mainstream writers, but as a devious Jewish critic to boot. In Wagnerian fashion, the "Germanized" Jew—in this case, Julius Korngold—is understood to be an imposter, a cultural parasite in the "genuine" German body politic:

> Before little Erich Wolfgang Korngold was chosen to copy the whole of Mozart's story . . . his name was simply Erich. And it is indicative of the disgusting affair that, when it finally started, Mozart's name was quickly attributed to him. It would not at all be surprising if the former lawyer from Brünn were from now on called Julius Leopold and [like Mozart's father] writes a treatise on playing the violin.[26]

What appears to have particularly outraged this writer is the notion that the young Mozart and the young Korngold might truly warrant discussion in the same breath. Worse still, in this critic's mind, is the notion that Korngold might even have surpassed Mozart:

> Of course, a comparison comes soon with the young Mozart, and the father's pride . . . is compounded by the assertion that Erich Wolfgang is actually more than Wolfgang Amadeus, since [Mozart] composed in the sense and in the style of his time, but [Korngold] follows completely new ways. . . . In no time, one of the members of the "charming" clique for whom a Jewish Beethoven is not enough, and who would hastily construe a Jewish Mozart in addition, rashly wrote that just now, when so many musicians find themselves lost in dead ends, one had finally come along who knows the right exit.

Such attitudes, so publicly expressed, were undoubtedly painful and infuriating annoyances to Julius Korngold and every other member of Vienna's community of assimilated Jews, with their thoroughgoing identification with German culture. But we do well to bear in mind that these voices remained on the margins of high culture and polite society and were powerless to prevent Jewish representation in greatly disproportionate numbers in Vienna's rich musical life.[27] Still, there were times when mainstream writers on music—whether they were Jewish, like Korngold and Graf and a number of the city's other leading critics, or, like Kalbeck, were not—did feel compelled to engage the anti-Semitism they found in their midst.[28]

One such case, part of a larger story that merits close examination, involves Erich's Piano Trio in D Major, Op. 1, composed in 1910. A strikingly mature work for a boy of thirteen, the Trio was a clear advance over *Der Schneemann*. "Compared with this child we are all impoverished," Richard Strauss is supposed to have said upon first hearing it.[29] The Trio's first Viennese performance was given in the Bösendorfer Hall on December 11, 1910, in a concert of new works by Austrian composers that was sponsored by *Der Merker*. Julius, who continued to be wary of allowing Erich's music to be performed in Vienna, permitted this performance under the impression that it was to be a private affair, designed to promote the new publication. The concert was anything but. Glowing notices from Munich, where the Trio premiered on November 4, made Erich's work the most highly anticipated piece on a program that also included music by Zemlinsky, Alma Mahler, and Karl Weigl, among others. Indeed, the inclusion of the Trio induced a veritable who's who of Vienna's political, social, and cultural elite to attend, including the writers Arthur Schnitzler, Hermann Bahr, and Felix Salten, and the composers Carl Goldmark, Oscar Straus, and Oskar Nedbal. The newspapers even saw fit to treat the event like a society affair by publishing the names of the many notables who were present.[30]

As with *Der Schneemann*, here again there was a split in critical opinion between Kalbeck and Graf. For Kalbeck, the Trio provided new evidence that the "splendid boy [*Prachtjunge*] whose mighty talent remains a mystery related to nature," was fast "approaching a significant future."[31] The critic describes each of the four movements in some detail, noting, for example, how in the opening Allegro there is "no patchwork, no stuffing, not a weak bar anywhere"; everything is arranged in accordance with the composer's "self-will." The other three movements came in for similar high praise. Most notable, however, was Kalbeck's decision to send his readers off with a striking biblical citation from Luke 2:47: "'All who heard

Figure 3. Carl Goldmark in 1902.

him were astounded at his understanding and his answers,' it was said of the twelve-year-old boy Jesus. May Erich Wolfgang increase in wisdom, age, and grace with God and the people! He will not be lacking in laurels."

Standing in complete contrast to this image is the picture Graf paints of an unseemly venue of musical commerce: "What shall we say when a boy, a strong and precocious musical talent, takes the plunge into the modern musical market, where circus people and fire-eaters sit in bright-colored, painted booths behind the shouting barkers?"[32] The critic reminds his readers that he had never denied the boy's extraordinary musical gifts, even if, in his review of *Der Schneemann*, he had made no secret of his belief that Erich's propensity for "quirky" harmonies and "irregular, twitching" rhythms had a "corrosive effect" on the musical style, like rust on metal. "If [in *Der Schneemann*]," Graf continued, "those distortions and discolorations . . . could be interpreted as expressions of boyish cockiness," now, with the more mature new piano trio, it had become clear that "artificiality and intricacy" were in fact part and parcel of the young composer's style—and this, clearly, Graf does not see as a good thing. "This composing boy," he writes, "is a true child of his time in that the bizarre and nervous nature of modern music exerts a strong appeal on him, because he feels a kindred element in these problematic elements of music."

Richard Robert, writing in the *Wiener Sonn- und Montags-Zeitung*, was similarly critical of the Trio's "precocious harmony," finding it to be unnatural, bizarre, and contrived. "It would be good for the little maniac for dissonance to take to the mineral springs with Joh. Sebastian Bach (I know of no better teacher)." Indeed, Robert suggests that further publications and performances—Julius's doing, the reader is presumably meant to infer—should be put aside for the time being to allow the boy to continue his studies in search of "simplicity and purity."[33]

The principal objection made in David Josef Bach's review for the *Arbeiter-Zeitung*, Vienna's voice of social democracy, recalled in its own, more politicized way, Graf's criticism of the atmosphere surrounding the concert:

> It is to be hoped that the little Korngold will be a musical matter; then he must be saved from becoming a social sensation. Success, loud public recognition can also be beneficial to the youngest composer and therefore can probably also be granted to young Korngold. But if our public concert life has in and of itself less and less to do with art, and more and more to do with the sensationalism of unmusical snobs, of liquid capital and its parasitic following, then Erich Wolfgang

Korngold should at least learn to distinguish judgment from a lack of judgment, and discerning listeners from audiences of the worst kind. In the end, all this was confused. Little Korngold's power of discrimination will not be sharpened if raving mad idiots [*tobsüchtige Schmücke*] strive to confuse him with irreverent comparisons, when attendance lists are published, as if it had to do with a ball or a charity bazaar, not with art and a young artist.[34]

The generally lukewarm reception of Erich's Trio by more than one Viennese critic provides the context for the note his father sent to Max Kalbeck in response to Kalbeck's rather more heartening review:

With tears still in my eye, I sit down to thank you wholeheartedly for your lovely, warm words about my Erich. When someone like me by virtue of his position has to struggle again and again against adversity, misinterpretation, and anger in a matter that really should silence the evil instincts of human nature, words like yours are doubly fortunate. . . . May your wishes concerning the child be fulfilled![35]

Julius's frustration is palpable. He seems to interpret any questioning of the circumstances under which Erich's music was making its way onto Viennese programs as evidence of an unwarranted and unfair belief—a triumph of the "evil instinct of human nature"—that all this was happening so early and so rapidly not because of the boy's merit as a composer, but only because of the power and influence his father wielded as the city's leading musical tastemaker. Rather than allowing that some criticism may have been made honestly by fair-minded critics in the course of doing their jobs—not by Graf, perhaps, but certainly by others—Julius took it all personally. Now it was not only Graf, his bête noire, but also the likes of Robert and Bach and others who, in his mind, were against him. Given his obvious conflict of interest, Julius could not fight back in print against this perceived injustice, so he registered his protest privately by withdrawing his membership in the Vereinigung Wiener Musikreferenten (Association of Viennese Music Critics). This soon led a minority faction of the association to respond in a condemnatory letter intended to goad Julius into public argument. Advised by a journalist friend—Kalbeck is a likely candidate—of the inflammatory nature of what was contained in the letter, Julius reportedly left it unopened. And though the charges made in the letter were retracted a year later, it did little to lessen the breach.[36]

Meanwhile, the noted satirist Karl Kraus, whose hatred for what he saw as the perniciousness of Vienna's daily press (and of the *Neue Freie Presse* most of all) permeated his writings, entered the fray on 31 December 1910 with a biting essay titled "Der kleine Korngold."[37] Kraus began by fantasizing about intervening in "the family life of the old Korngold" and using a pair of pinchers "to excise the demon who compels this father, like William Tell, to deliver critical shots to the head of his child"—strong evidence, he believes, that "musical politics is the meanest and most dangerous of all aspirations arising in any field of art." Kraus is convinced that all the recent attention paid to "the little Korngold" by "every independent virtuoso, every trio, piano tuner, and organ grinder" merely reflects a desire to curry favor with "the old Korngold." One critic in particular comes under Kraus's direct fire in this regard:

> Herr Max Kalbeck, that colleague who has remedied in their children what he has inflicted on the men of music, that man from the era of Wagner and Bruckner hatred who has not yet discovered the late Hugo Wolf but does not want to let it be said that he has misjudged a new-born Korngold, has the goodness to write down the passage: "'All who heard him were astounded at his understanding and his answers,' it is said of the twelve-year-old boy Jesus.' May Erich Wolfgang increase in wisdom, age, and grace with God and the people! He will not be lacking in laurels."

Kraus immediately scoffs at this audacious comparison, first "because the audience that crucified Jesus is enthusiastic in the Bösendorfer Hall"—Jews were always disproportionately represented among Vienna's concert-going public—and second "because the modest world fame to which the [Christian] salvation doctrine could be brought could not be compared with the sensation produced by the miracles of the little Korngold."[38] Clearly impugning Kalbeck's and Julius's integrity at the same time, Kraus adds for good effect: "At least at the time [of Jesus] correspondents did not receive telegraphic orders from their editors to give a favorable report. It is also mortifying to imagine what part in the comparison [with Jesus] father Korngold plays, and one has to assume it does not suit him. He prefers the part of the old Mozart, and he did not hesitate to take it on in a feuilleton."

The feuilleton in question had appeared in the *Neue freie Presse* two months earlier. In it is Julius's discussion of a "Mozart Evening" recently given in the auditorium of Vienna's newly inaugurated Urania, an educational institute with a public observatory. Among other items, the bill included Mozart's youthful singspiel *Bastien und Bastienne*, composed at the age of twelve. Julius writes at some length to justify the many actions Leopold Mozart took on behalf of his prodigy son: "Leopold Mozart . . . fought like a lion for his child and considered it his duty to defend the prodigy against lies and underestimation. You have to read the letters Leopold Mozart wrote at that time from Vienna in order to gauge the tribulations he faced, and how stubbornly he argued for his cause. 'He was guilty of convincing the world of this miracle,' he wrote in one of them."[39]

All this was too good for Kraus to pass up, so he shared his wicked take on the many parallels that could be drawn between Leopold Mozart and Julius Korngold:

> One must see how poorly the young Mozart, who was born with talent but without a press, comes off in the comparison, and one may wonder what would have become of this other Wolfgang if his father, like the elder Korngold, had had his hand in the divine game. . . . [Father Korngold] has already supplanted the young pseudo-Korngold of the eighteenth century and introduced the genuine Mozart of the twentieth.[40]

Later, alluding once more to Kalbeck's review, Kraus offers Julius some advice:

> I do not know if the criticism that praises the chubby lad as a "splendid boy" whose "mighty talent remains a mystery related to nature" is valid. I do not know whether it is instead a secret related to the *Neue freie Presse*, that is, an editorial secret and a family secret at the same time. In any case, it should stay that way. If the little Korngold "is approaching a significant future," then the genius-correspondence of the father will not stand in the way. But if he is just a freak of nature, his presence is not worth the hype.[41]

A few weeks after the appearance of Kraus's article, *Der Merker* weighed in on the controversy, one that had been set into motion, after all, by its concert of December 11. In his article "Zum Wunderkindproblem" (On the Child Prodigy Problem), Richard Batka begins by noting that events of recent weeks and months had led many in Vienna to compare the accomplishments of young Erich with those of Mozart, adding that, for some, such a comparison was not only impudent but blasphemous.[42] He quickly dismisses this criticism by making the obvious point that no one was comparing "the lad in short pants with his Op. 1" with "the immortal creator of *Don Giovanni* and *Zauberflöte*," and that it could only be left to the future to determine what significance might eventually be attached to the mature Korngold vis-à-vis "the German musical genius of light and love." Rather than stopping there, Batka continues by suggesting that if the history of the young Mozart were not seen through the rose-tinted glasses of anecdotal wisdom, then it would be discovered that even Mozart was only human, that he had benefited from certain deceptions made on his behalf by his father, and that the "hymns to the *Wunderkind*" sung in 1765 were not altogether different from those sung in 1911. This leads Batka to conclude: "Perhaps those principled persons who are discontented with the present and praise times past [*laudatores temporis acti*] will take these facts to heart. No one today can say whether a Mozart will one day come from the young Korngold. But one is arguably justified in drawing parallels between the early stages of their lives without running the risk of committing artistic sacrilege, not as a "blind" supporter of modernism, but as a perceptive appreciator of the good, but scarcely better, old times."

Batka's article drew a strong response a few months later in the radical German-nationalist *Der Scherer* from a critic named Karl M. Klob.[43] Klob set out to debunk what he characterized as Batka's attempt to convince an unbelieving public that stories telling of Mozart the child prodigy were largely hype, whereas those telling of the miraculous Korngold were entirely believable. Klob undertakes a nearly point-for-point rebuttal of each of Batka's claims, arguing for the young Mozart's superiority every step of the way. As for the role of Leopold Mozart in advancing his son's career, Klob argues that "all this 'Barnum-like' hype of Mozart's father"—the reference here is to Batka's characterization of a promotional piece Leopold planted in the London *Public Advertiser* on 11 July 1765—"is refreshing compared with the objectionable fawning [*Wohldienerei*] with which critics and music writers who are friends of father Korngold, or else want to be, engage in standing up for the boy prodigy. And that is the most undignified and despicable thing about the whole story of this modern child prodigy."

Like Kraus, Klob intimates that Max Kalbeck was among the offenders: "Critics such as the conservative Max Kalbeck who screw up their faces at an augmented triad write hymns of praise to the compositions of the young Korngold, which because of their modern character they would properly be obliged to 'savage.' Critics who deliberately attack truly brilliant composers (such as Hugo Wolf!), or are dead silent about truly striving talents,

Figure 4. Erich and his parents, ca. 1911.

are now cheering for this child." Then, in a footnote, Klob, again recalling Kraus, cites Kalbeck's likening of the young Korngold to the boy Jesus when he demonstrated his insight and wisdom before the teachers assembled in the Temple. "Would all this happen," Klob asks,

> were Korngold Jr. not the son of the music correspondent of the *Neue freie Presse*? Probably not! Or maybe yes! But then the matter would cost the father a pretty piece of money. Yet, on the contrary, Herr Korngold profits from it because *Der Schneemann* brings royalties and the Trio will also find some buyers. The most repulsive thing about the Korngold matter is the "propaganda" that the liberal journalists make for the alleged genius out of sycophancy toward Korngold the father. Where is there something like this in the story of Mozart's youth?

To prove the injustice of it all, Klob turns finally to the unfair advantages over Mozart enjoyed by the young Korngold. Whereas Wolfgang Amadeus's first compositions were brought out by "a very modest Parisian publishing house," Erich Wolfgang's appeared in the prestigious Universal Edition, "a firm for which only the best is good enough," a circumstance Kolb attributes, once again, to the influence of Julius Korngold. "Where will it lead," Klob asks in conclusion, "if even a critic as good as Herr Batka tries to correct history in favor of a little composing Jew? Israel should not be surprised if the 'shame of the century' increasingly gets the upper hand among the truly German nationalists. However, the Jews may then thank their native acolytes [*konnationalen Trabanten*] for promoting the anti-Semitic movement."[44]

This could not go unchallenged, and so in May Batka responded with a rebuttal that concluded in a forceful tone:

> And now I ask Herr Klob: what entitles him to accuse a critic, who up till now he treasured as "fair, intelligent, and deserving," of "sycophancy" and "gratuitous service" to a colleague? What prevents him in this case from assuming such an openly expressed and represented evaluation, even if it were to be erroneous, is the result of an objective testing and an honorable conviction? And finally: what is one to call someone who, blithely, without the slightest evidence, blames a hitherto "excellent" critic for having suppressed better knowledge out of consideration for an influential man? "Undignified"? "Despicable"? As you like.

And all because of a little composing Jew! So that's it! Herr Klob apparently sticks to Lessing's Patriarch. . . . [45] Would "truly German-nationalist-minded men" think it more appropriate if I were to keep my good opinion of the artistic phenomenon to myself because by chance it happens to concern a non-Aryan? I was taught in the *Burschenschaft* to sing: "Whoever knows the truth and does not say it is truly a cowardly wretch." Along with many other discerning musicians, I allow myself to consider the little Korngold a biological miracle and his Trio a work of genius, whether that brings joy to the father or distress to others. And so God commanded, Herr Klob![46]

Over the next few years, leading up the outbreak of the Great War, Vienna would hear each of Erich's major new instrumental works. On November 13, 1911, Artur Schnabel performed the Piano Sonata No. 2 in E Major, Op. 2. A year later, on November 17, 1912, Weingartner led the Vienna Philharmonic players in a performance of the *Schauspiel-Ouvertüre*, Op. 4. And a year after that, two more new works were introduced within a span of three weeks' time. On November 8, 1913, the Sonata in G Major for Piano and Violin, Op. 6, was performed by the visiting duo of Artur Schnabel and Carl Flesch, and on November 30, the Sinfonietta in B Major, Op. 5, received its world premiere with the Vienna Philharmonic, led by Weingartner, to whom the work was dedicated. Although there was little Julius could do to prevent visiting artists from performing whatever they wished on their Viennese concerts, he did make a strong effort, again to no avail, to dissuade Weingartner from performing his son's music in the Philharmonic concerts. As the conductor put it in an essay published a few years later: "I had to fight fiercely with his father, who could not rid himself of the idea that my advocacy for his son was out of place in Vienna, while I steadfastly held the opinion that a truly significant talent should be promoted without taking incidental circumstances into consideration."[47]

The Sinfonietta was the work that brought the first phase of the composer's career to a close. As such, it is an appropriate work with which to conclude our considerations here. Despite the diminutive used in its title, this is a major composition of nearly forty-five minutes' duration. Yet, despite its temporal dimensions and wide array of orchestral forces, this is no real symphony. To be sure, its four movements are unified by a recurring theme—a five-note "motto of the cheerful heart," based on a series of rising fourths—and the whole abounds in motivic connections of all kinds. But as suggested by the name Erich gave his motto, the music does not seem *echt symphonisch*, at least not in the sense in which that concept had come to be understood. Indeed, as some early critics noted, certain passages sound rather more operatic or balletic in nature, like music for the theater, not for the concert hall. In short, this work was neither fish nor fowl.

The Sinfonietta came up at least twice in Julius's correspondence with Max Kalbeck. In a letter of 29 November 1913, the day of the public dress rehearsal, Julius responded to a report he seems to have received from Kalbeck concerning a woman who had complained to him about Weingartner's decision to perform Erich's new work:

> It is a pity you cannot let her know how the venom flowing from ignorance or malice against a boy who has the misfortune not only of being an anomaly, but also of being my son, is stopped cold by the warm recognition of friends, to whom, thank heavens, so many musicians, music lovers, great artists—recently Richard Strauss—are staunchly joined. Nevertheless, Erich Wolfgang, as shown by his youthful, sky-blue Sinfonietta, which was greeted in the rehearsal today by the Philharmonic with stormy applause—they play it superbly—goes about composing oblivious of it all.

Julius goes on to say that he was expecting to receive similar "hate mail" (*Drohbriefe*) regarding the matter. And it was not only letters of this kind that rankled, but also what he thought would be the "rabble-rousing [*Hetze*] of certain colleagues (Robert, Graf, Bach, etc.)."[48]

In the event, Graf left no review. And while those by Robert and Bach are somewhat lukewarm—both critics, for example, hear Puccini in the slow third movement, and, as Bach wrote, "a symphonic Puccini is a contradiction in terms"—their reviews are respectful and have little "rabble-rousing" about them.[49] Robert does sound a note of concern, however, when he mentions the mixed reception that followed the performance: "Although the Sinfonietta . . . offered not the slightest reason for demonstrations, it was applauded—the composer had to appear several times on the podium—but also hissed. This was certainly out of place in the case of a young musician in whom the bells of the future ring."

The following day, shortly after the concert had concluded, Julius adopted a tone of irritation and exasperation in another letter to Kalbeck:

After the dress rehearsal, I wrote with all bitterness: these are very bad people! What crudeness does it require to attack a boy, a half-child, in whose brain originated this three-quarter-hour-long, in many cases entirely new music, orchestrated with the most distinctive feeling for sound—despite all the anti-Semitism and all the conspiring (from members of [illegible] and students of the academy) as revenge for [illegible]. There's no doubt that the shamefulness of the midday concert . . . will be repeated. How right I was, on account of Vienna's "peculiarity," to balk with my hands and feet against the "world premiere" in the Philharmonic Concerts! But eventually Erich and his work will survive that too, and I am relying on the fairness and also on the indignation of his friends and supporters.[50]

The "peculiarity" mentioned was almost certainly the "shame of the century" Weingartner had in mind when he looked back on his years spent working in a city where "the treacherous seed of racial hatred had sprouted richly."[51]

Kalbeck, one of those "friends and supporters" on whom Julius was relying, waited nearly a week before publishing his review, and when it came it was long, detailed, and characteristically poetic. Like Robert, he acknowledged the unfavorable response from a relatively small part of the audience, although he played down its significance as the work of "some apparently professional malcontents."[52] At greater length than either Bach or Robert, Kalbeck considered the question of just what kind of music this was: "We don't believe the Sinfonietta . . . has gone straight from the theater into the concert hall: it does not bear its name in jest and willingly surrenders to the cyclic form." But as he reflects on its progression from the "imaginative, not to say fantastical, modestly aspiring Allegro" to the "brilliant Scherzo that unleashes the mad magic of the Walpurgis Night," to the "tired Andante, onto which an obstinate four-bar melody hangs like a heavy twilight butterfly on its flower," and finally to the outcome of the "episodic final movement," he has to wonder whether the journey has not all been just "a colorful dream." This prompts him to ask: "In the end, was it the god of dreams and poetry who alienated the Sinfonietta from its original vocation?"

Yet Kalbeck sees in the young Korngold someone who held the potential to be true to that vocation, someone in whom rang, to recall Robert's turn of phrase, the bells of the future of the symphony:

> To make his beautiful inspirations ever stronger and stouter, to arrange them ever more richly, to make them more and

more supple, until he has won from them the last compelling personal expression of their and his being—may our glorious young hero consider that to be his talent's next and foremost task! From the backdrop of the Sinfonietta poet will emerge a symphonist who recognizes and fulfills the highest law of art in the calm balance between freedom and necessity, in the complete intermeshing and interpenetration of content and form.

With this peroration, we are reminded of our point of departure, the essay Kalbeck wrote three years earlier in celebration of the Vienna Philharmonic's fiftieth anniversary. Then he had looked forward to the day when a young genius would come whose work the orchestra would find worthy of being introduced to the world. The Sinfonietta had now been given its world premiere by that very orchestra, and it was certainly a worthy piece. But, for all its attractiveness, it was not yet the symphony Kalbeck seems to have been awaiting. In fact, Vienna and the rest of the world would have to wait another forty years for such a work to come from the composer's pen.

Written between 1947 and 1952, the Symphony in F-sharp, Op. 40, received its world premiere on October 17, 1954, in a radio performance by the Vienna Symphony Orchestra, a performance so under-rehearsed that Erich tried to have it called off. He was never to hear the symphony again. If the Sinfonietta had been neither fish nor fowl, this new work was a like a fish out of water, a fiercely uncompromising composition of late-Romanticism written during the same period that saw, among other radical postwar developments, the rise of the Darmstadt School and of John Cage's indeterminacy.[53] With his father's death in 1945, Erich had in effect assumed the mantle of the old Korngold. The fate of his magnificent but ill-timed symphony, however, would have been far happier had it appeared when Kalbeck called for it, in the years when the young Korngold, the astounding little Erich Wolfgang, was still taking Vienna by storm.

Appendix:
Ernst Decsey, "Concerning Our Youngest Composer"
Neue freie Presse, 27 February 1910

One must have the courage to believe in miracles.[54] Whether it is the sky-tingling waters of the Yellowstone Park or the hot springs of artistic talent —only if you believe in miracles can the fullness and greatness of nature be grasped. A few weeks ago, such a miracle arrived in my home, three green volumes of music and three attestations that the mysterious original power that we call the deity or nature has not died, and that the miraculous is borne out, as in the days of Pascal, of Mozart.

So, there were three green volumes of music, and I thought, Peters or Universal Edition, new "numbers," new reviewing burdens.[55] And I sighed as you sigh in the case of new numbers and new reviewing burdens. But the first read-through shows that these are not numbers; and the first play-through shows that these are reviewing pleasures! New music and a new man. There was a sonata, three movements, D minor; there were six character pieces, held together and explained by the name of Don Quixote; there was a delightful pantomime "The Snowman," a piano score with text. Three triumphs at one stroke, and it is the effortlessness of the success that indicates talent.[56]

The sonata raced across the piano. It really was racing, for this well-orchestrated "black" piano piece is charged with energies: you imagine it as having to do with a conqueror, a present-day hero. It is a *Sonata Eroica*, blooming from two themes: a stormy masculine theme with passionate semitone harmony and jagged rhythms, and a second theme of a gentler, more thoughtful feminine character. (Two figures of unforgettable countenance that require a skillful "dramatist" to juxtapose in this manner.) In the continuation and development everything a musician can value in a musician is found: the exciting dramatic conflict of the themes, no empty turns, no beating around the bush with "passagework," no filler, but rather a unity of character, confidently made form, in short, a sonata movement with all the traditional parts and driven by the spirit of the modern age. Then a scherzo in the rosy contrasting key of D major, and a trio whose harmonic daring goes after conquests, yet is so logical that one must speak of a strong will, not of idiosyncrasy or arbitrariness. Finally, the last movement: twenty variations on a theme by A. v. Zemlinsky, a last movement that shall not be called "last and least" because in the strictness of the form, in the binding of the passacaglia-like style, the "Conqueror Sonata" reaches the summit, its highest inner strength.[57]

This sounds completely new. Who was the man who wrote it?

But there was still the pantomime. And it showed a completely different compositional countenance. The cunning Pierrot asserts his character, outwits the old Pantalon, dresses himself up as a snowman, abducts the little Columbine.[58] In this theater shine all the suns of humor. The music scurries adroitly, all the rhythms are dance-like. A waltz is struck up, so that you see skirts flying and sing and play and whistle along with it. And at the same time, you discover art in abundance and notice how the snowman alters his musical shape when his dramatic task is changed, dancing in the manner of a waltz, standing petrified in *Don Giovanni* harmonies (when he appears as a "guest" in Columbine's room), appearing in the manner of a fugue, in double and triple iteration (when three snowmen appear as faces before the excited Pantalon).

In the sonata, the conqueror character; in the pantomime, the Eulenspiegel humor, the Gozzi atmosphere—who was the man who, like his snowman, is capable of this double appearance?[59] I covered the title page and guessed. A friend who was listening, himself a creative musician from an erudite home, began to advise me: it must be a modern musician. Perhaps from the Debussy School. Perhaps of the Scriabin tendency. But a master in any case. The harmonic expression is so exotically colored, the whole so idiosyncratic—it is miraculous. No, I had to say, it is not miraculous. It is a miracle. For he who wrote the sonata and pantomime is named Erich Wolfgang Korngold, now twelve years old, but a boy of eleven when he wrote most of these notes. . . . I flipped open the sonata and found the following explanation in the preface: "This piano sonata is published not for the purpose of bringing it to the public, but rather to be distributed privately to musicians and musical experts in numbered exemplars exclusively for the purposes of appraisal. It was composed by a boy in his eleventh and twelfth years. Erich Wolfgang Korngold was born on May 29, 1897 in Brünn. He wrote down the first movement of the sonata in the summer of 1909, and the third by the beginning of 1909. The middle movement was begun at the end of 1908 and brought to completion in October 1909."

The other volumes said something similar—it was therefore a miracle, a genuine miracle. This music had swelled forth from a child, or shall we say, a half-child. You stand with an uncanny feeling before such mental and technical maturity, which we do not want to limit by calling it precocity. You stand with an uncanny feeling and are almost giddy when you think of the boy who writes such manly thoughts, and then of the "big," that is, grown-up (not great) musicians who often write such childish things.

Erich Wolfgang Korngold, the composer of this sonata, the six characteristic pieces, and the *Snowman* pantomime, has grown up, mind you, in a musical atmosphere. He is the son of the music critic of the *Neue freie Presse*, who, in order to do what was most imperative, forwarded the works of the boy to musicians and music lovers, in particular to those who are non-resident [in Vienna] and allowed the child to speak for himself. In this way, too, I became acquainted with the musical miracle, and, following the case with keen interest, I also came to know opinions that accorded with my impressions.

A music scholar of the first rank, Professor Hermann Kretzschmar in Berlin, passed judgment: "Even among the most extraordinary examples of musical precocity, that of your son remains phenomenal. As to modernity and virility of style, the only analogy that springs to my mind is that of the young Handel." Richard Strauss read Erich Wolfgang's compositions with the greatest astonishment and confesses: "The first feeling that overcomes you is horror and fear that so precocious a genius should be able to follow its normal development, which one would wish him so sincerely. This assurance of style, this mastery of form, this originality of expression in the sonata, this harmony, it is all truly astonishing. . . ." Engelbert Humperdinck also speaks of a maturity of creative power that almost frightens him: "If I were not to see it in black and white, I would consider it impossible." Artur Nikisch does not know what he should marvel at first, the flourishing invention, the imagination, or the boldness of the harmony: "My God, what all will this genius give to the world if it develops normally? May the Almighty only grant health to this exceptionally gifted human being—then there will be nothing to be afraid of. . . ." And in a similar tone other significant musicians of our time responded to the music parcel, for example Ferdinand Pfohl ("If this child develops in a progression in line with his achievements so far, he will someday leave his mark on his time"), Paul Marsop ("To me the advanced development of the mental faculty seems inconceivable"), and countless others.

What is peculiar, actually self-evident, is what resounds from most of these responses: the feeling of terror and fear triggered by this uncanny instance of precocity. And yet this miracle is also natural. It was Goethe who gave it expression: "Musical talent may well show itself earliest of any; for music is something innate and internal, which needs little nourishment from without, and no experience drawn from life. . . . But how would the divinity find everywhere opportunity to do wonders, if it did not sometimes try his powers on extraordinary individuals, before whom we stand astonished, and cannot understand whence they come?"[60]

With these words of wisdom, the dynamism of the natural wunderkind E. W. Korngold is also explained. A quiet boy with good, dark, dreamy eyes, whom you look at again and again and yet do not see at all. A boy who has been a musician since he was five years old. In his eighth year he had already advanced to the point of jotting down his own musical thoughts, and in his tenth year he surprises us with a kind of dramatic cantata, whose text he had a fellow schoolboy write, music full of mysterious harmony and of a gloomy, even ghostly atmosphere.[61] For several years a good master, Robert Fuchs, has been his counterpoint teacher; a musician of the likes of Alexander v. Zemlinsky, his teacher of piano and form.

Erich Wolfgang Korngold has not been talked about publicly yet. But if he has been kept away from the public so far, it will no longer be possible to prevent the public from pressing toward him. The *Schneemann* pantomime, a piece ready to be performed with no further ado, has already become known in Viennese musical families, and a performance of Erich Wolfgang's most recent work, a splendid piano trio, will certainly become known. Yet this work might encourage the timid to believe in the miracle of this boy, this gifted child who, one wishes, should draw energy from the forest, mountain, and sea, draw energy from nature, for he has to live long for his art.

NOTES

1. Max Kalbeck, "Wiener Philharmoniker," *Neues Wiener Tagblatt*, 24 April 1910. All translations are mine unless otherwise noted. For his assistance with a handful of passages, I am grateful to Peter Krapp.

2. Original German: "die Gemüter förmlich revolutioniert." Josef Reitler, "Wiens musikalische Atmosphäre und die Stadt der Tonheroen," *Österreichs Illustrirte Zeitung*, 21 August 1910. In 1910 Reitler was a sub-editor and part-time music critic at the *Neue freie Presse*.

3. For the father's take on Erich's extraordinary childhood and youth, see Julius Korngold, *Die Korngolds in Wien: Der Musikkritiker und das Wunderkind* (Zurich: M & T Verlag, 1991), 117–86. This memoir was published posthumously, but shortly before Julius's death the portions of it devoted to Erich's boyhood and youth were published in English translation. See Julius Korngold, *Child Prodigy: Erich Wolfgang Korngold's Years of Childhood* (New York: Willard, 1945). Other helpful sources include Brendan G. Carroll, *The Last Prodigy: A Biography of Erich Wolfgang Korngold* (Portland, OR: Amadeus Press, 1997), 21–93; and Guy Wagner, *Korngold: Musik ist Musik* (Berlin: Matthes & Seitz, 2008), 39–84.

4. J. Korngold, *Die Korngolds in Wien*, 118; and *Child Prodigy*, 11.

5. J. Korngold, *Die Korngolds in Wien*, 122–23; and *Child Prodigy*, 17–18. These two versions of Julius Korngold's memoirs give different dates of the first encounter with Mahler (1906 and 1907, respectively). I have followed the 1907 date since it accords with a near-contemporaneous report in the *Neue freie Presse* by Ernst Decsey, as well as with the recollections of both Mahler's and Korngold's widows. See Alma Mahler, *Gustav Mahler: Memories and Letters*, 3rd ed., ed. Donald Mitchell, trans. Basil Creighton (Seattle: University of Washington Press, 1975), 152; and Luzi Korngold, *Erich Wolfgang Korngold: Ein Lebensbild* (Vienna: Verlag Elisabeth Lafite, and Österreichischer Bundesverlag für Unterricht, Wissenschaft und Kunst, 1967), 11.

6. See, for example, Julius Korngold, "Gustav Mahler," *Neue freie Presse*, 4 June 1907.

7. For Erich's recollection of his years of study with Zemlinsky, see Erich Wolfgang Korngold, "Erinnerungen an Zemlinsky aus meiner Lehrzeit," *Auftakt* 1 (1920–21): 230–32. For a complete translation, see "Recollections of Zemlinsky from My Years of Study" in this volume. See also Carroll, *The Last Prodigy*, 48–50; and Lorraine Gorrell, *Discordant Melody: Alexander Zemlinsky, His Songs, and the Second Viennese School* (Westport, CT, and London: Greenwood Press, 2002), 33–34.

8. Felix Weingartner, "Ein Phänomen der Frühreife," *Almanach für die musikalische Welt 1914–15*, ed. Leopold Schmidt (Berlin and Leipzig: Herbert S. Loesdau, 1914), 155–64, at 158–59.

9. The present whereabouts of these testimonial letters is unknown, but we can assume they were among the more than two thousand letters to Erich and Julius Korngold seized by the Nazi authorities in 1938. See Carla J. Shapreau, "The Vienna Archives: Musical Expropriations During the Nazi Era and 21st-Century Ramifications," Institute of European Studies, University of California, Berkeley, 8, https://escholarship.org/uc/item/0q71b0p2. Excerpts from some of the letters can be found in, among other sources, Julius Korngold, *Die Korngolds in Wien*, 129–31; idem, *Child Prodigy*, 29–32; and Carroll, *The Last Prodigy*, 42–44.

10. A. B. [August Beer], "Ein musikalisches Phänomen," *Pester Lloyd*, 16 February 1910.

11. Richard Specht, "Erich Wolfgang Korngold," *Der Merker* 1/10 (25 February 1910): 427–30. A musical supplement to this issue includes the last movement of the sonata and one piece from *Don Quixote*; for a brief discussion on it, see 443–44.

12. Ernst Decsey, "Vom jüngsten Komponisten," *Neue freie Presse*, 27 February 1910. An annotated translation of Decsey's article appears at the end of this essay. See also Decsey, "Ein neuer Komponist," *Signale* 2 (March 1910): 329–31.

13. Erich Wolfgang Korngold Collection, Music Division, Library of Congress, Box 16, Folder 5. Beginning with the *Schauspiel-Ouvertüre*, Op. 4 (1911), Korngold would orchestrate his own scores.

14. "Künstlerische Soirée bei Baronin Bienerth," *Neue freie Presse*, 15 April 1910; "Die musikalische Soirée bei Baronin Bienerth," *Neue freie Presse, Abendblatt*, 15 April 1910; Paul Zifferer, "Gesellschaft im Modena-Palast," *Neue freie Presse*, 19 April 1910; "Das Wohltätigkeitskonzert im Ministerratspräsidium," *Neue freie Presse*, 21 April 1910; and "Die Wohltätigkeitsvorstellung im Ministerratspräsidium," *Neues Wiener Tagblatt*, 28 April 1910. I have taken my characterization of Vienna's second society from Brian Vick, "The Vienna Congress as an Event in Austrian History: Civil Society and Politics in the Habsburg Empire at the End of the Wars against Napoleon," *Austrian History Review* 46 (2015): 109–33, at 117; see also David Conway, *Jewry in Music: Entrance to the Profession from the Enlightenment to Richard Wagner* (Cambridge: Cambridge University Press, 2012), 120–25.

15. Felix Weingartner, *Lebenserinnerungen*, 2 vols. (1923–29; repr., Hamburg: Severus, 2013–14), 2:160–62.

16. Ibid., 2:189–90.

17. "Alter Musikus," *Wiener Montags-Journal*, 23 May 1910.

18. "Das Aktionsprogram des Hofoperntheaters für die Saison 1910/11," *Neue freie Presse*, 20 June 1910.

19. Max Kalbeck, "Hofoperntheater," *Neues Wiener Tagblatt*, 7 October 1910, from which the quotations in the following paragraph are taken.

20. Max Graf, "Hofoper," *Neues Wiener Journal*, 5 October 1910, from which the following quotations are also taken.

21. Making sense of this snide remark requires knowledge of the ballet's plot; a synopsis appears in note 58 below. Graf is referring here to Pantalon's drunken dream, which occurs near the end.

22. Lis Malina, *Dear Papa: How Is You? Das Leben Erich Wolfgang Korngolds in Briefen* (Vienna: Mandelbaum Verlag, 2017), 42–43 (italics in the original).

23. In his memoirs, Julius refused to name this antagonist, referring to him instead as "Iago" (J. Korngold, *Die Korngolds in Wien*, 144). In the abridged English edition of the memoirs, Graf is identified more neutrally as a "colleague" (Korngold, *Child Prodigy*, 52–53).

24. Karl Schreder, "Hofoper," *Deutsches Volksblatt*, 5 October 1910.

25. A. H., "Das musikalische Wunderkind: Der Schneemann des kleinen Erich Wolfgang," *Ostdeutche Rundschau*, 6 October 1910, from which the next two quotations are taken.

26. Before moving his family to Vienna, Julius practiced law in his Moravian hometown of Brno/Brünn. His prodigy son's name is entered as Erich Wolfgang in the registry of births maintained by the city's Israelitische Cultusgemeinde (Jewish Religious Community).

27. For a succinct discussion of Vienna's Jews at the turn of the century as both cultural insiders and social and political outsiders, see Steven Beller, *The Habsburg Monarchy* (Cambridge: Cambridge University Press, 2018), 211–20, esp. 216–20.

28. And not only music critics—see my discussion of this matter with respect to Goldmark, in David Brodbeck, *Defining Deutschtum: Political Ideology, German Identity, and Music-Critical Discourse in Liberal Vienna* (New York: Oxford University Press, 2014), 290–308.

29. Quoted in Alma Mahler Werfel, "Mein Leben war Leidenschaft: Memoiren aus Wiens grosser Zeit," *Die Weltwoche* (15 July 1960): 23.

30. The report from Munich is found in *Neue freie Presse*, 11 November 1910. Listings of the notables in attendance at the Viennese performance are given in *Neue freie Presse*, 12 December 1910; and *Der Morgen*, 12 December 1910.

31. M. K. [Max Kalbeck], "Merker-Konzert," *Neues Wiener Tagblatt*, 13 December 1910, from which the next few quotations are taken.
32. Max Graf, "Novitäten im Konzertsaal," *Neues Wiener Journal*, 13 December 1910, from which the other quotations in this paragraph are taken.
33. rbt. [Richard Robert], "Novitäten-Konzert," *Wiener Sonn- und Montags-Zeitung*, 12 December 1910. Alas, the English translation of "little maniac for dissonance" fails to capture the word play of the original: "kleiner grossen Dissonanzwüterich."
34. D. B. [David Josef Bach], "Novitätenkonzert," *Arbeiter-Zeitung*, 14 December 1910. The sneering reference to the publication two days earlier of such attendance lists in the *Neue freie Presse* and *Der Morgen* is obvious.
35. Korngold to Kalbeck, 13 December 1910, Julius Korngold Collection, Leo Baeck Institute, Center for Jewish History, New York, AR 2946, 10.
36. Korngold, *Die Korngolds in Wien*, 146–49; Wagner, *Korngold: Musik ist Musik*, 66–68; Carroll, *The Last Prodigy*, 65–66. Robert later turned up the heat in a biting feuilleton titled "The Case of Korngold." There he writes: "Dr. Korngold divides the whole musical world into two camps: artists who perform Erich Wolfgang [and] critics who praise his works with blind and deaf enthusiasm—and those who do not. . . . Dr. Korngold now practices criticism only from the point of view of the father." Richard Robert, "Der Fall Korngold," *Wiener Sonn- und Montags-Zeitung*, 11 May 1914. For a longer translation and discussion of this feuilleton, see Carroll, *The Last Prodigy*, 67. Carroll does not appear to recognize that Robert was a leading music critic, as well as pianist and teacher.
37. Karl Kraus, "Der kleine Korngold," *Die Fackel* 12 (31 December 1910): 1–3, from which the next several quotations are taken. On Kraus's hatred of the press, see Wilma Abeles Iggers, *Karl Kraus: A Viennese Critic of the Twentieth Century* (The Hague: Martinus Nijhoff, 1967), 94–119. For a more recent study, see Paul Reitter, *The Anti-Journalist: Karl Kraus and Jewish Self-Fashioning in Fin-de-Siècle Europe* (Chicago: University of Chicago Press, 2008).
38. On Kraus's complicated relationship with the Jewish Question, see Iggers, *Karl Kraus*, 171–91; and Reitter, *The Anti-Journalist*, passim.
39. J. K. [Julius Korngold], "Konzerte, *Neue freie Presse*, 31 October 1910. The letter quoted at the end is dated 30 July 1768 and addressed to Lorenz Hagenauer; see *The Letters of Mozart & His Family*, vol. 1, ed. Emily Anderson (London: Macmillan, 1938), 129–34.
40. Kraus, "Der kleine Korngold," 2.
41. Ibid.
42. Richard Batka, "Zum Wunderkindproblem," *Der Merker* 2/8 (1911): 337–40, from which the following quotations are taken. Batka, with Richard Specht, was a co-founder and co-editor of the journal.
43. Karl M. Klob, "Zum Wunderkindproblem," *Der Scherer* 13 (2. Ostermond [April]-Heft 1911): 4–7, from which the following quotations are taken. The citation of the month of publication in accordance with the old Germanic calendar—Ostermond instead of April—is emblematic of the publication's political orientation. See also André Banuls, "Das völkische Blatt 'Der Scherer': Ein Beitrag zu Hitlers Schulzeit," *Vierteljahrshefte für Zeitgeschichte* 18 (1970): 196–203; and Eugene Davidson, *The Making of Adolf Hitler: The Birth and Rise of Nazism* (New York: Macmillan, 1977), 11–13.
44. *Schmach des Jahrhunderts* (Shame of the century) was a bimonthly Berlin journal devoted to the fight against anti-Semitism.
45. In Gotthold Ephraim Lessing's play *Nathan der Weise* (1779), the famous eighteenth-century plea for religious tolerance among the Jews, Christians, and Muslims set in medieval Jerusalem, the Patriarch is a cruel and fanatical Christian.
46. Richard Batka, "'Scherer'-Schererein" ('Scherer'-Annoyances), *Der Merker* 2/16 (1911): 689–90, at 690.

47. Weingartner, "Ein Phänomen der Frühreife," 160–61, quoted in J. Korngold, *Die Korngolds in Wien*, 158.
48. Korngold to Kalbeck, Julius Korngold Collection, Leo Baeck Institute, AR 2946, 19. This undated letter was written, as noted, on the day of the dress rehearsal, November 29.
49. rbt. [Richard Robert], "Drittes philharmonisches Konzert," *Wiener Sonn- und Montags-Zeitung*, 1 December 1913; and D. B. [David Josef Bach], "Konzerte," *Arbeiter-Zeitung*, 13 December 1913.
50. Korngold to Kalbeck, 30 November 1913, Julius Korngold Collection, Leo Baeck Institute, Center for Jewish History, New York, AR 2946, 13.
51. Weingartner, *Lebenserinnerungen* 2:163.
52. Max Kalbeck, "Musik," *Neues Wiener Tagblatt*, 6 December 1913, from which the following quotations are taken.
53. Giselher Schubert, "Die Sinfonie in Fis: Korngold und das Problem des Sinfonischen in der Orchestermusik seiner Zeit," in Arne Stollberg, ed., *Erich Wolfgang Korngold: Wunderkind der Moderne oder letzter Romantiker?: Bericht über das international Symposion Bern 2007*, ed. Arne Stollberg (Munich: Edition Text + Kritik, [2008]), 87–100.
54. This article was translated and annotated by me. Ernst Decsey (sometimes spelled Décsey, b. 1870, Hamburg; d. 1941, Vienna) was an Austrian writer and music critic. In 1899, after studying law at the University of Vienna and music at the Vienna Conservatory, he became music critic for the *Grazer Tagespost*, later rising to become the paper's editor-in-chief in 1908. In 1920 he succeeded Max Kalbeck as the regular music critic of the *Neues Wiener Tagblatt*, a position he held until 1938, when he was let go by the Nazi authorities on racial grounds. He was the author of several novels and short stories, as well as of a number of biographies of composers and musical performers, perhaps most notably Hugo Wolf and Anton Bruckner.
55. The reference here is to the Peters Edition, Leipzig, and the Universal Edition, Vienna.
56. In July 1910 Julius Korngold sent copies of all three works to the Library of Congress. These are catalogued in the Performing Arts Division under the call numbers M23.K85 (Piano Sonata), M24.K86 (*Don Quixote*), and M1523.K72.S3 (*Der Schneemann*). This copy of the sonata, however, eventually went missing and has not been found. My thanks to Catherine Rivers, Music Specialist in the Library's Music Division, for her assistance in this matter.
57. "Last and least"—presumably the expression "last but not least" is intended—is given in English in the original. The passacaglia was originally composed as a freestanding exercise in C minor in the spring of 1909 as part of Erich's lessons with Zemlinsky; this is one of the works Erich played for Weingartner later that year. The autograph of this version carries the inscription "Beendet [Completed] 30.IV.1909." This manuscript was recently acquired by the Music Division, Library of Congress, and is housed in its Erich Wolfgang Korngold Collection; it has not yet been catalogued. On Mahler's suggestion, Erich later transposed the movement into D minor for use as the finale of his sonata.
58. A synopsis, adapted from Henry Lowell Mason, *Opera Stories* (Boston, 1910), 92–93, follows: A poor fiddler, Pierrot, loves the beautiful Columbine, whose guardian uncle, Pantalon, does all he can to upset the match, as he himself wishes to win the heart of his niece. Columbine is kept a prisoner in her chamber, her one joy being to look down from her window onto the Nicolo Market, longing for a sight of Pierrot. As Pierrot chances by her window Pantalon arrives with two servants and drives Pierrot away. Pantalon searches the stalls of the marketplace for something that will appeal to the fancy of his niece. His rude taste leads him to choose a life-size figure of the evil Krampus, which the servants carry to her, despite the teasing of a number of street urchins. As Pantalon goes on another errand, the urchins begin a snowball fight, while some of them

make a great snowman with arms outstretched toward Columbine. It waxes late, and Pierrot, with his violin, serenades Columbine, who is now too fearful to appear at the window. As the awkward Pantalon reappears, Pierrot hides behind the snowman. Pantalon, seeing the latter, is amused almost to death; he bows and scrapes and assumes, in frolic, a similar position. The lovesick Pierrot gets an idea from this, and after Pantalon has left he takes the snowman away, arrays himself in white, and takes the place of the snowman, with arms outstretched and eyes looking longingly to the window of his beloved.

The scene changes to Columbine's chamber. Pantalon is angry that his niece continually looks at the snowman, and he commands the figure to enter the house. The figure does not need a second bidding and straightaway is heard stomping up the stairs. Pantalon, overcome with fright, calls his servants, but they, too, are motionless with fear. He rushes out, but shortly returns dressed as the devil, thinking this to command the situation. To gain courage he takes several long sips of wine, and now, wonderful to relate, sees not only one snowman but two, three, four, and then a whole battalion who dance wildly about him. Dazed and overcome he falls into a heavy sleep. The snowmen leave, while Pierrot and Columbine rush out of the house. Pantalon, recovering his senses, runs to the marketplace but is greeted by the distant horn of the coach that bears the happy pair away. He tears his hair in despair and throws himself in anger upon the real snowman, which the thoughtful Pierrot had put back in its place.

59. Decsey passes over *Don Quixote* without remark. These pieces were not commercially published until 1995, when they were released by Schott.

60. Johann Wolfgang von Goethe, *Conversations of Goethe with Johann Peter Eckermann*, trans. John Oxenford, ed. J. K. Moorhead, intro. Havelock Ellis (1930; repr., New York: Dover, 1998), 382, entry for 14 February 1831. The subject of discussion here was Mozart.

61. This was surely a reference to *Gold*, the cantata that had so impressed Mahler three years earlier.

"You must return to life": Notes on the Reception of *Das Wunder der Heliane* and *Jonny spielt auf*

CHARLES YOUMANS

A gifted, successful composer of opera, still young, romantic in musical style and intellectual disposition, perplexed by a growing rift between his creative inclinations and the bustling modernity around him, heads west, to the New World, gambling optimistically and a bit desperately that his creative ability, a product of profound devotion to Occidental culture, can be adapted to the vibrant artistic milieu of America. Max, the melancholy protagonist of Ernst Krenek's *Jonny spielt auf* (*Jonny Strikes Up*, 1927), had more than a little in common with Erich Wolfgang Korngold, jazz or no jazz. Krenek too would find his way to the New World, having lived through the private doubts and "transformation" (Susan Cook's term) on which the autobiographically conceived Max was modeled.[1] These three had an artistic dilemma in common, and a quest, irrespective of the fact that only two of them were chased from Europe by barbarians. A new world had replaced the old, and it required a different, revitalized music. "What was the *Kunstidealist* doing in the land of the dollar?" asked Julius Korngold in his obituary for Mahler.[2] His son would also raise that question, and provide an answer of sorts.

For opera composers in the late 1920s, the genre itself encapsulated the problem, and it saw a bewildering array of proposed solutions.[3] Korngold's *Das Wunder der Heliane* (1927), his intended magnum opus and the other major event of Vienna's 1927–28 season, was, like *Jonny*, a high-profile document of this "opera crisis."[4] Reasonably enough, the two works have been read as antithetical: what could a "jazz opera" (so described by everyone but the composer) featuring a blackface bandleader and a slapstick death by train have to do with a "timeless" (Korngold's word) morality play culminating in not one but two resurrections? In *Heliane*, Korngold set out to eclipse the Mahler of the Second and Eighth symphonies, with "unending, unreserved affirmations of eschatalogical truth and pious purity" (Richard Taruskin), couched in a "feast for the ear, prepared with fabulous skill and lavish generosity by a well-endowed talent manifestly giving its All" (Robin Holloway). *Jonny*, conversely, offered "corporeal elation and spiritual nihilism, a tonic for the tired and the disillusioned, for people who felt betrayed by the lie of transcendence" (Taruskin), by means of music seemingly determined to leave the feelings cold: "The musical norm is omni-purpose atonality crossed with *Neue Sachlichkeit* functionalism; the jazz is equally colourless" (Holloway).[5]

If ever a black-and-white reading fit the bill, it would seem to here. As I hope to demonstrate below, however, early critics saw a more nuanced range of concerns, regardless of their newspaper's angle, and they reacted to the works through a common frame of reference that today is all but forgotten. The stylistic differences that strike our ear so powerfully were acknowledged, but they were not primary. Rather, they were folded into a wider conversation—about genre, style, commerce, modernism, celebrity, and influence—that emerges when considering a thicker sample of the reception.

"Is grand opera itself necessary today, or even possible?"[6] That this question could be posed in a positive review of *Jonny*, at that date the greatest box-office draw in the history of the German stage, and answered with a contented "no," suggests an attack from the inside. But Krenek, it is worth remembering, went on to compose some sixteen more operas, to Korngold's single example after *Heliane*; in 1927, in other words, both composers were invested in the genre's future, artistically and commercially.[7] Krenek faced accusations of selling out with *Jonny*, and these stung, but Korngold was just as eager for his work to be popular—and with twenty-six Vienna performances by June 1930 (compared to thirty-five for *Jonny* through 1931) and productions in twelve other cities, *Heliane* was anything but a failure.[8] In the back of each composer's mind, of course, was *Wozzeck*, which had rolled out in 1925 as an artistic triumph and a solid business proposition, proving that living opera was still possible and that artistic risk could find its reward.

What did it mean to be "modern" at this historical moment? Who and what represented the present, and the future? *Jonny* proved more decisively than ever that the "atonals" did not own the avant-garde in Central Europe—and any reader of the journal *Anbruch* would recognize this as a truism.[9] We will see that the reviews of both operas particularly emphasize stylistic heterogeneity, with the tendencies of Schoenberg's school folded in among a rich variety of approaches—an obvious enough observation with Krenek, but less so for Korngold, whose last work before *Heliane* was

Figure 1. Ernst Krenek ca. 1925.

the *Vier kleine Karikaturen für Kinder*, Op. 19 (1926), playful experiments with the styles of Schoenberg, Stravinsky, Bartók, and Hindemith.[10] Wagner, too, still hovered in the mind, complemented now by an equally pressing concern, the canonical contemporary Richard Strauss, whom Schoenberg would describe in 1923 as "*the only revolutionary* in our time."[11]

Figure 2. Erich Wolfgang Korngold in 1927.

In supporting that provocative remark Schoenberg would lump together *Intermezzo* and *Elektra* as works that defined the era and would retain their status, a judgment that would be richly confirmed by critics' preoccupation with Strauss, especially *Salome*, *Rosenkavalier*, *Ariadne*, and the two works named above, in reviews of both *Heliane* and *Jonny*.

To their first listeners, then, these operas embodied much more than the confrontation between monumental late-Romantic redemption kitsch and pop music–inflected modernist atonality. They engaged with a rich variety of issues, which overlap freely in the two works and were described by the composers themselves as well as by listeners, by critics, and even by the operas' characters, whose words and actions can be read as negotiations of aesthetic ground. Teasing apart these elements reveals an extraordinary kinship, with *Heliane* and *Jonny* unexpectedly homologous, if not cut from the same cloth.

Korngold's decision to compose an opera on *Die Heilige* (The Saint), a "mysterium" by the piteously short-lived Hans Kaltneker (1895–1919), was made "in a little *Konditorei* on the Wiedner Hauptstraße," where the composer brought Luzi Korngold, watched her read the play, and asked if she thought it would make a suitable operatic subject.[12] To have the new bride deciding Erich's projects was the stuff of Julius's nightmares, though in this case the father was unusually successful in keeping his petty judgments to himself, apart from a snide characterization of the subject matter: "sexual difficulties, similar to those that featured in [Kaltneker's] other works."[13] Later it would emerge that the poet had written the play with Korngold specifically in mind, as many aspiring librettists must have done.

What set this work apart was the "curious mixture of chastity and sensuality," of "simultaneously pure and erotic love," a risky hybrid that Luzi (and presumably Erich) heard as well in the voice of Lotte Lehmann, the first Heliane.[14] The plot deals with a nameless Stranger, jailed and awaiting execution for spreading hope and joy among an oppressed people. On his last night he receives a visit from Heliane, the wicked Ruler's virgin wife, who eases the condemned man's final hours by granting his requests to see her hair, then her feet, and finally her entire naked body. The relationship's brisk intensification appears headed beyond the visual—in fact, the Stranger asks, "Will you let me sink myself into you, so that I know nothing more, know nothing, feel nothing, know nothing, suffer nothing, but you, only you, only you?"—but in the nick of time she retires to an adjacent chapel, to "pray for you, and for myself."[15] Meanwhile the Ruler arrives, unaware of his wife's presence, and offers a deal: clemency, if the Stranger can teach him to gain his wife's sexual consent. Heliane overhears the conversation and, predictably aghast, steps from the shadows, revealing what seems an obvious betrayal and finding herself commanded by the Ruler to face his tribunal on charges of infidelity.

So much for Act 1. The remaining two acts, in brief, involve Heliane's defense, encapsulated in "Ich ging zu ihm" (I went to him), the opera's best-known excerpt, where she claims chaste motivations while the music hints otherwise; the Stranger's suicide with Heliane's knife; the dismissal of the court by the Ruler, who orders Heliane to undergo, "before God," the "trial of the bier," with freedom her prize if she can resurrect the Stranger (end Act 2); a crazed demonstration by the *Volk* in anticipation of Heliane's miracle; her failed attempt at resurrection, which breaks down in her revised account of the fateful encounter, that is, a confession of her "human" feelings for the Stranger; the latter's miraculous return from the dead in spite of Heliane's apparent guilt; her murder by the Ruler, who then runs away; and finally, exhaustingly, her own resurrection by the Stranger, who takes her hand as they float to heaven.

Intentional comedy is in short supply, but otherwise the work has something for everyone—most notably, blasphemy, guaranteed to arouse strong feelings since legally speaking it represented a potential crime. This possibility was raised directly by the critic Max Springer in the pages of the *Reichspost*, eliciting a lengthy and self-evidently panicked response from the composer. Even the accusation itself was newsworthy; the *Wiener Sonn- und Montags-Zeitung*, for example, quoted Springer's charge of "lewd sultriness" in Heliane's disrobing, a dramatic choice that "would have to offend not only the sensibilities of a faithful Catholic, but those of any Christian-feeling person at all."[16] Korngold protested vociferously, if not entirely credibly: "Nowhere in my opera does this death-overcoming love have the character of sensual, sinful lust or wantonness," a comment that flatly contradicted his character's own exasperated confession at the moment of truth in Act 3: "I can't do it, I can't do it! I loved him!"[17] Korngold subsequently cited that very line as proof of a crisis of conscience and "repentant doubt," and then asked, dangerously, regarding the premiere that took place in Hamburg on October 7: "Could a story grip and move its audiences, as has been demonstrated in Hamburg and now also in Vienna, if it contained elements that violated religious feeling?"[18]

The answer, as the composer seemed to know and *Jonny* would soon prove beyond doubt, was an emphatic "yes." That confession of bad behavior was one of the work's selling points, so much so that it was spelled out explicitly in the synopsis provided by *Radio-Wien* for listeners of the live broadcasts: whereas in Act 2 Heliane explains her nudity as an act of "great compassion" (in the words of the anonymous synopsis-author), Act 3 is driven by the self-incriminating confession, which, offered as she looks at the Stranger's body on the bier and prepares to attempt his resurrection, leads the onlooking *Volk* to demand justice through her death at the stake.[19] What the synopsis leaves out, and what could hardly be missed, is that we in the audience are already implicated in her sin in Act 1, when

Figure 3. Leopold Sachse and Egon Pollak, director and conductor of the Hamburg world premiere of *Das Wunder der Heliane*, with Korngold and librettist Hans Müller after the dress rehearsal on October 7, 1927.

we gaze at her along with the Stranger and hear him plead, "Give me the miracle [*Wunder*] of your radiant white body," a none-too-subtle play on the title that would not be out of place in an operetta at the Theater an der Wien.[20]

Violating religious feeling was good for business, then, if one staged it properly and had energetic press coverage (positive or negative). Indeed, plenty of commentators came to Korngold's aid, including the same anonymous critic who quoted Springer's charge; he would go so far as to spell out the work's moral: "that on earth only one thing, love, has the power to work miracles, and that here below all existence remains appearance [*ein Gleichnis*], decipherable at the moment when one crosses over into that other, higher life."[21] From a publicity standpoint such rationalizations were necessary, to explain away the scandal but also to keep it alive in an acceptable guise. This much Korngold had learned from the example of Strauss; before *Salome*, Strauss was a well-known composer, successful and established, but afterward he was a phenomenon, firmly installed as the leader of his generation. And everything Strauss achieved, Korngold wanted: artistic respect and accomplishment, to be

Figure 4. Program for the Viennese premiere of
Das Wunder der Heliane at the State Opera.

sure, but also broad public success, built on the foundation of a masterpiece ensconced in the repertories of all the major theaters in Austria and Germany. Thus, undeterred by Mahler's difficulties with *Salome* and the Viennese censors twenty years earlier, Korngold set off on the same road.

Strauss had been something of a musical godfather to Korngold ever since reviewing juvenilia that the cautiously proud Julius had sent around to various musical authorities asking for their unvarnished opinion of his son's potential.[22] In a response of 3 January 1910, the famously laconic Strauss positively bubbled over with enthusiasm:

> Today I received your son's compositions and have read them with the greatest astonishment. This case hardly calls for mere congratulations: the first feeling that seizes one, when one hears that this was written by an 11-year-old boy, is that of awe and concern that so precocious a genius would be able to follow its normal development, which one would wish him so sincerely. This assurance of style, this mastery of form, this characteristic expressiveness in the sonata, this bold harmony, are truly astonishing. How happy you must feel![23]

In subsequent years Strauss would follow Korngold's progress closely, and the two occasionally met, as in a 1912 visit described by Julius in which the teenager used Zemlinsky's analytical methods to explain progressions in *Salome*, eliciting the composer's amused response, "I never noticed that myself."[24] Whatever Julius's fury at Strauss's 1919 appointment as co-director of the renamed Vienna State Opera, and however sharply he criticized his administrative choices, he did not forget Strauss's many kindnesses to Erich and to himself, recalling that Strauss took time during his 1921–22 trip to the United States to write a note to Julius on the success then being enjoyed by *Die tote Stadt* in New York.[25] For his part, Korngold would dedicate to Strauss his first mature independent symphonic overture, *Sursum corda*, a subject on which a symphonic poem had been written by Alexander Ritter, Strauss's own mentor.[26]

All of this goes some distance toward explaining why Korngold should have built his magnum opus as a pastiche of allusions to Strauss. It was predetermined, personally, musically, and professionally. Bruno Walter acknowledged this reality when in his foreword to Luzi's biography he summed up Korngold's creative nature by stating that *Heliane* was his greatest work and Strauss was his main influence.[27] Walter knew that in *Heliane* the debt went well beyond *Salome*. The final duet, which Julius called a product of "an inspired hour . . . a fully formed gift from above," plainly recalls Ariadne and Bacchus's ecstatic transfiguration—without, however, the distancing effect of Strauss's onstage audience.[28] The overbaked symbolism of *Die Frau ohne Schatten* makes itself felt throughout, not only in unrestrained musical opulence but in characters lacking names, in earthly suffering contrasted with magical wonders, and in otherworldly effects of harmony and timbre that startle by their peculiarity.

The most thoroughgoing parallel with Strauss, it turns out, is one that almost no one noticed: *Guntram* (1894), his ill-fated first opera. An unrepentant Wagnerian collage with clear allusions to everything from *Tannhäuser* and *Lohengrin* to *Die Meistersinger* and *Parsifal*, *Guntram* tells of a medieval minstrel who brings hope to an oppressed *Volk*, gets on the wrong side of their tyrannical ruler, the cruel Duke Robert, falls in love with the Duchess, kills the Duke in self-defense, then renounces his beloved to seek a Schopenhauerian redemption in asceticism. On several counts this strange and little-performed work, on which the young Strauss spent a considerable part of his creative energies over a period of six years (1887–93), and with which he believed he would assume his place as the leader of Austro-German music—a work that Korngold certainly knew both in musical content and biographical context—left a distinct impression on a composer attempting the same thing at exactly the same age (*Guntram* and *Heliane* were premiered in the years when their composers turned thirty).

The explicit socialist dimension of *Guntram*'s plot, an element resonant with certain of Strauss's lieder from the mid-1890s (for example, the "Lied des Steinklopfers"), found an echo in *Heliane*'s suffering populace, whose plight and anger would have impressed operagoers accustomed to seeing impoverished Viennese stampeding bread wagons and fighting in the streets over milk.[29] The critic for the *Arbeiter-Zeitung* saw this theme as deeply embedded in the opera, even with the choice of Kaltneker, whom he identified as a hero of the working class. In all three of Kaltneker's finished plays, the writer claimed, "there resonated a voice that is distinct and understandable first and only to the workers—a pure, noble voice, that knew how to speak the unspeakable and to make the incredible credible and clear."[30]

As in *Guntram*, this element lent the story a modern, realistic dimension that critics of *Heliane* likewise noted. In *Der Morgen* this feature accounted for the opera's impact: "Powerful is the explosive strength of the work's drama, powerful the realism of the crowd scenes, powerful the choruses that he carries upward to high C-sharp."[31] Ferdinand Pfohl, whose review of the Hamburg premiere was published as a feuilleton in the *Neue freie Presse* when Julius discreetly recused himself, likewise drew attention to the "realistic fury of the folk scenes, the hysterical scream of the great masses, their ecstasy, their fervor, their abandon, their anger, their outrage."[32] For Pfohl, realism was balanced with the idealistic dimension that readers of that newspaper would have expected at the State Opera: "In poetry and music, in character, intellectual content and mood, in form and color, *Heliane* shows the hallmarks of a simultaneously modern-realist and modified Romantic style."[33] The former constituted a distinct, substantial element, then, albeit one that gave way to a reassuring final duet "lead[ing] upward to a transcendental sphere of consecration and transfiguration."[34]

Guntram would also be a model in creating distance from Wagner by means of the variety of its Wagnerian sources; constructed as a "monstrous fantasy on Wagner's complete works," its swirling allusive chaos would be heard by thoughtful listeners as paradoxically new, personal, and removed from Wagner.[35] Korngold's similarly freewheeling intertextuality suggests that he knew the pressure of composing with a head full of someone else's works; the Dance of the Seven Veils–like exhibitionism leads here to an attack of conscience, a reunion with the Jochanaan figure, a Bacchus-Ariadne happily ever after, and a mystical symbolic fairy-tale transcendence, even as the Alberich-like Ruler explicitly renounces love at the discovery that his Elisabeth is also a Venus and, in her power over him, perhaps even a Kundry. Or, in the words of the critic for *Freiheit!*, it was a mélange of the "love and heroic lives" (*Liebes- und Heldenleben*) of Lohengrin, Tannhäuser, and Tristan, "but Korngold has always remained 'himself,' he creates something new without wanting to be 'different,' he is no epigone of Wagner, but an individual spirit."[36]

By 1927 it was more than apparent to Korngold and indeed to any culturally aware composer that old materials could be used to make new art, and that one could establish a personal identity through the idiosyncratic manipulation of recognizable preexisting styles. The juxtaposition of stylistic references would be a hallmark of the opera, widely remarked by critics, who often pointed to the leading lights of contemporary music, including the avant-garde. Along with a typically healthy dose of Schreker and Puccini—Korngold was by then known as the "Viennese Puccini," and the second act's debt to *Turandot* was obvious—were moments of Debussy, Stravinsky, Delius, and even quasi-atonality, in sufficient quantity that *Heliane* could be attacked as having produced a sort of anti-neoclassicism, that is, that Korngold had used up-to-date stylistic materials to produce an old-fashioned music. "Could one hold that Korngold signifies a *further development* of older operatic music, or is his music a *repetition* of the old, if also with new means? Can one in fact make old music with new means?"[37]

The question, then, was not whether Korngold was open to the technical "advances" of his modernist contemporaries, but to what ends he was applying those techniques. That he made use of them, albeit in a personal style drawing on a rich palette of influences, was considered a given. Here even Pfohl put his cards on the table, claiming to hear modernist means put to good ends. In the Act 1 love scene, "with its fairy-tale iridizing orchestral colors and gentle-as-breath sounds, a play of the softest

Example 1. *Das Wunder der Heliane*, Act 1, scene 4.

dissonances gives off a poetic fragrance without equal" (Example 1).³⁸ At the height of the choral outburst in Act 3, with the brass divided into three groups and playing in three different keys, "the terrible against the immense and elementary, the gratingly dissonant together with the consonance of the human throng, has rarely before been represented with greater force" (Example 2).³⁹ Others heard Debussy-like passages:

Example 2. *Das Wunder der Heliane*, Act 3, scene 1.

"Korngold has accomplished the salvation of the seventh. He loves this interval tenderly, often luxuriating in a veritable harem of sevenths in parallel motion" (Example 3).[40] Likewise, there were meter changes reminiscent of Stravinsky: Korngold was "the phenomenal technician of the present, who can fashion what and how he wants. He reigns sovereign over all means. The richness of rhythm, of interesting (and always architectonically well-grounded) meter changes, of tonal flexibility, makes the score a true miracle-work [*Wunderwerk*]" (Example 4).[41]

Korngold's own words indicate that his deployment of modern means was witting. In his Opus 18 songs, which he called "character studies for my new opera," the composer explored atonality as a way of broadening his expressive palette for the opera:

> Harmonically speaking, *Heliane* is more radical than *Violanta* and *Die tote Stadt*. By no means do I isolate myself against

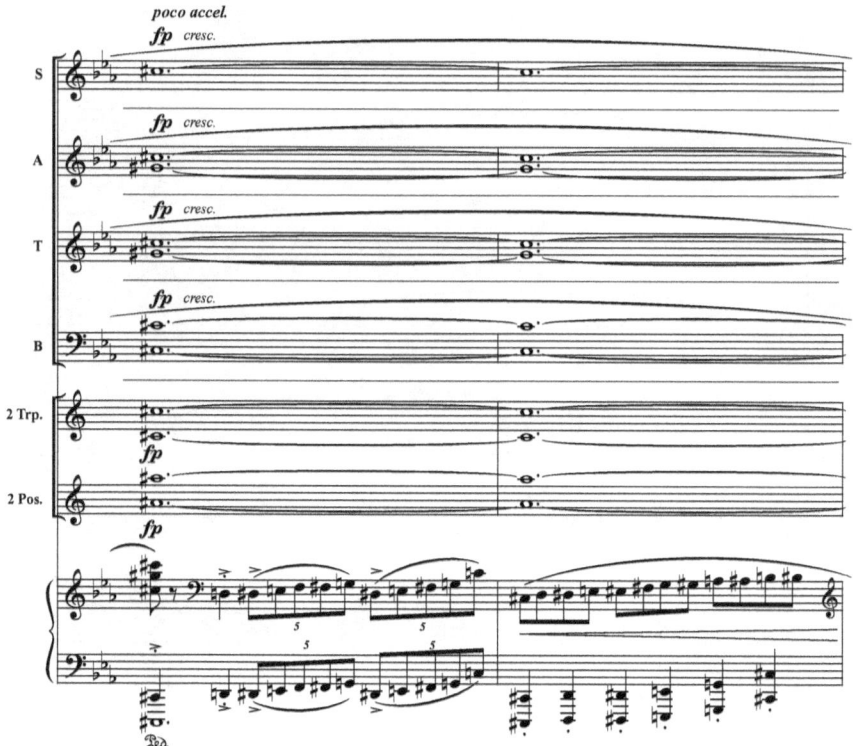

Example 2. continued

the harmonic enrichments which we owe to, say, Schoenberg. But I will not give up claim to the eminent expressive possibilities offered by "old music." In my Kaltneker songs, there are places that one might designate as truly atonal. I do not subscribe to any one doctrine. My musical creed may be called the inspired idea. With what displeasure one hears this concept nowadays! And nevertheless, how could artificial construction, the most exact musical mathematics, triumph over the fundamental strength of the inspired idea![42]

Here Korngold embraced the "atonals," his father's archenemies, while simultaneously maintaining faith with the Straussian concept of the *melodischen Einfall* (melodic idea or inspiration). He sought, in a word, to be modern, or modern enough—to acknowledge the current state of the material while openly retaining his connection to those traditional factors that gave the art its power. In basic orientation this perspective is

Example 2. continued

not unrelated to Schoenberg's ostensible conservatism in "Brahms the Progressive," which, while delving more deeply into technical matters, argued for a union of tradition and novelty.

Julius himself provided evidence that Korngold took such claims seriously, with the complaint that his son had an "inexplicably early infection of that musical degeneration that would soon start to shake the tonal foundations of music."[43] Korngold was a regular participant in meetings of the International Society for New Music, founded by Rudolph Réti and Egon Wellesz in 1922, even as his father was regarded as the group's main enemy.[44] At a concert of the Incorporated Society of Contemporary Music in Venice on September 5, 1925, his String Quartet in A Major made a strong impression.[45] Schoenberg's Society for Private Musical Performances also included music by Korngold.[46] With his quirkily catholic compositional tendencies, Korngold used old music in new ways, but also new music in ways that at least on the surface seemed antiquated. And he would maintain consistently—though we cannot know whether

Example 3. *Das Wunder der Heliane*, Act 1, scene 4.

he truly believed it—that old and new were of no consequence to him. What mattered was reaching his audience.

It is difficult to imagine a sharper contrast with *Heliane* than *Jonny spielt auf*, the first and paradigmatic *Zeitoper*. Set in "a central European city, Paris, and the Alps during the 1920s," the opera populates itself mainly with artists: Max, a successful but troubled opera composer; Anita, a glamorous singer in need of more fame and more love; Daniello, a celebrity violinist living the good life; and Jonny, a black jazz-band violinist unconstrained by morals or inhibitions of any kind. Onstage we see modern settings (a hotel corridor, a train station), machines (a loudspeaker, an arriving train, a car that points its lights at the audience), and newspaper-worthy events presented with cool objectivity (Daniello's death beneath the wheels of a locomotive, accidental or self-inflicted, is barely noticed by the other characters). All possible resources are marshaled

Example 4. *Das Wunder der Heliane*, Act 3, scene 4.

to bring the characteristic features of contemporary urban life into the sanctified, timeless museum-atmosphere of the opera house.

The central dramatic problem belongs to Max, and it focuses our attention from the start on the challenges and purpose of being an artist in the present-day world. When the curtain rises we find Max wandering near a glacier, singing a banal paean to his beloved natural surroundings and seeking an answer to ill-defined melancholic longings. He rescues Anita, they fall in love, she travels to Paris to perform his opera, and a sex farce ensues in which Jonny steals Daniello's Amati violin and Anita and Yvonne

Example 4. continued

(a mischievous chambermaid) pair off for one-night stands with Daniello and Jonny respectively. The next day Anita returns home, but her infidelity sends Max again to the glacier, which sings to him (beautifully, all sides would admit) before being interrupted by Anita's voice heard through a loudspeaker, a siren that seconds the glacier's call to Max: "You must return to life." Back in town, high jinks ensue: Anita and Max board a train for America, while Daniello is left as a corpse on the tracks and Jonny plays the Amati atop a globe as the onlookers dance and a chorus announces

Figure 5. Cover of printed score, *Jonny spielt auf*.

fatefully, "The glittering New World comes across the sea and conquers old Europe through dance."[47]

Krenek would protest consistently that *Jonny* was not a *Jazzoper*; rather, the work came from his five-year "neo-Romantic" period, with Max as the protagonist and his music the work's central aesthetic statement.[48] To at least some contemporaries the claim was plausibly sincere and aesthetically reasonable, notwithstanding the shock of hearing jazz performed in an opera house by an actor in blackface. Jazz lends atmosphere, in this reading, and it is delivered by a buffoon (albeit a dangerous one), along the lines of Ochs and his waltzes in *Der Rosenkavalier*. Julius saw the potential for this very comparison, and he confirmed its believability by attempting to undercut it: "Were the waltzes in *Rosenkavalier* directed at a 'will of the time?'[*Zeitwillen*]"[49] Yes and no, one might say, but in any case the basic intent of creating ambience with popular dances seems ordinary and uncontroversial. The critic for *Das kleine Blatt* spelled out the point:

> Initially the opera patron is taken aback when he encounters, in the house where he is accustomed to hearing the melodies of the great classical masterworks, or the metaphysically imbued operas of Wagner, the sounds of a jazz band and a saxophone. But if one thinks a bit more deeply, one recalls that the dances used in comic operas of earlier times were also contemporary, and thus the crime of the young, ingenious poet-composer Ernst Krenek is not so great. It is as though he had thrown open a window and allowed the fresh air to purify the dusty atmosphere of the opera of today. In any case: is there an opera of today?[50]

This last line brings us closer to Max's problem, and Krenek's. If Max is treated as an object of affectionate parody and a gentle exercise in self-criticism on the part of Krenek, the character's dilemma—What purpose can I serve in this world?—is nonetheless real. Anita, for her part, is no less concerned with fundamental questions, most affectingly when she philosophizes, Marschallin-style, after her affair with Daniello: "One should live the moment as though none would follow."[51]

Approaching serious matters by means of comic irony was of course a straightforward and long-established Romantic technique, which Krenek's critics recognized as such. Rather than timeliness or objectivity, the reviewer for the *Arbeiter-Zeitung* heard echoes of Tieck, as the composer strove "for the practice of a highly Romantic irony, a joking game [*Scherzspiel*] not without deeper feeling, and, if you will, not without deeper significance . . . . 'Have you tried to treat the comical as grave, the grave as comical? . . . ,' says Tieck. There can be no better motto for *Jonny spielt auf*."[52] The irony extended as well to musical style, which ranges widely and none too subtly, as was noted in a matter-of-fact characterization in *Das interessante Blatt*: "There is little to be seen in terms of a uniform style; each scene is designed

Figure 6. Vera Schwarz, Alfred Jerger, and Koloman von Pataky, lead performers of the first Viennese production of *Jonny spielt auf* at the State Opera on December 31, 1927. *Das interessante Blatt*, 5 January 1928.

in a musically distinct way."[53] Krenek would later claim to have taken this approach deliberately, in emulation of Berg, who at least for this brief period would be a more important model than Schoenberg, thanks to an eclectic disposition:

> For my ostensibly reactionary exploits, I also fabricated a little theory to the effect that the newly discovered means of musical expression, that is, the atonal vocabulary, should not prevent the use of the old ones, and that it should be possible to restore the old vocabulary to its original power and freshness, through something vaguely mystical which I called *Urerlebnis*, or primordial experience. In this I hoped to differentiate myself constructively from my fellow modernists of the Schoenberg school who promoted the idea that the new idiom had superseded the old and rendered the meaningful use of the old resources impossible. Only Alban Berg was striving for a synthesis in accordance with his conciliatory, warmhearted temperament, but he arrived at different results.[54]

Neoclassicism was in the air, it seems, or at least something vaguely like it, but Krenek apparently felt a kinship with the Second Viennese School that he did not want to sever entirely, and so he looked for a broadly accommodating middle ground. No doubt his attraction to Berg had both aesthetic and commercial motivations—which is not to accuse him but merely to say that it produced effective music, music that could reach listeners without compromising itself with respect to substance. This was the spirit that allowed and encouraged the appropriation of jazz; the subject matter was relatively unimportant, as we see from Krenek's claim that *Leben des Orest* was the only true "jazz opera" in his output.[55]

Julius, in a twelve-column, five-page feuilleton published the day after *Jonny*'s premiere, and typical not only for its acerbic wit but for its deep, painstaking engagement with the work, heard a different model for Krenek's ostensible innovations: Richard Strauss. "This succession of brief pictures in everyday tone, this dialogue in everyday prose—is it not lifted from Strauss's *Intermezzo*?"[56] In dramatic organization, in its libretto (written by Krenek himself), and above all in its music, Julius heard a second-rate imitation of a work and a composer he deeply admired, notwithstanding the battles over his opera administration. "For its musical as well as its scenic form, *Jonny* likewise depends on Strauss's *Intermezzo*, except that with Strauss we have a masterfully constructed, continuously flowing, motivically and melodically saturated, easily mobile dialogue- and interlude-music, but with Krenek—the opposite."[57]

Echoes of Strauss were heard as well by the critic of the *Neues Wiener Journal*, but here in a pejorative description of *Jonny* as a straightforward revival of traditional operatic organization, again along the lines of *Rosenkavalier*, "it proceeded as normally as other operas," and, as in the model, emptied of any content "from which one could expect instruction, moral principles and higher philosophy."[58] In *Der Morgen* one could likewise find the complaint that "this opera has nothing to do with a worldview."[59] The charge of an unapologetic emptiness, where "the dehumanization and mechanization of art again takes a powerful step forward," was easily shifted from Strauss to Krenek, particularly given the parodic elements, however tenderhearted, in the common treatment of Max and the amusingly idealistic composer in *Ariadne*.[60] Max's glacier music can no more be taken at face value than can Strauss's opera within an opera, and that was a source of frustration to many listeners.

Is that why Krenek turned away from Zeitoper so quickly after *Jonny*? Within five years he would return to the Schoenbergian fold. Did he take Julius's criticism to heart? The accusation of "mendacious Romanticism" apparently stung.[61] "To leave no doubt about the untruthfulness of these mountain-sentimentalities, the author lets us see the hotel terrace nearby the glacier, with jazz and dance music for good measure."[62] Here an

Charles Youmans

Figure 7. Program for the Viennese premiere of *Jonny spielt auf*.

authority figure, perhaps the most powerful force in Krenek's native city, accused him of musical lies, of betraying his art. And beneath the satire, Julius claimed, lay something sinister: "The nigger [*Der Nigger*], the bringer of jazz culture, triumphs with a stolen violin over Beethoven's Europe? This does not seem to be a satirical punch line."[63]

Paul Bekker, on the other hand, was in a position to grasp the point, having mentored Krenek in 1925–27 and witnessed his absorption of influences that culminated in *Jonny*. Like Krenek, Bekker believed that the success of *Jonny* was based on a massive misunderstanding: "The fact that the whole sprang from an ironic purpose was overlooked, as was the serious intent of the lyric parts."[64] Walter Henry argued similarly in *Anbruch* shortly after the premiere that *Jonny* was, in the words of Susan Cook, "more than a jazz opera or a work concerned only with mirroring its time"; the grotesque celebration was meant rather to redirect its audience toward symbolism rooted in both Jungian personality archetypes and a Nietzschean conflict between the Dionysian Jonny and the Apollonian Max.[65] (*Intermezzo* meets *Die Frau ohne Schatten*, more or less.) Certainly, the composer of *Jonny* rejected Weill's inclination, inspired by Busoni, to write music that maintained a determined independence while studiously avoiding illustration of the action on the stage.

Read carefully, the early reception of these two markedly different operas seems to warrant a reconsideration of what they have in common. That they had conspicuous differences and were in direct competition was obvious from the beginning, even to the Austrian tobacco authority, which produced cigarettes named for both operas at the time of their premieres. "Mine is more expensive," Korngold would observe, noting its golden mouthpiece.[66] The striking contrasts presented commercial opportunities and offered each composer a chance to galvanize support among segments of the ticket-buying public. But that conflict obscured interrelationships that deserve wider acknowledgment than they have received.

Korngold and Krenek were precocious, prolific composers who did not quite live up to their potential, and who found their careers diverted in ways they could not predict or control. They were also composers who hoped with their music to reach people—as many as possible—whose lives they aimed to improve through thoughtful, even provocative engagement with important moral and spiritual questions. In the context of Vienna in the 1920s this meant for both a need to address the clash between the sexual and spiritual sides of human nature, and to let the chips fall where they may. A sex-crazed "Negro" jazz musician using a stolen violin to "conquer Europe" was bound to ruffle feathers, but Heliane's compassionate striptease, revealed by the character herself in Act 3 as an act of blasphemy, was hardly a lesser act of artistic daring. Anita cannot suppress her libido either, but she takes the discreet step of channeling it away from Jonny and toward the white, upper-class, artistically legitimate yet unsavory Daniello. Heliane uses *Mitleid* as a cover for an autoerotic reverie that inevitably undercuts the subsequent transfiguration—"Papa's masturbatory fantasy," in Taruskin's words.[67]

Salvation also figures centrally in both works; the protagonists depart for an ideal space, whether we call it heaven or America, that facilitates a synthesis of the sexual and the spiritual. Redemption unfolds in both cases through male confrontation—Jonny vs. Max, the Ruler vs. the Stranger—but with agency provided to the female characters, who seem inclined to consider more deeply than their male counterparts the philosophical stakes. And time is thematized for critical purposes in both operas, albeit from opposite sides: *Jonny*'s obsession with the contemporary ("We are disappointed by the lack of an airplane," Julius would complain) brings Max's problem into focus, while *Heliane*'s exaggerated timelessness reduces an element of the Expressionist worldview to a tactic for producing bourgeois escapism.[68]

If we look past the timeliness of jazz, as Krenek urges us to do, which of these composers had a keener sense of the musically modern, and the musical future? Korngold would be the driving compositional force in the emergence of film as the most vibrant musico-dramatic genre of the twentieth century. His film scores would be built on the mature style established in *Heliane*: a superficially Wagnerian sumptuousness detached from the spiritual or philosophical agenda and made to serve the carefree ends of Hollywood romance and historical adventure. Was Julius right, then, that after *Heliane* Korngold lost his desire to compose? Or did he rather find it easier than Krenek to shed the chains of Romanticism and lead music toward a lightness in which it could be appreciated for its own superficial interest and its rejection of deeper responsibilities? In which old music could be new, in other words, and nothing more than itself, going "back to life?"

From this standpoint, Krenek's return to atonality in 1933 would be simultaneously a high modernist and a Romantic retrenchment, a return to an ostensibly new style now over twenty years old and devoted to aesthetic ideals that were considerably older still. It would be Krenek, rather that Korngold, who continued trying for decades to resuscitate the institution of meaningful, large-scale, spiritually significant opera—first with *Leben des Orest* (1928)—ground already trod of course in *Elektra* (1909), Strauss's most advanced work by Second Viennese standards—then in *Karl V*, an opera devoted to regeneration, and then through continued attempts at least through *Pallas Athene weint* (1955) and *Der goldene Bock* (1964). From a distance, Krenek, post-*Jonny*, seems positively Heliane-like. Having shed her clothes in human feeling, Heliane attempts to recover a piety that cannot hide its hollowness. Having set Europe ablaze with a collage of rootless styles, Krenek attempted to rejoin the idealists but could not help but remind all sides that the world had moved on.

But was Wagner's style old enough to form the basis of a Korngoldian neoclassicism—old means for new music? Strauss had been pursuing such a project since the late tone poems; indeed, he inaugurated it with *Guntram*, where with calculation he turned Wagnerian style against its own aesthetic goals. But this project, conspicuous and witting as it was, has not been easy to discern in Strauss, or at least not easy to accept, and Korngold would learn even more bitterly the dangers of mixing enormous talent, a desire for public success, and ambivalence toward the sacralization of music.

NOTES

1. Susan C. Cook, *Opera for a New Republic: The* Zeitopern *of Krenek, Weill, and Hindemith* (Ann Arbor: UMI Research Press, 1988), 84.

2. Julius Korngold, "Was sollte der Kunstidealist im Lande des Dollars?," *Neue freie Presse*, 19 May 1911; quoted in Michaela Feurstein-Presser and Michael Haas, eds., *The Korngolds: Cliché, Critic and Composer* (Vienna: Jüdisches Museum der Stadt Wien, 2007), 31.

3. Surveying the hodgepodge of operas premiered between 1922 and 1928, Paul Bekker vented his frustration that the group "reveals no community of spiritual impulse behind its varied manifestations—in fact, hardly permits of any organized approach to its consideration." New works from this period include Franz Schmidt's *Fredigundis* (1922), Julius Bittner's *Das Rosengärtlein* (1923), Franz Schreker's *Irrelohe* (1924), Hindemith's *Cardillac* (1926), Alban Berg's *Wozzeck* (1925), Hans Gál's *Das Lied der Nacht* (1926), and two highly contrasting operas from Richard Strauss: *Intermezzo* (1924) and *Die ägyptische Helena* (1928). Paul Bekker, *The Changing Opera*, trans. Arthur Mendel (New York: W. W. Norton, 1935), 257. On operatic diversity in the 1920s and its specific relationship to Korngold, see Brendan G. Carroll, *The Last Prodigy: A Biography of Erich Wolfgang Korngold* (Portland, OR: Amadeus Press, 1997), 197.

4. For example, Ernst Schliepe, "Krisis in der Oper," *Signale für die musikalische Welt* 89 (1931): 1238–41; Hans Stieber, "Die Krise im deutschen Opernschaffen," *Rheinische Musik-und-Theater-Zeitung* 27 (1926): 8–9; and Julius Kapp, "Gibt es eine Krise in der Oper?," *Blätter der Staatsoper* 9 (April 1929): 10–12. See Cook, *Opera for a New Republic*, 9; and Jenny L. Jackson, "Musical Style as a Representation of Social Milieu: The 1927 Premieres of Ernst Krenek's *Jonny spielt auf* and Erich Wolfgang Korngold's *Das Wunder der Heliane*" (M.A. thesis, University of Iowa, 2001), 23.

5. Richard Taruskin, "The Golden Age of Kitsch," in *The Danger of Music* (Berkeley: University of California, 2009), 255–56; Robin Holloway, "Korngold and Krenek," in *Essays and Diversions II* (London: Continuum, 2007), 103.

6. *Arbeiter-Zeitung*, 6 January 1928, 6.

7. With *Die Kathrin* (1939) Korngold completed his output of three full-scale operas and two one-acters.

8. Guy Wagner, *Korngold: Musik ist Musik* (Berlin: Matthes & Seitz, 2008), 242.

9. For example, in a report on a lecture given by Krenek just after *Jonny*'s premiere: "One should not look on him as a leader of the atonals; even those who went to the opera loaded with negative expectations would have had to see that for the most part the music did not sound as awful as they anticipated." See "Krenek spielt auf. . .: Ein Vortrag des Jonny-Komponisten im Kulturbund," *Neues Wiener Journal*, 4 January 1928, 3.

10. If these small pieces were "child's play," as Brendan G. Carroll describes them, they nonetheless forecast a range that would make its way into *Heliane* and would not go unnoticed by critics. Carroll, *The Last Prodigy*, 190.

11. Arnold Schoenberg, "New Music" (1923), in *Style and Idea*, ed. Leonard Stein, trans. Leo Black (New York: St. Martin's Press, 1975), 137. Emphasis in original.

12. Luzi Korngold, *Erich Wolfgang Korngold: Ein Lebensbild* (Vienna: Verlag Elisabeth Lafite, and Österreichischer Bundesverlag für Unterricht, Wissenschaft und Kunst, 1967), 37.

13. Feurstein-Presser and Haas, *The Korngolds*, 89.

14. Luzi Korngold, *Erich Wolfgang Korngold*, 49.

15. Act 1, scene 4.

16. *Wiener Sonn- und Montags-Zeitung*, 31 October 1927, 4.

17. Erich Wolfgang Korngold, "Nochmals: 'Das Wunder der Heliane,'"*Reichspost: Unabhängiges Tagblatt für das christliche Volk*, 11 November 1927, 8. Heliane's line is from Act 3, scene 2.

18. *Reichspost*, 11 November 1927, 8.

19. *Radio-Wien*, 23 March 1928, 929.
20. "Gibt mir das Wunder Eures leuchtend weißen Leibs." Act 1, scene 4.
21. This passage makes an ostentatious reference to Goethe's Eternal Feminine. *Wiener Sonn- und Montags-Zeitung*, 31 October 1927, 4.
22. The reactions of Strauss, as well as Engelbert Humperdinck, Arthur Nikisch, Hermann Kretschmar, Karl Goldmark, Arthur Seidl (and Seidl's students at the Leipzig Conservatory), and others are described in Wagner, *Korngold: Musik ist Musik*, 57–59.
23. The full text of Strauss's letter, now held at the Bayerische Staatsbibliothek, appears in translation (here slightly modified) in Carroll, *The Last Prodigy*, 43. An excerpt of the original can be found in Wagner, *Korngold: Musik ist Musik*, 57.
24. Julius Korngold, *Die Korngolds in Wien: Die Musikkritiker und das Wunderkind—Aufzeichnungen von Julius Korngold* (Zurich: M & T Verlag, 1991), 237.
25. For Julius's published statements of gratitude, see ibid., 237–38.
26. Ritter's *Sursum corda! Eine Sturm- und Drang-Phantasie* was published in 1896 by Joseph Aibl, the Munich publisher of many of Strauss's early works.
27. Bruno Walter, "Erich Wolfgang Korngold zum Gedächtnis," in Luzi Korngold, *Erich Wolfgang Korngold*, 6–7.
28. Julius Korngold, *Die Korngolds in Wien*, 291.
29. Egon Gartenberg, *Vienna: Its Musical Heritage* (University Park: Pennsylvania State University Press, 1968), 225.
30. D. J. Bach, *Arbeiter-Zeitung*, 8 November 1927, 3.
31. *Der Morgen*, 31 October 1927, 8.
32. Ferdinand Pfohl, *Neue freie Presse*, 11 October 1927, 3.
33. Ibid.
34. Ibid.
35. *Münchener Bote*, 19 November 1895.
36. *Freiheit!*, 28 December 1928, 7.
37. *Arbeiter-Zeitung*, 8 November 1927, 3.
38. *Neue freie Presse*, 11 October 1927, 3.
39. Ibid.
40. *Der Morgen*, 31 October 1927, 8.
41. *Neues Wiener Journal: Unparteiisches Tagblatt*, 30 October 1927.
42. *Neues Wiener Tagblatt*, 23 May 1926; portions quoted in Julius Korngold, *Die Korngolds in Wien*, 354; full excerpt in Carroll, *The Last Prodigy*, 193–94 (translation modified).
43. Feurstein-Presser and Haas, *The Korngolds*, 35.
44. Ibid., 86; see also Wagner, *Korngold: Musik ist Musik*, 226–27.
45. Carroll, *The Last Prodigy*, 188.
46. Wagner, *Korngold: Musik ist Musik*, 229.
47. Translation from liner notes to *Krenek: Jonny spielt auf*, with Heinz Kruse, Alessandra Marc et al., Gewandhaus Orchester Leipzig, cond. Lothar Zagrosek, in *Entartete Musik: Music Supressed by the Third Reich*, CD, Decca, 436 631-2 (1993).
48. Ernst Krenek, *Horizons Circled: Reflections on My Music* (Berkeley: University of California Press, 1974), 25.
49. *Neue freie Presse*, 1 January 1928, 3.
50. *Das kleine Blatt*, 1 January 1928, 12.
51. Part 1, scene 4.
52. *Arbeiter-Zeitung*, 6 January 1928, 6.
53. *Das interessante Blatt*, 5 January 1928, 17.
54. Krenek, *Horizons Circled*, 27.
55. Ibid., 25.
56. *Neue freie Presse*, 1 January 1928, 3.

57. Ibid.
58. *Neues Wiener Journal*, 4 January 1928, 3.
59. *Der Morgen*, 2 January 1928, 4.
60. *Reichspost*, 1 January 1928, 13.
61. *Neue freie Presse*, 1 January 1928, 2.
62. Ibid.
63. Ibid.
64. Bekker, *The Changing Opera*, 282.
65. Walter Harry, "Zeitliches und Überzeitliches in *Jonny spielt auf*," *Anbruch* 10 (January 1928): 14–17; quoted in Cook, *Opera for a New Republic*, 106.
66. Luzi Korngold, *Erich Wolfgang Korngold*, 49.
67. Taruskin, "The Golden Age of Kitsch," 255.
68. *Neue freie Presse*, 1 January 1928, 3.

Acoustic Space, Modern Interiority, and Korngold's Cities

SHERRY LEE AND SADIE MENICANIN

Late in 1901 a four-year-old Erich Korngold moved with his family from Brno, a compact, moderately sized town of a little over 100,000 people, to Vienna, a swiftly expanding and briskly modernizing city over ten times the population of his hometown. Then numbering about 1,700,000 including its still-spreading suburbs, Vienna was to exceed two million within less than a decade. Granted, Brno was hardly a backwater; rather, the effectively bilingual southern Moravian capital—mostly German-speaking in the central city, Czech-speaking in its suburbs—had flourished with rapid industrialization throughout the nineteenth century. It was the location from which rail transport had begun in the Czech lands with the arrival of the first train from Vienna in 1839, and it had also, since the late 1860s, boasted the first Czech tram service; by the time the Korngolds left it had more than doubled in size over the course of a half-century and had two universities. It was without doubt a modern urban center, and yet, in comparison to the Viennese metropolis, the contrast must have been striking.

Notwithstanding the pessimism of retrospective accounts such as Stefan Zweig's *Die Welt von Gestern* (*The World of Yesterday*) or George Clare's *Last Waltz in Vienna*, daily life in Vienna in the early part of the twentieth century was nothing if not lively, even if its bustle and vitality could not completely conceal the decaying of the empire that such authors so colorfully evoked.[1] Its impression on the senses would have been anything but moribund. Peter Payer has described this era as "The Age of Noise" in Vienna: both newcomers and longtime residents found it an increasingly sonorous and frequently cacophonous environment.[2] More than twenty years previously, music critic Eduard Hanslick had groused about the "piano plague" inflicted by enthusiastically "tinkling dilettantes" upon the ears of the musically sensitive in the city (granted, he was being a bit tongue-in-cheek).[3] Hanslick was, in this instance, registering amateur music as environmental sound—and indeed as noise. Such a complaint was likely out of date by

1901, considering not only the likely decline of amateur playing with the rise of sound-recording and reproduction technologies such as the gramophone, but also the ongoing increase in a battery of other urban sounds that added to the clamor, sometimes all but drowning out the acoustic past. Ineradicable alterations to the urban soundscape stamped "modernity" with the immutable characteristic of "noisiness." Today, a growing number of studies of "sound history," "auditory history," "audio cultures," and the like are situating Western and Central Europe within a historiography of modernity focused on the changing sonic dimensions of a society and culture characterized by urbanization, industrialization, mechanization, and developments in media.[4] In this burgeoning historical sketch of the auditory cultures of the past, Vienna takes its rightful place among—and despite undeniably distinctive features, comes to sound similar to—other major European capitals in an age when urban quiet, let alone silence, was becoming increasingly rare.

Julius Korngold may have been Hanslick's literal successor, but even if the ideological torch of expert musical listening was well and duly passed on from one critic to another, there is little trace of complaint about sound affliction in the urban environment within Julius's recollection of his own and his son's careers in the energetically buzzing Viennese metropolis. At the turn of the century anti-noise campaigns were ramping up, having begun with public debate on sound nuisances as medical professionals became aware of the health dangers posed by noise. New auditory emanations marking the soundscape of Vienna around 1900—from sources post-dating Julius's prior sojourn in the capital during the years of his education—included the automobile and the electric streetcar, which replaced the steam-powered streetcars of the 1880s (themselves replacements for the horse-drawn streetcars in use since the mid-1860s). Such sounds irritated the notoriously noise-averse Gustav Mahler, who was clearly attentive to the sonic environment, and was beleaguered by the emanations of urban and rural soundscapes alike.[5] Yet Mahler's ardent critical champion Julius Korngold penned his memoirs about the city almost as though there was nothing to be heard there but its concert music, this despite the fact that the *Neue freie Presse* for which he wrote frequently joined Vienna's other leading liberal newspapers, such as *Die Zeit* and the *Neues Wiener Tagblatt*, in publishing articles concerned with the growing loudness of city life. The non-musical sonic environment may have been physically heard, but it was not listened or attended to in the critic's idealized musical sphere. Perhaps the senior Korngold's preoccupation models the ideal immersion in art that he wished for his prodigious son as well. As if he could not only be shielded from too early exposure as a musical "genius," or from the sounds of those aesthetically undesirable cultural spheres of the lowbrow popular or the modernist avant-garde—but his ear, attuned solely to music, could remain deaf to the broader acoustic emanations of a modern urban life exterior to the concert hall, the opera house, or the domestic music room.

William Cheng has suggested that aspects of our understanding of Erich Korngold as a *Wunderkind* have contributed to the predominant reception of the composer as a figure "hopelessly estranged from the postwar *Zeitgeist*," and of his works as fundamentally apolitical, lacking "social timeliness."[6] We agree, and would argue even further that this occluded perception extends to a near-exclusion of many aspects of contemporary urban existence from the picture of his experiences and his aesthetic. But Korngold lived his whole life in modern urban environments. Surely his aesthetic output, and indeed, the listening experience of his audiences who lived and heard within those same spaces, must have been shaped in many ways by the conditions of twentieth-century metropolitan life in all its acoustic complexity. This facet of Korngold's world, the inevitable resonance of sonic modernity within the spaces of modern identity, compounds the critical challenge to both the composer's own ostensible naïveté and his music's apparent political neutrality. After all, as Jonathan Sterne has asserted, "Sound is an artifact of the messy and political human sphere."[7]

Granted, there are reasons for the persistence of romanticized perceptions that overlook the necessary embeddedness of Korngold and his music in the "messy" and noisy realities of his environs. For instance, the recognition of Korngold's talent exempted him from active service in the Great War, so though he was drafted into the Austrian army and participated in the war effort, leading the regimental band and giving concerts to raise money for the Austrian War Relief, he was insulated from the real-world trauma of combat. Ultimately, the war had relatively little impact on his compositional activity.[8] There are also those dramatic elements of his operas, with historical settings or steeped in nostalgia, that readily convey the sense of an aesthetic sensibility attuned to pastness, despite their origins during wartime or in the interwar years when trendy *Zeitoper* leapt onto the stage. Further, the coexistence within his compositional language of traditional characteristics alongside advanced and innovative features is aptly summarized in his own well-known statement, offered as commentary on *Das Wunder der Héliane* in 1927: "By no means do I isolate myself against the harmonic enrichments which we owe to, say, Schoenberg. But I will not relinquish claim to the eminent possibilities offered by 'old music.'"[9] At the same time, it is well worth remembering that Korngold was actively engaged with the new sound technologies that were proliferating during the growth of his career, from the live recordings he made for piano rolls with various companies to, of course, his many years of influential work in the hyper-efficient sound film industry.[10]

Thus, Korngold's complex relationship to modernism combines both progressive and apparently conservative or even backward-looking elements. Julian Johnson argues that this combination is not really a case of modern vs. anti-modern contradictions, but rather that such tension is precisely characteristic of the phenomenon of modernism itself: "A music history that divides composers into conservative and progressive groups obscures the fact that the whole of musical modernity takes place in the slippage between the idea of a stable past and the sense of a disjunct present," he asserts. "Works which foreground this contradiction are arguably more articulate about history than those that insist on an exclusively progressive quality since modernity is not defined by the progressive alone, but rather the constant tug between the progressive and regressive." It is in this sense that Johnson references Korngold's music as a sonic emblem of such modern tensions: "*Die tote Stadt* (1920) [is] as articulate about the precarious present as the Neoclassicism of Stravinsky. . . . His willfully nostalgic music is not peripheral to the experience of modernity in the twentieth century but, precisely in its constant turn to memory, absolutely central."[11]

Die tote Stadt is our principal interest here, too, and we imagine that a juxtaposition of two urban spaces like those of Korngold's modern Vienna and the historic Bruges in which the opera is set might capture, in a sense, this tug between modernity and pastness in Korngold's aesthetic outlook: one a metropolis rapidly advancing in terms of both population and architectural growth and technological modernization, the other a town at the end of a long period of commercial decline and thus quintessentially defined by pastness, even in its contemporary bid for modernization. In what follows we consider the relationship among urban modernity, theories of the subject and its psyche under the pressures of modern life, and their resonances in both Korngold's opera and its literary source text—all in terms of various configurations of acoustic spaces, whether exterior, interior, or in liminal spaces in between.

Georg Simmel's 1903 essay "The Metropolis and Mental Life" is probably the best-known and most influential fin-de-siècle study of the effects of urban modernity on the individual's physical, emotional, and psychological being. The essay's recurring references to psychology and the "nerves" highlight its historical proximity to the early development of psychoanalysis and the pseudo-medical discourse of neurasthenia, a psychopathological weakness (mostly among intellectuals and the cultivated upper classes) resulting from nervous exhaustion attributable to ambient noise and the stresses of urbanization. Concerned with "the intensification of emotional life due to the swift and continuous shift of external and internal stimuli" on the senses of the metropolitan individual, Simmel emphasized the nature of "the adaptations made by the personality in its adjustment to the forces that lie outside of it."[12] The individual's necessary response to the acute demands of city life on the nerves, he theorizes, is the development of a capacity for "the protection of the inner life against the dominations of the metropolis."[13] According to Anthony Vidler, Simmel "characterized the 'psychological foundation, upon which the metropolitan individuality is erected' . . . as *spatial by definition*,"[14] and indeed, it is clear from Simmel's articulation of "emotional life" versus "outside forces" that a conception of interiority and exteriority is at work in his diagnosis of the conditions of urban existence. Simmel's emphasis on the nature of space as a projection of the subject interests Vidler, and us, too.[15] Though Vidler's principal interest in art and architecture yields a distinctly visual focus, we are eager to reassert the importance of sound, because architectural spaces, landscapes, city streets, and domestic interiors are all acoustic spaces as well.

Holly Watkins has deftly drawn together conceptions of architectural and sonic space in a fresh consideration of the influence of Viennese architect Adolf Loos on the thought and music of Arnold Schoenberg.[16] Watkins highlights the significance of the relationship between concepts of interior and exterior for both artists' responses to their times, providing a model for a spatial understanding of music in relation to other cultural spheres of Austro-German modernism. Whereas Loos's 1910 polemic against decorative ornamentation and the development of his architectural style "facilitated a retreat inward," she argues, Schoenberg's own later notions of the interior dimensionality of twelve-tone musical space constituted a similar "inward turn" in the 1920s and '30s.[17] Her discussion demonstrates the historical viability of creative spatial conceptions of private, subjective interiority versus external stimuli that span from Simmel's and Loos's turn-of-the-century theories through Schoenberg's interwar compositions and beyond. It is crucial to recognize that these multifaceted conceptions of space as projections of the subject implicate both the psychological interiors of the individual *and* the metropolitan exteriors in which the subject lives and moves. The sensory dimensions of urban existence, including the sonic, exert pressures that shape the experience of the subject, who may either embrace the exterior world of variegated urban stimuli and dwell among them, like the nineteenth-century *flâneur* incessantly pacing the streets, or withdraw protectively into a domestic interior or the interiority of the mental life. Or perhaps both at once, as is the case for the protagonist of Georges Rodenbach's archetypal symbolist novella *Bruges-la-morte*, on which Korngold's *Die tote Stadt* is based.

Simmel wrote his classic essay just a decade after the 1892 publication of Rodenbach's immensely popular tale about Hughes Viane, the morbidly grieving widower obsessed with a woman who resembles his dead wife. In his relentless pacing of the streets of Bruges, a city chosen because the unmoving waters of its canals seem dead to him just like his love, Hughes bears a notable resemblance to the French *flâneur*, that literary city stroller with no profession but to dwell in the cityscape.[18] His obsessive immersion in the psychological depths of grief and his self-insulation in a closed, silent house or the interior of his own brooding psyche also identify him as one of the neurotic subjects of early psychoanalysis and symbolist and decadent literature. He may even be diagnosable as a neurasthenic, given his oversensitivity to sound stimuli: "He needed infinite silence. . . . Those suffering from mental anguish can be hurt by noise too."[19] It is true that, from the perspective of the twentieth century's second and third decades, both the *flâneur* and the neurasthenic of the late nineteenth century have come to appear more as relics of their historical moment than as contemporary figures. Yet perhaps surprisingly, according to James G. Mansell, references to the fin-de-siècle concept of neurasthenia and its cultural manifestations, from J. K. Huysmans' notorious literary representation of sensory decadence behind closed doors to the neurasthenic Proust's famous cork-lined room, became more frequent after the Great War in the medical and sociological discourses mobilized by interwar anti-noise campaigns, even if the notion of "neurasthenia" per se was no longer considered an appropriate medical diagnosis.[20] The interwar popularity of *Die tote Stadt* must be understood in this context, one in which any stirrings of prewar nostalgia among the operagoing public could have been amplified by ever-growing concerns about the dangerous assault on their senses and their health of modern mechanized sound, so ubiquitous in the spaces of their metropolitan lives. Otherwise, the protagonist of Korngold's operatic smash hit may well have appeared as merely *passé* to most modern citizens of those fast-paced and noisy urban centers of postwar Hamburg, Cologne, and Vienna, where the opera was premiered,[21] as much an outdated relic as the cobbled streets, canals, and ever-present church bells of the historic city of Bruges that housed and embodied Hughes's obsessive immersion in the lost past.

It was Rodenbach who, in 1892, declared Bruges to be dead. For many this could hardly have seemed fair, as Bruges was at that time making concentrated efforts at modernization, not least in the shape of an up-and-coming tourist industry. Bruges became one of the world's first tourist destinations in the latter part of the nineteenth century, a port of call for English and French visitors in particular, and around the turn of the twentieth century its successful development was distinctly future-facing. An organization called "Bruges Forward: Society to Improve Tourism" had been established by 1900, according to Stephen Victor Ward, and was "only one of several competing local organizations wishing to promote tourism. . . . Already, since the 1890s, many attractive Belgian resort posters had been issued, as elsewhere prepared by varying combinations of local and railway initiatives."[22] Even though the population was down to a quarter of what it had been at the height of the "Golden Era," the long trend of decline (since around 1500, when the silting-in of the Zwin Channel brought an end to its great age of maritime trade) was waning even as Rodenbach was penning his portrait of a town in its death throes.[23] Christian Berg notes that the city authorities of Bruges and Rodenbach's contemporary Flemish writers alike much preferred the perspective of the town as a thriving part of the wider modern revival of Flanders, rather than as a kind of mausoleum. According to poet and translator Will Stone, it was because of this resistance to Rodenbach's persistent vision of melancholia and deathly torpor, combined with the affront of his seemingly traitorous adoption of Paris and the French language as his literary milieu, that a Rodenbach memorial has never appeared in Bruges.[24]

Yet paradoxically, it was Bruges's thriving past upon which its robust tourist industry was being built. Nicholas Royle's introduction to *The Bells of Bruges* (the English translation of Rodenbach's final novel, *Le Carillonneur* of 1897) enumerates some of the audible features of the cityscape in its modern incarnation, in summertime especially, crammed as it was with visitors from around the globe. In addition to "pealing bells and crying gulls," he notes "the slap of rubber on stone as cars and, predominantly, bicycles negotiate the cobbled streets and leafy squares. The babble of the rabble, tourist hordes speaking in many tongues. The hoteliers and bartenders, ticket sellers and turnstile operators will answer you, it seems, in whatever language you use to address them."[25] These include some relatively distinctive sonorities, then; cobbled streets in particular, being far from the modern norm, sound a collision of past and present. Bruges's prospering new tourist industry was predicated on marketing it as a modern destination through its enduring pastness and the status of its contemporary spaces as well-preserved relics.

When it came to selling Bruges, it is likely that the potential for an acoustic realization of Rodenbach's imagined spaces played a significant role in selling Korngold on the project of composing and staging the dead city. In Rodenbach's portraits of Bruges, the city's deadness is certainly evidenced in the pastness so manifestly visible in its most renowned features—the canals, cobbled streets, and medieval buildings—but also, undeniably, in its soundscape. This is composed variously of timeless natural sounds such as wind and rain, of historical, cultural, and social sounds such as the all-important church bells that "scatter the air with sound dust," and notably, of silence: the silence of Hughes Viane's house, of Bruges's sacred spaces and its near-empty streets. Vienna's architecture, some have noted, had the effect of rendering its street spaces "canyons, which became deeper and deeper the closer one moved toward the city centre," and in which its urban noises reflected and rebounded from stony walls and surfaces, sound being "held together and amplified" by high buildings.[26] In contrast, Bruges's canals, streets, and bridges contained only quiet. Rodenbach identified silence as a common theme throughout all his work. His long poem *Le Règne du silence*, published the year before *Bruges-la-morte*, is in part a preparatory meditation on the quietude of the novel to follow, which is shot through with references to sound and stillness. "The silence of the canals is a 'lesson' to Hughes Viane," suggests Stone. "Any noise that erupts threatens to injure this state of muted melancholy resignation. . . . Ironically only the bells of Bruges are permitted to break this silence."[27] In fact, it is not only the sound of bells that disturbs the city's stillness. The religious procession, important enough for Rodenbach to feature it in both *Bruges-la-morte* and later *Le Carillonneur*, is a public event that fills the otherwise empty and silent streets with motion and sound: not only bell ringing, but voices, singing and chanting, and the motion of many bodies and objects. The exhibition character of the springtime Feast of the Holy Blood turns the interiority of spirituality outward and heightens the contrast between them. This apparent reversal only reaffirms the nature of the relationship between the exteriority of city space and the private interiority of which it forms an extension. In his poem "Du silence," Rodenbach had referred to Bruges as a "soulscape," an intriguing concept that effectively construes the city environment as a physical externalization of an interior, immaterial aspect of individual being.[28] Just as the chanting of religious celebration and the ringing of sacred bells externally render audible an interior realm of spirituality and belief in the soul, the dark depths of the still canal waters are readily readable, for Hughes and for us, as materializations of his inner state. In Eduard Cairol's words, "The image of the dead city turns in on itself and implies . . . closure or seclusion into an interior space on one hand, and into silence on the other. Certainly, sleepy cities with frequently deserted streets, like Bruges, allow public space to be seen as an extension of private space. The decadent mentality, faced by the strife of the exterior world, looks for its refuge in them."[29]

Clearly, then, the space of Bruges itself is crucially important to Rodenbach's novel. As many commentators have noted since, the author went so far as to accord it the status of a central character in the tale: "In this study of passion, we also wanted to evoke a City, the City as an essential person, associated with moods, who advises, dissuades, and determines [the protagonist] to act. Thus, in reality, this city of Bruges that we have chosen appears almost human."[30] When considering the translation from texted to musical-dramatic narrative, the question of the role that those spaces played in Korngold's conception arises quite readily, and testimonies conflict as to whether Korngold had ever visited Bruges before the opera was written. Luzi Korngold thought not. In her 1967 biography of her husband, citing her memory of the 1921 Vienna premiere of *Die tote Stadt*, she made particular mention of the second act "in which Bruges, the 'dead city,' becomes the leading actress. Bruges, where Korngold had never been; yet he had been able to paint a visionary picture of it that puts us right in the middle of the old Flemish city."[31] Korngold himself stated in a program note that the opera was inspired by the atmosphere of Bruges, which he may have meant literally, or only in reference to the city's fictional portrayal. Yet Julius Korngold suggested that the family had indeed been there in the summer of 1913, when they holidayed in Westende on the Belgian coast:

> From Westende, it was only a short trip to Bruges, Rodenbach's *Dead City*, for which a few years later Erich was to find a music of melancholy and ecstasy. He experienced its milieu, stood by the gloomy canals, heard the bells, and saw the Beguines walking the lonely streets.[32]

Julius's undeniably poetic account still seems plausible enough, as it is only about 15 kilometers from Westende to Ostend and about the same distance again from there to Bruges (on a modern road map; he does not mention how they traveled). The younger Korngold did write a short letter to his maternal grandparents from Westende on 22 July 1913, complaining that he was bored (as teenagers do), exclaiming over the great width of his bed in their lodgings (though the room itself was not large), grousing about the food, but noting that the sea was beautiful, if cold for swimming. However, apart from a passing mention of work correcting the proofs of his Sinfonietta, which would be premiered under Weingartner

Figure 1: The city of Bruges in Georges Rodenbach's *Bruges-la-morte*, with intersecting canals, bridge, residential houses on the right and the Begijnhof on the left (led to by the bridge), and the bell tower in the distance.

in Vienna's Musikverein later that year, it is a fairly inconsequential communication and gives no hint of other excursions in the region.[33] But even if he had not visited the place that summer, the images in Rodenbach's book could have supplied Korngold with multiple views of Bruges, for *Bruges-la-morte* is one of the first works of fiction to be illustrated with photographs (see Figure 1).[34] Rodenbach's preface to his novella emphasizes the importance of including photographs of the city's actual environs within its pages in support of his conception of the city as central to the narrative and not merely its atmospheric backdrop. Thus, if Korngold could not recall the cityscape from his own memory, some of those photos could have suggested a context for the following suggestion that the composer sent to Alfred Roller in a letter of 4 August 1920, concerning the stage design for Act 2 of *Die tote Stadt* (referred to as "den Brüggeakt"; see Figure 2):

> For the Bruges Act, I would like to submit a <u>new</u> proposal (from my librettist) to you, my honorary *Hofrat*, for your kind consideration. How would it be if the <u>main</u> channel, into which a channel <u>arm</u> flows near the bridge, were to bend <u>backwards</u>? So that one could have a prospect of the characteristic Bruges houses in perspective on both sides of the canal? I probably express myself vaguely (I don't want to discuss my <u>drawing</u> talent!!) but I hope that you will understand me anyway. It's an <u>idea</u>![35]

Tempting as it is to speculate, it probably matters little in the end whether Korngold had ever really "been there" before his effort to evoke the space of the city in orchestral sound and dramatic space. *Die tote Stadt*'s atmospheric wind machine and its evocative tolling church bells could just as well have been products of informed imagination as of memory. Julius and Erich co-wrote the libretto, and the changes they elected to impose on Rodenbach's narrative include the names of central characters—Hughes is renamed Paul, his unnamed dead wife is christened Marie, his housekeeper is called Brigitte rather than Barbe, and his wife's lookalike, the dancer Jane, becomes Marietta—plus the creation of some new ones, Paul's friend Frank and Marietta's theatrical companions, none of whom exist in the novella. But among the challenges that arise in the task of putting the tale of *Bruges-la-morte* onstage, the issue of space looms large. Highly significant is the idea of consigning the events of Act 2 and most of Act 3 to a dream, a stroke that effectively renders Paul prey to a fantastic and violent unconscious rather than portraying him as an actual

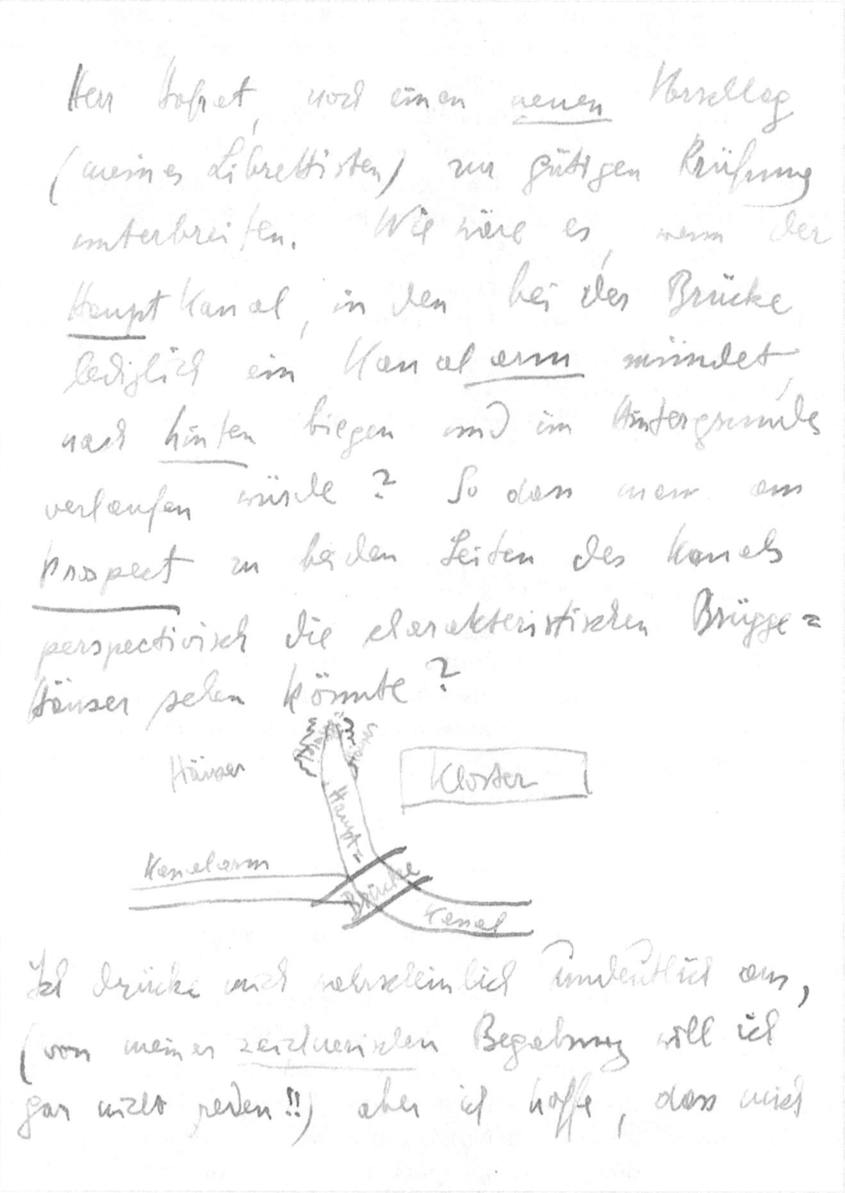
Herr Hofrat noch einen neuen Vorschlag (meines Librettisten) zur gütigen Prüfung unterbreiten. Wie wäre es, wenn der Hauptkanal, in den bei der Brücke lediglich ein Kanalarm mündet, nach hinten biegen und im Hintergrunde verlaufen würde? So dass man am Prospect zu beiden Seiten des Kanals perspectivisch die charakteristischen Brügge=Häuser sehen könnte?

Ich drücke mich wahrscheinlich undeutlich aus, (von meiner zeichnerischen Begabung will ich gar nicht reden!!) aber ich hoffe, dass mich

Figure 2: Korngold's letter to Alfred Roller that includes a sketch of the Bruges setting of Act 2 of *Die tote Stadt*, indicating the city's main canal (*Haupt-Kanal*) lined with houses (*Häuser*), a smaller canal branching off it (*Kanalarm*) near a bridge (*Brücke*), and the thirteenth-century beguinage (*Kloster*) off to the right. All these elements are visible in a similar spatial configuration in the photo from Rodenbach's novel, but as though viewed from the opposite direction.

murderer when he melodramatically strangles Marietta with a plait of Marie's hair. Establishing these events as imagined, taking place in the separate, interiorized "space" of Paul's mind, effectively distances them from the events of reality. At the same time, these psychologically interior dream-events are precisely those that take place in the "exterior" narrative space of the city of Bruges. Dramatic-spatial delineations are thus both the means to confronting the challenge of staging the novel and rendering the conceptual significance of the "Dead City." A reconfiguration of the narrative setting was essential to operatic adaptation. Hughes/Paul cannot plausibly pace the city streets and quaysides within the confines of onstage space. What can be thematized within the scope of the opera house is the fundamental distinction between inside and outside—the contrast and continuity between interior and exterior physical spaces, the quiet and safe domestic enclosure and the sonorous city street—that is emblematic of the modernist condition of subjectivity and its retreat to interiority in the face of urban exposure and sensual onslaught. Arguably, the operatic version intensified these contrasts beyond their existence in Rodenbach's text, by rendering the Bruges setting of Acts 2 and 3 almost entirely within Paul's psyche, yet within the context of that dream, distinguishing it almost invariably as an external, public space. In the opera, the city is no empty and silent reflection of Paul's fixation on the stillness of death, but rather an actively resonant space enlivened with sound.

Ben Winters has discussed "the demarcation of narrative space" in relation to Korngold's film music, a sense of which Korngold was "particularly adept at providing . . . supplying not only information of geographical or temporal relevance but also outlining spatial relationship[s] between characters and locations."[36] This concept of the acoustic demarcation of narrative-dramatic spaces is interesting in the case of the composer's best-known opera. Since the operatic stage supplies (or dictates) a particular type of space, Korngold's acoustic delineation of dramatic settings, concepts, and relationships on that stage is one facet of acoustic space to consider. But he also made use of his sonic arsenal to suggest other spaces that are either less literally existent in the stage world or exceed its physical boundaries and invoke spaces beyond what can be seen on the boards. In *Die tote Stadt*, an opera that floats within a dreamlike nostalgia, Korngold strategically harnesses acoustic space and blurs boundaries between inside and outside, contributing to the establishment of atmosphere and the plotted ambiguities between dream and reality. He engages with acoustic space in multiple ways, starting with his numerous exploitations of the boundary between offstage and onstage. These manipulations can variously function as a realist extension of the stage into exterior spaces, or support the establishment of dreamlike settings and, ultimately, an ambiguity between interior and exterior modes of existence. Die tote Stadt is shot through with offstage voices and sounds, many of which contribute to its occasionally hallucinatory atmosphere and encourage the audience to question what is presented as "real." A relatively straightforward instance of offstage sound occurs early in Act 1, just after the visiting Marietta performs the famous lute song for Paul inside his rooms. A group of Marietta's friends makes its way past the window on the street below. Singing and laughing merrily, their offstage voices suggest a carefree realm well outside Paul's claustrophobic obsessions. After all, the city of Bruges must extend beyond the stage; Korngold's setting facilitates the suspension of disbelief as required of us in the unwritten contract between audience and operatic spectacle. The offstage sound of the exterior world is a gesture of verisimilitude, but over the course of Die tote Stadt that same extended acoustic space comes to represent something more than a realistic urban environment. As an extension of another kind, from which emanate supernatural and ineffable expressions of sentiment without logical explanation, it effectively upends the initial offstage establishment of a realistic, outside urban space.

In addition to exceptional sound placement on- or offstage, Korngold's strategic employment of particular timbres and instruments frequently portrays acoustic-spatial qualities of distance or removal that are tied to the dichotomy between exteriority and interiority and, within Paul's unconscious, to the "fantastical gap" between his dream and reality.[37] The orchestra pit is itself an acoustic space that usually has a defined relationship to that of the stage, a relationship simultaneously integrated and separated, though presumably invisible to the operagoer. Further, an orchestra, especially one as large as Korngold's, is a potent generator of a sense of musical space. Korngold's orchestration is highly detailed. To no small extent he, like some other composers of that era, including Franz Schreker, used the orchestra as a kind of meta-instrument—a richly variegated one, to be sure—and this tendency to treat his orchestration in terms of timbrally vivid masses of sound renders an overall palette characterized by a high degree of timbral blend. The major exceptions, though, the true standouts in his orchestral language, are indeed the distinctive markers of the Korngold sound: the harps, the range of percussion instruments, and especially the keyboards, including celesta, harmonium, organ, and Korngold's own instrument, the piano. And finally, perhaps most important for Die tote Stadt, there are the bells. Resistant to timbral blending, all of these instruments provide unique registral capacities for suggesting spatialization in sound. Their unique qualities, combined in some scenes with special placement, render them especially effective acoustic markers of narrative space. Even when some instruments and effects are not literally distanced by exceptional physical location, they nonetheless evoke a spatial dimension that comes to be associated with the acoustic space of the dream: these include the bells, also the celesta, and notably, high string tremolos. Interspersed throughout the opera, timbral and motivic suggestions of a dreamlike acoustic space come to be associated with Paul's unconscious. And when such special timbral elements are used in conjunction with offstage sound, Korngold effectively superimposes different types of acoustic spaces.

Bruges itself is introduced in the transition to the second act with the sonority of bells, heard for the first time. This act particularly intrigues us because it transitions from inside Paul's domicile to the streets of Bruges—a move outside—and at the same time marks his shift into the dream world—further into a psychic interior. Appropriately, it is colored by atmospheric acoustic effects in space, both onstage and off. Bells reinforce the narrative's gothic mood and its religious theme, and also contribute to a realistic sense of setting: listeners are enveloped in the resonant acoustic space of the dead city. In the remarkable prelude to Act 2, Korngold's score specifies "low bells on stage," which renders them a part of the space of the scene. However, even though the curtain goes up partway through this interstitial music, the stage remains dark, densely veiled as if by mist, and the stage direction in the libretto notes that "the ringing of bells has already begun before the scene becomes clear." The bells are initially audible within a liminal space—another fantastical gap—located apart from the rest of the orchestral sound but still invisible to the audience. This ambiguity simultaneously reinforces the bells' association with the real-world urban space of Bruges and with the quality of unreality that characterizes the interiority of Paul's dream. Their placement within Paul's imagination also includes their spectral association with the beloved dead, Marie.

Marie, *die Tote*, is granted a form of presence within the opera, albeit a ghostly one, beyond Paul's memory and the many physical relics—numerous photographs, her large portrait, the enshrined (or entombed) plait of her hair—which fill the interior room in the house dedicated to her.[38] This operatic Marie has a voice and, briefly, an embodied existence in the stage world. She is only overtly present aurally or visually from the end of Act 1 into the prelude to Act 2, and is characterized by a unique treatment of acoustic space; excised from any living body, her voice emanates from undefined spaces. When she appears to Paul as a vision near the close of Act 1, Korngold does not clarify whether her voice is on- or offstage; but by the end of the scene the composer specifies that Marie fades into the background, "*in Nebelschleier hinein*," into the veils of mist, from which she sings her final words to Paul. This stage direction implies that Marie's body disappears, though her voice remains. The deliberate elimination of the visible source of the voice generates a tension between presence and absence that is established through a play of acoustic versus visual spaces. Finally, her voice alone, with no visible presence, sounds from offstage at the beginning of the prelude to Act 2—exceptionally, for preludes are usually acoustic spaces at the margins of drama, occupied exclusively by instruments. Marie is thus relegated to a purely acoustic space whose in-betweenness is liminal in more than one respect.

However, before she disappears from view at the end of Act 1, Paul sings that he senses her in the sights and sounds of Bruges, invoking the bells: "You are with me, forever, always. You are in this dead city, you sound in its bells, you rise from its waters." The bells themselves do not toll at that moment, but just as Marie's disembodied voice is heard in the Act 2 prelude, so too are the bells heard for the first time, slightly after her voice ceases. Their sounding in this transitional space between acts, and between real, imagined, and dreamed events, marks them as acoustically overdetermined. They are the real sounds of Bruges, and they constitute the audible index of Paul's fantasized association of the town with the dead. As in Rodenbach's novel, "The town, once beautiful and beloved too, embodied the loss he felt. Bruges was his dead wife. And his dead wife was Bruges."[39] Paul even speaks directly to the bells in the first scene of Act 2 as he lurks outside Marietta's apartment, accusing them of haunting his conscience.

The tolling of bells is a signal, too, in the offstage religious procession whose sounds and voices dominate Act 3. By then, notably, the juxtaposition of on- and offstage sound has increased in prevalence from its first occurrence in Act 1, and throughout the second act. The entrance and exit of Marietta's theater troupe in Act 2, for instance, bookending the nested performances of the famous "Pierrot Lied" and the embedded resurrection scene from *Robert le diable*, are denoted by degrees of vocal distance. Korngold's stage directions—"One can hear the dancing company in boats, laughing and singing"—suggest that the audience (and Paul) should hear the troupe before seeing them, implying that they are approaching from an unseen distance, their voices perhaps echoing off the walls of the canal. They exit in much the same fashion, their festive singing marked "*verklingend*," fading away, so that the sound bleeds over the border of on- and offstage space. And the "Pierrot Lied," sung by Marietta's friend Fritz, is accompanied by a wordless offstage chorus of eight sopranos. Not fixed to any narrative action, they project an ineffable sense, requiring no explanation or logic but contributing a kind of auditory spectacle that suits the nostalgic text of Fritz's song, dwelling on the enchantment of distant lands. Moreover, the religious procession of the Feast of the Holy Blood, passing in the street outside Paul's window and replete with children's and adult choirs and tolling bells, marks the culminating use of offstage space in *Die tote Stadt*. Once more, through the manipulation of acoustic space, the streets of Bruges materialize sonically as a real exterior as well as an unreal dreamscape. The procession dominates a significant portion of the third act, and the illusion of a slow, drawn-out physical approach is created by voices sounding "*aus der Ferne*" (from the distance) and growing ever louder. Gradual amplification is accomplished with crescendos and an accumulation of voices, beginning with a seraphic children's choir, then proceeding through the addition of women's and men's voices. The entrance of the children's chorus behind the scene is marked with the floating, spatially dislocated gesture of the string tremolo, a specially coded timbre that sounds somehow above and removed from the orchestra due to its elevated register, but also through its absence of metrical definition. Coupled with a simmering conflict between Paul and Marietta inside his house, the procession grows ever louder from outside the window, with more and more voices joining in. As the public space of Bruges, sounding its sacred past, intrudes into the private space of Paul's enclosed existence, Korngold's layering of disparate acoustic spaces escalates the dramatic tension to an explosive degree. It is released only in violence, when Paul strangles Marietta, finally silencing her and the orchestra at once. Throughout *Die tote Stadt*, from the first act to the final scene, the strategic evocation of acoustic space through special orchestral timbres and the harnessing of offstage spaces is essential to Korngold's establishment of a murky relationship between exteriors and interiors, whether physical or psychological, or both at once.

This consideration of Korngold's multifaceted creative engagement with the delineation of distinctive acoustic spaces could extend well beyond *Die tote Stadt*. Think of his next opera, *Das Wunder der Heliane* of 1927, drawing on a sonorous-spatial palette similar to that of *Die tote Stadt*, with the use of organ, bells, and disembodied voices offstage. Set in an unnamed place at an unidentified time, it retreated further from social reality into myth, mysticism, and psychological depths, in the very year that Ernst Krenek's *Jonny spielt auf* juxtaposed its protagonist's psychic isolation with the trappings of acoustic modernity ranging from jazz to sirens. Or contemplate Korngold's opportune migration in the 1930s from Europe's Old World threatened by rising fascism, his translation to the New World urban spaces of Los Angeles with its affluent, technology-forward film studios, and the narrative-dramatic screen spaces he profiled in sound.[40] Neither wartime and post–Second World War America nor the war-shattered spaces of Vienna (including its bombed opera house) to which Korngold finally returned, temporarily, in 1949, were less noisy than they had been when the century was young. Rather, they were ever more clangorous, with the ongoing acceleration of urban growth and technological modernization. If one hears Korngold's later works as acoustic echoes of his earlier ones, the common historical verdict that his late-Romantic style was obsolescent within a serialist midcentury is all too easily rendered. In other words, the change in reception of the Korngold sound is an index of the politicization of sound in culture. Cultural and artistic modernisms, however, are plural and eclectic, and the nostalgic turn to acoustic spaces of interiority and pastness is a response to modernism no less than modern in itself.

NOTES

Many thanks to Joseph L. Clarke and Gregory Lee Newsome, both of the University of Toronto, for their insightful contributions to the development of this essay.

1. Stefan Zweig, *Die Welt von Gestern: Erinnerungen eines Europäers* (Stockholm: Bermann-Fischer Verlag, 1944); George Clare, *Last Waltz in Vienna: The Destruction of a Family, 1842–1942* (London: Macmillan, 1981).
2. Peter Payer, "The Age of Noise: Early Reactions in Vienna, 1870–1914," *Journal of Urban History* 33/5 (2007): 773–93.
3. Eduard Hanslick, "Ein Brief über die 'Clavierseuche,'" in *Suite: Aufsätze über Musik und Musiker* (Vienna, 1884).
4. For a rich sampling of insightful historical sound studies in a European context during the Korngolds' era, see Daniel Morat, ed., *Sounds of Modern History: Auditory Cultures in 19th- and 20th-Century Europe* (New York and Oxford: Berghahn Books, 2014).
5. For a consideration of Mahler's complex relationship to acoustic modernity, see Sherry Lee and Thomas Peattie, "Extraordinary Listening (Mahler—and Franklin)," in *Music, Modern Culture, and the Critical Ear*, ed. Nicholas Attfield and Ben Winters (London and New York: Routledge, 2018), 29–50.
6. William Cheng, "Opera *en abyme*: The prodigious ritual of Korngold's *Die tote Stadt*," *Cambridge Opera Journal* 22/2 (2011): 121.
7. Jonathan Sterne, *The Audible Past: Cultural Origins of Sound Reproduction* (Durham, NC: Duke University Press, 2003), 13.
8. See Brendan Carroll, *The Last Prodigy: A Biography of Erich Wolfgang Korngold* (Portland, OR: Amadeus Press, 1997), 379n12.
9. Erich Korngold, *Neues Wiener Tagblatt*, 26 May 1926, quoted in ibid., 194.
10. For an informative comparison of the studio system developed in Hollywood in the 1930s with efficiency-driven "factory production" models, see Ben Winters, "Korngold and the Studio System," chap.1 in *Erich Wolfgang Korngold's "The Adventures of Robin Hood": A Film Score Guide* (Lanham, MD: Scarecrow Press, 2007), 5–15.
11. Julian Johnson, *Out of Time: Music and the Making of Modernity* (New York: Oxford University Press, 2015), 113–14. See also Walter Frisch, *German Modernism: Music and the Arts* (Berkeley: University of California Press, 2005), 5.
12. Georg Simmel, "The Metropolis and Mental Life" (1903), trans. in *The Blackwell City Reader*, ed. Gary Bridge and Sophie Watson (Oxford and Malden, MA: Wiley-Blackwell, 2002), 11.
13. Ibid., 12.
14. Anthony Vidler, *Warped Space: Art, Architecture, and Anxiety in Modern Culture* (Cambridge, MA: MIT Press, 2001), 68–69; our emphasis.
15. Ibid., viii.
16. Holly Watkins, "Schoenberg's Interior Designs," *Journal of the American Musicological Society* 61/1 (2008): 123–206.
17. See ibid., 129–30 and 197–98.
18. Notably, *flânerie* was (and is) a distinctly male occupation; as Anke Gleber makes clear, the female *flâneur* is recognized merely as a streetwalker. See Gleber, "Female Flanerie and the *Symphony of the City*," in *Women in the Metropolis: Gender and Modernity in Weimar Culture*, ed. Katharina von Ankum (Berkeley and Los Angeles: University of California Press, 1997), 67–88. Indeed, Hughes encounters the dancer Jane, his beautiful and pious wife's golden-haired double, in the street; his subsequent treatment of her is as a courtesan or "kept woman," scarcely distant from that of a prostitute.

19. Rodenbach, *Bruges-la-morte and The Death Throes of Towns*, trans. Mike Mitchell and Will Stone, with introductions by Alan Hollinghurst and Will Stone (Sawtry, Cambridgeshire, UK: Dedalus, 2011), Kindle edition.

20. See James G. Mansell, "Neurasthenia, Civilization, and the Sounds of Modern Life: Narratives of Nervous Illness in the Interwar Campaign Against Noise," in Morat, *Sounds of Modern History*, 278–302.

21. *Die tote Stadt* was premiered simultaneously in Hamburg and Cologne in 1920 and in Vienna in 1921.

22. Stephen Victor Ward, *Selling Places: The Marketing and Promotion of Towns and Cities, 1850–2000* (New York: Routledge, 1998), 40.

23. Rodenbach's essay "Agonies de villes," which also focused on Bruges, dates from three years prior to *Bruges-la-morte*. It is published in an English translation by Will Stone as "The Death Throes of Towns," together with Mike Mitchell's translation of *Bruges-la-morte* (Sawtry, Cambridgeshire, UK: Dedalus Books, 2005).

24. The 1903 statue by Georges Minne that was intended for the Begijnhof is instead located in Ghent. See Will Stone, "Rodenbach Remembered?" in Rodenbach, *Bruges-la-morte and The Death Throes of Towns*.

25. Nicholas Royle, "Introduction," in Georges Rodenbach, *The Bells of Bruges*, trans. Mike Mitchell (Sawtry, Cambridgeshire: Dedalus Books, 2008), 9.

26. Payer, "The Age of Noise," 775–76.

27. Will Stone, "Introduction" to "The Death Throes of Towns," in Rodenbach, *Bruges-la-morte and The Death Throes of Towns*.

28. See Lynn Pudles, "Fernand Khnopff, Georges Rodenbach, and Bruges, the Dead City," *The Art Bulletin* 74/4 (1992): 637; and Dorothy M. Kosinski, "With Georges Rodenbach—Bruges as State of Mind," in *Georges Rodenbach: Critical Essays*, ed. Philip Mosley (London: Associated University Press, 1996), 155.

29. Eduard Cairol, "Decadence and Mass Culture: The Novel as a Panorama—The Case of *Bruges-la-Morte*," *Journal of Literature and Art Studies* 5/7 (2015): 484.

30. Georges Rodenbach, opening "Avertissement" to *Bruges-la-morte* (Paris: Ernest Flammarion, 1892), 10 (capitalization as in original). Technically, the work's first appearance was in serial form in *Le Figaro*, but the Flammarion text is its first edition as a book.

31. Luzi Korngold, *Erich Wolfgang Korngold: Ein Lebensbild* (Vienna: Verlag Elisabeth Lafite, and Österreichischer Bundesverlag für Unterricht, Wissenschaft und Kunst, 1967),

33. When the couple visited Bruges together late in 1954, Luzi's sense was that it was the first time he had been there.

32. Julius Korngold, *Die Korngolds in Wien: Der Musikkritiker und das Wunderkind—Aufzeichnungen* (Zurich: M&T Verlag, 1991), 193.

33. See Lis Malina, ed., *"Dear Papa, How Is You? Das Leben Erich Wolfgang Korngolds in Briefen* (Vienna: Mandelbaum Verlag, 2017), 52–53.

34. For a study of the use of the photograph in early modernist literatures see Paul Edwards, *Soleil noir: Photographie et littérature des origines au surréalisme* (Rennes: Presses universitaires de Rennes, 2008).

35. Note that Korngold maintains the subterfuge of "my librettist." The nonexistent "Paul Schott" was invented by the Korngolds to disguise the fact that Julius and Erich wrote the libretto in collaboration. The original letter is held in the collection of the Theatermuseum Wien, HS_AM47414Ro, https://www.theatermuseum.at/de/object/fb12595fe3/.

36. Winters, *Erich Wolfgang Korngold's "The Adventures of Robin Hood,"* 37.

37. This formulation is Robyn Stilwell's, from his essay "The Fantastical Gap Between Diegetic and Non-Diegetic," in *Beyond the Soundtrack: Representing Music in Cinema*, ed. Daniel Goldmark, Richard Leppert, and Lawrence Kramer (Berkeley, Los Angeles, and London: University of California Press, 2007), 184–204.

38. For a discussion of the relationship between the photographs and relics of the protagonist's dead wife and the use of photographs of Bruges in Rodenbach's text, see Michael Newman, "Dead Mirrors: Relics and Photographs in Georges Rodenbach's *Bruges-la-Morte*," *Photographies* 4/1 (2011): 27–43.

39. Rodenbach, *Bruges-la-morte*, Kindle edition.

40. Peter Franklin offers an insightful consideration of Korngold's complex relationship to "serious-minded modernis[m]" within the context of his emigration to California and his successful Hollywood film work in "Modernism, Deception, and Musical Others: Los Angeles circa 1940," in *Western Music and Its Others: Difference, Representation, and Appropriation in Music*, ed. Georgina Born and David Hesmondhalgh (Berkeley and Los Angeles: University of California Press, 2000), esp. 154–59.

Korngold and Jewish Identity in Concert

LILY E. HIRSCH

Within the perceived "Korngold Renaissance" that began toward the end of the 1980s, Erich Wolfgang Korngold is performed in the context of music suppressed during the Nazi era.[1] These concerts in turn routinely index a conception of Jewish music and Jewish identity connected to the Holocaust.[2] In April 1987, Korngold was included in a "Holocaust Memorial Concert" performed by members of the Los Angeles Philharmonic at the Gindi Auditorium in Bel-Air.[3] In March 1998, the Salt Lake Jewish Community Center sponsored a "celebration of Jewish music," including Korngold's and others' music, labeled during the Nazi era *entartete Musik* (degenerate music).[4] In March 2015, the Atlanta Jewish Music Festival put on "Music of Resistance and Survival: A Holocaust Remembrance Concert," with songs of the ghetto and concentration camps as well as compositions by Felix Mendelssohn and Korngold.[5] And on August 20, 2015, in Madison, Wisconsin, the chamber music group Bach Dancing and Dynamite Society performed music by "two composers who died at Auschwitz" as well as a piece by Korngold. The concert was part of the project "Performing the Jewish Archive," which was designed to recover "lost" works by Jewish artists. Reporter Gayle Worland described the event as a whole under the heading "Uncovered Jewish Music Taking Stage in Madison." In one 2004 article on the composer's "comeback," Korngold was labeled a "Jewish Mozart," an epithet related to critic Eduard Hanslick's early verdict on the young composer: "The little Mozart!"[6]

Events and descriptions such as these frame the reemerging Korngold as a Jewish composer of Jewish music and victim of the Holocaust. At the same time this packaging reinforces such categorization, a cyclic process with little substance. Some authors recognize this cycle as a dangerous oversimplification or potential exploitation of a complicated past. Michael Haas, author of *Forbidden Music*, identifies this risk as a "heffalump trap" involving the "re-ghettoization of Jewish composers": "Mirror-imaging

Nazi policies in order to resurrect the composers they banned may be inevitable, but taking them from one ghetto and plunking them into another can be a real danger."[7] Historian James Leoffler offers another advisory edict in the context of Soviet music: "We must first start by asking what we gain, and what we lose, in applying our cultural labels to . . . historical music."[8]

So how should we present the performances of the music of composers connected to the Nazi era? How do we do right by them and their past in concert? In some ways, composers like Korngold do not make it easy. Korngold was a victim of anti-Semitism and Nazi politics, but he was also able to leave for Hollywood before the Holocaust. Though he was of Jewish origin, he was not observant, but a secular Jew, with all the convolutions that entails. As professors of public policy Barry Kosmin and Ariala Keysar argue, "Jewish secularism contains conflicting ideologies; so its ranks encompass a variety of Jewish nationalists, assimilationists, cultural cosmopolitans, and political universalists. As a result . . . teasing out and differentiating the secular from the religious and even more the irreligious from the areligious among [secular] Jews is a difficult task."[9] Korngold wrote two pieces linked to Jewish religious observation: *A Passover Psalm*, Op. 30, and *Prayer*, Op. 32. Yet Korngold did not view himself as a Jewish composer, nor see his music as Jewish, a category he might have defined and related to in many different ways.

Musicologist Ruth HaCohen has traced Jewish music's historical dismissal to conceptions of noise.[10] But Jewish music has also been linked to liturgical music, music connected to Israel, or music composed by Jews. It has also been associated, as Leon Botstein asserts, to the Nazi era. He writes, "It is nearly impossible to define and undertake the study of any aspect of the history of Jews in Europe without grappling with the brutal facts of their ultimate fate: the successful extermination of peoples and cultures between 1933 and 1945."[11] In reality, the making of Jewish music is a heterogeneous practice—one that changes over time and space, based on local negotiation and thinking about the category.[12]

Recently, at the national meeting of the American Musicological Society, Howard Pollack offered some aid to those researching composers with a complicated sense of Jewishness. To approach the subject, he recommended four pertinent questions:

1. How is the subject related to Judaism and Jewish culture?
2. How do *others* regard the subject or his or her work as Jewish?
3. How does *the subject* regard his or her person or work as Jewish?
4. How does the *investigator* regard the subject or his or her work as Jewish?[13]

In this chapter, I will let these queries guide me as I navigate Korngold's connections to Jewishness, the role played by external factors in the political context of his career, and the impact of both on his music and musical activities. I will highlight in particular a little-known correspondence with musicologist Anneliese Landau, who, in 1942, asked him directly: "How is your approach to the question of a Jewish style in music?" In so doing, I hope to convey an understanding of Korngold's relationship to Jewish music and his Jewish identity with the nuance that this complex and sometimes contentious issue deserves.

Question 1: **The Subject and Jewishness**

Korngold's parents, the critic Julius Korngold and his wife, Josephine, did not practice the Jewish religion. The family "saw themselves," according to biographer Jessica Duchen, "first and foremost as Austrians"—a notion of national identity not unusual for the Jewish bourgeoisie of the time.[14] The anti-Semitism of Vienna had an impact on the inhabitants' sense of place. Especially after the crash of 1873, a virulent anti-Semitism dovetailed with a general distrust of modernization.[15] Nevertheless, this external pressure did not prevent Jews from a thorough assimilation.[16] While some Jews endeavored to make their transition complete through conversion, the Korngolds did not view this step as necessary. Michael Haas argues that they "were inclined to dismiss confessional adherence to the point of neither leaving, nor converting and simply ignoring what they saw as a personal expression of a redundant religious practice."[17] Indeed, though they never joined a synagogue, the Korngolds did not contradict their official listing as "Israelis" or "Mosaic," a category to which they were assigned by the Austrian civil service.[18]

In his musical career, Korngold wrote only two pieces with overt Jewish connections. The *Passover Psalm*, Op. 30, is set to a Hebrew text, composed for solo voice, chorus, and orchestra, and the *Prayer*, Op. 32, is based on a text by Jewish writer Franz Werfel (Alma Mahler's third husband), for tenor, women's choir, and organ. The rabbi Jacob Sonderling commissioned the works. He had left Germany in 1923, settling first in New York before moving to Los Angeles in 1935. He then led a Reform synagogue on Fairfax Avenue—the Fairfax Temple—which served German and Austrian émigrés. In that position, he would commission works from Arnold Schoenberg and Erich Zeisl as well as Korngold.[19] Duchen notes, "Rabbi Jacob Sonderling seems to have been an artistically enlightened and imaginative individual, and supportive of Los Angeles' immigrant artistic population."[20] His correspondence with Korngold about the compositions reveals this engagement as well as his interest in music and direct role in the creation of these works.[21]

Sonderling's commission and Korngold's Jewish background provide some justification for treating Korngold as a Jewish composer, in concert and otherwise. Korngold's association with Gustav Mahler (a point to which we will return) also points toward that Jewish connection. My discussion here, however, also considers identity formation in the negative—that is, in response to anti-Semitic criticism, the turmoil of the Nazi era, and other people's relationship to Korngold and his music.

Question 2: Outside Attitudes

In 1926, Korngold was discussing plans to stage his opera *Das Wunder der Heliane* with the opera director in Nürnberg, Bertil Wetzelsberger. At the same time, the National Socialist Party was holding a congress in the city. His wife, Luzi, recalled, "With fearful forebodings, I watched the Nazis stamping past my window in their torch-lit demonstrations and listened to their pounding marches. As I heard the dull drumbeat mixed with the high-pitched sound of the piccolo, an inexplicable fear gripped me concerning Erich."[22] When Hitler came to power, Korngold's adaptation of Leo Fall's *Die geschiedene Frau* was in performance at Berlin's Theater am Nollendorfplatz. The show would close early, resulting in what Haas dubs an "intriguing" lawsuit.[23] Subsequent opportunities in Germany disappeared. Korngold took refuge in his family's retreat in Austria's Salzkammergut, focusing there on the composition of his new opera *Die Kathrin*. In a letter of 6 December 1934, Ludwig Strecker of the music publisher Schott, explained his reluctance to publish the work: "Only yesterday, Furtwängler, Kleiber, and Hindemith have resigned from all of their posts and they stand accused of being 'too Jew-friendly.'"[24] Korngold's music, according to the infamous "Entartete Musik" exhibition in Düsseldorf in 1938, was then banned as "degenerate" alongside other works condemned as jazz or Jewish.[25] In Theo Stengel and Herbert Gerigk's *Lexikon der Juden in der Musik* (1943), Korngold, who had made popular arrangements of operetta, was disparaged for his musical appropriation of the beloved composer Johann Strauss, reworkings that supposedly included jazzy additions.[26] It did not matter that Korngold was not a jazz enthusiast; pseudo-musicology made the Nazi case. To enforce the artificial divide, Strauss's own Jewish connections had been erased, his ancestry no longer available in official records.[27]

In 1937, before the annexation of Austria, Korngold's opera *Die Kathrin* was scheduled to premiere with the Vienna State Opera under the direction of Bruno Walter. But the premiere would have to wait, eventually taking place in Stockholm in October 1939. Because of the "threatening situation," this would be the only premiere of his work that Korngold would miss.[28] The reviews were mixed and at times decidedly anti-Semitic: "The emigrant Jew Korngold's disgusting opera *Kathrin* is performed, while Swedish composers are forced to have their works performed abroad. . . . The libretto is a typically Jewish mishmash . . . a typical example of what Jewish cultural Bolshevism can achieve."[29]

Meanwhile Korngold's music, and specifically his arrangements, had already attracted the attention of Max Reinhardt, who had offered Korngold an escape from the Nazi threat: Hollywood. In 1934, Korngold agreed to score the film adaptation of Shakespeare's *A Midsummer Night's Dream*. As Bryan Gilliam points out, while the Nazis attempted to sever *A Midsummer Night's Dream* from its Jewish connection—the music of Felix Mendelssohn—Korngold worked to expand the effect, creating his score by incorporating Mendelssohn's incidental music as well as other music by the composer along with original passages of his own.[30] After the film was completed, Korngold returned to Austria, but, when a telegram arrived on January 22, 1938, requesting Korngold's immediate reengagement in Hollywood, Korngold viewed it as "an omen."[31]

Once settled in the United States, Korngold would suffer from another prejudice against his music, in particular his film music, one related to the anti-Semitic dismissal of his work. As Naomi Pfefferman wrote in 1999, "The work that Korngold composed in Hollywood after fleeing the Nazis was spurned as 'kitsch.'"[32] In Nazi Germany, the denigration of film music overlapped with the denunciation of Jews—an argument encapsulated in Pfefferman's choice of the word *kitsch*, a category of special censure during the Nazi era.[33] Gilliam highlights one Nazi writer's assertion—an extension of "Wagner's strategy"—that "Jewish musicians made ideal film composers." Their perceived unoriginality presumably lent itself to the construction of a "musical wallpaper."[34] Richard Taruskin ties such denigration to Korngold's operatic music, in particular the "decadent" *Das Wunder der Heliane*, labeling it a "kitsch cousin."[35]

Would this criticism affect Korngold's own relationship to perceptions of his work's Jewishness? How did the political context and his forced emigration shape Korngold's self-identity, as a Jew and émigré? And how did Korngold himself view Sonderling's commission? The émigré musicologist Anneliese Landau carried on a lengthy correspondence with Korngold in the course of research for her book on Jewish composers, published in 1946.[36] Their letters are particularly valuable as an attempt to reveal Korngold's own attitude toward his music and identity shortly after external factors had forced him to confront these issues in a new way.

Question 3: **The Subject on Jewishness and Jewish Music**
Though Korngold grew up unobservant, he would have been aware of an unofficial societal divide between Jews and non-Jews. Haas describes "wealthy, talented Jewish circles that created a parallel social universe to haut-bourgeois non-Jewish Vienna."[37] This separation extended to marriage practices, Jews and converted Jews often finding matches among themselves. The composer Richard Strauss suspected this societal circumscription affected Julius Korngold's music criticism and would accuse him of primarily supporting his "fellow Israelites."[38]

External factors would convert Korngold's rather passive awareness of his Jewishness into something more, something unavoidable; it would become one of his life's deciding factors. And that effect would color his self-identity and attitude toward life as an émigré. In the United States, Korngold and Luzi embraced their new home in Toluca Lake in northern Los Angeles. Korngold described his work with Warner Bros. positively: "I feel very happy as an artist here. No one tells me what to do. I do not feel part of a factory. I take part in story conferences, suggest changes in the editing when it is dramatically necessary to coincide with musical structure. It is entirely up to me to decide where in the picture to put my music. . . . And the studio heads never make the acquaintance of my music until the day of the sneak preview."[39] However, the Korngolds socialized in Los Angeles primarily with other Austrians and Germans, and, in so doing, maintained some Viennese customs, including the *Jause*, an afternoon ritual of coffee and pastries.[40] We see this ongoing connection to Austria and Korngold's Austrian self-identity in many of his film scores. According to Ben Winters, these films display an idealized Austrian nostalgia.[41] But news of the reality in Austria depressed Korngold and he would try to help everyone he could escape Nazism, often writing affidavits pledging financial support. According to Duchen, "Korngold signed so many affidavits for would-be immigrants that eventually the authorities refused his name as guarantor."[42]

In this way, Korngold was an exile as much as an émigré. This distinction is important. Barbara Zeisl Schoenberg recognized that scholars have had a tendency to subsume German-speaking émigrés under a single heading.[43] But each émigré would have a distinct past and a specific relationship to a new home—a place of exile for some, of refuge for others. The experience of emigration, then, varied vastly and the terms employed by those who fled further reflect this variation. German historian Jost Hermand explains, "Those who were more or less apolitical usually used the term emigrants. The activists, on the other hand, preferred terms such as exiles, displaced persons, or outcasts."[44] Hermand interprets the distinction as an effort to emphasize the necessity of emigration, the lack of choice involved. After all, exile is by definition a process of forced banishment—a forced move that continues in the new land. Accordingly, that new land is a place of asylum, rather than a home, and exiles may someday return to their "real" home.[45] Applied to Bertolt Brecht, Hermand points out, "The word emigrant sounded too much like a 'voluntary expatriate.'"[46]

The term *exile* also differentiates those émigrés who remained dissatisfied from those who fully embraced their new home. Some authors have assumed that among émigré artists, musicians might most easily overcome exile since music is supposed to be a universal language that easily translates.[47] But many German and Austrian composers suffered in the United States. Another Viennese émigré composer, Eric Zeisl, called Los Angeles a "sunny, blue grave."[48] For Zeisl, emigration was exile. The term also has some merit in Korngold's case. Korngold was very much conflicted, working in a new home while imagining a return, though he recognized that a true return was impossible, and that considering himself an exile was little more than a nostalgic fiction: Austria would never be the same after the war.

How to reconcile Korngold's music with this complicated Austrian émigré/exile status? Luzi Korngold observed, "It was as if he had made a vow that he would write no more music, except for film music, as long as horrors were weighing on the world."[49] But this sentiment stands in opposition to Korngold's own words in 1940: "Never have I differentiated between my music for the films and that for the operas and concert pieces."[50] Moreover, in 1941 he composed the two Jewish works unrelated to film, *A Passover Psalm* and *Prayer*. Duchen imagines that these pieces were a welcome change: "He had not been formally commissioned to write anything other than film music for a very long time."[51] But could the Jewish context have attracted the composer as well?

In 1945, Korngold would participate in another similarly suggestive musical endeavor—a concert featuring the works of other émigré composers under the auspices of the Jewish Centers Association in Los Angeles. In charge of the event was Anneliese Landau, music director for the Association since 1944. She had received her doctorate in musicology from Berlin University (now Humboldt University) in 1930, and had lectured on music over early German radio. After Hitler assumed power, she was fired as a Jew and then worked in the Berlin Jewish Kulturbund, a closed cultural organization created by and for Jews, before emigrating to the United States.

Landau contacted Korngold and visited him at his home to discuss the event; he suggested for the concert his popular suite *Much Ado About*

INTERNATIONAL COMPOSERS CONCERT

A Musical Salute to the United Nations Security Conference

On April 24, 1945, at 8:15 P.M.

AT THE

WILSHIRE EBELL THEATRE
In Los Angeles

★

SPONSORED BY

The Jewish Centers Association
OF LOS ANGELES

ARRANGED BY

DR. ANNELIESE LANDAU
Music Director of J. C. A.

★

PROCEEDS OF THIS CONCERT WILL BE USED FOR THE FOUNDATION OF A RECORD LIBRARY AT THE JEWISH COMMUNITY CENTERS IN LOS ANGELES

★

——————— JEWISH CENTERS ASSOCIATION ———————
OFFICERS:
MEYER E. FICHMAN, EXECUTIVE DIRECTOR

JUDGE IRVIN STALMASTER	DR. MAURICE SMITH	LEONARD CHUDACOFF
PRESIDENT	FIRST VICE-PRESIDENT	SECOND VICE-PRESIDENT
MRS. I. PELTON	MAX FIRESTEIN	SECRETARY
THIRD VICE-PRESIDENT	TREASURER	MRS. S. GLICKMAN

MRS. LEE S. KESTENBAUM
CHAIRMAN OF MUSIC COMMITTEE

Figure 1. Program for the International Composers Concert.

Nothing for violin and piano, composed in 1918–19. Amiable and helpful, according to Landau, he also offered to play the piano part himself. He would ask his friend, Henri Temianka, a virtuoso violinist and conductor, to play the violin part.[52] The concert itself—the "International

Composers Concert," at the Wilshire Ebell Theatre—presented works by nine composers in total, all from Europe: besides Korngold, Ernst Toch, Arnold Schoenberg, Louis Gruenberg, Paul Dessau, Mario Castelnuovo-Tedesco, Ernest Bloch, Darius Milhaud, and Maurice Ravel, with his "Kaddish" in memory of Franklin D. Roosevelt (see Figure 1). In keeping with the politicization of music in the United States at the time and the music of émigrés in particular, a subtitle was added—"A Musical Salute to the United Nations Security Conference"—honoring the international meeting of delegates from forty-six nations in San Francisco, which began on April 25. At its close, the conference would establish the United Nations—a striking moment of international cooperation during the last days of the Second World War.[53] In this way Korngold to some extent accepted the label Jewish—as he would at other concerts organized by Landau, such as her Broadway Melodies Pop Concert, on July 29, 1945, at the Beverly Fairfax Jewish Community Center.[54] In a letter of 23 July 1943, Luzi offers a comparable example, describing her attendance at the "Jewish thing" (*jüdischen Sache*), a performance at the Hollywood Bowl of the dramatic pageant *We Will Never Die*, with music by Kurt Weill. The spectacle, on July 21, included a public listing of Jews who had contributed to civilization. As she reported to her husband, he was announced as part of a small group of contemporary composers.[55]

Does this activity, along with the Sonderling commission, point toward a new interest in Judaism, Jewish identity, or Jewish music? Could Korngold have experienced something like the Jewish recommitment of that other Austrian composer, Arnold Schoenberg? On July 21, 1933, Schoenberg had attended a meeting for exiled Jews in Paris. A speaker at the gathering insisted that those assembled must not react to Hitler with the same extreme nationalism. Schoenberg disagreed; he believed strongly that Jewish nationalism was exactly the right course of action.[56] Just three days later, Schoenberg, who had in 1898 converted to Protestant Christianity, returned to the Jewish faith during a ceremony witnessed by the painter Marc Chagall.

Korngold's granddaughter, Kathrin Hubbard, doubts that Korngold experienced any such reorientation and instead remained non-observant. She wrote, "I know that my grandfather was a strictly secular or assimilated Jew, if you like. He did not practice the religion, was not observant of Jewish holidays and did not attend synagogue services. In point of fact, he especially loved Christmas holidays, and took great pleasure in wrapping elaborate amounts of gifts with a table designated for each recipient." She recalled seeing her grandparents' marriage certificate: "They had to declare whether they were Jewish, Christian or 'nothing.' ... Suffice to say, they checked the 'nothing' box."[57]

Before her trip to Toluca Lake, Landau had written to Korngold as part of her research for a book on the role of Jewish composers in music titled *The Contribution of Jewish Composers to the Music of the Modern World*.[58] The book included study guides and recommended recordings, and was commissioned by Jane Evans, the first full-time head of the Cincinnati-based National Federation of the Temple Sisterhoods. During her time in office, Evans also began the publication of a newsletter, *Topics and Trends*, and organized a radio program on Jewish liturgical music before turning her attention to larger issues of war as well as the needs of the Jewish community in what was then Palestine.[59]

In a letter dated 28 December 1942, Landau asked Korngold a series of questions, in her somewhat unidiomatic English, including:

> How is your approach to the question of a Jewish style in music? Have you ever thought of it? Or are you just a musician, with everything else of minor importance—as I believe you are, and most of us are, although Hitler wants urgently to trace Judaism in every little bit of our being and doing. Do you agree with Ernest Bloch: "I consider these pages of my own, in which I am at my best, are those in which I am most unmistakably racial" or do you agree with Gustav Mahler: "Ich bin Musiker, darin ist alles andere enthalten" [I am a musician; everything else is covered by that]?

One of Landau's other questions, about Korngold's "personal remembrance of Gustav Mahler," inspired an emotional response from the composer when he responded—in German—about a week later. Since childhood and even before, he had been connected to Mahler. The Jewish fathers of Julius Korngold and Gustav Mahler were both from the Czech province of Moravia, and Julius Korngold greatly admired Mahler, as would his son. In 1906, when Erich was ten, Julius took him to play for Mahler his early cantata for solo voices, chorus, and piano, entitled *Gold*. Julius reported that, as the boy played, Mahler "began to pace hastily to and fro, then run to and fro in that limping rhythm, peculiar to him when he was excited. He cried over and over again: 'A genius!'"[60] The story, now legend, ends with Mahler recommending that Korngold study with the conductor, composer, and teacher Alexander von Zemlinsky. In this way Erich Korngold would endeavor to pursue his musical objectives, fulfilling a childhood wish of 1910: to grow up to be Mahler.[61] On December 14, 1943, when his friend the director Max Reinhardt died, Korngold performed his own arrangement of Mahler's "Urlicht" at the memorial service.⁶² He would also remain close to Mahler's wife, Alma. On 17 December 1946, he asked her in a letter if he might dedicate to her his Violin Concerto in D Major, Op. 35, which would be premiered by Jascha Heifetz on February 15, 1947.⁶³ In his letter to Landau, Korngold shared with her his early declaration that, as a boy, he had wanted to be Mahler. He also described the sadness he felt upon Mahler's death. It "distressed" him for weeks.⁶⁴

As for works other than film music, Korngold listed Lieder (Opp. 29 and 31) as well as his *A Passover Psalm*. The latter provided a segue into Korngold's consideration of his "position on Jewish music." Unsurprisingly, he sided with Mahler's "I am a musician" above all rather than Bloch's "unmistakably racial" music being his best, though with amendment: "I can here vary Mahler and say, I am an *opera composer*; everything else is covered by that," he wrote, adding that "my 'Passover Psalm' is the work of an opera composer, the same way that Verdi's Requiem is a work of an opera composer, moreover an Italian one."⁶⁵

Landau was the only person known to have asked Korngold directly about his attitude toward Jewish music—and he answered with resolution. He viewed his music as beyond designations of race or religion; his identification as a composer trumped all. He would hint at a similar sentiment when, in 1953, he wrote, "I, myself, do not believe in the mistaken thesis that art should mirror its time. . . . No, I am much more inclined to believe the opposite: the genuine artist creates at a distance from his own time, even for a time beyond."⁶⁶ He thereby distinguished his attitude toward composition from that of his early rival Krenek—a composer of *Zeitoper*—as well as Schoenberg, with his recent cantata *A Survivor from Warsaw* (1947). Korngold underscored his belief that music inhabits its own realm, and corrected individuals who attempted to see in his works a reflection of his historical experience. In commentary about his postwar Symphony in F-sharp, Op. 40, Korngold wrote, "The composer characterizes his new symphony as a work of pure, absolute music with no program whatsoever, in spite of his experience that many people—after the first hearing—read into the first movement the terror and horrors of the years 1933–1945, and into the Adagio the sorrows and suffering of the victims of that time."⁶⁷ Hubbard shared that, once in the United States, Korngold was often asked by reporters about his opinion of Hitler. He would reply, "I think Mendelssohn will outlive Hitler." Based on the response, she concluded, "As you can see, for him, everything was in the context of music."⁶⁸

Korngold's reasons for agreeing to fulfill Sonderling's commission or participating in Landau's concerts clearly do not confirm a new devotion to Jewish identity or music. Perhaps Korngold felt a sense of duty or responsibility to the local Jewish community, a sense of shared fate. As Korngold's father wrote in a letter to his son in early March 1938, "We live . . . in difficult, infuriatingly threatening times and must, like the Jewish families once in the ghetto, stick together more than ever."[69] More likely still, the experience of emigration may have provided a feeling of connection. Conductor Alexander Kahn, for one, argues that the similar experience of composers in exile could create a sense of solidarity, linking in this way the composers Korngold, Zeisl, and Ernst Toch.[70] The link to Toch may be particularly instructive.

Korngold and Toch shared a similarly complex relationship to Jewishness. The Viennese Toch had been a professor of composition at the Mannheim Conservatory of Music and in 1927 saw the successful premiere of his one-act chamber opera *The Princess and the Pea* at the Baden-Baden festival in Germany. Five years later, Toch was almost killed when a group of young people attempted to hit him with their car near Potsdamer Platz, a bustling intersection and popular square in Berlin. His only supposed crime: he looked too Jewish. In the spring of 1933 Hans Wilhelm Steinberg was busy preparing Toch's opera *Der Fächer* (The Fan) for performance in Cologne. Members of the Gestapo interrupted the rehearsal, grabbing the baton right out of the conductor's hand.[71] Once in the United States, Toch was included in Landau's International Composers concert and was also approached by Sonderling, who would use Toch's music for the Passover Festival at the Fairfax Temple in Los Angeles.[72] Additionally, Toch would contribute to the *Genesis Suite*—another collaboration among émigré artists, this time in cooperative composition, that premiered seven months after Landau's 1945 concert.[73] Toch never reaffirmed his commitment to Judaism or Jewish music. Indeed, he actively rejected Schoenberg's decision to do so, telling the composer, "Why should the Nazis have to tell me that I am a Jew and must be a Jew? I am who I am."[74] In the exchange of correspondence between Toch and Landau, Toch—much like Korngold—responded that he was "utterly at a loss as to how even to define Jewish music in what we call 'art-music.'"[75] In a speech in 1957, titled "Some Viewpoints of the Composer," given under the auspices of the Jewish Centers Association, Toch insisted that good art was independent of specific affiliations, national or otherwise; it could be religious, but such a religion, he maintained, was not tied to a specific denomination.[76] According to Kahn, Toch's work with Jewish institutions was a compromise: "It seems likely that Toch was attracted to commissions being offered to him by Jewish organizations at least in part because they provided him with sorely needed income."[77]

Korngold did not have the same financial need, thanks to his thriving film career. But the notion of compromise still seems relevant. Korngold may not have identified as a Jewish composer but he surely felt a sense of solidarity with others involved with Jewish institutions, especially émigrés. His identity was in this way defined by his experience and external pressures. But fundamental to that identification, in addition to his Austrianness, was his music. As his wife confirmed in a letter to Helene Thimig, an actress and the wife of Max Reinhardt, "His art is his life."[78]

Question 4: The Investigator
After emigration Korngold, though still unobservant, was increasingly connected to his Jewishness through social interaction, prejudice, as well as the need for work. Although he did not view his works as Jewish, others did—in some cases based on anti-Semitic stereotypes and tropes. In reference to Pollack's final question about the investigator's assumptions of the Jewishness of Korngold and his music—a question Pollack calls "the riskiest of all"—I myself am deeply skeptical of the entire enterprise of assigning fixed identities to music. Only if the composer him- or herself attempts such a labeling will I recognize it, and then only to some extent. With that perspective, and in conclusion, I ask: How should concert organizers approach the performance of Korngold's music?

In 2015, Charles Krauthammer, chairman of Pro Musica Hebraica, and Edward Rothstein, critic for the *Wall Street Journal,* engaged in a pertinent debate. Rothstein had reviewed a concert devoted to classical Jewish music sponsored by Pro Musica Hebraica, an organization dedicated to Jewish music; the program featured Korngold as well as the composers Jerzy Fitelberg and Mario Castelnuovo-Tedesco. In the review, Rothstein asked, "Aside from the creators' shared background, in what way were these works 'Jewish'?" Krauthammer, in response, urged audiences to look at the full body of Pro Musica Hebraica's work, insisting that "what emerges is a body of work of unmistakably Jewish character." Rothstein maintained that a focus on racial or sexual identity can reduce "the variousness and diversity of human experience to a monochrome template of victimization and claims for recompense." But, still, he was not ultimately at odds with Krauthaummer: "When it comes to works of art, there are indeed times and contexts in which a measured and appropriate attention to identity can reveal aspects that we may not have registered before, help bring to light hitherto unnoticed lines of influence, and compel us to see or hear things from a different perspective." And, this music, he wrote, was "Jewish in a biographical way—and not just because of the composers' birth but because of how their lives followed similar trajectories."

To me, both "Jewish character" and "Jewish in a biographical way" seem problematic qualifications. Yet these composers are indeed linked. Fitelberg, born in Warsaw, escaped the Nazis, settling in New York. Castelnuovo-Tedesco, an Italian composer, was also forced to flee. Like Korngold, he worked as a film composer in Los Angeles and performed in Landau's 1945 concert, playing piano for his "Dances of King David." The link then may have some basis as a helpful means of organization and marketing. Many of these composers benefited from such attention, as conductor James Conlon has insisted. Conlon has addressed that need with his "Recovered Voices" project in Los Angeles, but he also looks forward to seeing the need fulfilled. In "Recovering a Musical Heritage," he explains, "I now perform this music regularly, in the hope that it will find its place in the standard repertoire."[79] This repositioning or supposed last step—one without specific Jewish or Nazi-related label—may prove impossible, dependent on a "standard" or even canonic repertoire that has irrevocably splintered, if it was ever whole in the first place. But that label-less acceptance would be especially significant in the case of Korngold. That is, it would align with Korngold's own attitudes toward his identity and composition. After all, as he himself insisted, he was "an opera composer; everything else is covered by that."

Appendix

Anne L. Landau, Ph.D.
34-59 Eighty-ninth Street
Jackson Heights, New York

[New York] December 28th 1942

Dear Mr. Korngold:
The National Federation of Temple Sisterhoods has asked me to write the Program Study Material for this winter on the topic: THE JEWISH CONTRIBUTION TO THE MUSIC OF THE MODERN WORLD.

The last and main chapter of this book will be devoted to Music in America. Each chapter will be provided with a detailed bibliography and a list of recordings, so that the local units of the organization (there are 385 sisterhoods) might be influenced to purchase the available material for their discussion-forums.

Since I missed you in New York, would you do me the great favor to answer me the following questions at your earliest convenience, and via air-mail?

1. When did you come over to this country and what have you been doing since then?

2. Are you connected with Warner's for good? And are you writing just now music for a new picture, and if so, for which one?

3. What is with *Kathrine*, will it come out at the New Opera Co. definitely?

4. Have you written shortly and are you writing other music than music for pictures?

5. How is your approach to the question of a Jewish style in music? Have you ever thought of it? Or are you just a musician with everything else of minor importance—as I believe you are, and most of us are, although Hitler wants urgently to trace Judaism in every little bit of our being and doing. Do you agree with Ernest Bloch "I consider these pages of my own, in which I am at my best, are those in which I am most unmistakably racial" or do you agree with Gustav Mahler: "Ich bin Musiker, darin ist alles andere enthalten"?

6. Would you tell me something about your personal remembrance of Gustav Mahler? (Wenn ich Sie um etwas beneide, dann darum, dass Sie diesen Menschen persönlich kennen durften!)

7. Do you know Oscar Levant personally, who sketches so delicately the scene with you and Mr. [James] Cagney in his "Smattering of Ignorance"? And how do you see him? By the way—is he Jewish, I assume he is?

8. How is your approach to Copland? and Marc Blitzstein? Do you happen to know Jerome Kern personally, and if so, what do you think of him?

Please forgive my bothering you so very much, I just want to make you write, and if there are some other points you want to speak about, by all means, please do so! Your Austrian Period I followed up to your collaboration with Reinhardt's "Schoene Helena," which I saw in Berlin. "Die tote Stadt" I saw in Vienna in 1923. Between these two performances there are 10 years, which mean to me: study, promotion, position at the "Funkstunde/Berlin" and "Deutsche Welle," and—many lectures including your music.

Let me have your answer as soon as possible—and thanks for all the trouble you are taking!

Sincerely yours,
[Anneliese Landau]

Hollywood, 5 January 1943

Dear Madam,[80]
I have the feeling that I may answer your friendly letter—for which I want to thank you very much—in *German*, in which case your answer will arrive all the faster, so I will get on with it!

I came to America for the first time in October 1934—at the request of *Reinhardt*—and since then three times back to Vienna, on "quota" since 1936, and since 1938 uninterrupted in Hollywood. I passed my *citizenship exam* about a year ago and am now awaiting the swearing-in . . .

Below you will find my musical scores for film
Midsummer Night's Dream (Reinhardt) Warners (1934–35)
Give Us This Night (Kiepura) Paramount (1935)
Captain Blood (Flynn) Warners (1935)
Anthony Adverse (March) Warners (1936) (Academy award)
Another Dawn (Flynn) Warners (1937)
Prince and the Pauper (Flynn) Warners (1937)
Robin Hood (Flynn) Warners (1938) (Academy award)
Juarez (Muni-Davis) Warners (1939)
Elizabeth and Essex (Davis-Flynn) Warners (1939)
The Sea Hawk (Flynn) Warners (1940)
The Sea Wolf (Robinson) Warner (1941)

Kings Row (Sheridan) Warners (1941)
The Constant Nymph (Boyen-Fontaine) Warners (1942)
My next picture is supposedly going to be *Devotion* for Warners: a biography of the Brontë sisters (*Wuthering Heights*).

I cannot currently say with certainty that my new opera *Kathrin* is going to be performed by the New Opera Co., as the company is currently fighting for its existence . . .

Besides my film music and incidental music for Goldoni's *The Servant of Two Masters* for Reinhardt (for which I used motives by *Rossini*), I composed in recent years the Shakespeare Songs Opp. 29 and 31 (the *Narrenlieder* from *Twelfth Night*) as well as "A Passover Psalm," Op. 30, for solo soprano, choir, and small orchestra.

This last piece leads naturally to an answer for your next question: what I think of Jewish music. I could do a variation on Mahler and say, "I am an opera composer—and that covers it all." So too is my "Passover Psalm" the work of an opera composer, as is Verdi's Requiem (and an Italian one at that).

My memory of Mahler goes back to my childhood and will stay forever fresh in my mind. I had an immeasurable admiration for him, and, when asked as an eight-year-old what I "wanted to be," I used to reply, "Maestro Mahler."

I played my (back then hypermodern) compositions as a ten-, eleven-, and twelve-year-old to him on the piano, and I remember well his incredulous amazement . . . I experienced and thoroughly enjoyed the premiere of the Eighth Symphony in Munich in 1910. I also saw two Mozart dress rehearsals earlier at the Vienna Court Opera. His death in the spring of 1911 left me distraught for weeks. The only losses that moved me comparably were those of two revered friends and masters, Nikisch and Puccini.

Let me take a deep breath . . .

And now as a coda:

I met Mr. Oscar Levant at the house of Salka Viertel, Greta Garbo's friend, in 1935. In reality, the clumsy scene between me and Cagney never happened, and it does not say much for Mr. Levant's taste and inventiveness. His presence is highly overrated by many—himself included; his behavior is not collegial and outright rude, though I do believe he is a good piano player and a gifted musician.

I am not personally acquainted with Copland and Blitzstein and I also know little about Copland's music. On the other hand, I very much like Jerome Kern's charming character and find his talent as a composer equally charming. I see his operatic work on the same level as that of

Oskar Straus, whom I consider the most talented of the Vienna operetta period after Johann Strauss.

I believe I've exhausted your catalogue of questions as well as the writer and reader of these lines. Too bad we were not in touch in New York! I would be happy to hear from you again. With kindest regards and good wishes for 1943

Yours humbly,
Erich Wolfgang Korngold

NOTES

1. Brendan G. Carroll, *The Last Prodigy: A Biography of Erich Wolfgang Korngold* (Portland, OR: Amadeus Press, 1997), 367.

2. For more information on the link between "suppressed music" and Jewish music, see Lily E. Hirsch, "Righting and Remembering Past Wrongs: Music Suppressed by the Nazis in American Concert Performance," *Music & Politics* 10/1 (2016).

3. Marc Shulgold, "Holocaust Remembered in Berlin," *Los Angeles Times*, 26 April 1987.

4. Jeff Manookian, "A Celebration of Jewish Music in S.L.," *Salt Lake City Tribune*, 8 March 1998.

5. David R. Cohen, "AJMF: Holocaust Message in the Music," *Atlanta Jewish Times*, 5 March 2015, http://atlantajewishtimes.timesofisrael.com/ajmf-holocaust-message-in-the-music/.

6. Julius Korngold, *Child Prodigy: Erich Wolfgang's Years of Childhood* (New York: Willard Publishing, 1945), 11.

7. Michael Haas, "Where to Start or How to Start? (Part 1)," The OREL Foundation, http://orelfoundation.org/index.php/journal/journalArticle/where_to_start_or_how_to_start/.

8. James Loeffler, "'In Memory of Our Murdered (Jewish) Children': Hearing the Holocaust in Soviet Jewish Culture," *Slavic Review* 73/3 (Fall 2014). See also James Loeffler, "Why the New 'Holocaust Music' Is an Insult to Music—and the Victims of the Shoah," *Tablet*, 11 July 2013.

9. Barry A. Kosmin and Ariela Keysar, "American Jewish Secularism: Jewish Life Beyond the Synagogue," *American Jewish Yearbook* (2012), 5. Thanks to Amy Wlodarski for this reference and for her thoughtful discussion of the complexity of representing Jewish identity in biography at the national meeting of the American Musicological Society, November 9, 2017, in Rochester, NY.

10. See Ruth HaCohen, *The Music Libel Against the Jews* (New Haven: Yale University Press, 2011).

11. Leon Botstein, "The Jewish Question in Music," *Musical Quarterly* 94/4 (Winter 2011): 441.

12. See Tina Frühauf and Lily E. Hirsch, Introduction, in *Dislocated Memories: Jews, Music, and Postwar German Culture*, ed. Tina Frühauf and Lily E. Hirsch (New York: Oxford University Press, 2014), 3.

13. Howard Pollack, "Jews, Music, and Biography," paper presented at the American Musicological Society National Conference, co-organized by Lily E. Hirsch and Amy Wlodarski, Rochester, NY, November 9, 2017, forthcoming in *Musica Judaica*.

14. Jessica Duchen, *Erich Wolfgang Korngold* (London: Phaidon, 1996), 12–13.

15. See Leon Botstein, "Introduction: The Tragedy and Irony of Success: Locating Jews in the Musical Life of Vienna," in *Vienna: Jews and the City of Music, 1870–1938*, ed. Leon Botstein and Werner Hanak (Annandale-on-Hudson: Bard College, and Vienna: Wolke Verlag, 2004), 13–19.

16. Duchen, *Erich Wolfgang Korngold*, 12–13.

17. Michael Haas, "The False Myths and True Genius of Erich Wolfgang Korngold," ForbiddenMusic.org, 18 July 2015, https://forbiddenmusic.org/2015/07/18/the-false-myths-and-true-genius-of-erich-wolfgang-korngold/.

18. Ibid.

19. Kenneth M. Marcus, *Schoenberg and Hollywood Modernism* (Cambridge: Cambridge University Press, 2016), 165.

20. Duchen, *Erich Wolfgang Korngold*, 194.

21. Sonderling to Korngold, 8 March 1941. I thank Daniel Goldmark for sharing this letter.

22. Quoted in Carroll, *The Last Prodigy*, 191.

23. See Michael Haas, *Forbidden Music: The Jewish Composers Banned by the Nazis* (New Haven: Yale University Press, 2013), 219.

24. Quoted in ibid., 240.

25. The jazz element was a central feature of the exhibition's attack on Kurt Weill and Ernst Krenek. Greta Beigel, "It Wasn't Music to Their Ears: An Exhibition Opening Thursday Re-creates the Nazis' 1938 Denouncement of 'Degenerate' Composers," *Los Angeles Times*, 17 March 1991, http://articles.latimes.com/1991-03-17/entertainment/ca-690_1_music-history.

26. Theo Stengel and Herbert Gerigk, *Lexikon der Juden in der Musik* (Berlin: Bernhard Hahn Feld Verlag, 1943), 153.

27. See Bryan Gilliam, "A Viennese Opera Composer in Hollywood: Korngold's Double Exile in America," in *Driven into Paradise: The Musical Migration from Nazi Germany to the United States*, ed. Reinhold Brinkmann and Christoph Wolff (Berkeley: University of California Press, 1999), 239.

28. Luzi Korngold, *Erich Wolfgang Korngold: Ein Lebensbild* (Vienna: Verlag Elisabeth Lafite, and Österreichischer Bundesverlag für Unterricht, Wissenschaft und Kunst, 1967), 79.

29. Quoted in Carroll, *The Last Prodigy*, 293.

30. Gilliam, "A Viennese Opera Composer in Hollywood," 226.

31. Luzi Korngold, *Erich Wolfgang Korngold*, 268.

32. Naomi Pfefferman, "Music That Heals," *Jewish Journal*, 15 July 1999, http://jewishjournal.com/old_stories/1854/.

33. See Natalia Skradol, "Fascism and Kitsch: The Nazi Campaign Against Kitsch," *German Studies Review* 34/3 (October 2011): 597. For a discussion of "entartete Kitsch," see Ruth Holliday and Tracey Potts, *Kitsch! Cultural Politics and Taste* (Manchester, UK: Manchester University Press, 2012), 13–15.

34. Gilliam, "A Viennese Opera Composer in Hollywood," 229.

35. Richard Taruskin, "The Golden Age of Kitsch," in *The Danger of Music and Other Anti-Utopian Essays* (Berkeley: University of California Press, 2010), 260.

36. Anne L. Landau, *The Contribution of Jewish Composers to the Music of the Modern World* (Cincinnati: National Federation of Temple Sisterhoods, 1946).

37. Haas, "The False Myths and True Genius of Erich Wolfgang Korngold."

38. Ibid.

39. Quoted in Barbara Zeisl Schoenberg, "The Reception of Austrian Composers in Los Angeles: 1934–1950," *Modern Austrian Literature* 20/3–4 (1987): 135.

40. Anneliese Landau, "Pictures You Wanted To See—People You Wanted To Meet," in "Memoirs" (unpublished), 128. Author's collection.

41. See Ben Winters, "Swearing an Oath: Korngold, Film, and the Sound of Resistance?" in *The Impact of Nazism on Twentieth-Century Music*, ed. Erik Levi (Vienna: Böhlau, 2014).

42. Duchen, *Erich Wolfgang Korngold*, 178.

43. Schoenberg, "The Reception of Austrian Composers in Los Angeles: 1934–1950," 141.

44. Jost Hermand, *Culture in Dark Times: Nazi Fascism, Inner Emigration, and Exile*, trans. Victoria W. Hill (New York: Berghahn Books, 2013), 174. These distinctions are of course fluid. See, for example, Ben Shephard, *The Long Road Home: The Aftermath of the Second World War* (New York: Alfred A. Knopf, 2011).

45. Reinhold Brinkmann, "Reading a Letter," in Brinkmann and Wolff, *Driven into Paradise*, 5. See also David Kettler, *The Liquidation of Exile: Studies in the Intellectual Emigration of the 1930s* (London: Anthem Press, 2009), 1, 17–22.

46. Jost Hermand, *Culture in Dark Times*, 174.

47. Ibid., 238.

48. Schoenberg, "The Reception of Austrian Composers in Los Angeles: 1934–1950," 136.

49. Quoted in Alexander Gordon Kahn, "Double Lives: Exile Composers in Los Angeles" (PhD diss., University of California, Berkeley, 2009), 177.
50. Quoted in ibid., 174.
51. Duchen, *Erich Wolfgang Korngold*, 194.
52. Landau, "Memoirs," 126–28. See also Lily E. Hirsch, *Anneliese Landau's Life in Music: Nazi Germany to Émigré California* (Rochester, NY: Eastman Studies in Music, University of Rochester Press, 2019).
53. Hirsch, *Anneliese Landau's Life in Music*.
54. Thank you to Daniel Goldmark for sharing this concert's program.
55. Liz Malina, ed., *Dear Papa, How Is You?: Das Leben Erich Wolfgang Korngolds in Briefen* (Vienna: Mandelbaum Verlag, 2017), 236–37.
56. See Kahn, "Double Lives: Exile Composers in Los Angeles," 84.
57. Kathrin Hubbard, email to author, 10 July 2017.
58. Landau, *The Contribution of Jewish Composers*.
59. See Pamela S. Nadell, "National Federation of Temple Sisterhoods," *Jewish Women's Archive*, http://jwa.org/encyclopedia/article/national-federation-of-temple-sisterhoods.
60. Luzi Korngold, *Erich Wolfgang Korngold*, 18.
61. Duchen, *Erich Wolfgang Korngold*, 43.
62. Kahn, "Double Lives: Exile Composers in Los Angeles," 195.
63. Malina, *Dear Papa, How Is You?*, 248.
64. Anneliese-Landau-Archiv 792, Akademie der Künste, Berlin.
65. Ibid.
66. Erich Wolfgang Korngold, "Faith in Music!," Foreword to Ulric Devaré, *Faith in Music* (New York: Comet Press, 1958; orig. 1956), viii.
67. Quoted in Carroll, *The Last Prodigy*, 348.
68. Hubbard, email to author, 10 July 2017.
69. "Wir leben, Ericko, in schweren, unerhört bedrohlichen Zeiten und müssen, wie einst die Judenfamilien im Ghetto, mehr zusammenhalten als je." Malina, *Dear Papa, How Is You?*, 202.
70. Kahn, "Double Lives: Exile Composers in Los Angeles," 6.
71. Dorothy Lamb Crawford, *A Windfall of Musicians: Hitler's Émigrés and Exiles in Southern California* (New Haven: Yale University Press, 2009), 5–14.
72. Marcus, *Schoenberg and Hollywood Modernism*, 167.
73. Ibid., 238–39.
74. Quoted in Diane Peacock Jezic, *The Musical Migration and Ernst Toch* (Ames: Iowa State University Press, 1989), 65.
75. Toch to Landau, 18 December 1942, Anneliese-Landau-Archiv 703, Akademie der Künste, Berlin.
76. Ernst Toch, speech delivered at Jewish Music Council of Los Angeles, sponsored by Jewish Centers Association of Los Angeles, Anneliese-Landau-Archiv 508, Akademie der Künste, Berlin.
77. Kahn, "Double Lives: Exile Composers in Los Angeles," 110-11.
78. "Seine Kunst sein Leben ist." Luzi Korngold to Helene Thimig, 30 August 1946, in Malina, *Dear Papa, How Is You?*, 244.
79. James Conlon, "Recovering a Musical Heritage: The Music Suppressed by the Third Reich," The OREL Foundation, http://orelfoundation.org/journal/journalArticle/recovering_a_musical_heritage_the_music_suppressed_by_the_third_reich.
80. Korngold's response is in German. It has been translated by Elisabeth Staak.

New Opportunities in Film: Korngold and Warner Bros.

BEN WINTERS

In the early 1990s, BBC Radio 4 broadcast a comedy series called *The Masterson Inheritance* that each week told a chapter in the historical saga of "a family at war with itself." It was based on (deliberately ridiculous) audience suggestions, and it was claimed that "dialogue, music, and sound effects" were all improvised.[1] The historical setting would vary each week, but once the expository material and the title for the episode had been established, a soaring orchestral string- and horn-dominated theme punctuated by cymbals and bells would begin. The music returned to end each half-hour episode. No mention was ever made of the composer, but the opening titles were in fact taken from Korngold's score for the Warner Bros. film *Deception* (1946). In addition, the series repeatedly used Korngold cues from *The Sea Hawk* (1940) to underscore (often humorously inappropriate) love scenes and scenes of (melo)dramatic excess.[2] The sense of something already familiar about Korngold's Hollywood style is perhaps what prompted the writers to choose his music in the first place—though it is somewhat ironic that a radio series that often attempted to create an air of the distant past should choose as its title theme music from *Deception*, one of the few Korngold-scored films with a contemporary setting. Nonetheless, the richness and evocativeness of Korngold's Hollywood style was indeed considered suitable for a satirical melodrama that also conjured a sense of pastness. In addition to the material from *Deception* and *The Sea Hawk*, other Korngold cues, from his scores to *Anthony Adverse* (1936), *Devotion* (1946), *Of Human Bondage* (1946), *Kings Row* (1942), *Juarez* (1939), *The Private Lives of Elizabeth and Essex* (1939), and *Escape Me Never* (1946) were heard, though more sparingly.[3]

Such uses of Korngold's film scores are of course part of the scores' reception history, a reception history that also includes the output of self-confessed Korngold fans like John Williams and the recordings of Korngold scores undertaken by Charles Gerhardt in the 1970s, which undoubtedly furnished the radio series with its musical material. But despite the relatively large number of scores represented by these incidental cues, *The Masterson Inheritance* gives only a flavor of the breadth of Korngold's film output. There is more to his music than the heraldic pomp and soaring love themes perhaps most often associated with Korngold's name in the movies, and the more one studies his scores—and examines the complexity of the manuscript materials—the more one appreciates the stylistic range his music encompasses. In this essay, I will sketch an overview of Korngold's film output that draws attention to the variety of scenarios for which he provided music and the kinds of musical gestures and techniques he used to help him meet their dramatic demands. In many ways these techniques represent a significant expansion from the range demonstrated by his operatic output; in that sense Korngold's Hollywood career was not a regression from the culturally engaged world of opera but represented an opportunity to develop his gifts as a musical dramatist. After a brief summary of Korngold's working practices, I will explore the sound of his scores—including his use of particular orchestral colors—and his ability to score a variety of narrative scenarios, before I outline some aspects of his approach to scoring, including his thematic technique. In what follows, I will refer to the original cue numbering system used by Warner Bros., which identified cues using an alphanumeric system. A cue labeled 6C, for instance, would indicate the third music cue in reel 6 of the film. I have also indicated an approximate timing for the scene where possible to help readers locate the scene in home-entertainment versions of the films.

Korngold contributed to a total of twenty-two film scores between 1934 and 1954. With the exception of *Magic Fire* (Republic Pictures, 1956), *The Rose of the Rancho* and *Give Us This Night* (Paramount, both 1936) his scores were written for a single studio, Warner Bros., between October 1934 and October 1946. He initially worked in Hollywood during the winter seasons of 1934–35, 1935–36, and 1936–37, before his immigration to the United States as a result of the Anschluss in his native Austria, after which point he took on work year-round (if never on a permanent basis). Figure 1 shows Korngold's Warner Bros. identity card, which was issued in February 1943. As a result of working almost exclusively for one studio, the vast majority of score materials for his films survive in the Warner Bros. Archives at the University of Southern California. When these are consulted alongside accompanying production files and in conjunction with sketch materials and other documents held in the Korngold Collection at the Library of Congress, it presents a well-documented picture of the composer's working life—one that was far more engaged with

Figure 1. Korngold's Warner Bros. identity card.

the sometimes mundane realities of studio-era compromise and collaboration than previous accounts were prepared to admit.

Korngold's main work on a film tended to begin once production was complete—though a large number of films had elements of "prescoring," which would require Korngold to write and record music before filming, such as the songs sung by characters in *The Private Lives of Elizabeth and Essex* and *The Sea Hawk*, the former of which required the composer to be on set.[4] Prescoring was most apparent in cases where the narrative focused on composers and where the story involved the composition of a piece of music, the completion of which was necessary before production finished—as was the case with *The Constant Nymph* (1943), *Escape Me Never*, and *Deception*. For other films Korngold's main work would start after production had finished, though his involvement with a film had usually been decided before this point. Working to a copy of the film, and with the help of cue timing sheets prepared by a music editor and occasionally some music spotting notes,[5] he would sketch themes, and write out a reduced piano score. Such documents are remarkable in revealing Korngold's composition process as an act of assembly in which only the most essential elements are written down, and in which extensive shorthand markings indicating copying and transposition are employed. From Hugo Friedhofer's oral history, it seems that Korngold would pass these documents to his amanuensis Jaro Churain to copy and hand on to orchestrators.[6] The number of orchestrators he worked with during his film-scoring career was impressively large and included, among others, Simon Bucharoff, Milan Roder, Leonid Raab, Bernhard Kaun, and Ray Heindorf along with a familiar name from his Viennese past, Ernst Toch, who worked on the Brontë sisters' biopic, *Devotion*. Undoubtedly, his most long-lasting association was with Hugo Friedhofer, an orchestrator who subsequently embarked on his own Oscar-winning career as a composer. Korngold also continued to adjust orchestrations on the scoring stage as he conducted, and such changes in his own hand are frequently apparent when consulting the full-score manuscripts for his films. In addition, the process of synchronizing music to image was one to which he increasingly applied mechanical timing aids. This began with his work for *Juarez* in early 1939; indeed, his manuscripts are littered with punch markings and frame rates that provide a visual metronome at the start of cues or at tempo changes, and helped him calculate the lengths of fermatas.[7] He was also fully involved in scoring music for his films' trailers, and sometimes in creating bespoke orchestral overtures to be used for premieres or recorded for the roadshow formats of his films, where such extra music befitted the theater-like presentation style of a limited-run showing before a film went on general release.[8] In short, Korngold was fully engaged with the everyday life of being a musician for hire at a prestige film studio.

Korngold was not paid an exorbitant amount for his work, contrary to prevailing myths about the composer that tend to emphasize the unusual aspects of his film work. Contracts and pay records reveal that between his 1936 contract and his work on *Escape Me Never* in 1945, his pay remained exactly the same—a relatively modest $12,500 for twelve weeks' guaranteed work, usually paid weekly at a rate of $1,041.66. Max Steiner, as a full-time salaried composer at Warner Bros., in contrast, enjoyed regular pay raises: his pay increased from $1,500 a week in 1937 up to $2,000 a week in 1946.[9] Admittedly, Korngold did not work all year, contributing to two or at most three projects a year. In November 1940, having worked only on *The Sea Hawk* that year, he was obliged to ask for $4,166.66 (four weeks' salary) in advance against his next picture.[10] Nor are Korngold's contracts in any way unusual for a freelancer: they do not make any concessions to his "high-art" credentials, and his music belonged to Warner Bros. in the same way as any other composer's. Thus his score for *Juarez* was reused in part to score *The Mad Empress* (1939) to help settle a legal dispute with a rival filmmaker,[11] and substantial portions of his score for *Another Dawn* were cut at the behest of the Executive in Charge of Production, Hal Wallis.[12] The idea that Korngold was some special case in Hollywood who enjoyed a preeminent position and special

Figure 2. Bound copy of Korngold's manuscript short score for *The Sea Hawk*.

concessions is unsupported by the documentary evidence and is arguably in the service of romantic mythmaking. At the same time, it is clear that Korngold had the support of men like Wallis and associated with Jack Warner and other studio executives: a wonderful example of this relationship is the copy of his piano short score for *The Sea Hawk*, which he presented as a Christmas present to Jack Warner in 1940 bound in a geometric Art Deco design in blue, silver, red, green, and black, with gold name plate (see Figure 2). Moreover, his status as another (albeit important) cog in music chief Leo Forbstein's "well-oiled machine," as studio orchestrator and frequent Korngold collaborator Hugo Friedhofer memorably described the workings of the studio's music department, is not to denigrate the opportunities that scoring pictures for Warner Bros. offered him for artistic expression.[13]

The Sound of Korngold's Hollywood

Korngold contributed scores to a variety of films for Warner Bros., ranging from historical swashbuckling adventures—*Captain Blood* (1935), *The Prince and the Pauper* (1937), *The Adventures of Robin Hood*, *The Sea Hawk*—and historical costume drama like *The Private Lives of Elizabeth and Essex* and *Devotion*, to contemporary or near-contemporary melodrama, such as *Between Two Worlds* (1944), *Another Dawn* (1937), or *Deception*. In terms of their sound world, these scores are perhaps best known for their melodiousness and brassy exuberance: the fanfares and heraldic main titles of films like *The Private Lives of Elizabeth and Essex*, *The Adventures of Robin Hood*, *The Sea Hawk*, and *Kings Row* exemplify this. The more one studies his output, however, the more one recognizes the astonishing variety of textures and sonorities his scores offer—whether it be the lush string textures of *Devotion*'s love theme, the skittish xylophone and harp music to characterize Thorpe's monkey in *The Sea Hawk*, or *Another Dawn*'s evocation of a desert sandstorm. Korngold might utilize small ensembles to create delicate effects—such as the whistling string harmonics and thumping heartbeat of Tessa's attacks in *The Constant Nymph* or the piquant xylophone semitonal dissonances used to match the sound of Morse code in *Another Dawn* (as heard in cues 22A and 22B, 43:48)—or he might employ the resources of the full orchestra, as with the entrance of the Queen in *The Sea Hawk* (cue 4B, 33:19), the battle music from *Robin Hood* (cue 11B, 1:34:29), and the remarkable chromatically-saturated climax of *Between Two Worlds* as Ann searches for Henry (cue 12C, 1:47:57).

Undoubtedly, Korngold's facility with a variety of harmonic styles and approaches to musical texture allowed him to construct music to suit all kinds of narrative situations. He could write music to be brightly optimistic using relatively simple harmonies—as with Randy's theme in *Kings Row*, Nora's theme in *Of Human Bondage*, or large parts of *The Adventures of Robin Hood*—or deploy the full resources of the kind of Straussian and Mahlerian harmonic complexity that characterizes his operas. The chromatic infilling of Ann's theme in *Between Two Worlds* is one particularly compelling example of this, as are the love scenes between Denis and Maria in *Anthony Adverse* or between Parris and Cassie in *Kings Row*, while the military marches of *Another Dawn* could almost have been extracted from a Mahler symphony. Indeed, Korngold's status as a displaced Viennese artist is heard throughout his output, whether in the waltzes of *The Adventures of Robin Hood* or the forest scenes of *The Prince and the Pauper*, or in his direct evocation of turn-of-the-century Vienna in *Kings Row*.[14] Moreover, Straussian parallel chord writing is often a characteristic of his harmonic and textural palette—something to be found in the fanfares of *The Private*

Lives of Elizabeth and Essex or in certain character themes, such as Fenella's in *Escape Me Never*, Branwell's in *Devotion*, Mildred's in *Of Human Bondage*, or Dr. Gordon's in *Kings Row*—while *The Sea Hawk* includes almost direct quotation from Strauss's *Der Rosenkavalier*.[15] Yet Korngold does not confine himself to the musical language and influences of his Viennese youth. He was certainly capable of exploiting the more modernist language he had explored in his Opus 18 songs in the 1920s. The knife fight in *The Adventures of Robin Hood* (cue 10A, 1:24:47), for instance, is constructed using semitonal clusters and one could also point to the chromatic angularity of Prior's theme in *Between Two Worlds*, or some of the passionate outbursts of violence in *Of Human Bondage*, in which chains of parallel chords feature semitonal dissonances.[16] Moreover, parts of *The Sea Wolf* project little sense of tonality and might thus be described as modernist. Korngold also makes use of musical fragmentation—a disruption to surface rhetoric often associated with musical modernism—to characterize the mental illness of Cassie Tower and Louise Gordon in *Kings Row*. In addition to these touches of musical modernism, Korngold was not averse to exploring more popular idioms: he could turn his hand to jazz, often making use of saxophone sonorities, as in a jazz-harmony theme of sexual desire associated with Julia in *Another Dawn*,[17] and even try popular song. Although an early attempt at the instigation of Hal Wallis to write something for commercial release, using material from *Another Dawn*, produced a melody that, as lyricist Al Dubin pointed out, "no one but an operatic singer could sing," he later wrote two songs for *Escape Me Never*, including "Love for Love," which received a number of commercial recordings.[18]

Korngold deployed this technical facility with the language of music to create a variety of moods appropriate to narrative requirements. His ability to score comic scenes—or even to create comedy where little is apparent—might perhaps be surprising to those familiar only with the serious mood that characterizes his best-known operas, *Die tote Stadt* and *Das Wunder der Heliane*, although such parodies as the *Vier kleine Karikaturen für Kinder* and the comic opera *Der Ring des Polykrates* reveal a humorous streak was always there. Examples of musical humor can be found in the golf game in *Another Dawn* (cue 5, 13:03)—a comic set piece that largely avoids thematic material but manages to puncture John's pompous bravado and sporting ineptitude with busy xylophone textures, extremes of register, and Mickey Mousing—and in the music heard in the Inn in *Devotion* (cues 2B and 2C, 12:00) that scores Branwell Brontë's drunkenness with lopsided stomach-churning lurches in typical parallel chord writing (see Example 1). When Branwell presents his caricature sketch to its intended recipient (hoping to secure money for another drink) the point-of-view

Example 1. Branwell Brontë's drunken music in *Devotion* from the piano-conductor score.

shot of the sketch presents the same musical phrase in trumpets armed with Harmon or "wah-wah" mutes. Equally, *Devotion* offered an opportunity to score almost nightmarish drama. The music of Emily Brontë's supernaturally prescient dream—which we also hear prefigured when she relates it to Arthur Nichols—is chillingly realized. When it returns at the climax of the narrative to underscore her death (cue 11C, 1:43:39), it is a dialogue-free musical moment of enormous power. Beginning with harp and vibraphone glissandi evocations of the wind that rustles the curtains in her death room, we hear the opening fifths of Emily's own theme in bells before the ominous lurching trombone third-less triads from the dream return (outlining a series of tritone progressions) along with the stormy theme associated with the house Emily calls *Wuthering Heights*, highlighted with xylophone and celesta color. A nervous repeating falling chromatic figure in strings then gives way to an equestrian topic that combines the recorded sound of horses' hooves with a rising musical representation of the same in marimba triplets as Emily's mounted "black rider" approaches. He appears to terrifying string trills with a triumphant trumpet intoning a minor version of Emily's theme over stacked thirds in trombones. The horse's tramping feet are suggested by aggressive xylophone chords before the growing frenzy of more brass statements of the *Wuthering Heights* theme treated sequentially, and underpinned by bells, gives way to a typically Korngoldian gesture of fragmentation and sequential repetition—a common way he increases tension. The scene finishes with a final statement of Emily's ascending fifths theme and a series of major seventh chords before the horse-triplets whisk Emily away to her death. There is then a remarkable moment of emotional release, as we see Emily's body lying in her chair: the music dissolves via harp glissandi and a tritone horn variant of the "sisters theme" into a moment of charged pathos as the theme proper is heard in funeral bells in Korngold's favorite key of F-sharp major. Charlotte Brontë then bids her beloved sister farewell having "found the meaning" with the man Emily loved (Nichols). It is a remarkable sequence.

Pathos is also a characteristic of many moments in *Between Two Worlds*, such as the moment when the vicar Bunny's heartbreak at having lost the opportunity to forge a new beginning is given new meaning by his assigned role in the afterlife, or when Benjamin's joy in recalling the old friends he is to be reunited with—and the recollection of his love, now lost, for his wife, whose selfishness and social climbing has doomed her to an eternity of loneliness—come into painful conflict. These moments are emotionally affecting almost entirely as a result of Korngold's score.

Key to the variety of Korngold's sound world is the composer's sensitivity to orchestral tone color, for which he had long been known. His early symphonic works and operas had revealed a predilection for tuned percussion, and although Korngold undoubtedly allowed his orchestrators at Warner Bros. a certain amount of creative freedom when interpreting his short scores, his pencil indications of instrumentation nonetheless indicate a continued fondness for tuned bells, celesta, xylophone, and marimba. Bells dominate the ends of a number of scores, including *Escape Me Never*, *Kings Row*, and *Between Two Worlds*, and in *The Sea Wolf* (cue IC, 03:28), rising and falling figures in marimba create an oppressive atmosphere to match the fog as Leach is rowed out toward the *Ghost*. Korngold also took advantage of opportunities that newly invented instruments offered him. Thus the vibraphone—an instrument with an electric motor that had been developed in the 1920s and which Korngold used in his fifth opera, *Die Kathrin*—became a mainstay of his film work.[19] Indeed, it is likely that it was through Hollywood that he was introduced to the instrument, which had previously been used primarily in vaudeville and jazz: it features in *Another Dawn*, on which he worked before completing the orchestration of *Die Kathrin*. Other examples can be found throughout Korngold's scores. In evoking Wolf Larson's crippling headaches in *The Sea Wolf* (cue 3A, 19:46), for instance, vibraphone and marimba play distinctive ascending and descending broken half-diminished seventh chords, while in *Devotion* we hear the vibraphone prominently in the scene in which Emily recounts her dream to Nichols. This cue was orchestrated by Hugo Friedhofer (3F, 27:57), but Korngold himself orchestrated a retake of this section that introduced solo marimba and the shimmering vibraphone E-minor chords that end the scene. Significantly, Korngold also embraced the Novachord, an instrument often described as the world's first polyphonic synthesizer.[20] For some this may be a surprise given the associations of some forms of electronic music with high modernism.[21] Nonetheless, Korngold appears to have recognized and employed the distinctive timbral qualities of the instrument. He first made use of the Novachord during January and February 1941 when working on *The Sea Wolf*, and besides blending it effectively with other instruments, he also highlights its unearthly sound. In cue 2A (10:01), for instance, its lower register intones the theme that signifies Wolf Larson and his ship, the *Ghost*, as it makes its first appearance out of the fog. Korngold also used the instrument extensively in *Between Two Worlds*—where its more ethereal qualities are germane to the narrative situation, a metaphysical story of the journey to the afterlife—and in *Devotion*, where it features in some decidedly more earthbound cues. It is also heard prominently in the melodramas *Of Human Bondage* and

Deception: in the latter, its sustaining qualities are most obvious in the aftermath of Christine's murder of Hollenius as, horrified, she contemplates his body (cue 10A, 1:32:00). In short, the Novachord became a staple of Korngold's orchestral palette.

Korngold's Scoring Technique

Besides providing him with new orchestral colors such as the Novachord, film offered Korngold the opportunity to hone dramatic gifts forged in the opera houses and theaters of Europe. Thus the vast majority of his scores were strongly thematic in their construction. Indeed, given the large percentage of film his music underscored, it is unsurprising that he should draw upon techniques familiar to him from opera to help construct the amount of music often required. Having said that, it is undeniably the case that—with a few prominent exceptions—the signifying associations between character and/or emotion and theme are usually much clearer in his films than in his operas. It is usually not too difficult to label themes or to recognize their associations with particular characters. A score like *The Private Lives of Elizabeth and Essex* features a number of themes for the Queen (including one for her sorrow), a theme for Ireland, and a theme for the ring that is a symbol of Elizabeth's love for Essex (among others); while in *The Sea Hawk* even Thorpe's ship, the *Albatross*, is given personality through its own theme. Sometimes these character themes might appear to be applied rather literally. For example, in cue 3E of *The Sea Hawk*—the banquet scene aboard the *Albatross* (24:54)—as Doña Maria crosses conversational swords with Errol Flynn's Captain Thorpe, Korngold's score juxtaposes the openings of their contrasting themes, before a reference to the Queen prompts a statement of her musical moniker, one that is closer in tone to Thorpe's manly heroism than Doña Maria's implied femininity. Yet these musical incipits are combined skillfully to create a convincing and integrated musical texture; indeed, the reduction of full themes to a "head motive" that can quickly signify is a practice that Korngold uses throughout his output to create complex thematic textures that may draw a number of themes together. In *Anthony Adverse*, for instance, when Don Luis returns from the spa ready to begin his honeymoon, a strutting version of his music combines and contrasts with fragments of Maria's music which are then sequentially developed, as she readies herself to flee with her lover; while in *Between Two Worlds*, conversations between Lingley, Mrs. Clivedon-Banks, and Mrs. Midget are characterized by frequent statements of their respective themes (cue 5C, 41:35).

Korngold's themes are never the mere calling cards familiar from Adorno and Eisler's somewhat one-dimensional critique of the technique,[22] and his scores all rely on some form of thematic transformation, combination, variation and/or development. Changes of tempo and mode are most common—as with the mournful versions of Bunny's and Pete's theme in *Between Two Worlds* when they realize they are dead (cue 7B, 59:53), or a much faster scherzando version of Gemma's theme in *Escape Me Never* (cue 3C, 20:00) as she is chased by Caryl—but other kinds of transformations are also employed on a regular basis. An early cue in *Kings Row* (1C, 01:52) comprises a series of variations of Parris's theme to accompany Parris and Cassie's childhood swim, and a further variant is heard when Parris, Randy, and Drake swing on the rings in the ice house (1G, 09:35). Moreover, the musico-dramatic treatment of such material is often subtle and lends an extra hermeneutic layer to the narrative. Themes can be varied in order to trace the changing fortunes of characters: thus the journey of Essex's theme in *The Private Lives of Elizabeth and Essex* from optimistic heroism at the beginning of the film, as he returns triumphantly to London, to tragic acceptance of his fate as he faces the ax at the end of the narrative, is particularly striking. When Drake McHugh loses his fortune in *Kings Row*, his theme is cast in the minor, and fragments of it treated to sequential development (cue 8D, 1:15:20). Similarly, Anthony's theme in *Anthony Adverse*, which is first heard before his birth, serves him throughout his many adventures from childhood to fatherhood, adapting to his surroundings. When Anthony is at his lowest point in Africa its harmonies and intervals are warped to reflect his distance from his own moral identity (cue 34-B, 1:26:40). Piccolo's illness and death in *Escape Me Never* likewise alters and fragments his theme, which is then further developed as his grief-stricken mother, Gemma, gradually faces up to the reality of his death (cue 11C, 1:30:24); and Julia's theme in *Another Dawn* is subjected to a number of harmonic, metrical, and rhythmic transformations at various points as she struggles with her illicit feelings for Denny Roark. Themes can also evolve across the course of a narrative to the extent that their transformation reflects a permanent change to the characters. Toward the end of *The Adventures of Robin Hood*, Robin's fanfare theme develops to move the character further away from the music associated with the Merry Men to realign him with the music of others of his class, the themes of King Richard and Maid Marian.[23]

More often, though, thematic variation is a more temporary state of affairs. In *Juarez*, the Mexican song "La Paloma" is manipulated harmonically to suggest Carlota's madness: the music as performed in Mexico is depicted as crossing the ocean (cue 16B, 1:56:44) where it is "heard" by Carlota, albeit strangely altered by her damaged subjectivity. Seemingly called to the window by its obsessive repeating phrases, Carlota appears to reestablish the unwarped version of the song (and, by implication, her

Figure 3. Korngold conducting his music for *The Adventures of Robin Hood*.

own sanity) via a transformational harp glissando before crying out in anguish, apparently in knowledge of the fate of her husband. Indeed, this is also an example of the composer working skillfully with existing compositions alongside generating new thematic material, something he did with his very first score, *A Midsummer Night's Dream* (1935), which involved arranging both Mendelssohn's incidental music to the Shakespeare play and other pieces by the composer, in addition to writing a number of original cues. But many other scores required him to work with preexisting material either because of concerns about time, as with the use of Liszt's symphonic poems *Mazeppa* and *Prometheus* in *Captain Blood* or his own symphonic poem *Sursum Corda* in *The Adventures of Robin Hood*, or due to production practicalities. On *Anthony Adverse*, for instance, he needed to work with Aldo Franchetti's pastiche of a Puccinian operatic excerpt, which was supplied and filmed for an opera-house sequence before Korngold was engaged to work on the film. With *Juarez*, however, basing Juarez's theme on the Mexican national anthem (albeit loosely) seems to have been a deliberate compositional choice. Likewise, the decision to score the backstage reunion between Christine and Karel in *Deception* with Schubert's "Unfinished" Symphony, which is being performed onstage, is a masterstroke.[24]

Figure 4. Korngold's punch markings in the short score for *Of Human Bondage*.

One of the chief areas in which scoring for films differed from any thematic techniques developed in the opera house was in the close synchronization between onscreen events and musical gesture. As alluded to above, this is something that required Korngold to make use of mechanical timing aids—both in terms of cue sheets notated with precise timing information for use when composing, and through punches in the actual film stock to provide a visual metronome and visual synchronization points when recording music to film. It allowed Korngold to match changes in narrative location with precise changes in music, or to match character themes with the appearance of the character in question. Figure 4, for example, shows a page from Korngold's short score for cue 2C (19:27) in *Of Human Bondage* that reveals the necessity of synchronizing a change of shot—marked "Cut"—with Philip Carey's theme. Korngold asks for a warning punch at a distance of 18 frames to help him synchronize the moment. Korngold also made use of overt moments of Mickey Mousing, a technique of close synchronization usually associated more with Korngold's colleague at Warner Bros., Max Steiner. In *Devotion*, for instance, Madame Héger's dismissive sweep of the torn pieces of Charlotte's poem off her desk is matched by an aggressive minor-ninth descending scale in violas (cue 6C, 52:53).

Another essential skill when working with film is the ability to create a sense of time and place, and this is something at which Korngold was also adept. Despite the popular conception of most of his scores as regal swashbucklers that are rooted in a romanticized version of the past—a viewpoint often emphasized by pointing to the *Kings Row* main title and a supposed misunderstanding of the regal overtones of a narrative set in small-town America—and of a musical language that made few concessions to the settings of the narratives, the composer was more than willing to help a film's narrative in the characterization of its spatial and temporal setting. He could certainly create a convincing sense of pastness, as with Marian's theme in *The Adventures of Robin Hood*, which was modeled on a sixteenth-century dance tune,[25] the pastiche songs of *The Private Lives of Elizabeth and Essex* and *The Sea Hawk*, or the coronation music in *The Prince and the Pauper*. In terms of geographical setting, he could also engage in overt Orientalism—as with the theme for the fictional military outpost in *Another Dawn* or the Bedouin love song heard in the same film, in the music for Panama in *The Sea Hawk*, for Havana in *Anthony Adverse*, or indeed for the Jamaican Port Royal in *Captain Blood*. Moreover, such Orientalism applies to individual characters: Don Alvarez's Spanish identity is never in doubt in *The Sea Hawk* thanks to Korngold's sinewy clarinet exoticism, while Neletta's ornamented flute theme in *Anthony Adverse* marks her out as both racially other and sexually dangerous. The moral identity of characters, too, was also revealed as much by their musical themes as by any aspect of their dialogue or costume: Brother François's severe and ecclesiastical B-flat-minor theme in *Anthony Adverse* signifies as quickly as Sally's innocent music in *Of Human Bondage*, the flirtatious and slightly effete theme for Monsieur Héger in *Devotion*, or Lingley's aggressive and menacing music in *Between Two Worlds*.

The ability to score action scenes was also vital for a composer working for Warner Bros., though undoubtedly it was not Korngold's favorite task. On occasion, one feels he is going through the motions, overly relying on sequential development—the horse chase in *The Adventures of Robin Hood*, for example, manages to spin out an extended cue based on minimal material, and Cooky's encounter with the shark in *The Sea Wolf* (rehearsal number 13 in cue 8C, 1:02:41) relies on a less-than-subtle ascending chromatic bass line for its effect. Often, though, such action scenes can be striking. In the scene in *The Sea Wolf* in which two vessels collide (08:24), Korngold opts for an almost Ivesian texture in which the recorded and insistent blasts of the foghorn combine with scurrying strings and major seconds in horns. As the ferryboat sinks, cascading strings combine with an ascending chromatic harmonic sequence in a passage reminiscent of the cue "The Flood" that he provided for *The Green Pastures* (1936) and that was subsequently reused in *The Sea Hawk* (43:00). Likewise, the archery tournament in *The Adventures of Robin Hood* is built on a minimal amount of fanfare material treated sequentially—though here the harmonic twists and close synchronization are enough to keep it constantly compelling. There are also thrilling moments in *Of Human Bondage* when Mildred Rogers explodes with rage at Carey's rejection of her advances. Having shouted at him as he leaves (cue 10B, 1:16:57), she then proceeds to destroy their shared rooms (cue 10C, 1:17:30), but the sustained violence of the scene is maintained primarily by Korngold's music, which seethes with chromatic melodies, dissonant superimpositions, and cross-rhythm accents. Especially notable among the action scenes are the duel sequences Korngold provided for *Captain Blood*, *Anthony Adverse*, *The Prince and the Pauper*, *The Adventures of Robin Hood*, and *The Sea Hawk*. The latter two, in particular, are finely controlled ballets that match the choreography of the stunt work and chiaroscuro cinematography with chains of sequentially developed and sometimes metrically irregular musical fragments; in the case of the *Robin Hood* duel, Korngold also provides built-in pauses to allow for the insertion of wittily delivered lines. As such, the duel set-piece is a particularly impressive example of Korngold's ability to integrate visual action, musical expression, and dialogue.

Action scenes are indicative of Korngold's ability to construct larger stretches of music without recourse to the musical forms of concert music. Indeed, a cue timing sheet for the *Robin Hood* duel (11C, 1:35:39) exists in the composer's hand showing his conception of its structure.[26] Often, he draws upon thematic material to facilitate such structuring. The attack on the treasure caravan in *The Adventures of Robin Hood* is one such example (cue 4C, 33:25): in a four-and-a half-minute set piece, Korngold presents us with the March of the Merry Men, the "Jollity" theme the Merry Men share with Robin, Sir Guy's theme, and Robin's own theme in a bravura display of compositional deftness that not only satisfies musically but, more crucially for a film score, also articulates and makes clear to the viewer the parallel editing of the scene. For a number of scores, however, Korngold was required to write works that would function within the narrative as the musical compositions of characters. Thus *The Constant Nymph* features a tone poem for alto, chorus, and orchestra, the successful composition of which drives the narrative in the same way as the ballet *Primavera* in *Escape Me Never*. Likewise, *Deception* centers on the composition of a cello concerto, which dominates the score and provides the majority of its thematic material. Film projects like these undoubtedly offered Korngold a route back to the concert hall, yet his post-Hollywood works constitute a concert-hall repertory transformed entirely by his experiences in Hollywood, as all made use of film-score material in ways that draw attention to the commonalities between these different kinds of compositional activity.

Korngold's film scores, then, are far more sophisticated than the overblown romantic or melodramatic excess that was crucial for *The Masterson Inheritance*'s improvised comedy, or indeed for the regal swashbuckling brassiness for which he is arguably best known. Even for those film composers for whom Korngold is cited as an influence—such as John Williams—it tends to be a narrow range of music that invites the comparison, usually the bombastic elements of *The Sea Hawk* and *The Adventures of Robin Hood*.[27] Yet when reviewing his corpus as a whole, it is in the combination of varied and sophisticated orchestral textures and colors, post-Straussian harmony, an expressive thematic technique, and close visual synchronization that Korngold's stylistic fingerprints are to be found. From that perspective, arguably few have attempted to follow him closely, and his scores remain somewhat isolated outliers in the film-score landscape. Ultimately, Korngold's ability to traverse the worlds of Hollywood and concert hall may prove to be his most enduring legacy: in reintegrating the sound of Hollywood with the genres of string quartet, concerto, and symphony in works written for the concert hall after the end of his Warner Bros. film-scoring career, he draws attention to the kind of narrative content that listeners have always found in so-called absolute music but that mid-twentieth-century criticism had sought to suppress. In that sense, Korngold's film scores are no mere cul-de-sac for a transported and moribund operatic style—nor solely a venerable model for film composers wanting to re-create a classic-era Hollywood aesthetic—but form a significant part of a larger critical history of music in the twentieth century and its relationship with popular culture.

NOTES

1. For more on *The Masterson Inheritance*, see https://archive.org/details/TheMasterson Inheritance.

2. Royal Brown named the first of these two repeated themes the "romantic theme," in *Overtones and Undertones: Reading Film Music* (Berkeley: University of California Press, 1994), 100; the second is a theme to accompany Spanish brutality, first heard in *The Sea Hawk* after Thorpe and his men have been captured and chained to the oars of a galleass (cues 9E and 9F). The audience's growing awareness of the intended meaning of these repeated *Sea Hawk* cues in *The Masterson Inheritance* often results in laughter as soon as they are heard. In addition, in the first episode, the closing titles elided *Deception*'s title music with the closing trumpet fanfare from *The Sea Hawk*.

3. Often it was the film's love theme (in *Devotion, The Private Lives of Elizabeth and Essex*) or (as with *Anthony Adverse* and *Of Human Bondage*) the theme for one of the principal female characters.

4. The studio's daily production reports reveal that Korngold was on set on June 13, 1939, and the difficulties with the song required a new set of lyrics. See "'The Private Lives of Elizabeth and Essex' Production— Daily Progress Reports," Warner Bros. Archives, University of Southern California.

5. Music spotting notes consist of instructions or suggestions for music's placement in a scene. At Warner Bros. in this period, these suggestions tended to come from Hal Wallis. Such spotting notes exist for *Captain Blood* (1935) and *Escape Me Never*. In the case of *The Constant Nymph*, Korngold was given a copy of the script in advance, which indicated the likely positioning of music in the narrative.

6. See *Hugo Friedhofer: The Best Years of His Life. A Hollywood Master of Music for the Movies*, ed. Linda Danly (Lanham, MD.: Scarecrow Press, 2002), 39. Only one score in Churain's hand is still extant: the copy of *Kings Row* held at the Library of Congress. See Erich Wolfgang Korngold Collection, Box 9, Folder 5.

7. I have detailed some aspects of this in "The Composer and the Studio: Korngold and Warner Bros.," in *The Cambridge Companion to Film Music*, ed. Mervyn Cooke and Fiona Ford (Cambridge: Cambridge University Press, 2016), 51–66. The studio also produced piano-conductor scores from the full-score manuscripts to aid the recording process, and these often contain valuable extra information.

8. Korngold provided a live overture for *Juarez* to be played for the world premiere at the Warner Bros. Beverly Hills Theatre on April 25, 1939. Examining the full score at Warner Bros. Archives, relevant cues (6A, 9E, parts of 10D, and Trailer Part 1) have been removed with a note indicating "use for overture." Likewise, Korngold also prepared live overtures for the premieres of *The Private Lives of Elizabeth and Essex* on September 17, 1939, and *The Constant Nymph* in July 1943. The *Constant Nymph* overture, rather than being assembled after the scoring process, was sketched out in Korngold's hand in short score and is preserved in the Erich Wolfgang Korngold Collection, Box 4, Folder 6, Library of Congress.

9. See "Max Steiner Payroll," Warner Bros. Archives.

10. See payroll notice in Folder 3103D, Warner Bros. Archives.

11. On 17 July 1939 *Juarez* producer Henry Blanke had written to Jimmie Gibbons asking him to "run the picture tomorrow morning at 10 o'clock with Mr. Forbstein and Mr. Torres so that Mr. Torres can point out to Mr. Forbstein the pieces of music that have to be eliminated and have to be substituted by something else which Mr. Forbstein has to put in on account of Torres not having applied for certain rights to use certain music now contained in the picture." See "Juarez" Legal, Warner Bros. Archives. As a consequence, cues including 4C, 9B, 9D, 11B, and 11C from *Juarez* appear to have been reused in *The Mad Empress* alongside other stock music owned by Warner Bros. The original music for *The Mad Empress*, by James Bradford, was removed—though Bradford himself claimed that some of his arrangements remained, something that Warner Bros. vigorously denied.

12. See "'Another Dawn' Story—Memos & Correspondence 1 of 2," Warner Bros. Archives. Wallis's cutting notes are dated 24 February 1937.

13. Friedhofer stated in his oral history that "Leo [Forbstein] was a master at running a department. He ran it so beautifully it could run itself. I can do no better than to quote from an interview I did with Tony Thomas several years ago. . . . 'We were all cogs in his well-oiled machine.'" Danly, *Friedhofer*, 70.

14. I have explored Korngold's Viennese nostalgia in "Swearing an Oath: Korngold, Film, and the Sound of Resistance?" in *The Impact of Nazism on Twentieth-Century Music*, ed. Erik Levi (Vienna: Böhlau Verlag, 2014), 61–76.

15. In cue 2A the signaling hail between the *Albatross* and the Spanish galleass involves parallel triads of C major, B-flat major and B major and matches Octavian's arrival bearing the silver rose in Act 2 of Strauss's opera (rehearsal number 15). Only the rhythm and chord spacing differs, and then only slightly.

16. In cue 10C (1:17:35), a chain of chromatically descending parallel major triads is supplemented by simultaneous flattened third and sixth scale degrees, creating chromatically altered thirteenth chords.

17. *Between Two Worlds* also makes prominent use of saxophone sonorities, though the gramophone recording—which plays a version of the music that Henry himself plays on the piano—was arranged by jazz trombonist Leo Arnaud.

18. See Al Dubin's memo to Hal Wallis, dated 18 March 1937, in "'Another Dawn' Story – Memos & Correspondence 1 of 2," Warner Bros. Archives. "Love for Love" was recorded by Andy Russell with Paul Weston and his Orchestra, and by Claude Thornhill's Orchestra with Fran Warren.

19. Again, pencil indications in the short scores reveal that the decision to use the instrument can be attributed to Korngold.

20. Thom Holmes, *Electronic and Experimental Music: Technology, Music, and Culture*, 4th ed. (New York: Routledge, 2012), 32. The Novachord was developed by Laurens Hammond and was first demonstrated in February 1939. His more famous instrument, the Hammond Organ, was also used by Korngold in *Kings Row*.

21. Susan McClary drew upon this image of the avant-garde composer seeking modernist isolation in the electronic studio in her article "Terminal Prestige: The Case of Avant-Garde Music Composition," *Cultural Critique* 12 (Spring 1989): 57–81. More recently, the long and subtle history of the relationship between new instruments (both electronic and "mechanical") with modernism has been explored by Thomas Patteson in *Instruments for New Music: Sound, Technology, and Modernism* (Berkeley: University of California Press, 2016).

22. Hanns Eisler and Theodor Adorno, *Composing for the Films* (London: Athlone Press, 1994).

23. See my discussion of this issue in *Erich Wolfgang Korngold's "The Adventures of Robin Hood": A Film Score Guide* (Lanham, MD.: Scarecrow Press, 2007), 121–22.

24. I discuss this scene, along with two other movie uses of Schubert's "Unfinished" Symphony in *Music, Performance, and the Realities of Film: Shared Experiences in Screen Fiction* (New York: Routledge, 2014), 161–71.

25. See my *Korngold's "The Adventures of Robin Hood,"* 73–75.

26. Reproduced in ibid., 84.

27. The oft-remarked resemblance between Korngold's main title for *Kings Row* and John Williams's main title for *Star Wars* (1977) is, I think, overstated, given that there are other models for Williams, including Miklós Rózsa's main title for *Ivanhoe* (1952). Moreover, the *Star Wars* main title's use of the so-called cowboy half cadence ♭VII–V might seem to connect it more obviously with the main title of *The Prince and the Pauper*, which likewise uses ♭VII harmony prominently, while in tone it is closer to the main title for *The Private Lives of Elizabeth and Essex*, whose third-related fanfares resemble the rebel fanfare motive used throughout the *Star Wars* films.

"The caverns of the human mind are full of strange shadows": Disability Representation, Henry Bellamann, and Korngold's Musical Subtexts in the Score for *Kings Row*

NEIL LERNER

The phrase "kings row" has a particular meaning to well-informed players of checkers: it refers to an opponent's first row of squares on the board, and if a player advances one of their checkers to that row, the piece is then marked as a king by having a second piece placed upon it. It is then granted the ability to move both forwards and backwards on the board, granting an advantage to the player with the king. The symbolic potential of the phrase "kings row" points to themes of advancement, mobility, and victory. Consider as well that aficionados of Erich Wolfgang Korngold and 1940s Hollywood film would also be familiar with "kings row" as the title of a black and white Hollywood film that features what many consider to be Ronald Reagan's finest work as an actor—and also a title that competes with the patronymic name "Herrmann" for most frequently misspelled word connected to film music. (No doubt many overzealous copy editors have thought they were doing an author a favor by correcting what they believed was a missing apostrophe.) The 1942 Warner Bros. production was based on a bestselling 1940 novel by Henry Bellamann, a writer whose career began not as a literary creator but as a music teacher and someone who, as professor and administrator, achieved considerable success at numerous institutions, some of them quite prestigious. Because the novel's content was thought to be too lurid for a Hollywood film under the production code—the novel's subject matter revolves around, among other topics, incest, sexual abuse, premarital sex, homosexuality, and rampant corruption—the story of how Bellamann's novel became a big budget commercial film has become part of Hollywood legend. Parts of Korngold's score have also been examined, but much remains to be uncovered regarding the way this music mediates the unsettling and sometimes horrific (and horrifically ableist) narrative.[1] *Kings Row*'s main character, Parris Mitchell, observes near the end of the film that "the caverns of the human mind are full of strange shadows," and in the film those strange shadows have the power of being accompanied by Korngold's remarkably sumptuous, complex, and effective music.

One of the principal pleasures of musicology and teaching is the privilege of sharing beautiful things with people who have not yet experienced them. (Is this not a chief reason why we value beauty?) As a college professor specializing in film music, I have had that experience when I teach the film *Kings Row* and Korngold's impressive and iridescent score. The reaction among students has been fairly consistent for over two decades: at first furrowed brows while trying to place why it sounds familiar, and then looks of shock and sometimes indignant concern as they make the connection between Korngold's stirring opening overture and some of John Williams's most famous film scores from the fourth quarter of the twentieth century. There is an unmistakable similarity between the melodic contour of the opening of *Kings Row* and the opening of the main title theme from *Star Wars*.[2] Both feature disjunct melodies that open with a prominent leap up a fourth and then up a fifth before descending by step, although after that point the melodic similarities evaporate (see Examples 1 and 2). The secondary themes in both are dissimilar, although the B section of *Kings Row* can be traced to the second theme in Williams's main title music for *Superman: The Movie*. Indeed, the score for *Kings Row* has become a canonic—if still relatively underexamined—example within the rather young discipline of film music studies, whose main historical narrative has been that of the transplantation of European symphonic and operatic musical styles into mainstream U.S. culture in the 1930s and '40s via the first generation of sound film score pioneers Max Steiner and Korngold, followed by numerous other European émigrés.[3] Because of the similarities between the *Kings Row* and *Star Wars* themes, and the subsequent mass circulation of *Star Wars*, there is a strong argument for *Kings Row* being, at least indirectly, the most influential and well known of all of Korngold's works.

Despite Korngold's central role in creating much of the Hollywood musical vocabulary that achieved prominence in the twentieth century, Korngold has been discreetly omitted from most twentieth-century music histories. If his work is mentioned at all, it is frequently the non-cinematic output, with the Hollywood writing being whispered about as a kind of historical embarrassment. Bryan Gilliam identifies three reasons for Korngold's exclusion from the modernist historical narrative as it developed after the Second World War: his reliance on a large, lush symphonic

Example 1. Opening of Korngold's music for *Kings Row* (1942).

Example 2. Opening of John Williams's score for *Star Wars* (1977). The orchestration, harmonic language, and melodic leaps bear similarities with the opening of *Kings Row*.

sound when smaller chamber ensembles had become the new standard; his retention of a tonal vocabulary when atonality became equated with progressive stylistic impulses; and, most significantly, his "migration into mass culture."[4] Ironically, though Korngold's compositional significance was undervalued in the 1960s and '70s because of his work in film, his influence and audiences grew precisely because of that work. An important moment in the renewal of interest in Korngold came in 1972, when his son George produced a recording of many of his film scores for RCA featuring the National Philharmonic Orchestra under the direction of Charles Gerhardt.[5] George Korngold's liner notes to this recording circulated the story of his father composing the regal theme for *Kings Row* only after learning the film's title and before he knew anything else about the story, setting, or characters.

Documents at the Warner Bros. archive offer a detailed history of how the novel was adapted into a film under the production code, as well as insights into casting and production decisions, but there is relatively little concerning just how Korngold went about his work. It is unclear, for instance, if Korngold ever read the original source novel by Henry Bellamann. What does emerge from those archival documents is that Korngold was aware of Bellamann, and his private words differed significantly from his public ones on this topic. A clipping from the *Los Angeles Daily News* of 22 October 1941, appears to have been sent to Korngold. It announced: "Here's something <u>unusual</u>: Henry Bellaman [*sic*], author of *Kings Row*, <u>heads west</u> to <u>help</u> Eric [*sic*] Wolfgang <u>Korngold</u> on <u>the scoring</u> of the movie adaptation of the novel at Warners."[6] A few days later, on October 25, 1941, Korngold sent a memo to a Mr. Taplinger (no doubt Robert Taplinger, the publicity director at Warner Bros.) on studio letterhead:

> Dear Mr. Taplinger:
> Thank you very much for your kind note regarding the photos taken for P.M.
> I am enclosing an amusing newspaper clipping.
> Isn't it too bad that Shakespeare couldn't do the same as Mr. Bellamann and "head west" just to help me score "A Midsummernightsdream"?[7]
> But, seriously: should I really <u>stop</u> working and wait for the arrival of Mr. Bellamann? Amazing isn't it, that he didn't seem to care about the script, the cast, shooting or directing—he is just crazy about music.
> Besides, he was on the faculty of the Curtis Academy of Music and I, myself, was professor in the music academy in Vienna—so, maybe, we'll win the <u>Academy Award</u> for 1941—together.
> However, if he shouldn't arrive in time to help <u>me</u>, I shall certainly be ready to "head east"—perhaps <u>I</u> could help <u>him</u> in writing his new book!!

Please forgive this outburst of sarcasm and once more thanks and best regards!

Sincerely yours,
Erich Wolfgang Korngold[8]

Korngold's decidedly snarky note corroborates what other writers have said about his reputation for wittiness, as when for instance Jessica Duchen described him as "having one of the sharpest and readiest wits about."[9] A generous interpretation of Korngold's sharp reaction would recognize that in the fall of 1941 he was in the midst of the crunch of having to generate a large orchestral score in under two months, and a war was going on in his home country that would soon extend to the United States with the attack on Pearl Harbor. We do not know precisely what happened with this heralded meeting of novelist and film composer, but Taplinger was too savvy a publicist to let the occasion go to waste. The press book for *Kings Row* contains a brief announcement with the title "Novel's Author Aids In Scoring *Kings Row*":

> Henry Bellamann, author of the best-seller, *Kings Row*, opening Friday at the Strand, travelled to Hollywood to consult with composer Erich Wolfgang Korngold on the scoring of the film version of the Bellamann novel.
>
> Bellamann, whose musical background before writing *Kings Row* includes teaching posts at the Curtis Institute of Music in Philadelphia and the Juilliard Musical Foundation, thus became the first author in modern times to help score the motion picture adaptation of his own novel.
>
> Reason for asking Bellamann to work with him on the scoring of the picture, according to Mr. Korngold, is that "he (Bellamann) has the feel of the characters, of the mood and of the story, deep in his heart—and that is where all good music comes from."
>
> Bellamann, born in Fulton, Missouri, in 1882, spent the first thirty years of his life as a musician and professor of music. He wrote his first novel, *Petenara's Daughter*, in 1926.[10]

The public face put on Korngold's earlier response was complimentary, if not wildly different in tone than his private one. This story begs the question of which other authors (in modern times or otherwise) also may have helped score the motion picture adaptation of their own novel. The list cannot be long.

"THE CAVERNS OF THE HUMAN MIND ARE FULL OF STRANGE SHADOWS"

Figure 1. Henry Bellamann.

Bellamann: Worthy Target for Korngold's Ridicule?

Were these private and public writings about and between Korngold and Bellamann sound and fury signifying nothing more than the machinations of Hollywood's publicity machinery, or might they point us to some new ways of reaching deeper understandings of both individuals? A deeper look into Bellamann's career reveals a figure who, though not nearly as famous as Korngold, was nonetheless highly accomplished in several different areas. His name will be familiar to scholars of Charles Ives because Bellamann was an early and important advocate, publishing "Charles Ives: The Man and His Music" in *The Musical Quarterly* in 1933, well before Ives was championed by Bernard Herrmann and Leonard Bernstein.[11] The 1920 edition of the *Grove Dictionary of Music and Musicians* contains the following entry:

> BELLAMANN, HEINRICH HAUER (Apr. 28, 1882, Fulton, Mo.), secured his general education at Westminster College in Missouri and the University of Denver. He then went to Paris, studying piano with Philipp and organ and composition with Widor. Since 1907 he has been director of the School of Fine Arts in Chicora College for Women at Columbia, S.C. He has interested himself in the advancement of modern French music in the South, and has presented for the first time in America many of the more important works by d'Indy, Widor, Debussy, Magnard, Labey, Roussel, de Sévérac, de Bréville, Chausson and others. He is an authorized representative of Philipp's method. His compositions include a piano-concerto, a violin-sonata, a piano-sonata, a piano-quartet and choral works. He has also written numerous magazine articles. In 1907 he was made Mus. D. by Grayson College (Tex.). His wife is an accomplished singer and since 1907 has also taught at Chicora College. He comes of a distinguished line of German musicians.[12]

Note that Bellamann's initial vocational path was that of a musician and teacher, and then an academic administrator. It may be revealing that the early part of his career, while a music teacher, finds him listed as "Heinrich," while his later literary work was published under the name "Henry."[13] An Imagist poet, his poems appeared in numerous publications, including some of the little magazines (like *Broom* and *The Dial*) that sought to advance modernism in the early twentieth century. His novels, on the other hand, were the result of work later in his life, after he had stepped away from his administrative posts. His first extended job was at the Chicora College for Women in Columbia, South Carolina. The arrival of Henry and his wife, Katherine, in 1916 was hailed with considerable fanfare in the *Greenville Daily News*, in a story with the header "Chicora to Have a Strong Music Department."[14] The editor-in-chief of the *Musical Courier* heaped praise upon the Bellamanns in 1916, writing:

> It is a pity that the music schools in the larger places cannot be situated like Chicora College and that many of them are compelled to look so much like factories or office buildings. It is a pity, too, that more of the conservatories do not have as modern, wide awake and progressive a head as H. H. Bellamann. He has studied in France and Germany, speaks French and German fluently, was a pupil of such men as Philipp and Widor, in Paris, and to this day keeps up an animated correspondence with Vincent d'Indy regarding the latter's famous Schola Cantorum and other musical matters.[15]

The writer went on to provide a dizzying list of composers performed by students who had been studying French music with Bellamann:

> The programs contained the names of Rhene-Baton, Schmitt, Delibes, Masse, Halevy, Debussy, Pesse, Godard, Paladilhe, Chausson, Hahn, Chaminade, Faure, Hüe, Bizet, Ravel, Alkan, Saint-Saëns, Frank, Vidal, Widor, Duparc, Philipp, Lacombe, Laurens, Massenet, Dell'Acqua, Dukas, Bemberg, De Severac, Chabrier, Pessard, Le Maire, Boisdeffre, Fontenailles, d'Indy, Moret, Leroux, Auguin, Pierné, Tours, Gounod.[16]

To bring such musical repertoire to the United States would in itself have been a remarkable achievement, but to do this kind of programming in South Carolina is difficult to comprehend. The Bellamanns' success in Columbia was such that within ten years, a correspondent for the *Musical Courier* presented a glowing report of the activities at Chicora: music classes had enrollments of 250 students, with demand requiring the employment of two new assistants, and a robust performance calendar.[17]

Bellamann left Chicora College in 1924 to become the chairman of the examining board of the Juilliard Musical Foundation, and in that same year he was named an officer of public instruction in France as well, which also made him a Chevalier of the Legion of Honor in recognition of his work advancing French music and culture.[18] He became dean of the Curtis Institute of Music in 1931, a position that lasted for only one year.[19] Jay Miles Karr, a Bellamann scholar and professor at Bellamann's alma mater Westminster College, in his native town of Fulton, Missouri, offered no explanation for his short tenure at Curtis other than to state wryly that in 1932 "differences with the director of the Curtis Institute of Music in Philadelphia, where he was then Dean, gave him the opportunity to withdraw from the administrative side of music and devote full time to writing."[20] Bellamann possessed the ability to explain specialized ideas about music to an audience outside of the academy, as he demonstrated with his articles in publications like *The Commonweal* and *The Saturday Review*. When evaluating the state of new compositions by U.S. composers, he began by acknowledging with some irony that new music, regardless of the composer's nationality, was already a hard sell: "There is no noticeable outcry for repeated hearings of Hindemith, Krenek, Berg, Resphigi, and others."[21] Although he does not mention Ives by name, he seems to be advocating for an Ivesian independence from the European tradition when he concludes that American composers were "often about as good a craftsman as his European colleague—but not always. . . . The American too often goes imitative and furnishes forth long and dull symphonies when it is rather obvious that his wing-spread is not equal to the flight."[22]

Bellamann's engaging prose style was on full display in his discussion of music criticism in *The Saturday Review*, an article in which he drew attention to the different standards for music critics and critics of music critics:

> If you are a music critic you are permitted to say that Mr. Unglaublicherklavierklopfer [roughly, unbelievable piano-knocker] is a bad pianist, that his readings are unintelligent, his fingers clumsy, his taste beyond hope, and that he should play for his friends, never for the public. But, if you are writing a brief opinion of the present status of music criticism the editor won't permit you to say that Mr. So-and-so is a feeble, futile, frustrated composer and is compensating himself by drubbing better men, or that he is a side-line teacher of singing or violin, praising where his blackmail has succeeded, blaming where it has failed, or that he is a pseudo-musicologist blowing up a fine dust of second-hand erudition to obscure his lack of sensitivity and understanding. No: the editor won't let you do that.[23]

Despite Bellamann's first-rate erudition and sensitivity, Korngold was annoyed at being asked to meet with him while composing for *Kings Row*. It's tempting to wonder if some of the skepticism that Korngold expressed in the memo to Robert Taplinger about Bellamann's musical stature may have been connected to Korngold's own issues with music critics, and one critic in particular: his father Julius, who disapproved of Erich's work in Hollywood.

From Novel to Film—Via the Hollywood Production Code
Most of the critical reception of *Kings Row* has been dominated by debates over how closely Bellamann's literary creation may have been to actual individuals and situations in his hometown of Fulton, Missouri.[24] The novel's opening page characterizes the fictional town of Kings Row as "A good town. A good clean town. A good town to live in, and a good place to raise your children," but then spends the next 674 pages casting doubt on that assertion.[25] The central character in the novel, Parris Mitchell, bears resemblances to Bellamann: he was born in the Midwest with an absent father figure, achieved recognition for his seriousness of purpose and affinity for music, and left his small hometown for transformative experiences as a young adult in Europe. Parris, an orphan, is raised by his grandmother, Marie Arnaut von Eln, who owns an orchard, and his friends include sexually precocious Drake McHugh, the tomboy Randy Monaghan, homosexual Jamie Wakefield, attractive but troubled Cassandra Tower, and the daughter of the overseer of the orchard's nurseries, Renée Gyllinson. Bellamann sets up Parris's coming-of-age through his navigation of the sexual possibilities presented by these characters, and generally follows the heteronormative and masculinist conventions of his day. The midwestern fin-de-siècle setting offers Parris adult role models who are lawyers, physicians, teachers, and clergy, and he proves himself to be a sensitive, hardworking student who becomes a serious student of the piano (in the film we hear him play Chopin and Beethoven) as well as medicine. We meet the lead characters when they are children—a feature retained in the film—and an especially important incident revolves around Cassandra's birthday party. Cassandra's father, the mysterious Dr. Alexander Q. Tower, has no patients and spends most of his time at home, taking care of his mentally ill wife. The wife of another doctor in the town, Henry Gordon, schedules her daughter Louise's birthday party at the same time as Cassandra's in order to ruin the event. Her ploy succeeds and Cassie is humiliated. Dr. Gordon has a history of performing surgery without anesthesia, and later it will be revealed that he views himself as a moral force who punishes sinners with his operations. Parris has his first sexual experience at the age of fourteen with Renée, though she is discovered by her father, an orchardist, who beats her and moves the family away from Kings Row. Parris has homosexual experiences with Jamie Wakefield, and learns that Drake has also spent some intimate time with Jamie, though both Parris and Drake will identify as heterosexual. As a young person preparing for medical school, Parris is tutored by Dr. Tower while also carrying on a secret sexual relationship with Cassandra.

Kings Row shows that Bellamann possessed an unusually perceptive understanding of Freud. He follows Freud's propensity for turning to Greek mythology in naming things, as he does with his characters of Parris and Cassandra (Cassie). In Greek mythology, Paris and Cassandra are important characters in the Trojan War described in the *Iliad*, and, significantly, both of them are children of Priam and Hecuba. In Bellamann's novel Parris and Cassie form an incestuous romantic triangle with Dr. Tower, who does more than become a surrogate father figure for the orphaned Parris. The novel, then, is working through some of Freud's most important claims about human sexuality and societal repressions of it vis-à-vis the Oedipus and Elektra myths.

In the film, cancer begins to claim the life of Madame von Eln, Parris's grandmother, and he experiences two large traumas within a few days: Dr. Tower, who had been sexually abusing Cassandra, murders her and then kills himself, and Madame von Eln reaches the end of her life (a death hurried along in mercy by Parris per the urging of von Eln's long-time servant Anna, who wishes to end her friend's suffering). Parris moves to Vienna to study the new field of psychiatry and the novel shifts its attention to Drake McHugh, who has been carrying on sexual liaisons with numerous women around Kings Row, though he decides he wants to marry Louise Gordon. The Gordons refuse to allow the union. Although Drake was the recipient of a large trust fund, he unexpectedly becomes part of the working class when his savings are embezzled by Lucius Curley, the local banker, yet another corrupt professional at work in Kings Row. Drake begins to see Randy Monaghan and they fall in love. Having landed a job at the railroad, Drake is injured by a passing train, and Dr. Gordon takes the opportunity to punish the young man he regarded as a sinner by amputating both of Drake's legs from the hip down. Randy begins a correspondence with Parris, who offers them some money that he was willed by Dr. Tower.

Upon returning to Kings Row, Parris discovers more about Dr. Gordon's sinister operations. Another friend of his, Peyton Graves, is involved in an extramarital affair with a young woman of color, Melissa St. George (her father was a wealthy white man and her mother was African American). Although part of the landowning and supposedly wealthy class, Peyton is actually in financial ruin, and when his lover offers him her surprisingly large savings (left to her by her father), Peyton commits suicide. Drake has responded to the loss of his legs with severe depression (he has Randy promise that he will never leave his house until he dies); his condition deteriorates when he learns he has cancer in his pelvic region, a condition suggested to be a result of Gordon's butchering. After Louise

Gordon begins to publicize her now deceased father's sadistic surgeries, Mrs. Gordon asks Parris to have her committed to the local asylum. When Drake's suffering reaches the point that palliative measures are no longer bringing him any relief, Parris approves the attending physician's idea of administering a lethal dose of morphine, mirroring the earlier mercy killing of his grandmother at the suggestion of her servant. Parris begins a romantic involvement with a new woman, Elise Sandor (whom he first mistakes for the long-departed Renée), and decides to stay in Kings Row.

Rich in lurid situations that would have been particularly shocking in the 1940s, *Kings Row* the novel ends in what the screenwriter Casey Robinson described as "a negative triumph at best," referring to the long list of dead or suffering characters and declaring that "the last 170 pages of Bellamann's novel is a story of defeat."[26] Robinson decided in the fall of 1940 to make significant changes to the screenplay on top of the already numerous changes the novel required in order to pass under the Hollywood production code, offering this justification:

> Especially in these days does one need to have faith in something. Little towns like Kings Row are America and one needs to have faith in America. Certainly there is evil in Kings Row, but there is good there also and one must believe that in the main the good will triumph over the evil for those who have courage and strength. Therefore, while we propose to use, in the main, the events of Bellamann's novel, we will shape them to a happier theme and conclusion. We believe that there will still be enough blood and tears and tragedy in the story to keep it from becoming Pollyanna on the Farm.[27]

Even with a more hopeful conclusion, the film offers an unusually harsh indictment of the hypocrisies and injustices occurring in the supposedly idyllic world of small towns in America. While eliminating plot elements like the mercy killings (Drake not only lives but has a moment of heroic overcoming at the film's end), Dr. Tower's incestuous sexual abuse, Cassie's nymphomania (as it was called in the novel), Jamie's queerness, and Peyton's interracial romance, the film still manages some surprisingly critical moments, as when the young Randy Monaghan announces, "it's a free country . . . I guess." This imaginary world, modeled on the real, still offered a rogues' gallery of criminal bankers and surgeons, but Robinson knew his market well enough to accommodate the need for a commercial feature film to provide the happy ending associated with a Hollywood product. That impulse in favor of pleasant fantasies and

Figure 2. Movie poster for *Kings Row*.

themes that could lift morale grew in the national mood after the surprise attack on Pearl Harbor, which delayed the planned December release of the film until the spring of 1942.

A Melodrama of Disability Horrors

Robinson's "blood and tears and tragedy" point in part to the film's status as a melodrama, a cinematic genre or mode common to many Hollywood films of that time, but also to the film's qualities as a relative of the horror film, coming in a decade during which Hollywood produced little that we would today recognize as horror (Val Lewton's films, such as *Cat People* of 1942, were notable exceptions). Clifton Fadiman's review of Bellamann's novel in *The New Yorker* refers to "the 'Dracula' elements" and concludes by saying he does not believe the "novel is a sound one, but it's interesting enough as melodrama. And you can't laugh off some of the shivers, as you can so easily in the case of Faulkner."[28]

Another subtle connection to horror films comes when Parris asks the elderly lawyer, Colonel Skeffington, if he thought it might be possible that

Dr. Gordon was maliciously operating on patients. Skeffington responds that "you wouldn't be shocked if you heard of it happening in some remote town in Europe"—the usual locale for the Universal horror films of the early 1930s, such as *Dracula*, *Frankenstein*, and their sequels. Following Robin Wood's definition of horror as a genre in which "normality is threatened by the Monster," *Kings Row* contains multiple monsters and threats to normalcy, all of them connected in some ways to anxieties about what constitutes a normal and healthy mind and body.[29] Both Cassie and Louise are labeled as psychologically unhealthy. But Drake's cruel maiming at the hands of Dr. Gordon—and Dr. Gordon's sadistic attempts at moral retribution, which points back to the moral model of disability, in which disability is understood as an exterior sign of a flawed internal character—occupies the central focus of the ways disability gets represented in the film. A response from an exhibitor who attended an advance screening is particularly revealing, as it predicts the new sensitivities of a domestic audience suddenly made aware of the imminent or existing casualties of war:

> Gentleman,
> I saw the preview of Kings Row. To my estimation it is an excellent picture. Particular credit should be given to the Director for the inspired and faithful performances of all principals.
> And yet I feel that under the present circumstances some important change should be made before it is nationally released.
> We are now at war and must face it practically. Unfortunately we shall have, or now already have, some casualties. Some boys may lose their limbs if not their lives. Some of their relatives, friends or loved ones may see the picture and to remind them of the gruesome fact will not be conducive to our intentions as an industry, placed with a responsibility of keeping up the morale of the nation.
> Couldn't Mr. Regan's [sic] accident be changed so that Mr. Coburn merely <u>fractures</u> the legs, and when Mr. Cummings returns from Vienna perform an operation that will make Mr. Regan [sic] regain the use of his legs. Mr. Cummings was pictured as an outstanding pupil.
> He can also direct that Mr. Coburn's daughter be sent to an institution where under the able care of a young physician, her mind is cleared and subsequently marry that young doctor.

It has been done before. And now more than ever we
need pictures with an ending that will rekindle our hope in
faith. The important part is that audiences will leave with a
happy frame of mind.

I realize it will entail a great expense. I'm sure that this
will not stop you, for your company has an excellent record
of patriotic service.[30]

Here then is a kind of evidence rarely found regarding a film's initial reception, a reaction to the loss of limbs in the film as being a trigger that could remind viewers of the actual loss of limbs that occurs with war. Even though the movie was not altered along the lines of what the exhibitor suggested, his letter shows the film's relevance as a triumphant overcoming narrative of Drake's reaction to the loss of his legs. Even today, the scene when Drake first awakens after the amputation and screams "Where's the rest of me?!?" is disturbing, in large part because of Reagan's superb performance, but also because of the synergy of cinematography and music.[31]

Before he directed *Kings Row*, Sam Wood had worked on another film about small-town America: *Our Town*. William Cameron Menzies, the production designer for *Our Town*, had the same role with *Kings Row*, although *Our Town's* musical score by Aaron Copland differs from Korngold's by imparting a pastoral quality that has come to be associated with certain representations of America in film and television music.[32] David Bordwell posits that Menzies was "one of the chief importers of German Expressionist visuals to the U.S.," and he points to things like his love of slashing diagonal compositions, worm's-eye viewpoints, close ups, and deep-focus photography, before concluding that "Menzies' films, though mostly not celebrated as classics, gave American cinema the permission to be peculiar."[33] The cinematographer for *Kings Row*, James Wong Howe, deferred all credit for the shots to Menzies:

Kings Row I loved doing. William Cameron Menzies designed
the sets and did the sketches for the shots; he'd tell you how
high the camera should be. He'd even specify the kind of
lens he wanted for a particular shot; the set was designed
for one specific shot only, and if you varied your angle by an
inch you'd shoot over the top. . . . Menzies created the whole
look of the film; I simply followed his orders.[34]

Kings Row has more than its share of peculiar moments, most of which occur visually, but a few of which find their correspondingly peculiar

Figure 3a. Foreground (books), middle-ground (Parris's profile), and background (Dr. Tower's shadowy visage) appear in equally deep focus.

Figure 3b. Another example of deep focus: foreground (pitcher and syringe) and background (Parris at his grandmother's bed) appear in equally sharp focus.

Figure 3c. An uncommon shot for a Hollywood film, with Parris's and Skeffington's heads relegated to the lower third of the frame.

Figure 3d. An expressionistic close-up, full of chiaroscuro and details of painful emotion, as Drake awakes to discover his extreme mutilation.

Example 3. Amid dissonant chords against syncopated rhythms in the low woodwinds, Cassie tells Parris about his grandmother's terminal illness.

moment in Korngold's score. See Figures 3a and 3b for examples of deep focus photography, Figure 3c for an unusual use of the bottom third of the frame, and Figure 3d for an expressionistic close-up.

The film's preoccupations with disability, with minds and bodies defined as abnormal and in need of either cure or erasure, along with its fixation on Freudian psychoanalysis, provided several opportunities for Korngold to write in a more expressionistic style than he normally did. Both Cassie and Louise are understood to be mentally unhealthy, with Cassie killed by her father and Louise threatened with lifetime imprisonment in an asylum by her father because of her threat to publicize his criminal surgeries. Cassie's neuroses are suggested through both actress Betty Field's twitchy gestures and eye movements and a musical motive that is rapid and chromatic (seen at the end of Example 5). In one scene where Cassie tries to tell Parris about his grandmother's terminal condition, Korngold rocks between dissonant chords against syncopated rhythms in the low woodwinds, creating an ominous effect not unlike the numerous low woodwind cues Bernard Herrmann had earlier created for *Citizen Kane* (Example 3).[35]

Mrs. Gordon solicits Parris's medical assistance for Louise, and the scene where they both go up to her bedroom, which Mrs. Gordon keeps locked from the outside, is underscored by an uncharacteristically atonal passage (Example 4). (See Appendix for a list of cue numbers and titles used by Korngold and his orchestrators.) Korngold's composition teacher, Alexander Zemlinsky, was also a teacher of Arnold Schoenberg. Erich's conservative father, Julius, had sought to keep his son from becoming friends with Schoenberg while they were in Europe, although

Example 4. An uncharacteristically atonal passage accompanies the scene in which Mrs. Gordon tells Parris about Louise's confinement and takes him to Louise's room.

when Erich and Schoenberg both ended up in Southern California during the war, they became unlikely friends.[36] Erich's son George told of a meeting between the two when Erich astonished Schoenberg by going to the piano and playing some of the latter's piano works from memory.[37] Korngold's reputation as a reactionary, tonal late-Romanticist out of place in the twentieth century has already been examined by Bryan

Gilliam and others. The biographer Brendan Carroll presents Korngold as a composer who never flinched from writing tonal music:

> The sense of tonality and key relationships is never completely absent from Korngold's music, no matter how exotic his harmonic pallette [sic] became or how ambiguous the chordal progressions. Even in his fourth opera, *Das Wunder der Heliane*—the final frontier of tonality as far as Korngold is concerned—this tonal certainty is ever present, acting as a guide for the ear no matter how convoluted the language becomes.[38]

However, his music for the cue "Louise's Bedroom" offers a brief but contradictory piece of evidence to any claims that Korngold created only tonal music. The film ends up omitting nearly all of the first three measures Korngold wrote, but an examination of the entire melody he intended shows him experimenting with serial technique.[39] The monophonic chromatic melody that rises upward as the characters ascend the stairs deploys nine of the twelve pitches available in the chromatic scale. The second four measures repeat the first four, but two octaves higher and transposed down a whole step. After the first eight monophonic measures, the cue shifts to a trilling motive that has widely been associated with Louise. If this is indeed a serial row, then it does not follow Schoenberg's rules, as it repeats pitches non-sequentially within itself. Even if these are only accidental similarities with Schoenberg's atonality, the dramatic result, with the music depicting Louise's apparent mental instability is effective, and Korngold's use of trilling pedal tones against unstable harmonies follows Strauss's earlier use of the technique in *Salome*.

Drake's progression from free-roaming playboy to a bed-ridden double amputee with severe depression, and finally to one with a positive attitude (Parris ostensibly cures him by reciting poetry to him, and in his reaction Drake demonstrates that he has grown up and not just grown older) receives a series of musical cues that reflect these different states, most memorably perhaps in the heroic music of triumph at the film's conclusion. The development of the main musical motives for Parris and Drake have been discussed in detail by Scott Murphy, but a brief examination of another motive, one that Korngold seems to have written as a signifier of the friendship of Parris and Drake, will show it to be one of the most important motives in the score.[40]

The Parris-and-Drake motive appears eight times throughout the score, most prominently after Drake awakes post-amputation and cries out for Parris, and then upon Parris's return from Vienna.[41] It first appears after

Example 5. The first appearance of Korngold's motive for Parris and Drake.

we follow the characters as young boys in an afternoon of play (swinging on the rings at the icehouse), and as they depart, they acknowledge their close bond of friendship (Example 5). The melodic contour darts down before moving more majestically and then excitedly. Menzies and Howe's careful composition of the image aligns Parris with a tree in the background—the tree appears to be an extension of Parris—and the tree is kept in the composition of the next shot, which shows the entrance to

Example 6. As Randy and Drake read a letter from Parris, Korngold rapidly alternates between their motives.

Example 6. continued

the von Eln nursery, where Cassie has been waiting for Parris. The subtle matching of Parris's body with a tree, and then the contrasting of a smaller tree and larger one, is balanced in the succeeding shots. These focus on the young Parris walking over the stairs (accompanied by a soft version of the score's main melody, which is also Parris's motive), and then dissolves into an elliptical edit advancing ten years into the future—revealing Parris's maturation by showing his adult feet walking back over the steps and again kicking at a rock, accompanied by the main title/Parris theme played much more loudly and powerfully than the first time.

A scene in which Drake reads a letter from Parris in Vienna offers a superb example of Korngold's tight connections between filmic motivation and musical score. Whenever a character is mentioned, the music highlights it with the character's motive (see Example 6). While Drake reads Parris's words to Randy, the music begins with Parris's motive. As it becomes clear in the letter that Drake has not revealed his financial misfortunes to Parris, the music plays Drake's motive, but in a minor key, and when Randy asks why Drake had not shared this important information with Parris, Drake responds that he wants to keep his friend, and the Parris and Drake motive begins to sound. At the moment when Randy states that she "loves his beautiful pride," part of Randy's motive sounds. As the scene returns to Parris's letter so does the music. Parris explains that his reason for pursuing the study of psychiatry in Vienna is connected to his history with Cassie, prompting her motive to sound. In the scene when Drake wakes for the first time after his amputation, Korngold adopts a more expressionistic quality to parallel the equally exaggerated visual flourishes, like the canted camera angles and close-ups (Example 7).

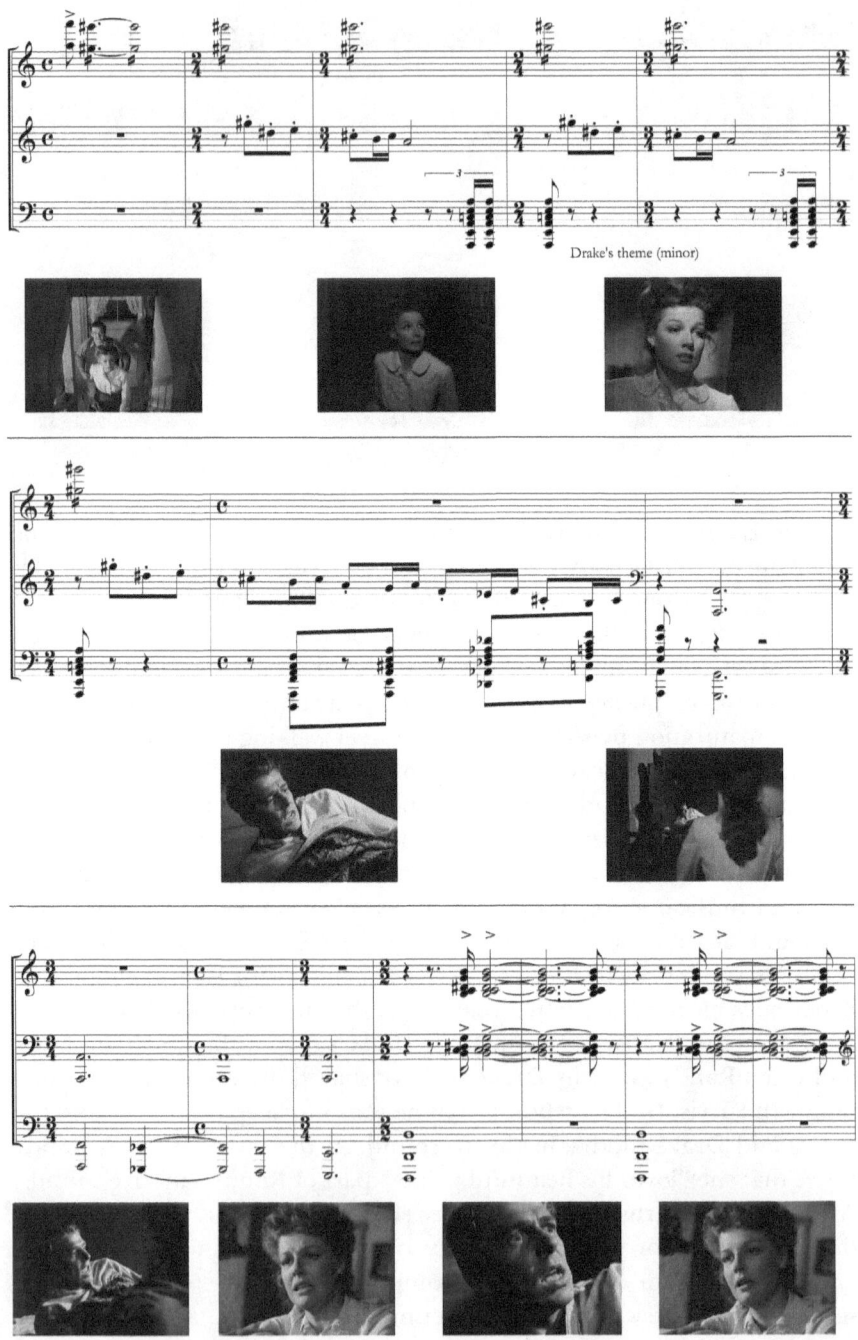

Example 7. Korngold punctuates Drake's reaction to his amputation with a sounding of the Parris-Drake motive.

Example 7. continued

As the shock of what has happened begins to sink in for Drake, he turns his head into a shadow and utters "Parris," as the Parris-Drake motive appears. That motive next occurs during Parris's return from Vienna, and as Parris runs into Drake's bedroom, the two men lock eyes and Parris rushes to Drake's side. After staring at each other for a few seconds, the two press their cheeks together as Randy leaves the room and recites Hail Marys in the hallway (Example 8).

This moment is one of the most euphoric and jubilant in the film, matched perhaps only by the earlier scenes of innocent play in the ice house (in which Korngold turns Parris's motive into a joyful waltz) and the final scene of Drake's heroic overcoming. Parris enters the final scene unsure if his decision to tell Drake about the unnecessary nature of the amputations would liberate his friend or send him into a deeper depression. Parris hopes to address what he has labeled Drake's "helpless invalid complex" through a curious reversing of Freud's talking cure—one in which the therapist does nearly all of the talking instead of the patient. Before he makes that revelation to Drake, he utters this cryptic declaration to him: "The caverns of the human mind are full of strange shadows." It is a line derived from one he utters to Randy in the novel: "The places of the human mind are full of strange shadows."[42] The words reflect Parris's psychoanalytical training and a Freudian understanding of the subconscious.

The film's representation of mental and physical disability follows the typical medical model of the time, which viewed a disability as an abnormality outside some statistically verifiable realm of normalcy, a dreaded condition that demanded medical intervention to cure, and short of that, erasure of the disabled person via institutionalization or, in the most extreme

Example 8. When Parris sees Drake for the first time after his amputation, and as they gaze deeply into each other's eyes, the Parris-Drake motive is heard again.

Example 8. continued

situations, euthanasia.[43] Cultural disability studies hold that persons with disabilities create anxiety for the temporarily able-bodied, and that anxiety can be relieved through a fantasy of the person with an impairment somehow overcoming the difference. While "overcoming" can have positive qualities, an important difference when applying it to a person with a disability is that unlike the overcoming of something like sociopolitical barriers of racial or economic difference, it reduces the person's body and mind into a disability to be cured or erased. Two of the best-known examples from the United States during the time of *Kings Row* are Helen Keller and Franklin D. Roosevelt, both of whom were celebrated for the way they were perceived to have overcome sensory deficits or paralysis, respectively. *Kings Row* reflects and amplifies those anxieties chiefly through the treatment of Drake and his amputation, but also through the mental illnesses of Cassie and Louise.

Kings Row offers parallel studies of masculinity: of the tyrannical and misogynistic patriarchs of Drs. Tower and Gordon, of Drake McHugh's promiscuity and privilege, and of Parris Mitchell's potential as a less tyrannical doctor/patriarch skilled in the practice of two Viennese imports: Beethoven (as studied by Parris) and psychiatry (typified in the film by a Viennese medical professor with a bit of a resemblance to Sigmund Freud). Korngold's marvelously multifaced score, one that defies categorization as simply post-Romantic and tonal, exhibits the composer's gift for sharply delineating characters as it works in close parallel with the ideas of the film. Probing deeper into the backstory of this powerful film and film score may indeed vindicate Korngold's assessment of

Bellamann's writing (in the official press materials) as coming from "deep in the heart . . . where all good music comes from," but it also leads us to the more troubling and bigoted arguments against homosexuality and disability that were sadly typical for Hollywood films of that era and later. These ideas haunt Parris's prescient remark that "the caverns of the human mind are full of strange shadows." Those caverns may provide resonant spaces for Korngold's memorable score, but unpleasant realities both lurk within as well as are made more palatable by those shadows.

Appendix: Cue Numbers, Titles, and Orchestrators in *Kings Row*

No.	Reel	Title	Orchestrator
1	1	A. Main Title	Hugo Friedhofer [HF]
2		B. The school	Milan Roder [MR]
3		C. Parris & Cassie	HF
4		D. Grandmother	HF
5		E. Cassy's [*sic*] Party	HF
6		F. Louise's Party & Drake	MR
7		G. Icehouse	MR
8	2	A. Operation	HF
9		B. Farewell-Parris Return	HF (6) & MR (10)
10		C. P. goes to Dr. Tower	HF
11		D. The Winter	HF
12	3	A. Last Will of Grandma	HF
13		B. Parris & Cassy and Drake & Louise	HF (5) & MR (10)
14		C. Dr. Gordon	HF
15		D. Drake's Exit	MR
16		E. Seduction Part I	HF
17	4	A. Seduction Part II	HF
18		B. Drake's Home	MR
19		C. Dreaming Voices	HF
20		D. Grandma & Anna	MR
21		E. Orchard-Dr. Tower	HF
22	5	A. Piano (underscoring)	None
23		B. Cancer	HF
24		C. Love Scene Part I	HF
25		D. Love Scene Part II	HF
26		E. Dead [*sic*] of Grandma	HF
27	6	A. Sunset	MR
28		B. Parris is packing	MR
29		C. Cassy	Bern[ard] Kaun [BK]
30		D. All is quite [*sic*]	BK
31		E. Nex[t] Morning	MR
32		F. Dr. Tower's Home	MR
33		G. Dr. Gordon	HF

Appendix: continued

No.	Reel	Title	Orchestrator
34	7	A. Farewell-Randy	Ray Heindorf [RH]
35		B. Flirt	RH
36		C. Wienna [sic]-Happy New Year	RH
37		D. Randy-Drake I	RH
38		E. Randy-Drake II	RH
39	8	A. Louise	MR
40		B. Drake is mad	MR
41		C. Bank	MR
42		D. Sale-Newspaper	MR
43		E. Randy's father	RH
44	9	A. Railway station & Parris' letter	HR
45		B. Randy	HF
46		C. Accident	MR
47		D. Dance	RH [the name "Perkins" is given in the Heindorf column]
48		E. Amputation	MR
49		F. Dr. Gordon-Luise [sic]	MR
50		G. Dr. Gordon-Luise cont.	MR
51		H. Drake awakes	HF
52		I. Vienna University	RH
53	10	A. Vienna Cabel [sic]-Randy's Decision	RH
54		B. The Letters across the ocean	BK
55		C. Parris comes back, and meets Drake	BK
56		D. Kings Row I	HF
57		E. Mrs. Gordon	MR
58	11	A. Luise's bedroom	MR
59		B. Dissolve	None indicated
60		C. Kings Row II	HF
61		D. Alice [sic]	HF
62	12	A. Bethowen's [sic] Pathetique	HF
63		B. Randy's Sacrifice	MR
64		C. Randy weeps	HF

Appendix: continued

No.	Reel	Title	Orchestrator
65		D. Parris Letter	HF
66	13	A. Parris-Alice [sic]	HF
67		B. I am the Captain of my soul	HF
68		C. Cast	HF
69	Trailer	I. Trailer Part I	MR
70	Trailer	II. Trailer Part II	MR
71	Trailer	III. Trailer Part III	MR
72	Trailer	IV. Trailer Part IV	MR

NOTES

1. Mark R. Scherer, "Where's the Rest of *Kings Row*?: Hollywood's Emasculation of a 'Grand Yarn,'" *Literature/Film Quarterly* 27/4 (1999): 255–62.

2. While the similarity between the opening melodies of *Kings Row* and *Star Wars* has been mentioned by too many scholars to list, a helpful starting point for the question of John Williams's originality is Jeremy Orosz's "John Williams: Paraphrase or Plagiarist?," *Journal of Musicological Research* 34/4 (2015): 299–319.

3. Despite the frequency with which *Kings Row* and *Star Wars* have been compared, there remains a dearth of sustained, in-depth studies of *Kings Row* from either literary or music scholars. The chief exception to this paucity is by Scott Murphy: "Korngold and *Kings Row*: A Semiotic Interpretation of Film Music" (Master's thesis, University of Kansas, Lawrence, 1994). Murphy provides background information on Korngold and the film as well as a transcribed short score based on his study of the conductor score; his project demonstrates the applicability of semiotic theories (from Christian Metz and Julien Greimas) to film music analysis, with selected scenes from *Kings Row* serving as his case studies. Brendan G. Carroll's biography of Korngold devotes about three of its 464 pages to *Kings Row*, mainly emphasizing the initial outpouring of fan mail asking about the music, an unusual response for any score in Hollywood and one whose prodigious size required the creation of a form letter particular to the *Kings Row* score. See Carroll, *The Last Prodigy: A Biography of Erich Wolfgang Korngold* (Portland, OR: Amadeus Press, 1997), 303–6. Bryan Gilliam situates Korngold within the larger context of other European émigrés who settled in Southern California during the war. Focusing on Korngold's reception vis-à-vis aesthetic modernism and in particular the idea of him experiencing two exiles, one from Austria and the other from opera, Gilliam provides a detailed look at the multiple leitmotifs that appear in a central seduction scene in *Kings Row* as evidence of the similarities between Korngold's compositional strategies for opera and film. See Gilliam's "A Viennese Opera Composer in Hollywood: Korngold's Double Exile in America," in *Driven into Paradise: The Musical Migration from Nazi Germany to the United States*, ed. Reinhold Brinkmann and Christoph Wolff (Berkeley: University of California Press, 1999), 223–42. Among film scholars, the most sustained attention to *Kings Row* occurs in Janet Walker's essay "Textual Trauma in *Kings Row* and Freud," in *Endless Night: Cinema and Psychoanalysis, Parallel Histories*, ed. Janet Bergstrom (Berkeley: University of California Press, 1999), 171–87; a version of that essay appears as "The Excision of Incest from Classical Hollywood Cinema: *Kings Row* and Freud," in Walker's *Trauma Cinema: Documenting Incest and the Holocaust* (Berkeley: University of California Press, 1999), 33–48.

4. Gilliam, "A Viennese Opera Composer in Hollywood," 223.

5. *The Sea Hawk (The Classic Film Scores of Erich Wolfgang Korngold)*, with the National Philharmonic Orchestra, cond. Charles Gerhardt, 33 1/3 rpm, RCA Red Seal LSC 3330 (1972). Carroll credits this recording as the inspiration for his biography of Korngold. It also appeared at a moment when a younger generation of filmmakers, including George Lucas and Stephen Spielberg, were just beginning to make movies that would later be classified in the category of the New Hollywood—a generation of creators who were keenly aware of earlier cinematic precedents from Hollywood and around the globe. The similarities to Korngold in John Williams's *Star Wars* were the result of Lucas seeking from Williams a re-creation of the swashbuckling sound connected with Errol Flynn films of the 1930s and '40s (i.e., Korngold's heroic scores). Continuing the interest in Korngold's film work as well as perhaps attempting to capitalize on the popularity of *Star Wars* (1977), an entire album devoted to *Kings Row* appeared in 1979, again with the team of George Korngold, Charles Gerhardt, and the National Philharmonic Orchestra (Chalfont Records SDG 305).

6. From the *Kings Row* clipping file, Warner Bros. archive, University of Southern California. The underlining, done in hand, comes from the original.

7. Korngold plays here with the title of Shakespeare's play in German, *Sommernachtstraum*.

8. *Kings Row* clipping file, Warner Bros. archive.

9. Jessica Duchen, *Erich Wolfgang Korngold* (London: Phaidon, 1996), 168.

10. *Kings Row* pressbook, State Historical Society of Wisconsin, University of Wisconsin, Madison.

11. Henry Bellamann, "Charles Ives: The Man and His Music," *The Musical Quarterly* 19/1 (January 1933): 45–58.

12. *The Grove Dictionary of Music and Musicians*, ed. Waldo Selden Pratt, vol. 6 (New York: Macmillan, 1920), 129. Bellamann was an unusually versatile and skilled scholar. In addition to teaching piano and music history, his language skills included German, French, and Italian, and at the time of his death in 1945 he was working on a translation of Dante's *Commedia*; his collection of three hundred volumes related to Dante was donated to Duke University. See Allan H. Gilbert, "Henry Bellamann Dante Collection at Duke," *South Atlantic Bulletin* 11/4 (February 1946): 8.

13. The 1917 volume of *Nodes and Becks*, the Chicora College yearbook, lists him as "Mr. Heinrich Hauer Bellamann, D. Mus., Professor of Piano, Organ and Theoretical Subjects." The 1911–12 prospectus for Chicora College provides an even more detailed title: "Mr. Heinrich Hauer Bellamann, D. Mus., Dean of the College of Music, Director of Musical Studies, Professor of Piano, Organ and Theoretical Subjects. Preparatory Teacher, by appointment, to Isidor Philipp, Paris Conservatoire." His first published book of poetry, *A Music Teacher's Note Book*, appeared in 1920 under the name "Henry," while the 1920 *Grove Dictionary* entry lists him as "Heinrich," further demonstrating the distinction between his musical and literary identities. It is notable that he maintained the Germanic name amid the anti-Teutonic sentiment that occurred in the United States during the Great War.

14. *Greenville Daily News* (SC), 14 September 1907.

15. "Variations on Themes Abroad and at Home," *Musical Courier*, 20 April 1916, 21.

16. Ibid.

17. "The Work of the Bellamanns," *Musical Courier*, 5 July 1917, 29.

18. "Juilliard Foundation Plans Explained," *Musical Courier*, 7 August 1924, 15;"Henry Bellamann Dean of Curtis Institute," *Musical Courier*, 19 September 1931, 23.

19. "Henry Bellamann Dean of Curtis Institute," 23.

20. Jay Miles Karr, "Rediscovering the Author of *Kings Row*," lecture presented October 18, 1979, in Fulton, Missouri, and revised in 1981. Manuscript from the Henry Bellamann Papers, South Caroliniana Library, University of South Carolina.

21. Henry Bellamann, "How Bad Is American Music?," *The Commonweal*, 26 October 1934, 605–6.

22. Ibid., 606.

23. Henry Bellamann, "From Poison to Elixirs: The Wide Range of Quality in Music Criticism," *The Saturday Review* 26 (30 January 1943): 20.

24. See Jay Miles Karr's introduction to *Kings Row* in the 1981 edition of the novel (Fulton, MO: Kingdom House, 1981), vii–xxv.

25. Henry Bellamann, *Kings Row* (New York: Simon and Schuster, 1940), 3. Bellamann's concerns about his novel being read as a *roman à clef* may be perceived in the strength of the denial he includes in the preface to the novel: "The town of Kings Row does not exist. The characters are imaginary. Kings Row resembles many towns of the period, but this is neither a picture of an actual place, nor is the story the reporting of the lives or behavior of living persons."

26. From the script treatment of 4 September 1940, MSS 99AN Series 1.2, box 217, folder 8, State Historical Society of Wisconsin, University of Wisconsin, Madison, 174.

27. Ibid., 175.

28. "Books: Knut Hamsun—Faulkner Made Easy," *The New Yorker*, 14 April 1940, 80–82.

29. Robin Wood, "An Introduction to the American Horror Film," in *American Nightmare: Essays on the Horror Film*, ed. Andrew Britton, Richard Lippe, Tony Williams, and Robin Wood (Toronto: Festival of Festivals, 1979), 15.

30. The handwritten letter, dated 31 December 1941, and from an exhibitor at Coney Island in New York, was forwarded to Jack Warner with an accompanying memorandum summarizing it. *Kings Row* clipping file, Warner Bros. archive, University of Southern California.

31. Reagan used the phrase "Where's the rest of me?" as the title for his autobiography, which he opens by recounting the shooting of that scene, explaining that "a whole actor would find such a scene difficult; giving it the necessary dramatic impact as half an actor was murderous. I felt I had neither the experience nor the talent to fake it. I simply had to find out how it really felt, short of actual amputation." Ronald Reagan and Richard C. Hubler, *Where's the Rest of Me?* (New York: Dell, 1965), 8.

32. For more on the differences between the musical languages in *Our Town* and *Kings Row*, see Neil Lerner, "Copland's Music of Wide Open Spaces: Surveying the Pastoral Trope in Hollywood," *The Musical Quarterly* 85/3 (2001): 477–515, esp. 491–94.

33. From David Bordwell and Kristin Thompson's blog, *Observations on Film Art*, "Foreground, Background, Playground," http://www.davidbordwell.net/blog/category/directors–menzies/.

34. Howe quoted in Charles Higham, *Hollywood Cameramen: Sources of Light* (London: Thames and Hudson, 1970), 88.

35. Examples for this essay were created from a combination of a study of Korngold's short score and the author's transcriptions. Cue titles come from the labor logs held in the Warner Bros. archives at the University of Southern California. The Appendix lists the cues and also identifies which of the four orchestrators were responsible for each cue.

36. Carroll, *The Last Prodigy*, 291–93.

37. Ibid., 291.

38. Ibid., 50–51.

39. Carroll briefly discusses an ascending twelve-note scale that Korngold uses in the climax of the Cello Concerto in C Major that Korngold wrote for a later film, *Deception*, commenting that "Bartók made a similar gesture at the end of his *Concerto for Orchestra*. Whether Korngold had ever heard this work at the time is unknown, but is unlikely." Ibid., 393.

40. Murphy, "Korngold and *Kings Row*," 58: "This author speculates that one of Bellamann's suggestions to Korngold could have been the use of a lyrical 'love theme' for the scenes with Drake and Parris, hinting at the homosexuality between the two male characters that is immediately obvious in the original novel but cut from the film version."

41. The timings in the film for the eight occurrences are: 12:09; 25:08; 53:00; 1:03:31; 1:28:56; 1:28:26; 1:37:14; and 2:02:57. A ninth appearance occurs in cue 28 but was not used in the soundtrack.

42. Bellamann, *Kings Row*, 548.

43. For more on the cinematic, and specifically musical-cinematic, representation of disability in 1940s Hollywood films, see my "Hearing a Site of Masculinity in Franz Waxman's Score for *Pride of the Marines* (1945)," in *The Oxford Handbook of Music and Disability Studies*, ed. Blake Howe, Stephanie Jensen-Moulton, Neil Lerner, and Joseph Straus (New York: Oxford University Press, 2016), 856–90; and "The Horrors of One-Handed Pianism: Music and Disability in *The Beast with Five Fingers*," in *Sounding Off: Theorizing Disability in Music*, ed. Neil Lerner and Joseph N. Straus (New York: Routledge, 2006), 75–89.

American and Austrian Ruins in Korngold's Symphony in F-sharp

AMY LYNN WLODARSKI

In the immediate aftermath of the Second World War, Erich Korngold turned to writing two works that he hoped would serve as a "bridge" back to his former world of concert music.[1] The first was his Violin Concerto, which he had begun in 1937 only to cease composition two years later as a musical protest against the Nazi Anschluss. According to his family, Korngold had "vowed not to compose what he called 'his own music' until Hitler was dead or overthrown," and thus the piece lay dormant in the composer's portfolio for nearly eight years as he furthered his career in film.[2] With the collapse of the Third Reich in May 1945, Korngold returned to complete it. The second work was his Cello Concerto (1946), which connected his work as a Hollywood film composer to the realm of his art music. Excerpts were first featured as diegetic music in *Deception* (1946), a film about a love triangle involving a pianist, a cellist, and a composer.[3] The cellist Eleanor Slatkin, who performed the excerpts for the film, would later present the entire concerto with the Los Angeles Philharmonic on December 29, 1946, two months after the commercial release of the film.[4]

Both concertos met with tepid reviews in the critical press, with the critic Olin Downes describing the Violin Concerto as a "Hollywood concerto" that was "fully orchestrated in the Straussian manner [with] melodies [that] are ordinary and sentimental in character; the facility of the writing is matched by the mediocrity of the ideas."[5] Another review lambasted the work's old-fashioned nostalgia, observing that "composition has travelled a long way from the idea of just writing some warm, romantic tunes."[6] Korngold saw such critiques as indicative of the stronghold that the modernists held within the press, commenting to Ross Parmenter that his concert works were intentionally "unmodern" and that he felt "out of sympathy with New York."[7] But critics such as Downes were not sycophantic devotees of modern music, as his admiring review of Shostakovich's First Symphony from the same concert demonstrates: "[It] kept a romantic and revolutionary spirit, in spite of the Wagnerisms of the slow movement and the influence of Prokofiev and others in various pages. It remains a youthful, earnest symphony, and its youth is contagious."[8] Rather, it was most likely the perception of overt commercialism and inauthenticity—a sense that Korngold was catering to the lowest common denominator—that irked Downes no end.[9]

Korngold had hoped that a return to Vienna might provide a more sympathetic audience—he had received word that the Staatsoper was interested in staging his opera *Die Kathrin* (1937)—as well as the chance to triumphantly "revive his music in Germany and Austria, where it [had been] forbidden by the Nazis."[10] But his struggle to reenter the European concert world was as difficult as it had been in the United States, albeit for a different set of practical and ideological reasons. A postwar revival of *Die tote Stadt* was cancelled due to a contract dispute among leading performers. His production of *Kathrin*, lauded by the audience in attendance, was dismissed as "old-fashioned" in the press and ultimately discontinued after only a handful of performances.[11] The German music publishing house Schott, which had unequivocally supported his compositional career before the war, grew increasingly reticent in the postwar period, whether due to the lack of a "Korngold-Publikum" within the market or inherent anti-Semitic attitudes at the publishing house itself.[12]

Korngold's Symphony in F-sharp, Op. 40 (1947–52) has often been presented as a final tragic premiere in the narrative of his postwar career.[13] Although dedicated to President Franklin Delano Roosevelt, Korngold insisted that the work had nothing to do with "the terror and horrors of the years 1933–45" nor the "sorrows and sufferings of the victims of that time."[14] Rather, his intention was to "show the world that atonality and ugly dissonance at the price of giving up . . . melody and beauty will result in ultimate disaster for the art of music."[15] Korngold offered the work to prominent émigré conductors such as Bruno Walter, Fritz Reiner, and William Steinberg only to receive "polite but chilly dismissals."[16] A Viennese premiere was finally secured with the Vienna Symphony Orchestra under the direction of Harold Byrns and scheduled for a 1954 broadcast on Austrian radio, but after the "final, hopeless rehearsal," Korngold begged his friend Heinrich Kralik to cancel the performance. Kralik answered that he "couldn't change the program overnight, in that the press and public had already been invited."[17] As Michael Haas reported, "The sloppiness of the performance was felt by Korngold to be overt belligerence aimed at himself and his musical values"—and thus he was right to fear its poor reception.[18] Some critics declared its neo-Romantic language out of touch with postwar realities, and no doubt the dedication to FDR irritated those whose sympathies lay quietly with the National Socialists or who had lived through the American bombing of the city.[19]

Within the literature, the most common explanation for the symphony's failure posits that the "rapid rise of the serialists to musical dominance" had relegated neo-Romanticism to the margins of postwar relevancy.[20] Brendan Carroll describes a conflict between an "artistic environment at odds with Korngold's philosophy [and] new musical trends incompatible with his melodic, tonal style."[21] Bryan Gilliam similarly argues that the European establishment had fully embraced modernism, and therefore Korngold was already "outdated in a progressive postwar world of concert music. The paradigm had shifted long before."[22] But such theories ignore the nuanced reality of musical culture in postwar Europe. As Stephen Downes notes, "After the Second World War, a heated debate developed between those advocating radical notions of innovative cultural advancement and those supporting conservative reconstruction."[23] Neo-Romantic works were still premiered and welcomed, but similar works by composers who had fled Europe met with particularly harsh criticisms.[24] Such insights suggest that Korngold was additionally stigmatized for any number of non-stylistic reasons: he was Jewish, the son of the late Viennese music critic Julius Korngold (whose sharp-tongued reviews had sunk more than a few careers), and a successful Hollywood film composer.[25]

Along these lines, I wish to consider that the symphony may have also suffered because its language was too unsettling, *too modern*, for postwar Viennese audiences. I offer that Korngold's compositional process and materials reflected a particular traumatic mode of modernism—*the ruin*—in which recognizable fragments from the past recall an uncomfortable or contested history of decay and destruction.[26] Andreas Huyssen recognized that the "catastrophic imagination and imaginary of ruins has accompanied the trajectory of modernity since the eighteenth century," but the specific tragedies of the mid-twentieth century prompted "writing of the ruins as a kind of micrology" against the grander claims of early modernism.[27] Functioning as postwar ciphers that demand a "renegotiation between overcoming the recent past and maintaining its memory as a way to avoid inhuman modernist fantasies," ruinous art forms betrayed the "temporal and spatial doubts that modernity always harbored about itself."[28] While some manifest as a "material fascination with destruction and demise," others constitute an aesthetic that enables the audience to "think about the historicity of our condition and even experience hope."[29] Korngold noted that his preference lay with the latter: "I do not believe in the mistaken thesis that art should mirror its time. . . . The true creative artist does not wish to re-create . . . the screaming of atom bombs, murder, and sensationalism."[30] But the symphony, in its quiet references to earlier repertories whose musical lives were deeply entangled in the modern historical moment, signaled its own disturbing relevance to the ruins of the time—whether the crumbling facades of Korngold's beloved Vienna or his experience in America as an exile in a state of fracture and suspension.

Until 1944, Vienna had lain outside the scope of the Allied bombing forces, but the invasion of Italy suddenly placed it within reach of the American flotillas located in Foggia. On March 17, the first air raid on the city commenced, followed by campaigns that would continue through 1945. Because most of the runs were not indiscriminate bombings but tactical missions, the city center was spared until March 12, 1945, when American bombers overshot their target (the nearby Floridsdorf refinery) by fifteen short flight seconds. The result was widespread damage to the cultural heart of the city. The Staatsoper, where Korngold had celebrated the Austrian premiere of *Die tote Stadt*, succumbed to a raging inferno; only the main facade, the grand staircase, and the Schwind Foyer with its famous murals survived the fire (see Figure 1).[31] As historian Jeffrey Diefendorf accounts, by the end of the war Vienna had seen fifty-two air raids as well as artillery fighting between ground forces. Twenty-eight percent of the city's buildings had been damaged and 4 percent entirely destroyed. In the end, 800,000 cubic meters of rubble would be removed to landfills outside the city's border.[32]

The visual impact was staggering to all who encountered it, and many read in its collapse and reconstruction metaphors for the modern condition in post-fascist Europe. In 1946, John Dos Passos issued an eyewitness report for *Life* magazine that detailed the extensive destruction of the city and wondered at the resurgence of Viennese music from among the ruins. Theaters had reopened and concerts were being played, but "the life that [was] starting up again in the ruins" felt strangely discordant. It had quickly taken on a "semblance of the old patterns" with performances by the Vienna Boys' Choir in the royal palace and the dignitaries of the court still singing "the cheerful Schubert Masses."[33] Two years later, American audiences would voyeuristically encounter the Viennese landscape as a "physical realm [with] no solidity or stability" in the film noir *The Third Man* (1948) by the British filmmaker Carol Reed. The cinematography captured a vision of Viennese history as ruinous—"always

Figure 1. Rubble at the State Opera House in Vienna after the war.

symbolically present . . . but irretrievably lost"—and jarred with the more elegiac tone of the narrator's opening voiceover: "I never knew the old Vienna before the war, with its Strauss music, its glamour and easy charm."[34] In both the *Life* article and the film, references to Romantic-era music amid the ruins heightened their fracture and revealed their aesthetic limitations within the postwar context.

Human ruins also lay among the destruction, not only of those killed in the bombardment but also of Jewish victims whose absence and symbolic reemergence among the rubble—as Philip V. Bohlman notes—recalled earlier crimes.[35] As Elizabeth Anthony observes, Korngold was one of nearly 130,000 Austrian Jews who had fled the Nazi regime between 1933 and 1945, and nearly 65,000 of those who remained had been murdered in anti-Semitic violence and the Holocaust. As a result, "the formal Jewish community, once more than 185,000 strong, counted fewer than 5,000 members by the end of 1945."[36] Jewish *Remigranten* found their own metaphors in the rubble, albeit of a different kind. In 1952, Robert Pick returned to Vienna to issue his own dispatch for the Jewish-American periodical *Commentary*. In the burn-streaked buildings of his former neighborhood, Pick found himself unwillingly transported back to Kristallnacht and confronted by a soundscape far less comforting than Schubert or Strauss. "This was my first return to Vienna since I had fled the place in 1938 amid the exultant howls of a Nazi mob," he wrote of the experience. "The two weeks I had already been in Europe had inured me to the sight of ruins: I distinctly remember that the [sight of the] burnt-out [synagogue] . . . did not really give me a shock. I had not forgotten the pogrom days of 1938, when this chapel had been put to the torch; and someone had told me it had not been rebuilt."[37]

Vienna's reconstruction (*Neugestaltung*) commenced almost immediately after the war. The city's destruction was seen as an "opportunity to introduce needed reforms into the urban fabric" and build from the ashes a "modern metropolis, a *Großstadt*, rather than . . . a historic capital."[38] But aesthetically the path forward was littered with ideological snares. Diefendorf notes that officials and architects wished to "reestablish continuity with [the city's] own progressive planning and programs of the 1920s . . . but without embracing any kind of radical modernism and rejecting all activities of the Nazi era."[39] As a result, designs were rejected that recalled the experimental modernism of the fin-de-siècle Vienna *Sezession*, the international style of the Bauhaus, and the neoclassical aesthetic preferred by Albert Speer.[40] City planners such as Karl Heinrich Brunner aimed to "protect the valuable old city image but not transform it into an open-air museum removed from daily life."[41] Whereas historically important buildings such as the Staatsoper fell under the jurisdiction of the Austrian state—which preferred the erection of historical replicas—new architectural designs sought to shun "false Romanticism" at all costs.[42] Thus by 1954 little progress had been made; architectural specters of the past—whether Romantic, modernist, or fascist—had proved difficult to avoid in designs for large-scale renewal. Like pedestrians who encountered rubbled obstructions in the *Gäßchen* (narrow lanes) of the old city, Viennese aesthetics found themselves at a precarious and politicized impasse.

This narrative corresponds with the time period of Korngold's symphony, from its inception to its ill-fated premiere, and provides a historical context for his personal encounters with the ruins of Vienna. That Korngold had not prepared emotionally for the devastation of his former home is evident in sources that predate his return to the city in 1949. In an interview in 1942, he expressed relief that he had not witnessed the swastika flying in Vienna, for it allowed him to "still dream of Vienna as it was."[43] For him, the city's *Gäßchen* were not rubble-strewn but brimming with the warmth of home; the city remained nostalgically preserved in his memory, as he explained in an optimistic and expectant note written before his departure:

> To be back in Vienna, back home again, after almost twelve years! It is, as it says in *Die tote Stadt*, a "dream of returning." And as if suspended in a dream, I wander through the lit, intimate, narrow *Gäßchen* of the inner city. I linger at the Michaelerplatz and the Heldenplatz, with its overpowering view of . . . the museum, the city hall, theater, and parliament. Finally, I stand filled with emotion before the beloved old opera house on the Ring.[44]

In May, after an eleven-year absence, Korngold and his wife, Luzi, returned to Europe, taking a route through the continent that had remained relatively intact. Their sojourn began in Paris—"unchanged [and] magnificent," filled with "real buildings" rather than the gas stations of Los Angeles—and wound through the undisturbed Swiss countryside to the Austrian border.[45] From there, the drive was "exciting and happy all at the same time. Every mountain, every river, every pension familiar—the entire landscape lovely and endearing."[46]

The Korngolds encountered their first ruins in the beautiful Salzkammergut region, where the family had their country estate, Schloss Höselberg, in the town of Gmunden. As Luzi recalled in her memoir, "Every store was still in the old place, and in the coffeehouse even the same waiter. Everything was unchanged. The only difference was that we had to stay in a hotel because forty Displaced Persons (DPs) were living in our Höselberg—poor, exiled, homeless people."[47] The refugees had been relocated from Ebensee, a former satellite camp of Mauthausen that had been converted into a refugee camp at the end of the war. But it is not the human desperation—the "catatonic families in every room"—that Luzi focuses on; it is the physical ruin of their beloved home.[48] "Our reunion with the dilapidated and crumbling estate was initially very sad. . . . The familiar musty smell of the walls mingled with the odor of unclean people; where gravel paths and garden beds had once been laid, now there were only garden allotments."[49] All of the furniture had been looted, even the front door ripped from its hinges and most likely used as fuel. A burst pipe had caused the dining room ceiling to collapse, leaving only two surviving words from the decorative emblem—"God avenges"—a metaphor of impending redemption and justice now stripped of any certainty by its disintegration.

Further displacement followed the Korngolds to Vienna, where they were forced to live in a hotel while they took up legal actions to reclaim their residence on Sternwartestrasse. Luzi first described their initial sense of alienation—"We lived as foreigners, as guests in the city in which our house stood"—but soon turned to the emotional impact of the ruinous landscape surrounding them.[50] Opening their hotel window, they peered with "excitement and curiosity" at the city before them, but the moment quickly turned sober:

> Before us stood the facade of the Vienna Staatsoper. If one hadn't known that the building was entirely burnt out inside, one might have expected to find a performance that evening in a festive brightly-lit house. Erich, whose heart hung heavy on the old opera house, turned away from it, shaking his head and with tears in his eyes.[51]

The overall sensation during their stay was that of a "ghostly return." "It was a 'dead city,'" Luzi recalled. "All of our relatives and nearly all of our friends had left or been killed."[52]

Also absent was the supportive circle that Korngold had enjoyed as a young prodigy, an emotional realization that caused existential distress for the composer. Upon leaving Vienna, the Korngolds drove through the "horrifically destroyed" landscape of Germany in order to visit with Ludwig and Willy Strecker at Schott's headquarters in Mainz. Despite a mutual exchange of sympathy and affection, the publishers' overall lack of interest in his current work struck the composer as a "symptom of the times" that made him feel like a victim.[53] "In the coming decades, I will no doubt be entirely erased from memory," he lamented to a friend in 1950. "One cannot fill a theater with the forgotten, the impoverished, and the emigrants."[54] After his return to Los Angeles in 1951, he would describe his sense of betrayal in the destructive language of the age: "What a rotten atomic world!"[55]

During Korngold's time in Europe, he sketched portions of his Symphony in F-sharp, but it was only in the relative peace of Hollywood that he found the necessary time to complete it.[56] The work consists of four movements—an opening Moderato; a Scherzo with Trio; an Adagio; and a Finale—scored for large orchestra with piano, celesta, and harp. In an unpublished commentary, Korngold sought to distance the work from any wartime associations. "[The] new symphony [is] a work of pure, absolute music with no program whatsoever," he contended, rejecting any connection to worldly events.[57] But as Daniel Chua recently argued, asserting the absolute blankness of a work is ultimately "an aesthetic strategy that claims for music the status of autonomy" while simultaneously signaling that it is "full of meaning" and "vacant signs of freedom" that can "inevitably assume multiple and contradictory meanings."[58] Lydia

Goehr similarly identifies the problem of inherent worldliness as the primary paradox of music from which one would typically deny any sort of extra-musical significance: "It expresses conflict because, while it assert[s] itself as a free or alternative means of expression, it would always also reflect through its materials the society that had given rise to it."[59]

This last point is particularly relevant to Korngold's symphony, given the amount of material borrowed from his earlier compositions that was integrated into the work. Robbert van der Lek and Mick Swithinbank note that Korngold's practice of reusing film music in his postwar concert music was well established by the time he began composing the symphony in earnest. In both his Violin Concerto and the Symphonic Serenade (1947–48), he had used excerpts from his film scores that could easily be converted into Classical and Romantic models.[60] But in the Symphony in F-sharp Korngold strove for a greater level of technical sophistication and therefore no longer restricted himself to quotations from a single film. Rather, he freely integrated material from various films into synergistic compositional blocks.[61] The Adagio is a case in point: it borrows heavily from scores for *Anthony Adverse* (1936), *Captain Blood* (1935), and *The Private Lives of Elizabeth and Essex* (1939), but the excerpts do not appear as discrete musical blocks. Instead, Korngold allows their material to overlap or revises them to create new musical effects from the original material.[62] The final product therefore does not resemble simplistic "arrangements in the sense of 'potpourris' or 'medleys'" but rather new conceptions that are "formally well-wrought . . . from works by a composer who was unable to forget a glorious past."[63]

The language Korngold used to portray both his state of mind and the symphony when writing to close associates suggests that he was also unable to forget the ruinous past. As he was finishing the symphony, he wrote to Joseph Marx with bitterness about his most recent encounters in Vienna: "My longing for the old homeland is hardly ardent after the awful experiences of my most recent stay."[64] In another unaddressed letter, the language of ruin becomes transferred to the musical content of the symphony itself. He describes the Scherzo as "a ghost-like, rapidly moving orchestra piece, twice interrupted: first by a heroic second theme in the horns and then by a calm and peaceful trio, somewhat like a lullaby."[65] The depiction of the opening theme as "ghost-like" seems odd at first, given its insistent tempo and character, unless one interprets Korngold's explanation more holistically: the movement is ghostly in that it is visited by two musical specters with uncomfortable associations to the wartime past, a fragment from his American exile and a reference to Arnold Schoenberg's Viennese period.

The first interruption, a heroic theme in the horns, derives from Korngold's film score for *Juarez* (1939), completed just before the outbreak of the Second World War. In this regard, one might read it as a ruin from his Hollywood repertory—an exilic fragment whose heroisms are soon dismantled by the repetitiveness of the new theme. Structurally, Korngold destabilizes the *Juarez* theme directly before the onset of the Trio, scoring its opening phrase as a *mezzo piano* solo in the first violin and flute (mm. 130–35). Weakened, it is easily overtaken by the aggressive forces of the original theme, which drive determinedly to a resolute C-major cadence. The moment is marked by a sustained silence, after which the Trio begins with the solitary entry of a solo horn on a C♯ pedal, suggesting an eerily remote harmonic realm rather than a "calm and peaceful" soundscape. Over this drone, Korngold scores a series of short phrases that wearily descend through chromatic motion, with the middle voice stretching to achieve a tension between the overall outline of a perfect sixth and the tritone relation produced in the final chord (Example 1). This thematic material also returns at the close of the movement, where Korngold subjects it to a process of exorcism similar to that which befell the *Juarez* theme earlier. After two short statements of the Trio's opening phrase, the full orchestra interrupts with an energetic rush to the final cadence, now punctuated by a blunt strike of the bass drum.

The Scherzo transmits its ruinous aesthetic not only through these processes of thematic conflict and dismantling, but also by a reference to the Viennese musical past. Generally, the Trio recalls the highly chromatic language of fin-de-siècle Vienna, but its opening recalls a specific figure and work: Arnold Schoenberg's *Verklärte Nacht* (1899). Schoenberg's piece begins with a similar drone, over which the strings slowly layer with diatonically descending sixths that repeat dirge-like throughout the opening. When the bass line first releases itself from monotony, the interval heard is also a tritone (C♯ and F) whose dissonance soon resolves back into the static pedal (Example 2). The possibility that *Verklärte Nacht* was a model for the Trio gains further weight when one considers Korngold's peculiar description of the tension-filled Trio as a "peaceful lullaby." His language intimates a nocturnal setting and the presence of a child, images that suggest some of the primary themes of Schoenberg's guiding poetic text, in which two lovers and an unborn child are transfigured by the glow of a magical night into a loving family.[66]

Many listeners in Austria certainly heard other remnants of Schoenberg's corpus in the symphony's first movement, which some reviewers freely associated with the modernist interwar period. Some identified the opening theme in Schoenbergian terms as a twelve-tone melody (despite the

Example 1. Korngold, Symphony in F-sharp, Op. 40, movement 2, Scherzo, mm. 144–46.

fact that it was not) set within a dissonant tritonal framework, while others spoke more generally about Korngold's "endeavor to achieve a modernist character" and his assimilation of "elements from the modern harmonic language" in the movement.[67] That some Viennese critics would have heard these echoes as unsettling seems likely, given their own uncomfortable role in Schoenberg's dismantling in the early 1930s. Joy Calico notes that an "organized anti-Semitic faction had torpedoed his academic career [in Vienna], and the press had regularly savaged his music as well as that of his students."[68] Soon thereafter Schoenberg secured a prestigious university position in Berlin, but he was ousted after the passage of the Civil Servant Law in April 1933, which barred Jews from holding academic positions within Germany. Left with few options, Schoenberg emigrated to the United States in 1933, where he lived until his death in 1951.[69] After the war, performances of his works became controversial political affairs in Vienna, where they complicated "hopeful signs of a return to normalcy [and] symbols of resilience and defiance."[70] Instead, his works functioned as musical ruins that reminded the public that this "Jewish native son [had been] shunned by his hometown and his music banned under the Third Reich" due to its supposed "degeneracy."[71]

Korngold's Adagio presented yet another set of uncomfortable ruins associated with his American exile and successful commercial achievements in Hollywood. Viennese reviews awkwardly sidestepped the Adagio's cinematic heritage and instead contextualized the work within a less controversial version of Austrian music history. In *Neues Österreich*, one critic labored to describe Korngold's musical genealogy as "firmly rooted in the soil of

Example 2. Arnold Schoenberg, *Verklärte Nacht*, mm. 1–6.

Vienna," the work of a "true Austrian composer" who had "remained lost in America for a time" but ultimately "found his way back to his homeland."[72] A review in *Die Furche* pointedly omitted any mention of Korngold's exile and instead highlighted the symphony's connection to the heritage of Viennese composers such as Anton Bruckner and Gustav Mahler.[73] But it was not only the Viennese press that strategically sought to whitewash Korngold's American exile from this reception history. Perhaps in order to avoid the charges of commercialism that had plagued the reception of the Violin Concerto, Korngold deliberately portrayed the Adagio as unrelated to his film corpus, writing that it was a "deeply emotional composition, which—in constant development—surges to symphonic heights of great expansion and concludes with an ecstatic 'Abgesang' (Aftersong)."[74]

Van der Lek and Swithinbank explain Korngold's parenthetical clarification of the German term *Abgesang* as a clumsy literalism that transmits the "impression of naïveté readily associated with the English of an immigrant."[75] But what if the composer had been intentional in his use of language and sought to subtly signal the Adagio's status as "music composed after"—that is, after exile, after war, after loss? In that case, the movement could be considered particularly ruinous, a symbol of both Korngold's own anxieties about his wartime corpus and the disquieting fact of his absence/reemergence in midcentury Austrian soundscapes. Moreover, the film scores from which he selected material were themselves burdened with the tragic weight of history. One hears in the scores the distinct influence of the *Ring* cycle and *Tristan und Isolde*, which comes as no surprise given Korngold's enthusiastic reverence for Wagner's operas. But his description of the Adagio as an *Abgesang* conjures up another compromised symbol: Walther's prize song from *Die Meistersinger von Nürnberg* and the opera's explicit ties to Nazi cultural propaganda.[76] Whether intended or not it is difficult, in the aftermath of the European catastrophe, to read these references as blank allusions. Their ecstatic vocabulary no longer leads optimistically to transfiguration in the manner of Isolde's *Liebestod*, but to the quickening horizon of impending ruin signaled by Korngold in the movement's ominous closing measures.

Not every reference in the work transmits a dissonant tone of hopelessness, a recognition that reflects Korngold's belief that postwar music should also strive to "uplift into the purer realm of phantasy" and bring about a vision of the future filled with "pleasure and exaltation, dedication and happiness."[77] One such pleasurable moment appears in the Finale, which reprises thematic material from the earlier movements (Example 3). It opens with a sprightly new theme that recalls the popular American wartime song "Over There," written in 1917 by George Cohan and repopularized in the 1942 film *Yankee Doodle Dandy* featuring James Cagney.[78] Its optimistic tone is confronted in a manner similar to that of the ghostly interruptions of the Scherzo, where Korngold allows the fateful opening bars of the Adagio to surface briefly (mm. 182–85) before transitioning to a restatement of the horn's angular theme from the first movement (mm. 192–98). As in the Scherzo, the challenged primary theme does not crumble under such external interruptions. Instead, the trumpets triumphantly

Example 3. Korngold, Symphony in F-sharp, Op. 40, movement 4, Finale, flute melody, mm. 5–9.

transform it into a fanfare that anticipates a quasi-recapitulation (mm. 207–73) and leads to a closing coda (beginning in measure 273).

The saturation of the movement with this lively tune could be read as Korngold's attempt to create a sense of optimism at the conclusion of the work, but the contrast between its vivacious realization and the original song's historical context (the American entry into both wars) complicates such easy reconciliations. Rather, it transmits another discursive mode associated with ruins that Robert Ginsburg identifies as the "inherent irony" created when a fragment with unsettling associations is transformed into a new aesthetic form that is "enjoyable for itself but [whose] function leaves the contrastive suggestion" of its trauma.[79] As the American-inspired theme blithely casts off the darker weight of the other citations, the ease of the encounter feels pleasurable, yet disjunctive. Its uncomfortable triumph presents itself as somewhat of a historical fiction, given the significant postwar challenges that were less facile to cast off in the political arena: the national shame of the Allied occupation of Austria (1945–55), the harsh emotional and physical aftermath of the war years, and the moral difficulty of "coming to terms" with the sins of Nazism. Through its seemingly innocent adaptation of a popular American mobilization song, the symphony, within the Austrian context, ultimately points to its own historical provocations.

The Finale's coda (mm. 280–301) provides one of the few genuine moments of peace and calm in the symphony, yet it is also concerned with ruin and reconstruction. The section reintroduces pastoral material first heard at the conclusion of the opening movement. Set in the key of E-flat and positioned at an equidistant remove from either pole of the central tritone (C–F#), Korngold's music creates a landscape filled with warm open fifths in the strings and rising-fourth motives in the overlapping winds (Example 4). The moment is reminiscent of two American models. Faint echoes of "Over There" can still be heard in the melodic material,

Example 4. Korngold, Symphony in F-sharp, Op. 40, movement 4, Finale, winds, mm. 280–91.

Example 5. Copland, *Appalachian Spring*, 1945, mm. 9–21.

but the overall setting evokes the opening of Aaron Copland's score for *Appalachian Spring* (1944–45), a Martha Graham ballet in which a citizen and his wife rebuild their home after the American Civil War (Example 5). Korngold presents the allusion without any ironic touches, and as such he conjures up the retrospective tone of Copland's original, which Elizabeth Bergman Crist describes as singing of "sadness of death before rebirth" and the "hope for a better peace after a bitter war."[80]

Although the creation of a nostalgic soundscape can create a "certain reflective distance from the past that can inform the construction of new ones," such remove does not ensure that the symphony ends on a comforting note.[81] As Crist notes with regard to *Appalachian Spring*, reconstruction necessarily recalls the moment of ruin that necessitated the rebuilding; as such, the wartime ballet "captured the anxiety of individuals and their community involved in a war" and was as much about what had happened as it was about "what might have been and what might yet be."[82] And just as *Appalachian Spring* was not without its musical "snakes in the garden"—the accumulating fourths that ultimately create a "delicate yet substantial dissonance that imbues the opening with a luminous tension"—Korngold also chose to end his symphony on conflicted terms.[83] A menacing *pesante* motive ushers in a fragment of the first movement's Schoenbergian theme, this time interrupted by a final statement of "Over There" that soars to the final cadence in F-sharp major. But the triumphant conclusion seems misplaced if not false, given everything that has preceded it. As such, it functions less as a firm resolution and more as a meditation on the persistence of trauma, the challenges of reconstruction, and the entanglement of Austrian and American historical memory in the postwar period.

In his essay "Layered Time," Amir Eshel writes that "the significant ruins of our time indicate both the . . . catastrophic and the fact that humans—weak and restricted as we might be—are still agents of our histories."[84] For ruins do not just represent material history, but also a "constructed relationship to questions of history, and its importance in the creation of the present."[85] The concern of the reconstructionist—or in this case, the composer who builds works from musical fragments with traumatic cultural significance—is therefore "clearly with posterity, with the afterlife, so to speak, of . . . individual lives" and perhaps also a "lament for his own frustrated hopes."[86] Edward Said contends that exiles like Korngold often felt "an urgent need to reconstitute their broken lives" and "reassemble an identity out of the refractions and discontinuities of exile."[87] As noted in the opening of this essay, Korngold had hoped that his postwar compositions would become musical bridges—pieces that would heal the geographic and psychological fractures that defined his own traumatized sense of identity.[88] But such an integrative healing never came to be, and instead postwar works like the Symphony in F-sharp are revealed as expressive sites of emotional ruin rather than sturdy paths back to a supposed golden age. As such, their critical failures stand as a testament to the devastation wrought by the war on Jewish émigrés such as Korngold, demonstrating that "more often exile destroys talent, or it means the loss of the environment that nourished the talent morally, socially, and physically."[89]

Precariously suspended between the past and the present and unable to assimilate fully into context aesthetically and/or politically, Korngold's postwar works hover uncomfortably between two worlds and yet belong fully to neither. They inhabit a specific ruinous moment in modernism that Matt Foley describes as "haunted precisely because the subject is left in-between choices, out of joint, still reeling from the . . . scars of loss."[90] Conceived in this awkward position, we might therefore understand the Symphony in F-sharp not as a compositional failure, but as a work of profound significance in its attempt to articulate the "unhealable rift forced between a human being and a native place, between the self and its true home"; its ruins speak of an "essential sadness [that] can never be surmounted" and are "permanently underlined by the loss of something left behind forever."[91] For, as the German intellectual Henry Pachter suggested in the most ruinous of terms, exiles like Korngold "were writing about ghosts, writing for ghosts, and gradually becoming ghosts."[92] Perhaps it was this quality that the conductor Dimitri Mitropoulous sensed in 1959, two years after Korngold's death and only a year before his own passing, when he declared the Symphony in F-sharp to be "the perfect modern work."[93]

NOTES

I am grateful to the following individuals for conversations that helped me conceptualize the framework for this essay: Abby Anderton, Martha Sprigge, Emily Richmond Pollock, Jessica Schwartz, Ariana Philips-Hutton, Tekla Babyak, and Lily Hirsch. All translations from the original German are mine.

1. Ross Parmenter, "He's Fed Up with Music for Films," *New York Times*, 27 October 1946, 69.

2. Bryan Gilliam, "A Viennese Opera Composer in Hollywood: Korngold's Double Exile in America," in *Driven into Paradise: The Musical Migration from Nazi Germany to the United States*, ed. Reinhold Brinkmann and Christoph Wolff (Berkeley: University of California Press, 1999), 223–42, at 228.

3. The film was produced by Warner Bros. and based on the French play *Monsieur Lamberthier* by Louis Verneuil. It starred Bette Davis (pianist), Paul Henreid (cellist), and Claude Rains (composer).

4. The performance was conducted by Henry Svedrofsky. See Korngold, Concerto in C Major for Cello, OREL Foundation, http://orelfoundation.org/works/worksDetails/Concerto_in_C-major_for_cello_and_orchestra2/.

5. Olin Downes, "Heifetz Features Work by Korngold: Violinist Introduces Concerto as Philharmonic Soloist—Efrem Kurtz Conducts," *New York Times*, 28 March 1947, 27.

6. Jessica Duchen, *Erich Wolfgang Korngold* (London: Phaidon, 1996), 211.

7. Parmenter, "He's Fed Up With Music For Films," 69.

8. Downes, "Heifetz Features Work by Korngold," 27.

9. Such a critique would be consistent with other criticisms levied by Downes against art music that drew too heavily from filmic conventions. See, for example, his critique of Schoenberg's *A Survivor from Warsaw* in Downes, "Schoenberg Work Is Presented Here," *New York Times*, 14 April 1950.

10. Parmenter, "He's Fed Up With Music For Films," 69. In a well-known instance, Korngold used the Nazi ban on his work to promote its contemporary value within postwar Vienna. As Brendan Carroll writes about the *Symphonic Serenade* (1947), "Furtwängler was under attack for his supposed Nazi sympathies. . . . Korngold [suggested] that it might be politically expedient for him to conduct a new composition 'by a Jew.' . . . This slightly devious tactic worked perfectly. Furtwängler wrote back at once . . . and urgently requested a score." Carroll, *The Last Prodigy: A Biography of Erich Wolfgang Korngold* (Portland, OR: Amadeus Press, 1997), 337.

11. Duchen, *Erich Wolfgang Korngold*, 212. As Andreas Giger explains, "The operas of Korngold, which had shown declining popularity before the war, could not have been ideal choices to conjure up the State Opera's glorious past. It therefore comes as no surprise that the Volksoper prepared the Viennese premiere of *Die Kathrin* with little enthusiasm and consequently without success." Giger, "A Matter of Principle: The Consequences of Korngold's Career," *Journal of Musicology* 16/4 (1998): 545–64, at 563.

12. Korngold to Dr. Hilbert, 2 November 1950, in *Dear Papa, How Is You?: Das Leben Erich Wolfgang Korngolds in Briefen*, ed. Lis Malina (Vienna: Mandelbaum Verlag, 2017), 262. See also Luzi Korngold, *Erich Wolfgang Korngold: Ein Lebensbild* (Vienna: Verlag Elisabeth Lafite, and Österreichischer Bundesverlag für Unterricht, Wissenschaft und Kunst, 1967), 95; and Carroll, *The Last Prodigy*, 346. For a discussion of Schott's political affiliations during and after the war, see Kim H. Kowalke, "Dancing with the Devil: Publishing Modern Music in the Third Reich," *Modernism/Modernity* 8/1 (2001): 1–41.

13. Carroll notes that earlier sketches for the main theme of the first movement appear on a score dated 1919 and conjectures that the theme was "first intended for

another composition and then rescued thirty years later for his Symphony in F-Sharp." Carroll, *The Last Prodigy*, 347.

14. Korngold, in ibid., 348.

15. Korngold, as cited in Brendan Carroll, *Erich Wolfgang Korngold, 1897–1957: His Life and Works* (Paisley, GB: Wifion Books, 1987), 14.

16. Michael Haas, *Forbidden Music: The Jewish Composers Banned by the Nazis* (New Haven: Yale University Press, 2013), 295. Haas notes that "the letters from [their] offices . . . make depressing reading."

17. Luzi Korngold, *Erich Wolfgang Korngold*, 97.

18. Haas, *Forbidden Music*, 294.

19. Lotte Lenya reported upon her return to Vienna in 1955: "By now we're used to the rubble, which they clean up religiously and indefatigably. What a determination to get on top again! But you can't find a single Nazi [here] today. It's as if there weren't any." See David Farneth, ed., *Lenya, the Legend: A Pictorial Autobiography* (New York: Overlook Press, 1998), 142.

20. Carroll, *Erich Wolfgang Korngold*, 14.

21. Ibid., 13.

22. Gilliam, "A Viennese Opera Composer in America," 228; see also Duchen, *Erich Wolfgang Korngold*, 201.

23. Stephen Downes, "Modernism in European Music," in *The Modernist World*, ed. Stephen Ross and Allana C. Lindgren (London: Routledge, 2015), 347–55, at 353.

24. Haas, *Forbidden Music*, 286.

25. Michael Haas, "The False Myths and True Genius of Erich Wolfgang Korngold," http://www.forbiddenmuisc.org; Giger, "A Matter of Principle," 556–59; and Brendan Carroll, "The Background of Korngold's Magnum Opus *Das Wunder der Heliane*," liner notes to *Korngold: Das Wunder der Heliane*, Radio Symphony Orchester Merlin, cond. John Mauceri, Decca 436 636-2 (1993), 26.

26. Here I wish to make a distinction between a "rubble aesthetic" and a "ruin aesthetic." Whereas rubble suggests the complete destruction or transformation of a whole into pieces that are almost unrecognizable, I contend that a ruin continues to possess recognizable forms or gestures that one can identify as a larger fragment from the past. Rubble is material to be cleared away, whereas a ruin requires further deliberation as to whether it is still useful. For excellent musicological work on the subject, see Abby Anderton, "Hearing Democracy in the Ruins of Hitler's Reich: American Musicians in Postwar Germany," *Comparative Critical Studies* 13/2 (2016): 215–31.

27. Andreas Huyssen, "Authentic Ruins: Products of Modernity," in *Ruins of Modernity*, ed. Julia Hell and Andreas Schönle (Durham, NC: Duke University Press, 2010), 17–28, at 19.

28. Ibid., 21; and Amir Eshel, "Layered Time: Ruins as Shattered Past, Ruins as Hope in Israeli and German Landscapes and Literature," in *Ruins of Modernity*, ed. Hell and Schönle,133–50, at 135.

29. Eshel, "Layered Time," 135. Adorno would recognize a similar modern aesthetic in the "hidden" references to Romanticism found in Berg's Violin Concerto: "Things that are modern do not just sally forth in advance of their time. They also recall things forgotten: they control the anachronistic reserves which have been left behind and which have not yet been exhausted." Theodor Adorno, *Quasi una Fantasia*, trans. Rodney Livingstone (London: Verso, 1992), 216. Berg's Violin Concerto was written in 1935 and bore the following inscription: "To the memory of an angel."

30. Korngold, "Faith in Music!," foreword to Ulric Devaré, *Faith in Music* (New York: Comet Press, 1958), viii.

31. "Vienna State Opera: History," http://www.wiener-staatsoper.at. The sets and props for nearly 120 opera productions and nearly 150,000 costumes were entirely destroyed in the blaze.

32. Jeffrey Diefendorf, "Vienna in Ruins," *Planning Perspectives* 8/1 (1993): 1–19, at 3.

33. John Dos Passos, "Vienna: Broken City," *Life*, 4 March 1946. See also Bernhard Wenzl, "An American in Allied-Occupied Austria: John Dos Passos Reports on 'The Vienna Frontier,'" in *Austria and America: Twentieth-Century Cross-Cultural Encounters*, ed. Joshua Parker and Ralph J. Poole (Zurich: LIT Verlag, 2017), 73–80, at 77. The description is similar to reports from Berlin, such as this one by British officer Richard Brett-Smith: "Amid the sour wreckage of a spotted city this music of a sweet and nostalgic nature was often to be heard." Brett-Smith, *Berlin '45: The Grey City* (New York: St. Martin's Press, 1967), 107. I am grateful to Abby Anderton for this specific reference.

34. Siobhan Craig, "*The Third Man* and the Wilder Side of Rubble," *Quarterly Review of Film and Video* 27 (2010): 193–209, at 202.

35. Bohlman refers to this symbolic reemergence as the "represence" of Jewish music in postwar Germany. For a theoretical discussion of "represence," see Philip Bohlman, "The Beginning of the End," in *Dislocated Memories: Jews, Music, and Postwar German Culture*, ed. Tina Frühauf and Lily E. Hirsch (New York: Oxford University Press, 2014), 265–76.

36. Elizabeth Anthony, "The First Returnees: Holocaust Survivors in Vienna in the Immediate Postwar Period," in *Lessons and Legacies XII: New Directions in Holocaust Research and Education*, ed. Wendy Lower and Lauren Faulkner Rossi (Evanston, IL: Northwestern University Press, 2017), 232.

37. Robert Pick, "The Vienna of the Departed: The Tale the Old Cemetery Tells," *Commentary* 16/2 (August, 1953): 153–57, at 153 and 154.

38. Diefendorf, "Vienna in Ruins," 3–4, 1.

39. Ibid., 10.

40. Ibid., 11. As Siobhan Craig notes, the visual aesthetics of Leni Riefenstahl and Albert Speer were "inescapable phantoms" in the period. "The trace of their unique and monstrous vision of the Nazi city necessarily permeated any later representations of Berlin and Vienna, the former capitals of Nazism." Craig, "*The Third Man*," 202.

41. Karl Heinrich Brunner, "Die Aufgabe der neuen Stadtplanung für Wien," as cited in Diefendorf, "Vienna in Ruins," 12. Brunner was appointed head of the city's planning department in 1948. He had left Vienna in 1929 to work on urban planning in Latin America and was therefore untainted by Nazi associations.

42. Diefendorf, "Vienna in Ruins," 12, 16.

43. Dorothy Lamb Crawford, *A Windfall of Musicians: Hitler's Emigrés and Exiles in Southern California* (New Haven: Yale University Press, 2009), 179.

44. Korngold, as cited in Luzi Korngold, *Erich Wolfgang Korngold*, 8.

45. Luzi Korngold to Helene Thimig-Reinhardt, 16 June 1949, reprinted in Malina, *Dear Papa How Is You?*, 251.

46. Luzi Korngold, *Erich Wolfgang Korngold*, 89.

47. Ibid., 89.

48. Ibid., 90. Luzi Korngold uses the word *vegetierte* to describe the families, suggesting both their suspension between life and death (a vegetative state) and their struggle to eke out a bare existence. Ebensee is located sixteen kilometers from Gmunden, at the southern tip of the Alpen lake. The concentration camp was liberated on May 6, 1945 and converted into a DP camp that mostly held Polish and Jewish peoples.

49. Ibid.
50. Ibid.
51. Ibid.
52. Ibid.
53. Ibid., 95.

54. Korngold to Dr. Hilbert, 2 November 1950, in Malina, *Dear Papa*, 262. Luzi would recall a moment that buoyed the composer's spirits right before their departure: As they

were having a drink at an establishment in Gmunden, a young man yelled to his girlfriend, "Quick! Sing *Die tote Stadt*.... That was Korngold! Hey waiter, that was Mr. Korngold!" See Luzi Korngold to Helene Thimig, 5 April 1951, in Malina, *Dear Papa*, 264.

55. Korngold to Marcel Prawy, 3 March 1953, in ibid., 268.

56. Brendan Carroll notes that Korngold threw himself into the project in order to "dispel his depression" brought on by his return to Vienna (*Last Prodigy*, 346). Luzi describes the process as filled with so much "passion and intensity" that the earliest drafts of the first two movements were finished quickly after their return to Europe (Luzi Korngold, *Erich Wolfgang Korngold*, 92).

57. Korngold, unpublished commentary intended for the aborted 1955 American premiere, as cited in Carroll, *The Last Prodigy*, 348.

58. Daniel K. L. Chua, "Beethoven Going Blank," *Journal of Musicology* 31/3 (2014): 299–300.

59. Lydia Goehr, *The Quest for Voice: On Music, Politics and the Limits of Philosophy* (Berkeley: University of California Press, 1998), 12.

60. Robbert van der Lek and Mick Swithinbank, "Concert Music as Reused Film Music: E. W. Korngold's Self-Arrangements," *Acta Musicologica* 66/2 (1994): 78–112, at 83.

61. Ibid., 104.

62. Ibid., 104–9.

63. Ibid., 110–11.

64. Korngold to Joseph Marx, 10 September 1952, in Malina, *Dear Papa How Is You?*, 266.

65. Korngold, unaddressed letter, n.d., Korngold Collection, Library of Congress, as cited in van der Lek and Swithinbank, "Concert Music as Reused Film Music," 102n27.

66. Schoenberg based his chamber work on a poem by Richard Dehmel, from "Weib und Welt." The verse reads: "Let the child you have conceived be no burden to your soul. O see, how brightly the universe gleams! . . . This will transfigure the other's child; you will bear it for me, from me; you have brought radiance on me, you have made me a child myself." Translation by Lionel Salter.

67. Giselher Schubert, "Die Sinfonie in Fis: Korngold und das Problem des Sinfonischen in der Orchestermusik seiner Zeit," in *Erich Wolfgang Korngold: Das Wunderkind der Moderne oder letzter Romantiker?*, ed. Arne Stollberg (Munich: Richard Boorberg, 2008), 87–100, at 89. See also Helmut Pöllman, *Erich Wolfgang Korngold: Aspekte seines Schaffens* (Mainz: Schott, 1998), 154. Carroll notes it is likely that this melody was written in 1919, well before Schoenberg's "discovery" of the twelve-tone technique, but its use of extended and angular chromaticism recalls the experimentation of the interwar period.

68. Joy Calico, *Arnold Schoenberg's "A Survivor from Warsaw" in Postwar Europe* (Berkeley: University of California Press, 2014), 41.

69. The Korngolds and Schoenbergs had long been acquaintances from their time in Vienna. Erich had been friends with Getrude, Schoenberg's daughter, when he was growing up. Though never close, the two families kept friendly relations during their time in Hollywood, sending congratulatory notes for birthdays and condolences in times of mourning.

70. Calico, *Arnold Schoenberg's "A Survivor from Warsaw,"* 47–48.

71. Ibid., 42.

72. Review of the Symphony in F-sharp, *Neues Österreich*, 20 October 1954, cited in Schubert, "Die Sinfonie in Fis," 90n9.

73. Review of the Symphony in F-sharp, *Die Furche*, 6 November 1954, cited in ibid., 89n9.

74. Korngold, unaddressed letter, n.d., Korngold Collection, Library of Congress, as cited in van der Lek and Swithinbank, "Concert Music as Reused Film Music," 102n27.

75. Ibid., 108.

76. See Thomas S. Grey, "Wagner's *Die Meistersinger* as National Opera (1868–1945)," in *Music and German National History*, ed. Celia Applegate and Pamela Potter (Chicago: University of Chicago Press, 2002), 78–104; and David B. Dennis, "'The Most German of All German Operas': *Die Meistersinger* Through the Lens of the Third Reich," in *Wagner's "Meistersinger": Performance, History, Representation*, ed. Nicholas Vazsonyi (Rochester, NY: University of Rochester Press, 2004), 98–119.

77. Korngold foreword to Devaré, *Faith in Music*, viii.

78. Giselher Schubert identifies that Korngold's most direct transcription of the song appears in the lower register instruments in mm. 83–86, at which point its status as a model for the first theme becomes retrospectively clear. See Schubert, "Die Sinfonie in Fis," 97.

79. Robert Ginsburg, *The Aesthetics of Ruins* (New York: Rodopi, 2004), 60.

80. Elisabeth Bergman Crist, *Music for the Common Man* (New York: Oxford University Press, 2005), 165, 166.

81. Sophie Thomas, "Assembling History: Fragments and Ruins," *European Romantic Review* 14/2 (2003): 177–86, at 182.

82. Crist, *Music for the Common Man*, 167.

83. Ibid., 172. Korngold's pastoral in E-flat is also in tritonal relation with Copland's *Appalachian Spring*, which is in the key of A major.

84. Eshel, "Layered Time," 135.

85. Thomas, "Assembling History," 181.

86. Ibid., 184.

87. Edward W. Said, "Reflections on Exile," in *Reflections on Exile and Other Essays* (Cambridge, MA: Harvard University Press, 2000), 173–86, at 177 and 179.

88. The terminologies of writing about exile culture are fraught with debate and have been well treated in musicological literature on the subject. See, for example, David Josephson, *Torn Between Cultures: A Life of Kathie Meyer-Baer* (Hillsdale, NY: Pendragon Press, 2012), 85–89; Hermann Danuser, "Composers in Exile: The Question of Musical Identity," in *Driven into Paradise*, ed. Brinkmann and Wolff, 155–71; and Stephen Hinton, "Hindemith and Weill: Cases of 'Inner' and 'Outer' Direction," in ibid., 261–78.

89. Henry Pachter, "On Being an Exile," in *The Legacy of the German Refugee Intellectuals*, ed. Robert Boyers (New York: Schocken Books, 1972), 17.

90. Matt Foley, *Haunting Modernisms: Ghostly Aesthetics, Mourning, and Spectral Resistance Fantasies in Literary Modernism* (Cham, Switz.: Palgrave Macmillan, 2017), 20.

91. Said, "Reflections on Exile," 173.

92. Pachter, "On Being an Exile," 19.

93. Nicholas Slonimsky, liner notes to *Erich Wolfgang Korngold: Symphony in F-Sharp, Op. 40*, Munich Philharmonic Orchestra, cond. Rudolf Kempe, RCA Red Seal, ARL 1-0443 (1974). I am not the first to assert that Korngold's symphony was modern in its aesthetic. Giselher Schubert makes a similar claim, connecting the work to a branch of modernism derived from the neoclassicism and "New Objectivity" of the 1920s as well as to a specific Viennese modernity exhibited by composers such as Gustav Mahler. See Schubert, "Die Sinfonie in Fis," 94–95.

Documents

Recollections of Zemlinsky from My Years of Study

ERICH WOLFGANG KORNGOLD
TRANSLATED BY
ELISABETH STAAK AND DAVID BRODBECK
INTRODUCED AND ANNOTATED
BY DAVID BRODBECK

The Austrian composer and conductor Alexander Zemlinsky (1871–1942) enjoyed an outstanding reputation as a private music teacher in late Habsburg Vienna. He is perhaps best remembered in this capacity for the counterpoint instruction he gave to his future brother-in-law Arnold Schoenberg. For a brief time, beginning in 1900, Zemlinsky taught Alma Schindler, with whom he had a love affair in the period before she began the relationship that would lead, in March 1902, to her marriage to Gustav Mahler. Among the last—and certainly the most precocious—of Zemlinsky's Viennese students was Erich Wolfgang Korngold, whose lessons were initiated in 1908 and continued for upward of two years until Zemlinsky departed Vienna to become the music director of Prague's New German Theater. Zemlinsky later recalled: "[Erich] began his tuition with me by practicing scales, and after one year he was already playing his first Beethoven sonata. Almost at the same time, he mastered harmony, and soon after this I began an analysis of form with him. He grasped all these things with uncanny speed, and in the second year we were analyzing Bach motets and such, and I was able to communicate with him as with a musician who had already learned all these things, but in fact much better, since an intuitive grasp is something quite different from theoretical knowledge. He was then eleven years old, child-like, warmhearted, and enthusiastic."[1] Korngold's affectionate recollection of his lessons with Zemlinsky, and of the man himself, appeared in 1921 in Prague's leading German-language music journal, *Der Auftakt*.[2] Translated excerpts have been published elsewhere, but the recollection below appears for the first time in a complete English translation.[3] All endnotes are editorial.

Recollections of Zemlinsky from My Years of Study

It was Gustav Mahler who advised my father to win over Alexander von Zemlinsky for my further musical education. I was eleven years old then and had been studying counterpoint under Professor Robert Fuchs for about two years.[4]

In addition to teaching me counterpoint, Zemlinsky casually took me through this or that movement, discussing matters of form and part writing, as well as piano playing, which I had been neglecting. It was a delightful education, free from all methodical restrictions, in which Zemlinsky appeared to be testing the limits of what to expect of me, how much of the usual and common course of study he could discard, be it simple or complex.

Soon my young imagination was marked by the fascinating imprint of this teacher—his fabulous musicality, the originality of his opinions and beliefs, the subtle irony of communication and conversation that emanated from this absolute authority who had captivated my heart. By the time Zemlinsky started teaching me, I had already composed, among other things, *Der Schneemann* for piano. Zemlinsky did not ask for my compositions and I did not show them to him. (When I included a set of passacaglia variations on a chordal theme he had given to me as a composition exercise as the finale of a sonata in D minor, this was done on the suggestion of Gustav Mahler, who, in 1909, had asked me to play this sonata and the variations.)[5]

On the other hand, Zemlinsky would not show me anything he was writing, no matter how often I begged him. "You are very hard to please," he remarked jokingly.

Crucial for my entire development and musical understanding of what you would call "modernism," toward which I was instinctively drawn from the start, was Zemlinsky's strict logic as applied to harmony, whether the freedom and boldness of chordal construction or the pursuit of remote pitch relationships among tones or Zemlinsky's particular technique of "delayed resolution." A natural and consequential forward movement of one tone—Zemlinsky's underlying principle—grants freedom to the next; he was especially strict about the logical sequencing of the bass line. Thus I owe Zemlinsky everything I learned about modern part writing and harmony, in particular authenticity rather than arbitrariness. For Zemlinsky, who I later realized was going through an artistic crisis of self-assertion against the new and enticing radical theories of his adored brother-in-law Arnold Schoenberg, it was basically impossible to hold back the genuine tonal feel. A chord "dragged" him, as he liked to say, from one pitch to the next.

Der Komponist des „Schneemann" erhält ein Standbild vor dem Hofoperntheater.

Figure 1. Caricature of the thirteen-year-old Erich as *The Snowman* (1910).

Back in 1910, he composed arrangements for *Kleider machen Leute*, an underappreciated, thoughtful opera with an enchanting, peculiar harmony and melodiousness influenced by Schoenberg's fourths and recent French music. As I studied this opera, I immediately grew very fond of it. I could not have been more pleased upon learning recently from Zemlinsky that he is at work on a revision that will make the opera theatrically effective. I am convinced that the work—which ranks high above contemporary production in inventiveness, originality, and refined, spirited technique—promises to be a huge success.[6]

After about a year and a half, Zemlinsky started to teach me orchestration. He spent little time on a general introduction to each instrument's nature and character, instead letting me jump into the deep end by assigning me the orchestration of Schubert lieder and piano movements by Beethoven. As chance had it, my composition *Der Schneemann*—played by me at the piano in April 1910 during a charity event at the governor's house, at the initiative of the publisher (Universal Edition), following a remark from the old Kaiser[7] (and despite the publishing contract) that it was now the state's property—had to be handed over to the Vienna Court Opera for a performance on October 4, 1910 (the Kaiser's birthday). At the request of Universal Edition, Zemlinsky took on the orchestration, parts of which were also introduced into my lessons, thus allowing me an excellent opportunity to see him at work firsthand.[8] An orchestration of my piano composition "Sieben Märchenbilder" (Seven Fairy-Tale Images) brought an end to my study of instrumentation technique, since in the summer of 1910 Zemlinsky left Vienna for a job in Prague, in whose music scene he would play such an important role.[9]

Thus I lost my adored and beloved teacher way too early—I was barely thirteen. It was in that same year of 1910, before the performance of *Der Schneemann*, that I had composed my Trio in D Major, which would become my official Opus 1, as well as the already mentioned "Märchenbilder" that became Opus 3 and a sonata for piano in E major that became Opus 2, the last of which I later dedicated to Zemlinsky. Though it was composed during the time he was teaching me, he would first learn about it through its publication and dedication. As early as summer break of 1911 I dared to work on the orchestration of my *Dramatic Overture*, Op. 4.

At this point, I cannot help but mention a funny incident. After I had finished working on that overture, my loyal foes and the envious—who at that time were of no small number (God be praised!)—had nothing better to do than credit the orchestration to Zemlinsky. You can imagine how sweet it felt when I arrived in Prague to see the piece performed with Zemlinsky conducting, and he asked me, "Well, Erich tell me honestly, did you really orchestrate this yourself?" A great sense of accomplishment for the student who had studied orchestration for only half a year, certainly, but an even greater one for Zemlinsky, the teacher!

How often have I complained, and complain still today, that my time with Zemlinsky was cut short by his departure for Prague! I had lost the most ideal teacher, the most compelling musical inspiration, the role model and paragon of my young years, but Vienna too had lost its most powerful musician. It is worth seriously considering whether the development of the gifted, young musical generation of Vienna might not have avoided some miscues and taken a better, sounder direction if only Zemlinsky had stayed, not to mention the influence exerted in the other direction, upon himself as an inventive musician.

Some have used malice in an attempt to undermine my relationship with Zemlinsky. Despite several such experiences, I am steadfast in my grateful adoration of Zemlinsky: teacher, conductor, and creator.

NOTES

1. Quoted in translation in Brendan G. Carroll, *The Last Prodigy: A Biography of Erich Wolfgang Korngold* (Portland, OR: Amadeus Press, 1997), 39.

2. Erich Korngold, "Erinnerungen an Zemlinsky aus meiner Lehrzeit," *Der Auftakt* 1/14–15 (1921): 230–32.

3. See, for example, Carroll, *The Last Prodigy,* 48–50; and Lorraine Gorrell, *Discordant Melody: Alexander Zemlinsky, His Songs, and the Second Viennese School* (Westport, CT, and London: Greenwood Press, 2002), 33–34.

4. The Austrian composer Robert Fuchs (1847–1927) was a well-known teacher of music theory at the Vienna Conservatory. There his students included, among other notables, Mahler, Franz Schmidt, Franz Schreker, Jean Sibelius, Hugo Wolf, and Zemlinsky. Erich was ten years old when, in 1907, Mahler recommended Zemlinsky as his teacher; he had turned eleven by the time the lessons with Zemlinsky commenced.

5. The Piano Sonata in D Minor, begun in 1908, was completed and first published privately the following year. See "Korngold Father and Son in Vienna's Prewar Public Eye" elsewhere in this volume.

6. Zemlinsky composed his comic opera *Kleider machen Leute* to a libretto by Leo Feld adapted from a novella by Gottfried Keller. Begun in 1907 and completed two years later, the work was given its premiere at the Vienna Volksoper under the composer's direction on December 2, 1910. It seems likely that young Erich would have been in attendance. For his father's review, see Julius Korngold, "Volksoper," *Neue freie Presse,* 7 December 1910. In 1921 Zemlinsky undertook a revision with an eye toward productions in Prague and Munich.

7. The late, long-reigning Austro-Hungarian monarch Franz Joseph I (1830–1916).

8. See the brief discussion in "Korngold Father and Son in Vienna's Prewar Public Eye."

9. Zemlinsky in fact remained in his position as a Kapellmeister at the Vienna Volksoper through the end of the 1910–11 season. Exactly when Erich's lessons ended, however, remains uncertain.

Notes for an Interview

ERICH WOLFGANG KORNGOLD
TRANSLATED BY ELISABETH STAAK
EDITED AND INTRODUCED BY KEVIN C. KARNES

Among thousands of documents preserved in the Korngold Collection of the Library of Congress are two typescript pages labeled, in an unknown hand, "Notes for interview" (*sic*), to which the same writer appended the provisional date of 1950, flagged with a manuscript question mark.[1] The document appears to record snippets of a conversation already in progress between the composer and an unidentified other: it opens with suspension points and is studded with them throughout, alternating with fragments of text that range in length from complete sentences to just four or five German words. Nowhere is the interviewer named or is the slightest hint at a location provided. Indeed, it is not even clear if the interview ever took place at all, or if the document records instead an imagined exchange between Korngold and an ideal interlocutor, perhaps in a kind of typed rehearsal for a conversation he anticipated upon his return to Austria. (Even his parenthetical notes indicating where recorded examples are to be played relay indecision, sometimes followed by one or even two question marks.) For all of its ambiguity, however, this curious document is invaluable, for it records what are probably Korngold's most extensive surviving statements on the concert and operatic music composed by his contemporaries, and of the sounds of avant-garde modernism, with which his own music was widely contrasted.

Korngold had given interviews before, but they had almost always focused narrowly on whatever projects he was working on at the time. He seems to have been reluctant to share his opinions about the music of contemporary composers, going only so far as to distance himself from musical modernism in a general way. "In no way does he consider himself to be a 'modern' composer," reported a Viennese interviewer in 1919. "Even Richard Strauss, [Korngold] says, told him once that he didn't know what people actually meant when they spoke of the 'modernity' of an artwork."[2] In contrast, in "Notes for an Interview," Korngold shares his unvarnished opinions of the music of Debussy and Berg, Wagner and Stravinsky, and even Arnold Schoenberg, with whom he socialized in California. He also reflects on what he found to be lacking in too much of contemporary music as a whole, and about what he felt his own compositions offered as an alternative.

Though provisionally dated 1950, Korngold's remarks might hint at earlier origins, for nowhere in "Notes" does he mention his final opera, *Die Kathrin*. In the document, he discusses or mentions *Violanta*, *Die tote Stadt*, and *Das Wunder der Heliane*, but not *Die Kathrin*, which by all accounts was at the front of his mind for nearly two decades beginning in the early 1930s. He began composing the opera in 1932, and his wife Luzi recalls that he worked single-mindedly on it during their visits to Austria from 1935 to 1938.[3] Even after its belated premiere in Stockholm in 1939, the composer remained focused on the work, dreaming of a performance in the United States during the war years and arranging for what would turn out to be a disappointing Austrian performance a decade later.[4] Whatever their origins and whenever they arose, several of the ideas Korngold floated in "Notes for an Interview" would be taken up and developed further toward the end of his life, in his introduction to Ulric Devaré's *Faith in Music*, included elsewhere in this volume.

Notes for interview
(ca. 1930)

... you can't ask me about modern music ... one always excuses it as a reflection of our time ... but that is nonsense ... did a Schubert, perhaps, bear the influence of his time and the great historical events that took place back then? Do you notice the Battle of Leipzig in his works? ... and Beethoven? His music exists outside of any time period and its events, aside from the dedication on the score of the *Eroica*, which Beethoven crossed out when the person he was originally honoring—Napoleon, namely—became overly symbolic of the times ... or Wagner and Verdi ... the invention of the railroad, which surely was more momentous back then than the invention of the engine and all that has developed from it (up to the airplane) has been for the present, finds no mirror in their works ... of course, there are a couple musical works in the literature that are relevant and magnificent despite their being reflections of their surroundings ... Debussy's *Pelléas et Mélisande* for example, and Alban Berg's *Wozzeck* ... though I consider these to be unique rather than trailblazing works, which therefore should not be repeated . . . it is certainly hard to imagine repeating *Tristan* . . . *Tristan*-music from a Wagnerian? . . . (record – part – beginning *Liebestod*?)

Q.: . . . *What is missing, in your opinion, dear Professor, in modern music?*

A.: . . . Above all, melody! Music is supposed to be a beautiful thing . . . Look, Johann Strauss played Wagner's "Magic Fire" music from *The Valkyrie* in coffeehouses (record). Who plays atonal or twelve-tone music in a popular concert, let alone in coffeehouses? . . . Puccini, Richard Strauss, now that's melody, that sounds beautiful . . . Puccini's operas and mine sold out the house at the Vienna Opera, not only in their first two performances but for eight to ten performances after the premiere . . . My first ballet, *Der Schneemann* (premiered in 1911) (record) . . . I was twelve years old then, and the audience was delighted . . . then *Violanta* (record) (premiere??) . . .
. . . then *Das Wunder der Heliane* (date?) (record??) . . . and finally *Die tote Stadt* (record—Lehmann, Tauber, etc.) (Jeritza?) (Orchestration of all operas!) . . . Of course, there have been some important phenomena in the world of music in the last thirty years . . . Schoenberg, who started out as a Wagnerian—look at *Verklärte Nacht* and *Gurrelieder* (record)—but who later blundered into a kind of formalism [*in einer Konstruktion*] and thus, in my opinion, into a dead end. And maybe the greatest of them all, Stravinsky—there's his *Petrushka* . . . My father did not write about ballet, and I, a young man, asked my father to take me to the performance of Stravinsky's *Petrushka* because I considered it bracingly new and significant. We were never unprogressive, neither my father nor I (record—*Petrushka*)

Q.: . . . *but wouldn't it be a little dangerous to look only for melody in music* . . .

A.: . . . of course not melody alone . . . but music is made of melody . . . and rhythm . . . and then a certain streamlike rippling [*Rieseln*] . . . if all of these come together, a little Beethoven can emerge . . . but without *all* of these? . . .
    Look at painting, for example—if reality is not that beautiful, why should one even consider drawing it? . . .
    Painters say, "This is how I see it." And musicians say, "This is how I hear it." But that is not enough. That's what differentiates artists from historians, whether in music, painting, or any art form—that they create something beyond the more or less photographic image of their era, something that stands above and beyond time and environment.

NOTES

1. Erich Wolfgang Korngold Collection, Box F, Folder 27, Library of Congress.

2. Karl Marilann, "Gespräch mit Erich Wolfgang Korngold," *Neues Wiener Journal*, 6 May 1919. Other published interviews include "Eine 'Schöne Helena' wird umgebaut . . . Ein neuer dritter Akt mit Happyend: Londoner Gespräch mit Erich Wolfgang Korngold," *Neues Wiener Journal*, 13 November 1931; and H. J., "Gespräch mit Erich Wolfgang Korngold," *Neues Wiener Journal*, 27 October 1933.

3, Luzi Korngold, *Erich Wolfgang Korngold: Ein Lebensbild* (Vienna: Verlag Elisabeth Lafite, and Österreichischer Bundesverlag für Unterricht, Wissenschaft und Kunst, 1967), 74–75. Luzi Korngold's recollections of the composition of *Die Kathrin* can be found in "A Farewell to Vienna" in this volume.

4. Korngold's hopes for an American performance are described in Ross Parmenter, "Famous at 13: Erich Korngold, Who Has Had Success as Composer for a Long Time," *New York Times*, 25 October 1942. On the Vienna performance of October 1950, see Guy Wagner, *Korngold: Musik ist Musik* (Berlin: Matthes & Seitz, 2008), 405–9.

A Farewell to Vienna

LUZI KORNGOLD
TRANSLATED BY ELISABETH STAAK
INTRODUCED BY KEVIN C. KARNES

"I am not a refugee," Korngold declared to the *New York Times* in 1942. "I'm grateful that I haven't seen the swastika in Vienna . . . and I am happy I had here a new country before I lost my own."[1] However Korngold described his status to his American interviewer, it is clear that his family's emigration in January 1938 had been unplanned. In June 1935, back in their summer home of Höselberg, the composer and his wife could already sense that their native Austria had become a "hostile" place, as the composer's wife, Luzi, would recall, with its hostility "partly underground, partly out in the open."[2] For the next three years, the couple would spend their summers in Europe, with Erich working hard on *Die Kathrin* and Luzi traveling and caring for their family. The balance of their months were spent in California, where Erich scored *Captain Blood*, *Give Us This Night*, *Anthony Adverse*, and parts of several other features. In the early autumn of 1937, their remarkable cycle of annual migrations seemed to have come to an end, as the family resolved to remain in Vienna for the better part of a year at the least, so that Erich could oversee the premiere of *Die Kathrin* at the Staatsoper under Bruno Walter. But the situation in the city troubled them. Luzi was hearing firsthand accounts of worrying political developments in Germany, and a series of friends had departed for the United States with no certain plans for return. Anticipating the opera's upcoming premiere, the *Neues Wiener Tagblatt* published a detailed synopsis of *Die Kathrin* on January 7, 1938, and Erich's work with the Staatsoper continued apace. Still, when the composer received an invitation from Warner Bros. to travel to Hollywood for the production of *Robin Hood* on January 22, the Korngolds took it as an omen, as Luzi would recall.[3] The premiere of *Die Kathrin* was postponed until the fall, and on January 29 they left for the States. Luzi's experience of these fateful years is recounted in the paragraphs below.[4]

By her own account, Luzi, born in 1900 as Luise von Sonnenthal, had first laid eyes on the composer when he was fourteen or fifteen years old. By that time, however, he had already figured in Sonnenthal family conversations. "Comparisons were always being made," she remembered, "to the famous wunderkinds of music—to Handel, the young Mozart, the young Mendelssohn." It was not until early 1917 that Luzi and Erich became acquainted, and things developed rapidly from there. By the summer of 1918, "people in Vienna had begun to gossip."[5] Luzi grew up in a family that had produced two generations of distinguished artists: actors, translators, and directors. Her grandfather Adolf, an actor, had served as artistic director of Vienna's celebrated Burgtheater in the 1880s.[6] Luzi was an actor herself, as well as a gifted singer, and she would prove to be a formidable writer, an eloquent chronicler of her life with Erich and an astute observer of the historical tides that shaped their life together. Against the objections of both sets of parents, the couple wed in a civil ceremony in Vienna's town hall on April 30, 1924.[7] She published her first memoir of their experiences together in 1960, three years after Erich's death.[8] She would elaborate that account into the volume from which the selection below is taken, which appeared in Vienna five years after her own death. Her book has remained a cornerstone of subsequent biographical writing on the composer. First and foremost, however, it records Luzi's own experience of creativity, emigration, and her family's journey through a changing world.

In this passage, we encounter the family just as they are settling back into Höselberg, Erich having recently completed work on Max Reinhardt's film adaptation of *A Midsummer Night's Dream* and turning his attention to *Die Kathrin*. "Erich Wolfgang Korngold has returned to Vienna, because he cannot get Vienna out of his blood," the *Wiener Montagblatt* reported. The same could have been said of Luzi.[9] Yet as her recollections make clear, the city they encountered in the spring of 1935 no longer felt like the city where they were wed. They immediately began thinking about laying "a path to a possible refuge in case of danger," and within weeks of their arrival the composer had already signed a contract to return to Hollywood for work on *Give Us This Night*. Over the course of their next several journeys back and forth across the Atlantic, Luzi repeatedly found herself contrasting the untroubled ease of their life in the United States with the sense of discomfort they felt in Austria—and, while in Europe, struggling to reconcile their memories of the city of their childhood with what they now sensed unfolding all around them. She recounts receiving the "fateful cable" from Warner Bros. in January 1938; their hasty departure for the States; and the almost surreal ease with which they settled back into their comfortable

Figure 1. Wedding photo of Luzi and Erich Korngold.

California routine, just as news of Austria's receptivity to Hitler's overtures began to roll in. At the end, Luzi wrestles with her memory of her own sense of ease in light of the experience of those family members the couple had left behind, whose own emigration they managed to arrange just in the nick of time.

In her first published statement on her life with Erich, Luzi recounted the start of their relationship, concisely and directly and in the third person. "In the spring of 1917, [Erich] got to know his future wife, Luzi Sonnenthal, granddaughter of the court actor Adolf Ritter v. Sonnenthal. From the very first meeting, there developed between these two young people a friendship and sense of connectedness that was unbreakable and would endure throughout their lives."[10] More than anything else, Luzi's memoir of the journeys she shared with Erich in 1935–38 testifies to her experience of that sense of friendship and connectedness, of the experience of a family whose destiny was altered by forces they could not control, but through which they endured.

Selections from *Erich Wolfgang Korngold: Picture of a Life*
Luzi Korngold

And Back to the USA

When he arrived in Vienna, Erich threw himself with passion into the arms of his *Kathrin*. He was able to be his old creative self again and worked raptly in his attic study for days on end, pausing only to visit the children's room every now and then. We had planned to go to Höselberg in the middle of June, and the journey there probably had an influence on his decision to sign the contract with Paramount [for *Give Us This Night*]. For the first time, the contrast between America, a country where we had traveled freely and carelessly for several months, and the partly underground, partly open hostility of Austria awakened serious doubts in him. Understandably, he did not want to cut off a path to a possible refuge in case of danger. My trust in him and his deliberations was so unshakeable that I would not for a moment doubt the rightness of his decisions. The ten years of my marriage had taught me to rely on his good reason and nearly infallible instinct.

This time, we decided to take our children to America. The Korngold grandparents were really upset, for they would miss not only their own son but the grandchildren as well, and for several months. Thus something of a pall was cast over the short time granted to us at Höselberg. We were supposed to arrive in America in August!

We began our journey to America on the *Ile de France*, this time together with our children and nanny. In New York, the all-too-familiar siege of news reporters awaited us; we were no longer bewildered or amazed, only a little disgruntled to have to stay in the blistering city for a couple of days, since Erich had meetings with Oscar Hammerstein about the movie to be shot [*Give Us This Night*]. At first pleasantly surprised by Hammerstein's manuscript, Erich declared shortly thereafter in Hollywood, "From week to week the book is growing worse. By the time we start shooting, it will be unusable." Unfortunately, he proved to be right. As was customary in Hollywood, multiple writers were hired to edit the script, which was passed from hand to hand until it came out a witless, clichéd "Hollywood musical" that could bring little joy to any musician working on it. Erich came up with pretty, lyrical music for [Jan] Kiepura's and [Gladys] Swarthout's numbers, but they were still considered too operatic and were not "hit" material.

This time around, we had rented a house in Beverly Hills from the start. A private tutor was hired for our older boy, who was taught in German, while the little one learned his ABCs with me and the nanny. We rediscovered old friends and made new ones. We had an active exchange with the Schoenbergs. Our children—Schoenberg's enchantingly beautiful baby daughter Nuria and our Schurli—forged a close friendship. I would bring Schurli over to the Schoenbergs in the afternoons when Erich was busy at the studio, or the Schoenbergs would drop Nuria at our house—often while we were away—and pick her up later. We adults were also frequently together, and every time, Schoenberg and Korngold got into serious debates about music. How could they not? Erich admired Schoenberg's mastery and even played some of his piano pieces by heart, but he could not really open himself up to a form of music that was so contrary to his own nature as an artist. I don't know what Schoenberg thought of Korngold as a composer. He once remarked, when Erich was still being called a "prodigy," that "Dr. [Julius] Korngold recommended Rudolf Kolisch [the violinist] to be my student. Why not his own son?"

During the winter, when Erich was already in the midst of recording the orchestra takes for the Paramount movie *Give Us This Night*, Warner Bros. approached him. They wanted Erich to write the music for a recently produced movie called *Captain Blood* (from a novel by [Rafael] Sabatini). Erich declined. First, he was still busy with his work at Paramount, and second, he did not intend to write any more film music. After urgent daily telephone calls, he was finally persuaded to at least screen the movie. And that's how, one night, we were shown *Captain Blood* and saw the very young Errol Flynn make his debut, when he had not yet fallen victim to Hollywood's sickness. It was an adventure film, but it was not without allure or a certain human charm. When we got home, Erich said, with the nervous anxiety that would later overcome him whenever he started working on any movie: "I can't do it! You have to go there and cancel for me!"

Obediently, I went to Mr. Forbstein, the music director, and broke the news to him about Erich's refusal. He listened to me kindly, patted my cheek, and said, "Don't worry, honey!" With that, I considered the matter settled. But Warners did not. They kept urging Erich, and promised . . . in short, I don't know how to explain it, since the material benefits weren't very tempting, either. But Erich gave in and all of a sudden was working on the score for *Captain Blood*. By day he was conducting recordings at Paramount, and by night he was at Warners, where within barely three weeks he composed the fresh and vivacious music that accompanies *Captain Blood*. On the last day of work, Erich had orchestra recordings from nine in the morning until seven at night, and after dinner he immediately went over to the "dub room" where they synched music and sound, staying there until half past five the next morning. Erich invited the technical staff to breakfast at Sardi's Restaurant, where despite the long and sleepless night everyone was lively and in good spirits. In finishing off their work on the film in such a festive manner (as he would do with all subsequent projects), Erich brought something new and unfamiliar into the lives of these men, who for the first time felt rewarded for fulfilling the work of their "daily routine." From the policeman at the entrance to the boss, everybody showed him affection: a mix of respect for his expertise and appreciation for his cheerful and humble personality.

Hal Wallis, the head producer and colleague of Jack Warner, quickly recognized Erich's dramaturgic talent and brought him in for discussions about dramatic issues—and by no means only relating to the movies he was scoring at the time. By now, Erich spoke English quite well, although he himself said that it's "not a language, but only an accent." In any case, he managed to make himself understood by way of this accent. Once again that spring, he declined a contract with Warners, for we still believed—more with our hearts than our minds—that we had a home we could return to [in Austria], which we did not want to leave behind. It was delusional, a lovely deception: the naive and confident "nothing-can-happen-to-us" attitude of happy people. In the wintertime, under the beaming California sun, we dreamed of the rain-soaked meadows of home. The ever-present, sweet scent of orange blossoms awakened in us a longing for the native chestnut trees and lilacs that would soon bloom at home. Soon, however, we would make the extraordinary discovery that a stay in Europe did not fully satisfy us, either. There, we imagined blossoming orange trees, colorful rock formations, and the deep, churning blue of the Pacific. In the end, we concluded with laughter that the times when we really felt most comfortable were those when we were between continents, in the midst of the ocean crossing.

In May 1936 we returned to Europe aboard the *Paris*. On the passenger list stood the names Stravinsky, Rodziński, and Koussevitzky.[11] During a walk on deck we ran into Stravinsky, who greeted Erich warmly in his amiable and casual way. Erich had been an enthusiastic devotee of this master since his early youth. When Stravinsky came to Vienna with the Ballets Russes and *Petrushka* for the first time—it must have been around 1911 or 1912—Erich was sitting in a box at the Opera with his grandparents. After the performance, the fourteen-year-old youngster was wild with excitement. He applauded like a fanatic until his shocked grandmother grabbed his hands, trying to stop his rowdy display. That same evening, Erich declared these words categorically to his father, who was not expected to review ballet: "You simply must go see *Petrushka*! There's never been anything like it!" Korngold senior obeyed his son's "command," and, for the first time in his life, wrote a full-length article about a ballet.

We enjoyed the summer months at our Höselberg with an ardor that now seems prescient. Our eyes took in the lush green of the fields, our hearts were beguiled and moved by the wildflowers, and the stream was like a vision. Wherever our gaze wandered, we said to ourselves: "Take that in! Don't forget anything!" This time around, our houseguests at Höselberg were Dr. [Ernst] Décsey and his wife. On lengthy hikes through mountains and valleys, we discussed the libretto for *Die Kathrin*.

As we did every year, we made a trip by car to the Dolomites and Italy. When we got back, Schurli was awfully sick, with a high fever but no symptoms. In Vienna, I immediately looked up the first pediatrician I could find, Prof. Knöpfelmacher, who diagnosed the boy with a tubercular infection of the hilar gland. "I recommend the California sun for parents who can afford it," Prof. Knöpfelmacher remarked. For our son, we could indeed afford the California sun, and the fact that the boy was advised to keep his distance from Vienna prompted Erich to telegraph his signature on his contract with Warners for *Anthony Adverse*, a movie that had been in the planning stages even before our departure. In October, we set sail aboard the *Rex*, an Italian steamer, bound for New York City.

In Hollywood, we watched with satisfaction how our youngster recovered quickly in the warm, radiant sun. Erich finished work on *Anthony Adverse*, for which he would win an Oscar in April. We didn't want to return to Europe until May, however, on account of our little one's health. At the time, Warner Bros. was producing the magnificent all-Black movie, *Green Pastures*, a simple yet wise tale, which would soon become famous, about how biblical events are mirrored in the curly hair of Negro children. The actors, an "all Negro cast," developed—according to the cast members themselves—a heartwarming intimacy with one another. Rex Ingram, who played the role of De Lawd, a handsome, tall man with short, gray hair, a twisted moustache, and dark, shimmering wet eyes, won us over as soon as we met him in person at the studio. Like all the other colored [sic] actors, "De Lawd" was not allowed to have his meals in the Green Room, Warners' dining hall. The choral director, [Hall] Johnson, who had studied the marvelous Negro spirituals with his singers and was famous in his field, was likewise banished to a cafeteria. Johnson was one of the most highly educated men I met in America. He was fluent in several languages, including German. He had mastered not only his position as choral director but also knew so much about music in general that it was a pleasure to have a conversation with him. So, Erich often skipped lunch in the Green Room and went instead to the cafeteria, seeking the company of "De Lawd" and Mr. Johnson.

Aside from the choral numbers, the finished film needed some background music, and Erich was asked to write it. Queried about his fee, he answered—to the amazement of Warner Bros., for whom business was just business—that he was staying in Hollywood for another month anyway and besides, he had fallen in love with *Green Pastures*, and that it would be a pleasure for him to do the music without any compensation. By now the film industry had come to see Korngold as an original and interesting personality, as a man who had already turned down several contract offers, yet who wanted to write music for free! To some, this seemed downright suspicious. The imagination of these "movie bigwigs" was too limited to see that there were more worthy and important things in life than collecting a weekly paycheck.

Short-Lived Happiness in Austria

When we next said our goodbyes to Hollywood, we believed it would be for a long time, if not forever. The premiere of Korngold's opera *Die Kathrin* was planned for the 1937–38 season, so we would be spending our first winter in Vienna since 1933. We were looking forward excitedly to the holidays at Höselberg, where Erich would complete his revisions of the work and orchestrate the score. Bruno Walter visited us during the summer, and Erich played his opera for him on the little piano in the bay window of our bedroom. Walter especially liked the gloomy, ominous soldiers' march, which also functions as an intermezzo before the second act, like a fever dream of the heroine, Kathrin. Walter, who was co-director of the Vienna State Opera in 1937, had officially accepted the piece [for performance]. Only the date of the premiere was yet to be settled, once the casting of the main roles had been determined.

After getting our gymnasium student, Ernstl, settled in Vienna, Erich, my sister Helene, and I returned to Höselberg, where our little one, who needed to keep his distance from the city, had been staying with his nanny. It was the first time we could enjoy fall—and later, winter—days at Höselberg. The house had an enchanting, musty smell of old wood and old brick walls; the silence was profound and interrupted only by the exhilarating sounds of children's voices, of our little Schurli and the custodian's son. Erich sat hunched over the revisions to his opera, and Schurli lay wrapped in a warm blanket under the fall sun. After our luxurious life in Hollywood we enjoyed the delightful sparseness of our stay in the country. We relished the farmer's dark bread and enjoyed the cider and the plum brandy produced on the Höselberg. It was another one of those "self-consciously happy" times that one never forgets . . .

Sometime in mid- to late October 1937, Helene Thimig called and invited me to see her in Leopoldskron [near Salzburg]. Max Reinhardt was already on his way to America, and Helene, who had brought an American car to Europe like we had, was supposed to take the car to Le Havre. In Hollywood I had been giving her driving lessons, yet she didn't dare drive over the Arlberg Pass without someone to accompany her, so I gladly agreed to help her out. When I arrived in Leopoldskron that late afternoon, the only other person there was an old friend, Frau Professor F. By then, Leopoldskron had shed its fall foliage. It was silent and cool, and life had moved indoors; we had supper in the wonderful old library. We were in a wistful, nostalgic mood, and maybe more than that: we sensed we were bidding a kind of irreversible farewell, if not to each other than to Leopoldskron, Salzburg, Austria. Frau Professor F., who hailed from Germany, was troubled and anxious, and even though she had not been persecuted for racial reasons, she sat between us like the incarnation of some obscure omen. We listened to her reports with discomfort, increasing alarm, and dread. Helene and I took our leave early. We excused ourselves quickly and retired to our rooms, depressed.

On the marvelous ride from Salzburg to Vorarlberg we allowed ourselves to be distracted from thoughts of the impending danger. The dark mood of the previous evening seemed as if it had been a bad dream. When we said goodbye, however, feelings of uneasiness and uncertainty overcame us. When and where would we see each other again?

Soon thereafter, Erich and I broke off our vacation in the country and returned to Vienna, where preparations for *Die Kathrin* were in full swing. The lead role of the opera was to be sung by Jarmila Novotná, but the tenor part was still pending. Jan Kiepura, who had been asked, had to decline because he was going to America in January. In the end, the premiere of *Die Kathrin* was postponed to March, in the hope that by then they would have found the right cast.

Farewell to Vienna

The day we received the fateful cable from Warner Bros. will never fade from my memory. It was our salvation from certain doom. We were supposed to meet at a concert where a pianist was playing Erich's third piano sonata. I was alone at home when the telegram with the offer arrived: "Can you be back in Hollywood within the next ten days to compose the music for *Robin Hood*?" I took the cable with me to the concert. Erich was running late. Finally, I saw him enter the house and take his seat in one of the back rows. Discreetly, I held up the missive. He shook his head in puzzlement. We had to wait until the concert was over before I could excitedly share the news with him. He looked at me with a start and said, "This is significant." He called [an official of the Opera] directly from the concert hall and told him about Warners' proposal. It was the end of January and they still hadn't found a singer for the tenor part. Dr. Eckman, the minister, said on the telephone, literally: "Herr Korngold, take this as an omen and go! In October I promise you a first-class premiere with Bruno Walter as conductor, and with Jarmila Novotná and Richard Tauber, who is available around that time. I will see to it immediately that you receive a letter guaranteeing the performance."[12]

It was late at night. Erich looked at me uncertainly and suggested that we go right then to the Imperial Hotel to find out what ships were sailing within the next five days. If it wasn't one of the really big ones, he would not leave during the winter. It turns out the ship was the *Normandie*, and Erich immediately reserved two cabins, since we would take Schurli with us, at the least. We had one day to pack our things into suitcases, to arrange our home and our affairs, and to bid farewell to family and friends. Ernst had to be left with our mother and my sister, as we didn't want to interrupt his gymnasium studies. The last friendly voice I heard on the telephone was that of Professor Knöpfelmacher, the pediatrician. And the first tragic report following Hitler's invasion of Vienna concerned him as well: he had found salvation by overdosing on sleeping pills.

Thus we began our eventful journey, which saw us held up or compelled to retrace our steps at every stop and border. We could not take the train because we still had the American car, which we had to bring back on account of customs. The roads were covered with ice and partly snowed in; it was bleak and bitterly cold, and I could drive only with the utmost care. After a rough sea voyage, we were finally relieved to take our seats on the train bound for California, on which we had an uneventful journey, thankfully. We hailed San Bernardino and its orange groves with joyful hearts, and when we arrived in Pasadena we were greeted on the platform by our beloved "family," Helene Thimig and Iphi Castiglioni, who had come to welcome us and give us a ride to Hollywood. We went directly to the Reinhardts: they had found a house for us close to theirs. Reinhardt always liked to maintain his "court" within close range. Erich, however, knew that serious work with Warners lay ahead, and he preferred living close to the studio. We found a house in Toluca Lake, five minutes from Warner Bros. We decided to rent it right away, since Erich could walk to the studio if he desired.

Already, on the following day, we were supposed to screen the finished film: an adventure story with a first-class cast (Errol Flynn again in the lead), childlike, fresh, cheerful, and sentimental, and as colorful as a picture book. Erich followed the movie's storyline attentively, but, I noticed, with increasing nervousness as well. Every time our eyes met, he shook his head anxiously. When we got home he broke into unrestrained despair. I had never seen him like this . . . "I can't, I can't do it!" he yelled in agitation. "Then just don't do it." I tried to calm him down. He looked at me with fear, made no response, and walked around all day with a worried look on his face. Finally, he made his way over to Mr. Wallis, lead producer for Warners, with a carefully composed letter of refusal in hand. He gave the letter to the man himself and asked forgiveness for having abandoned the project at the last minute. Mr. Wallis had no choice but to accept Korngold's refusal, and Erich came back home with a smile on his face. Over the upcoming week, freed of obligation, *Robin Hood* inspired all kinds of themes in Erich's mind, and he wrote them down. Reinhardt respected his decision, and we took comfort in knowing that at least Schurli could enjoy a healthy stay under the California sun. We planned to stay until spring, unrepentantly content, choosing to think of our situation in the best light possible.

One evening—it was February 12—Helene Thimig called. I answered her call upstairs while Erich, curious as ever, picked up downstairs in the hall. "Luzi," Helene said in a shaky tone, "it's all over. Schuschnigg is in Berchtesgaden."[13] At that moment the doorbell rang, and Mr. Forbstein, Warner's music director, strode into the house with these words: "Korngold, you *have* to do it!" Erich tried to explain that he'd already officially resigned [from *Robin Hood*] in writing. "That doesn't mean anything," replied Mr. Forbstein, waving his hand dismissively.

Still smarting from the devastating impression made by the phone call, Erich thought things over. Finally, he promised Forbstein that he would at least attempt to write the *Robin Hood* music. He did not want a contract. His conditions were that he would work and be paid on a week-to-week basis. "Then if I realize that nothing more is coming, I can quit with a good conscience; the music written up to then belongs to you," he explained. His proposal was accepted. Besides the ideas he had already written down, Erich also intended to use some themes from [his] *Sursum corda* [of 1919].[14] Thus he had already amassed a considerable amount of material before even really starting to work. The following evening, he sat down to work in the projection room.

Why we didn't do anything in the following days and weeks to save our Ernstl from the threatening situation in Vienna remains a mystery to me to this day. Our shortsightedness was so acute that we believed and hoped that the political situation in Vienna would calm down. Besides, we held a high opinion of our fellow countrymen, and we were convinced that what had happened in Germany could never happen in Austria. Erich worked from week to week; his mental balance returned to him along with his feeling of freedom. He wrote quickly and with inspiration and was already in the "dub room" by the beginning of March. When we heard the news that elections would be held in Austria on March 10, I initially believed, naively and happily, that little Austria would stand firm against Hitler. But Erich questioned my thinking. "He *has* to invade! Don't you see?" He added: "Hitler won't wait until the elections. It's too much of a risk."

Then came the horrible news from Vienna. On Friday, March 10, Hitler had attacked our homeland. Immediately we sent a telegram requesting that Ernstl, who had no passport (as a minor) but who did have a valid American visa, have his visa entered into my sister's passport and be brought to Switzerland. On Saturday night, when we didn't hear back, we called and learned that my in-laws had indeed registered Ernstl on their passport and would depart from Vienna in a couple of hours. My father-in-law had wisely procured a visitor's visa to the United States some time earlier. It is impossible to describe the worry, stress, and fear of those days—or the pain we felt for our "lost paradise." Alongside the support of our friends, particularly our "family," we had our first experience of the warm and human sympathies of the American people. Every single one of them made us feel that we were not alone in this difficult time. The telephone rang all day long: everybody wanted to help, and everyone lent us courage.

Finally, after months there came the long-awaited day on which Erich and I were to pick up his parents and our youngster from the train station. After the first year when our boys were still a little hindered by their European manners, they quickly put down roots and were soon indistinguishable from their countless little American friends. We, their parents, had so many reasons to be grateful, having understood only at that moment that we had been spared as if by a miracle.

NOTES

1. Ross Parmenter, "Famous at 13: Erich Korngold, Who Has Had Success as Composer for a Long Time," *New York Times*, 25 October 1942. I have reordered Korngold's sentences in the quotation.

2. Luzi Korngold, *Erich Wolfgang Korngold: Ein Lebensbild* (Vienna: Verlag Elisabeth Lafite, and Österreichischer Bundesverlag für Unterricht, Wissenschaft und Kunst, 1967), 70.

3. Korngold, *Erich Wolfgang Korngold*, 76; "Eine Volksoper Korngolds. Die Handlung der 'Kathrin,'" *Neues Wiener Tagblatt*, 7 January 1938.

4. Korngold, *Erich Wolfgang Korngold*, 70–78.

5. Korngold, *Erich Wolfgang Korngold*, 20, 30.

6. Unless otherwise noted, the information in this paragraph is drawn from Guy Wagner, *Korngold: Musik ist Musik* (Berlin: Matthes & Seitz, 2008), 112–22.

7. Although her surname might suggest otherwise, Luzi was raised in a largely secular Jewish household, as was her husband.

8. Luzi Korngold, "Erich Wolfgang Korngold (1897–1957)," in *Grosse Österreicher: Neue Österreichische Biographie ab 1815*, vol. 14 (Zurich: Amalthea-Verlag, 1960), 198–206.

9. "Erich Wolfgang Korngold: Hollywood, wie ich es sah," *Der Morgen: Wiener Montagblatt*, 13 May 1935.

10. Korngold, "Erich Wolfgang Korngold (1897–1957)," 201.

11. Alongside Igor Stravinsky, Luzi Korngold identifies Artur Rodziński, then conductor of the Cleveland Orchestra, and Serge Koussevitzky, who conducted the Boston Symphony Orchestra from 1924 to 1949.

12. Guy Wagner identifies the minister as Alfred Eckmann and the pianist as Robert Kohner in *Korngold: Musik ist Musik* (Berlin: Matthes & Seitz, 2008), 301.

13. Luzi Korngold refers to the meeting between Kurt Schuschnigg, Chancellor of Austria, and Hitler near the German town of Berchtesgaden on February 12, 1938. There, Hitler demanded and received major concessions from his Austrian counterpart, laying a political foundation for the Anschluss of March 11.

14. On Korngold's use of material from *Sursum Corda* in the score of *Robin Hood*, see Ben Winters, *Erich Wolfgang Korngold's "The Adventures of Robin Hood": A Film Score Guide* (Lanham, MD: Scarecrow Press, 2007), 97–102.

Composing for the Pictures: An Interview

INTRODUCED BY DANIEL GOLDMARK

The impetus for Korngold's first sojourn into film came largely at the hands of Max Reinhardt, the theatrical director-producer with whom Korngold worked extensively—and very successfully—during the 1920s and '30s, most famously on an adaption of Johann Strauss's *Die Fledermaus*, which played to great acclaim throughout Europe and eventually in the United States (rearranged and retitled *Rosalinda*). Hollywood came calling for Reinhardt as it had for so many talented European actors, directors, and other creative personages; in his case, Jack Warner invited Reinhardt to stage a performance of his famous production of *A Midsummer Night's Dream* at the Hollywood Bowl using Warner talent, including James Cagney, Olivia de Havilland, Joe E. Brown, Anita Louise, Dick Powell, and Mickey Rooney.

The success of the Hollywood Bowl event spurred Warners to pursue a screen adaptation of the production, with Reinhardt directing (sharing the duties with another European émigré, William Dieterle), and prompting Reinhardt to invite Korngold to Hollywood to arrange and reorchestrate Mendelssohn's incidental music for the play for use in the film. What was meant to be a quick job took months longer than expected. During this time, Korngold received and accepted other offers to work on films, and he and his wife, Luzi, also became enamored of their new surroundings, which ultimately became an advantage when a doctor recommended that their youngest son, Georg, repair to the warmer climes for his health.

Verna Arvey, herself a noted composer and librettist, conducted this interview with Korngold for the music journal *The Etude*. She does not mention his work on *A Midsummer Night's Dream*, maybe because it was not an original score. Prior to the interview, Korngold had also scored sequences for several films, as well as the full scores for *Captain Blood* (1935), *Anthony Adverse* (1936), and the only film musical he would ever work on, *Give Us This Night* (1936), collaborating with none other than Oscar Hammerstein II.[1]

Figure 1. Korngold and Reinhardt in 1934.

Arvey's identifying Korngold from the start as "the Viennese composer" shows that he had not yet become as closely associated with film as he would by decade's end. Indeed, much of the article focuses on the shifting place of music in the contemporary world (this being 1936), including the incredible suggestion—for the age—that film music was developing as a genre unto itself. Even with Korngold as one of its most visible and acclaimed practitioners, film music was still roundly disdained or ignored by music critics, who denied its status as a legitimate compositional form. Indeed, we know that Korngold's eventual turn to composing film music full-time during the war years led many critics to accuse him of having "sold out." While Arvey and others still looked at his work in film as a lark or even a whim, Korngold obviously took it quite seriously. Perhaps this is why Arvey completed her survey of Korngold's still-blossoming career with a prescient look forward: "Films have given Korngold a new outlet."

Composing for the Pictures
By the Noted Austrian Master, Erich Korngold
An Interview Secured Expressly for The Etude Music Magazine
By Verna Arvey
(1937)

Erich Wolfgang Korngold was born May 29, 1897, in Brünn, formerly Austria, now Czechoslovakia. Since 1901 he has resided in Vienna. He is the son of Dr. Julius Korngold, music critic for the Neue freie Presse *of Vienna. He began to take piano lessons at the age of six, and made his first attempts at composition when but seven. His teachers were Robert Fuchs and Alexander V. Zemlinsky. At the age of ten he composed a fairy-tale cantata, which he played before the amazed Gustav Mahler. His pantomime-ballet,* The Snowman, *was composed at the age of eleven. Many more compositions followed, in rapid succession. The youthful prodigy progressed so rapidly that before he had reached the age of twenty-three he had completed major works, such as the operas* Violanta *and* Die tote Stadt. *He became a conductor of his own works, as well as of the works of other composers. In 1924 he married a granddaughter of the actor Adolph Sonnenthal; and in 1930 he became a professor of the Wiener Staatsakademie für Musik. His biography was written by Rudolf Stephen Hoffmann and was published in Vienna in 1922. He is, at the time of writing (1936), still a young man.* —Editor's Note.

"Art is lonely to-day," declares Erich Wolfgang Korngold, the Viennese composer who was once termed the most amazing musical prodigy of the twentieth century. "The public is against great art. It wants something cheaper. Films and radio suffice to entertain it, since the opera and the symphony orchestra are not sources of joy to it.

"A musical difference in Europe and America? I am sorry to say that such a thing no longer exists. The days when people felt that all the world's culture dwelt on the other side of the Atlantic Ocean have long since passed. Of course, Europe is still more fond of opera than is America, though opera has declined there also, of late years. Still, there is not in Europe the dearth of operatic presentations that one finds in the United States, where there are only a few cities able to support opera for only a few months each year—and this is nothing. Opera is too expensive for these United States. It was always a luxury in Europe, though Europeans loved it too much to worry about the cost. Opera they must have! Emperors and aristocrats supported it."

A Far-Flung Audience

"Perhaps that is the difference between the music of to-day and that of yesterday. The modern composer writes his music for the masses of people, not for wealthy patrons. Beethoven, on the other hand, wrote his quartets for approximately four hundred people, most of whom were aristocrats. Today, hundreds of thousands of people hear the same quartets. Beethoven had no conception of what would happen when his music was played over the radio. Doubtless, his surprise would be great. Could he have foreseen such an event, perhaps he would have written differently, perhaps not. Who can tell? However, it is for the hundreds of thousands of listeners that the modern composer writes. That is why the results of his efforts are different. But, when one analyzes things, art itself has not changed in a hundred years. It is the mode of expression that has changed.

"For the young composer, there are now many dangers. The young composer should first study the old masters—not to copy them, you understand, but for background. Perhaps he should even go to Vienna for this. Then he should discover his own musical personality. He should not be disappointed, nor should he lose his energy and his ideals when he discovers how few opportunities there are now for sincere art. He must keep going; someday recognition and understanding will come. But the young composer should not write foxtrots. He should close his eyes to the films and his ears to the radio. He should simply write serious music, as the masters did: a real, a difficult question today, for writing entertainment music is not composing. Men like Mahler, Bach and Bruch were giants. Lehar is gifted, but he has nothing to do with music, in that sense. And those films! They are dangerous too, for they need so many musicians! They hire every composer they can find, with the result that many of them lose their best inspirations in pictures that will be scrapped tomorrow."

A Master Work

It must be explained that this interview with Korngold took place in the busy Warner Brothers–First National film studios in Burbank, California. Korngold is comparatively new to the film world, though he has underscored many major films since the signing of his contract. Therefore, like all sincere creators, this great composer is tremendously interested in the work at hand. His interest in films—a new form of musical expression—leads him to speak much of them. In like manner, as soon as he begins work on his new opera, he will speak of it constantly, since it will occupy his waking thoughts as well as his dreams. His current interest, however, is film music and the problems it offers.

Nevertheless, he need not be so concerned over the young composer in films; for the man who has something genuine to offer the world will not allow his mind to be contaminated with that sort of entertainment music. After all, they are two different things: writing film music, and writing art music. The approach to the one is that of a craftsman, to the other that of an inspired creator. The one factor that makes this evident is the amount of mechanics in film music—mechanics to which all the composers must conform in order to give their work a commercial value. Even Korngold, while he worked on the film *Anthony Adverse*, developing his new idea of pitching the music just underneath the pitch of the voices and rushing it into pauses in the dialogue, had to work with stopwatch in hand; for in such cases accurate and precise timing is of paramount importance.

Korngold is not worried only over young film musicians. He is worried also over the fact that in many cases too many composers are assigned to the same picture. Consequently, too many alien ideas creep in. He is disturbed over the fact that in a nonmusical picture, where there is, nevertheless, music, it is relatively unimportant. He feels that more recognition should be given it.

The King Condescends

The studio at which he works is justly proud of the acquisition of Korngold. The studio heads heard his music for *Captain Blood* for the very first time at the preview. They simply took it for granted that it was good and said nothing more about it. Fortunately for Korngold, he is said to be wealthy in his own right. He does not need the films, or the money they bring; so that, if they do not like what he writes, if his own work dissatisfies him, or if he does not like the picture, he stops work immediately. They evidently allow him to do so if he wishes, so great is their respect for him.

"I am already a noted composer," he says simply, in a matter-of-fact tone, with no visible conceit. Fame is not new to him. He has known it all his life. That enables him to dictate to those who pay him his salary, and to be independent so that he can return to Vienna to write his new opera, *Die Kathrin*, when the film work is finished. He may then return, if he will, to write the score for *Danton*, Max Reinhardt's scheduled screen undertaking.

Yet, to a certain extent, Korngold has had to adapt himself to Hollywood. When he first arrived, he told the producers flatly that it was impossible for him to work as hastily as other film musicians work. He insisted that he needed time for reflection, for mature deliberation, as well as time for his own creative work. Even he has had to make concessions. No longer can he create his own music while he is actively engaged in underscoring a film. That for *Captain Blood* was written in three weeks—surely, as he remarks, a "crazy" way to do things. Yet, he was pleased with the score, pleased that a suite from it would be published, and pleased with the writer's suggestion that it would be of interest to the general public to print the entire score, apart from the film, just as a screen scenario has lately been published in its original form.

In fact, Erich Wolfgang Korngold likes picture work.

"I play only the piano and the orchestra," says Korngold. Then he adds whimsically, "The orchestra is such a very nice instrument to play." When he composes, whether or not his music is intended for a film, he writes immediately as the completed music will sound. Thus, if his composition is orchestral, it is written in full score. He never writes for the piano and arranges an orchestral score from the piano copy. Of course, if his composition is intended for the piano, he would think of the piano first.

Genius and Simplicity

He is said to be tremendously popular with the other musicians in Hollywood. A legend has crept out of the studio recording room that discloses a reason for this popularity and sheds light on the amiability of this composer. He lifts his baton to open the rehearsal, and the entire orchestra, bent on a quiet joke, crashes into a discordant, loud, extremely wrong chord by way of greeting. Korngold merely smiles and says, "We'll take it again, gentlemen!"

The fact that his very first composition of note was a ballet is explained by Korngold as being because the ballet is the easiest form for a child of that age to comprehend. Despite his extreme youth when he wrote this ballet, the conductor did not change a single note of it. It is still performed, from time to time. Korngold now considers this initial ballet as being an important step toward his great ambition—the opera. He has written no more ballets since that time, because the opera form is more attractive. "Why write a ballet," he asks, "when it may be included in an opera with far greater effect? Opera is the combination of all the elements. After all, the inspiration for the dance comes from the music, not from the dance."

In Korngold's estimation, Stravinsky is the best of the living ballet composers. "After Stravinsky, there was no development, only imitation."

Korngold works extremely hard, and is his own worst critic. He is never satisfied with anything he does, though he is immensely pleased with the works of others. "No performance of my works is good. I have never heard a perfect performance of any of my operas!" he declares. If someone dares to opine, in his presence, that his new work will be greater than his last, he will demur. "Let us wait and see," he will say. The writer spoke of the reaction of another young composer, when he discovered faults of his own during a radio broadcast of one of his works. The other man in the room looked alarmed, as though a shrine had been desecrated by the speaking of another composer in the presence of the genius Korngold. But Korngold's own face gradually and boyishly lighted up as he said excitedly, "Yes, that's it! That is the way to feel! That is the way I always feel!"

Indeed, fame has given him confidence in himself, but it has not taken from him a certain boyishness that is inherent in all great men. Mention his composition *Rübezahl* to him and he will jump up spontaneously, run to the piano and play snatches of it rapidly and happily. If he is asked to sign an autograph book, he will first look over it in interested fashion, to see if it contains the names of anyone he knows. "Oh! Molinari!" he will cry. "I knew him! When I was conducting in Rome. And there is Hertz! I know him too."

Whither Going?

At the beginning of Korngold's amazing career (not so very long ago, one must admit) there was much discussion about him. Everyone acknowledged his precocity, though enemies once attributed his great success—and even his music—to his ambitious father, a renowned critic. True, there was no parental opposition here. Dr. Julius Korngold was happy over those musical leanings.

Contemporary modernists are wont to decry Erich Wolfgang Korngold's later works, to protest that he has not lived up to his early promise. The impression is given that Korngold (like the baby of the Mexican legend, who was born, spoke and died) came too early to the flowering of his genius, that he said what he had to say and never grew. "Sterility" is the word most often applied to him.

One might ask this pertinent question: "Should Korngold deliberately become an ultramodernist just because some zealous critics would consider that an advance over what has gone before?"

Films have given Korngold a new outlet. His music for them is beautiful and well scored. Perhaps in that medium he will regain whatever ground he has lost in the minds of certain of these critics. Then again, perhaps it is the critics themselves who will be forced to see matters in a different light.

Surely Erich Wolfgang Korngold is being led into the paths best fitted for him.

NOTES

1. Some details about Korngold's work on *Give Us This Night* can be found in Luzi Korngold's memoirs, reproduced elsewhere in this volume. Interestingly, the film was as close as Korngold would come to working on a hybrid form of the operas and operettas with which he was already so adept. Korngold apparently foresaw the film's mostly forgotten fate when he stated: "There have been some ordinary, program pictures which are forgotten after three months but which will be long remembered by musicians as containing some rare musical writing." This statement echoes his words from the same interview: "They hire every composer they can find, with the result that many of them lose their best inspirations in pictures that will be scrapped tomorrow." (Interview in press book for *Give Us This Night*, quoted in Jessica Duchen, *Erich Wolfgang Korngold* [London: Phaidon, 1996], 161.) Given the prevalence of this notion in his thoughts, we might surmise that this was more than a passing concern for the composer at the time.

"Give up your plans of coming home": Letters of a Viennese Father to His Son

JULIUS KORNGOLD
TRANSLATED BY ELISABETH STAAK
INTRODUCED BY BRYAN GILLIAM
EDITED AND ANNOTATED BY KEVIN C. KARNES

The letters that follow from Julius Korngold to his son and daughter-in-law reflect a tumultuous, even dangerous time for Erich and his extended family.[1] The famed Viennese opera composer had had a prestigious career on the international musical stage with such works as *Der Ring des Polykrates* and *Violanta* (both 1916), which premiered in Munich when he was only nineteen years old. *Die tote Stadt* was so highly anticipated that it received an unusual double premiere in Hamburg and Cologne on December 4, 1920; the Vienna premiere followed shortly thereafter, with Richard Strauss congratulating the composer backstage after each act.

Much of Korngold's early success was inseparable from his overbearing father, who was Eduard Hanslick's successor as music critic of Vienna's *Neue freie Presse* and, as such, one of the most influential voices in Viennese music. Like Leopold Mozart or Franz Strauss, Julius had great plans for his gifted son, who lived a sort of cocooned existence with his parents, insulated from material pressures and the worries of everyday life. On the positive side, Julius passed on to his son a rich knowledge of music, and Erich profited from his father's acquaintances with the major composers, conductors, and other musicians of his day. For example, Julius took the ten-year-old Erich to meet his friend Gustav Mahler, for whom he played one of his works. Mahler was stunned by his youthful brilliance and recommended that he should study with Alexander von Zemlinsky. But there was a downside to Julius's advocacy. Julius was a strident music critic who had no use for Viennese modernism, the so-called New Music, and had made many enemies, including Franz Schalk and Richard Strauss, co-directors of the Vienna State Opera. The turning point in the father-son relationship was when Erich began courting Luise (Luzi) von Sonnenthal, an actress and occasional screen star. Julius was aghast: his son would soon be joining up with the likes of theater people—and he would be distracted from composing. The Sonnenthals were a distinguished family in Viennese cultural circles, but that was not enough for Julius, who wanted no one to dilute the energy of his son's creative career.

By 1924, Erich had attained sufficient stature and financial independence that he asked Luzi for her hand in marriage. The marriage was a source of tension to the very end of Julius's life. To make matters worse, Erich, wanting a house of his own, took on arranging operettas to pay for it—in Julius's opinion, a further dilution of Erich's "serious purpose." The normally obedient son paid no heed to his father's distress and began creating a nest egg for a comfortable villa on the Sternwartestrasse, a lovely and quiet area near the Vienna suburb of Hietzing with easy access to the city center. His next opera, *Das Wunder der Heliane*, did not premiere until 1927. By then, his recalcitrant father had created significant friction between himself—and, by extension, Erich—and Strauss and Schalk. During this icy period of limited productions in his hometown, Korngold's widely successful arrangements of operettas by Johann Strauss for the Theater an der Wien attracted the attention of the great German stage director Max Reinhardt, who, among other things, collaborated with Korngold on an ambitious remaking of *Die Fledermaus* in 1929 for the Deutsches Theater in Berlin.

Hollywood at this time was going through a revolutionary period: the change from silent to sound film (and sound film music), from the modest attempts of film scoring in the *Jazz Singer* (1927) to original and innovative scores such as Max Steiner's famous work for *King Kong* (1933). In Germany, a political revolution was in motion, from the first Nuremburg Nazi Party rally in autumn 1927 to Hitler's appointment as chancellor in January 1933. Both of these trajectories changed Korngold's life dramatically. With the new National Socialist government and its official anti-Semitic policies, German stage venues were closed to Korngold's operas in 1933, and many German Jews, including Reinhardt, were forced to emigrate to the United States. But just as Germany was closing its doors, Hollywood had opened others. Reinhardt, now in Hollywood exile, had been hired to direct a production of Shakespeare's *A Midsummer Night's Dream* at the Hollywood Bowl, which led to a contract with Warner Bros. to produce a version for film. In 1934, he invited Korngold to come to California and compose the score, adapting Felix Mendelssohn's famous suite in his own distinctive style.

As the series of letters below remind us, Hitler cast a large shadow over Austria in the early 1930s. The Austrian parliament had been shuttered

Figure 1. Korngold with his parents, Josefine and Julius, in California, 1940.

in March 1933, when the country entered into the period of so-called Austro-Fascism, with Engelbert Dollfuss, head of the Christian Socialists, fighting off the Austrian Nazi Party on the right and the Social Democrats on the left. The press was censored, and in February 1934 civil war broke out—a turn that ended the Social Democrats' reign as a legally active political party. The following summer, Dollfuss was assassinated by a Nazi, and Kurt von Schuschnigg was appointed as chancellor. Schuschnigg maintained a dictatorship along the lines of Mussolini's in his delicate strategy to remain independent from Hitler and tolerate only a limited amount of anti-Semitism, allowing Jewish artists, writers, and intellectuals a haven from the fascist state to the north. These developments also meant a temporary reprieve for Korngold and his family—a measure of safety that, as these letters show, Julius hoped would continue as late as March 1938. Such hope was surely wishful thinking, given Schuschnigg's disastrous meeting of February 12 with Hitler in the German town of Berchtesgaden, when the German chancellor demanded that Nazis be allowed to serve openly in the Austrian government and that their fascist compatriots be released from prison.

In his letter to Erich of 23–24 February 1938, Julius is heartened by Schuschnigg's defiant speech on the 24th, promising that Austrians would fight courageously to maintain their nation's independence.

Schuschnigg made a number of last-ditch efforts to resist Hitler's maneuvering, but it was too late. By the time he penned his letter to Erich of 6–7 March, Julius saw the writing on the wall. By then, Toscanini had canceled his participation in the 1938 Salzburg Festival, and an Austrian premiere of Korngold's new opera, *Die Kathrin*, was in serious doubt. The father repeatedly urged his son to remain in California, perhaps to do further work with Reinhardt. Within four days of his writing the letter, Schuschnigg was forced to resign and a Nazi functionary was installed in his place. As Julius lamented, writing from Zurich on 15 March, the Germans were able to march into Austria wholly "without a fight." Julius had wisely obtained visas for himself, his wife, and their grandson Ernst, and together the family fled through Switzerland. The Nazis took over their home on Sternwartestrasse, with orders to burn Korngold's "degenerate" manuscripts upon seizing the house. Those scores were cleverly hidden inside published volumes of music by Brahms, Beethoven, and Mozart, however, and as a result survive today on deposit at the Library of Congress in Washington.

During this time, Erich was completing *Die Kathrin*, which would be his final opera, and decided to remain in Hollywood. With the Anschluss, the Korngolds' habit of summering in Austria and spending winters in Hollywood was brought to an end, and they bought a home in the neighborhood of Toluca Lake, large enough to house the extended family. The Anschluss dashed all remaining hopes of a Vienna premiere of *Die Kathrin*, and the hastily arranged first performance in Stockholm on October 7, 1939, met with a lukewarm response. Throughout the remainder of the 1930s and much of the 1940s, Korngold composed some of the finest scores in the history of Hollywood film music, establishing a distinct musical style that influenced film composers for generations to come. Some, like his father, might indeed have derided Korngold for composing film scores to support his family. But what choice was there, after all? Like Kurt Weill, Korngold was an artist who wrote for the love of his audience, not for any public esteem or sense of legacy he might attain. In contrast to his fellow émigrés Arnold Schoenberg and Paul Hindemith, he was entirely non-theoretical and poorly matched for a career in teaching. As Stephen Hinton notes, Korngold was a composer who knew no formal musical boundaries. As Korngold himself was fond of saying, "Music is music"— *Musik ist Musik*.[2]

Julius, a man of authority in Vienna, lived a life of dependence in Hollywood, speaking little English. Whereas the young Erich had lived under his parents' rule in Vienna, their roles were entirely reversed in California, and the Korngold household was full of domestic tensions. The

Korngold archive at the Library of Congress preserves several envelopes labeled, in Julius's angry handwriting, "To be opened only after my death!"

With the passing of both Hitler and his father in 1945, Korngold retired from film scoring and began composing, among other things, his Third String Quartet (1945), Violin Concerto (1946), Symphony in F-sharp (1952), and several lieder (1947). His son Ernst suggested that Erich might have felt that he owed something to his father, who was never sanguine about his son's Hollywood career.[3] By then, however, Erich's concert works were deemed outdated. But now, finally, more than a half-century after his death, Korngold's work is being reassessed.

Letters of Julius Korngold to His Son Erich
Winter 1938

I.

Wednesday, 23 February 1938,
the 8th letter

After I received your telegram yesterday, Ericko, I was unable to talk to Kerber, because he was too overworked.[4] Today he himself called and I read him your pessimistic cable. He immediately said that he is optimistic and has no doubt that *Kathrin* will be performed, and he told me to say hello whenever I got back to you. So kind of him.

Meanwhile, you will have received my seventh letter, in which I already shared the good news with you.[5] However—in times like these, who can be sure of anything?

Right now, England's swing toward a peaceful outcome has lifted spirits. While here in Vienna, demonstration after demonstration is heaped upon poor Schuschnigg, who is being strong-armed by military force and blackmail![6] His speech is pitted literally against H.'s Machiavellian monolog. The right-minded [*rechte*] Vienna wants to keep Austria the way it is—and thus, I believe, its Jews as well.

Thursday, 24 February

In any case, it's safe to say that nothing will happen to us Jews before the Salzburg Festival, because it's Austria's greatest source of income. They're trying to bring Toscanini around and [Bruno] Walter as well, who was hired in such haste that they had to write Toscanini a letter to calm him down! Honest! God only knows what concessions will be made to the Nazis <u>after</u> Salzburg! They say that Nazis <u>are permitted to work here</u> now (like regular residents), even though the law guarantees equality and freedom to all Austrians, including Jews, and even though battling against Jews—and Christianity—is intrinsic to the "Nazi world-view." It's an irresolvable conflict! Who can tell how much they'll give in to Hitler's pressure <u>after</u> Salzburg? There's fear that demonstrations alone would be enough to upset the "cultural" mission [of the festival], so some breathing room may be granted for culture. And for everything else as well, so long as nothing violent or "military"—or war—happens! But let's hope for the best! Especially if England pulls things together. And just now I'm reading that in November of last year, England and France agreed to act in case of an armed attack on Austria! That's why H. was wary of occupation and only made threats instead!! It's extraordinary, though, that Schuschnigg [illegible] the population [illegible] and to demonstrate for Austria's independence! Today, the day of Schuschnigg's speech, every house is flying the flag, a massive demonstration by the people for <u>Austria</u>! Yes, now we're finding the courage to resist! After this, everything shall remain as it has been! From somewhere outside—maybe [news about] Mussolini?—something has helped us to grow a spine![7] Take a look at Schuschnigg's speech! I even read in the *Prague Daily News* that Walter has telegraphed Toscanini to tell him that the safety of Austria's art is assured!! That applies to you as well. Hence Kerber's confidence!

So as long as this gangster doesn't risk a war, this limbo could be ongoing. On its own, without force, without violence, Austria will not surrender! No popular vote for H.! [End of the letter is missing.]

II.

6 and 7 March 1938

Erich, my dear child,
I feel very depressed. After yesterday's official radio announcements, I, like many others, felt the inevitability of events. Those well-meaning individuals at the top have the best of intentions, but people who see things

differently are running amok, taking on leading roles all over the place and preparing for what's to come. And even if they aren't yet able to agitate openly for annexation, aren't they being permitted to act in accord with their anti-Semitic worldview? And an order from outside might come at any moment. They even blame the Jews for the fact of Toscanini's cancellation, and thus for jeopardizing the profits from the Salzburg Festival. Demonstrations in small towns, brawling at the universities. I'm giving you only the <u>merest hints</u> [of the situation], intentionally and with caution. With a heavy heart, I've begun to doubt whether *Kathrin* will be performed, despite Kerber. Since they're now being allowed to openly proselytize their "worldview," one can only assume that calls to bar [the performance] will become more insistent. <u>God grant that I'm wrong!</u> The next couple of days will bring further developments. If not with respect to *Kathrin* itself, then with regard to the question of being overcome by dread of war if England fails to succeed in Italy, about which I'm growing ever more pessimistic. With great confidence I think about the <u>future</u> of your beautiful work, even if that means after the fate of Austria is decided, even if after a war! Even if <u>I</u> may not live to see it! For now, however, my beloved child, you really have to give up your plans of coming home! I say this with tears in my eyes, but please look for a permanent position, get an extended contract or find work at the Reinhardt School.[8] But you'll know better than I what's required, you know the situation in Hollywood, you have your friends! Someone like you, with your talent and extraordinary gift, is bound to be snatched up! The danger is too great to try coming back before summer. It could easily happen that things are set off suddenly and you won't be able to cross the border once we get dragged into it, which is possible and perhaps all but guaranteed. <u>It goes without saying that we will keep you posted about the situation!</u> I would immediately take Ernsti to Switzerland and out of harm's way, and there I'd await your instructions. <u>You can't be too careful these days!</u> I'm by no means the only one with dark thoughts. <u>Whomever</u> you talk to—everyone who can is considering what measures to take in light of the impending dangers! The Salzmanns plan to get out, and the Premingers too, Ottos, even the Fränkels are thinking about it.[9]

How much, my child, do I long for a letter where you share some news about your work! But I'll have to sit tight until you've finished with your heavy work. From Luzi's letters, which she promised upon your departure to send to [the family home on] Sternwartestrasse, I at least learn something, for which I am very grateful. Greetings to her and kisses to our beloved Schurli, whom I hope is recovering in the good climate, despite those awful floods.[10] We had a real scare until we got your telegram! We speak to Ernsti every day and are happy when he's with us or at an event. He's a good child, and very bright. The outfit his mother got him suits him very well, even the hunting hat. He looks picture-perfect. He got the 24 shillings for skis from me along with his allowance. His birthday will be celebrated sincerely! Just about the only real joy amidst my loneliness!

We live in difficult times, Ericko, full of unprecedented threats, and we must stick together more than ever—just like Jewish families used to do in the ghetto. I know, my child, that you won't let your parents perish amidst this threat to human dignity and existence, amidst the terror of a war against life itself. I'd be sure of that even if you didn't say it repeatedly yourself! My heart is filled with fear. Please, be well!

Your father, who loves you more than anything.

P.S. How are things with Reinhardt? Is he thinking of returning to Salzburg if there's no war? Obviously, <u>he's over 60</u> and doesn't [want to] risk anything. In Germany they just announced that <u>all officers have to serve their entire life, no matter their age</u>. It's easy to see how, while they're trying to make us accomplices to their belligerent entanglements, they might order that <u>anyone who served in the [First] World War</u> has to enlist. You understand. What did you think of the awful parrot fever that befell Thimig?[11] The poor thing! I hear she's doing better. Oh, I just thought of something else: Isn't Frau Reinhardt [Thimig] going to want to visit soon, to see her parents after all these experiences?

And if war has not already triggered my intervention mentioned above, couldn't Luzi travel with her to pick up Ernsti? If need be, pick him up in Switzerland, if he's there? Or are you thinking of Betti?[12] I only say all of this because you cannot come back <u>under any circumstance!</u> Ericko, listen to me! Just think about how I must feel writing this to you, telling you not to come back, not knowing if I will ever see you again. Understand from this just how bleakly I judge the current situation, how desperate my resignation is. Certainly, things could change, maybe a miracle happens, maybe God will save Austria, the world.

My blessings to you both, and may everything take a turn for the better! It's a <u>true godsend</u> that you are overseas during these times—everyone is saying that, without envy. <u>You have to use it wisely!</u> For your sake and for the sake of your children, wait until the storms have passed. And they will pass, though in my opinion not before we have a <u>short</u> yet catastrophic war. Don't think just now about your *Kathrin*—it will still receive its laurels. You see how I cannot speak. It's because of the stress, the feeling of desolation. Once more: God bless you and your loved ones!

III.

Zurich, 15 March 1938

Beloved, beloved children!
In the last two and a half days, great misfortune has befallen us and the world: revolution, occupation, the SA in the streets, in offices, and across the whole country, arrests, refugees, the proclamation of German laws, the first stripping of rights from Jews, etc. On Sunday—the last possible day, as later became clear—under imaginable stress, I dared flee with tickets to Paris, on the most dangerous route via [the Swiss municipality of] Buchs. I was stopped in Innsbruck. They took my passport because I am an "editor," they took me out of the coach—the entire train had to wait!—then let me go after all! A time-out in Zurich was doubtful, as Switzerland was closed to foreigners, then accessible after all, etc. Imagine us in such a situation! God helped us!

So far. What now? The questions: 1) How do we get our Ernstl to you?[13] We fled without return permits. The most important in that regard I will telegraph to you. 2) Where to live? 3) And how? Before recent events, I was able to secure some papers, because I had a hunch about what was going to happen. Thus I was able to give some money to Luzi's mother, Mama Sonnenthal, and also to leave some with Dr. Wolf and Aunt Anna as well as a couple hundred schillings with Hans.[14] I instructed Dr. Wolf to ask the *Neue freie Presse* for my pension—I wonder if he's getting it now?—(German officers are already working at the newspapers!) and from that as well as the money I've already given him (2,500 schillings) he's supposed to support Hans, Kornau, and our mortgage for the time being.[15] I also gave him authority over mail and money orders, mainly because of Ernsti's permits!

However, dear children, don't believe that you'll ever be able to return. Especially not you, Ericko and Luzi. Because you would never get out. They will declare Jewish passports invalid, just like they did in Germany. They will show you to the cage. And you, Ericko, have other things to fear as well, as I already told you. (Something can befall you as a German even in America, so get on with your citizenship! Or can Mexico possibly be considered in case of war?) As for us, if we do not use our passports before they expire (by the end of the year!) we can never renew them at a German office!!! I am terrified that I will never see you again if you don't send for us now, Ericko, as you have always assured me, to save your old parents' lives!

3) Pension and state benefits will be lost.[16] Furniture, the rest of the documents—yours, Ericko, and mine—everything will be lost for

refugees and "expatriates," as will surely be decreed! Your property, if you don't act quickly now (how and through whom?), will be confiscated once expatriation takes effect. <u>Is it not possible for you to become an American citizen as quickly as possible?</u> But what good is it all if we lose our homeland, human dignity, all that we achieved, our good name, freedom and physical safety, and on top of that the assets we've saved? This gruesome barbarity will be raging in Austria, of all places. Everything that was old Austria, all tradition, every last reminder of the past will be targeted and eradicated.

Where you are, Ericko, you have the chance to find new ways to make a living and receive new artistic honors! Here, old age must help me get over what I've lost! After some time, through Hans and Aunt Anna, I'll calmly dissolve what remains of our existing household (with Herma, whom I left with some money), and without raising suspicion (carefully, otherwise I would raise suspicion of escape. . .)[17] . . . I'll make sure that everything remaining is left in his charge, that the property is assessed, and that all the rest is placed in our safe-deposit box (afraid of spies, I took it out of the safe in time . . . !)[18] Yours and mine together are worth some 10,000 schillings, <u>which would otherwise be lost!</u>

Aunt Anna took the key to the safe-deposit box. I'm sure you will agree with this! How am I supposed to care for the poor lad if Dr. Wolf can't provide his living expenses because the pension's not paid or stops being paid? Awful, everything's awful, it doesn't bear contemplating. (The Swiss papers are already reporting the terror, the catastrophe, of those threatened with loss of life, the arrests and denunciations. *Sauve qui peut!*) And now, about the current situation. You can probably figure out why I sought refuge here. I withdraw cash to support the three of us—myself, Mama, and Ernstl. I hope it's going to be enough to sustain us through weeks of waiting for Ernsti's travel documents, even for months if necessary, and to pay for our tickets. If not, I will have to cable you to wire us money at the cable address we once used to wire you money! But I will write you about that before you answer by telegram with instructions. Those will be decisive. Otto [Preminger] escaped the same day, by way of Czechoslovakia (Milan?), which is also threatened. He's here now, didn't know that I'd also succeeded in escaping. Dr. Preminger and his wife sought refuge with their son. I will enclose some information.

For the Jews it will be worse than in Germany; they're importing ordinances ready to go. No, better to die than to live in such anguish and fear, nauseated seeing all this glorified hateful frenzy [*heroische Haß-Treiben*] everywhere around me. Imagine, children, I had to spend my last living days in such an atmosphere—even if <u>there were not real danger,</u> which is out of the question. And without the hope of seeing you, my loved ones! It's horrifying that one can [illegible]. Already they've announced on the radio the opening of <u>letters from abroad</u>. Already <u>on Monday, the borders were closed to Jews.</u>

I wrote you, Ericko, that I'd add Ernst's name to my passport. I tried to get a separate tourist visa for him but it wasn't granted because he would need a return permit. Finally, I had an American tourist visa entered into our passports, thinking that the visa would also apply for the child entered under my name, i.e., Ernsti. Tomorrow, I'll inquire about this at the American Consulate. If it's valid, then Ernsti's return is guaranteed. If you're waiting for the ship, play your parts, so they don't think in Washington that we didn't receive <u>our extension for return</u>. The times are so confusing. <u>The old extension for return is valid until April 12</u>, and that's important. <u>It's still valid</u>, and the document we mailed has to be [illegible] verified in the Washington lab [illegible]!! That's something that can be done, provided that Ernstl can travel on my tourist visa! Otherwise, we'd have to get a copy of the permit, which could take months. But war must not intervene.

Children, my mind isn't working, I feel utterly depressed, my diabetes has been getting worse on account of this <u>outrageous</u> stress that is overcoming hundreds of thousands in the same way. Nothing like this surprise attack two days ago has ever happened, never in the history of Austria. Austria simply collapsed, without a fight, through nothing but . . . In the final days there was already new anti-Semitic hounding in the papers—articles against Walter, etc. They chased Röbbeling out <u>on the first day</u>, etc., etc.[19] What poor souls we are! Believe me, how sorry I am for Luzi's mother! Hopefully she's on her way to Palestine with Nene, where they'll surely be allowed in![20] But this feeling of persecution, of difficult conditions, of separation from one's own! Thank God our Grandmother passed away in time!

We long for death every day, in exile now, in misery!

And my new book, my memoirs! I had to leave the manuscript in my <u>bag</u>, which has probably gone missing!

Oh children, I don't want to keep writing in such a confused state.

God bless you and Schurli, my beloved grandson! I'll have Ernstl write something to his mother. Goodbye and be well. God's blessing be with you, and maybe also with us!

Papa

Telegraph us if you have something to say about this letter!

NOTES

1. These letters are preserved in the Library of Congress. They are translated here from *Dear Papa, How Is You?: Das Leben Erich Wolfgang Korngolds in Briefen*, ed. Lis Malina (Vienna: Mandelbaum Verlag, 2017), 199–208.

2. See Stephen Hinton, "Hindemith and Weill: Cases of 'Inner' and 'Other' Direction," in *Driven into Paradise: The Musical Migration from Nazi Germany to the United States*, ed. Reinhold Brinkmann and Christoph Wolff (Berkley and Los Angeles: University of California Press, 1999), 261-78.

3. Author's personal communication with Ernst Korngold, May 1994.

4. Julius is describing interactions with Erwin Kerber, director of the Vienna Staatsoper from 1936 until 1940.

5. At some point, Julius apparently began numbering his letters to his son, with the present letter of 23–24 February 1938 being the eighth. It is unclear what Julius refers to with his reference to the seventh letter, and I have been able neither to find nor to identify it. There is certainly not much that would qualify as good news (*günstige Symptome*) in Julius's letter to Erich of one week earlier, except perhaps his passing reference to a "notice" (*Notiz*) about *Die Kathrin* appearing in the "*Neues Tagebuch*" (possibly the *Neues Wiener Tagblatt*) and the "Ricordi music journal" (probably *Musica d'oggi*). For Julius's letter to Erich of 16 February, see Malina, *Dear Papa*, 198–99.

6. Kurt Schuschnigg was chancellor of Austria from 1934 until the Anschluss in March 1938.

7. Julius is likely referring to talks leading up to the signing of the so-called Easter Accords of April 1938, in which the Italian and British governments agreed to collaborate loosely in Africa, the Middle East, and the Mediterranean. For the UK, the principal motivation for working with Mussolini was to keep him from concluding an alliance with Hitler.

8. Julius refers to the Max Reinhardt Workshop for Stage, Screen and Radio, founded in 1938 in Hollywood by the director and his wife, Helene Thimig. Korngold taught at Reinhardt's school from its beginnings, where he was joined on the faculty by a number of other émigré artists and performers.

9. Julius's note on the Premingers refers to the extended family of Otto Preminger, the Austrian-born director who had begun working for Twentieth Century-Fox in Los Angeles in the mid-1930s. The Fränkels were the soprano Luise von Fraenkel-Ehrenstein, to whom Erich dedicated his *Einfache Lieder*, Op. 9, and her husband, the diplomat and onetime composer Alfred von Fraenkel. The identity of the Salzmanns and the Ottos is unclear; it is possible that the latter clarifies Julius's reference to the Premingers, or that it refers to the family of Otto Witrofsky, the cousin of Julius's wife, Josefine.

10. Schurli was the nickname of Georg Korngold, the composer's younger son, who was then already in California with his parents.

11. Helene Thimig, Reinhardt's wife and a close friend of both Erich and Luise Korngold, had apparently come down with the pneumonia-like illness Psittacosis, also known as "parrot fever."

12. Barbara Wiskocil, whom the family called Betti, was the Korngolds' nanny who accompanied them to Los Angeles in 1935.

13. To refer to the composer's son Ernst, Julius uses the diminutive forms Ernsti and Ernstl interchangeably.

14. Hans (also Hanns) was Erich's older brother, the band leader Hans Robert Korngold. Aunt Anna was the actress Anna Kallina, sister-in-law to Julius's wife, Josefine Witrofsky. Josefine resettled with Julius in Hollywood shortly after the Anschluss. Hans fled to Switzerland and eventually joined the family in California. Anna's wartime

movements are less clear; she died in Vienna in 1948. Dr. Wolf was likely Emil Wolf, a friend in Vienna with whom Julius corresponded around this time.

15. Kornau was the stage name of Eduard Korngold, the younger brother of Julius, an actor and comedian in Vienna. Kornau remained in Vienna after the Anschluss, dying of unknown causes in February 1939.

16. Here Julius is attempting to answer the third question posed earlier in this letter, about how he would find the financial means to survive.

17. Julius's reference to Herma is obscure. Suspension points here and below are in the original.

18. The nature of the arrangement described here is unclear. We have translated Julius's *Kasse* as "safe-deposit box," reserving the English word *safe* for Julius's *Safe*, but it is uncertain whether he moved their cash and other effects from their private home into a bank or vice versa—or whether, perhaps, the transfer was made between other locations.

19. Julius refers to Hermann Röbbeling, who directed the Vienna Burgtheater from 1932 until the day of the Anschluss on March 12, 1938, when the newly installed Minister of Education, Oswald Menghin, immediately replaced him with the critic Mirko Jelusich.

20. Nene was Helene von Sonnenthal, one of Luise's sisters. After the war, she lived with her mother, Adele, in Hollywood, not far from the composer's home in Toluca Lake.

Some Experiences in Film Music

ERICH WOLFGANG KORNGOLD
EDITED AND INTRODUCED BY DANIEL GOLDMARK

This essay finds Korngold's world to be a drastically different place from where he sat for the interview in "Composing for the Pictures," just three years earlier. He and his family had made the trip between Hollywood and Vienna twice during this period. Korngold had scored several films, including all of *Another Dawn* (1937) and *The Prince and the Pauper* (1937), as well as sequences in *Hearts Divided* and *The Green Pastures* (both 1936). The family had spent the summer of 1937 at Schloss Höselberg, their country home, where Korngold worked on the opera *Die Kathrin,* which was scheduled to premiere in the coming year. In early 1938, Korngold received a telegram asking him to return to Hollywood yet again, this time to score *The Adventures of Robin Hood*. Initially interested in the project, Korngold turned down the assignment on seeing the film as it had, in his opinion, entirely too much action for a composer who focused on "heart, of passions and psychology."[1] Within days, however, the situation in Austria deteriorated to the point where the Korngolds realized not only that they could not return to their home, but that they had best make sure their older son Ernst, who had stayed in Vienna so as not to interrupt his schooling, left immediately, too, along with Korngold's parents, and flee not just Austria—but come all the way to Hollywood.[2] Faced with the prospect of being in California for the foreseeable future, Korngold ultimately agreed to score the film, which was released within two months' time. The score became not only his most acclaimed work for movies to date, but has since become the single work with which he is most associated; he also received an Academy Award for his efforts. By 1940, when this essay appeared, Korngold had also scored *Juarez* (1939) and *The Private Lives of Elizabeth and Essex* (1939).

The volume for which this essay was commissioned, *Music and Dance in California*, provided a veritable roundup of the state of the arts on the West Coast in 1940.[3] The book was meant to "give an adequate account of

Figure 1. From left to right: Korngold, Max Steiner, and Leo Forbstein. Max Steiner was probably the most famous of the "other composers" to whom Korngold compares himself, and Forbstein, the head of the Warner Bros. music department, was likely the "music-chief" mentioned below by Korngold.

the identity, the work, and the ideas of practicing musicians and professional dancers residing in California."[4] It begins with an essay by another European exile, Arnold Schoenberg; the more than sixty other contributors includes composer Ernst Toch, cellist Lajos Shuk, tenor Tito Schipa, and conductor Pierre Monteux. Several of the pieces focused on music for the stage and screen, with contributions from Nathaniel Finston, Meredith Willson, Ray Heindorf, Sigmund Romberg, and Gerard Carbonara, all prominent figures at the time in Broadway and Hollywood, although arguably none with a national reputation (excepting perhaps Romberg). Imagine the triumph the editors must then have felt when they learned that Korngold was going to write something. This essay remains the only piece in English in which Korngold shares his thoughts about his music in prose, rather than in an interview.

Given how little first-person testimony we have from Korngold regarding his work for film, this short document provides some extraordinary insight into the steep learning curve he faced when he first arrived in Hollywood. Korngold points out in the opening sentence that, though no one questioned his abilities as a composer for the stage and concert hall, he essentially knew nothing about the integration of music into film from a technical standpoint. He quickly mentions the composer's "most hated rival," the film's dialogue, as being distracting to the creation of the score, not to mention the sound effects, both of which typically end up dominating the music in traditional Hollywood soundtracks. As a composer of opera and operetta, Korngold had much experience in writing music that would express and articulate drama that was not yet realized—that is, his music came very early in the process of creating the drama, which was ultimately executed on stage and would change from performance to performance. Not so with cinema, in which Korngold received a largely completed record of a performance—the film itself—for which he would have to create a musical illustration of what he saw. No surprise, then, that he extols the virtues of writing music without needing to be tethered constantly to the restrictions of a click track[5] or even the finished film. Korngold also seems entirely aware of the fact that he is in the minority—perhaps even in a singular position in Hollywood—regarding the amount of deference he received as a composer. The ability to not only pick how many pictures he would score, but to go so far as to make suggestions for where the film might be edited at times, either to fit the music better or simply improve the drama, shows all too clearly the high esteem in which Korngold felt he was held as not merely a composer, but as a looming figure in the world of drama for stage and screen.

Some Experiences in Film Music
(1940)

When I came to Hollywood about six years ago, I knew no more about films and their making than any other mortal who buys his ticket at the box office. It was not even known to me that music—which happens to be my particular field—is only in rare cases recorded together with the picture, that is to say at the same time the camera photographs a scene. But my very first assignment, Reinhardt's production of *Midsummer Night's Dream*, was to make me familiar with all three music techniques. For this production, I had to make preliminary recordings, the so-called playbacks, of Mendelssohn's scherzo and nocturne, which were relayed over huge loudspeakers during the actual filming. Further, I conducted an orchestra on the stage for complicated, simultaneous "takes," and lastly, after the film was cut, I conducted a number of music pieces which were inserted in the completed picture as background music. In addition, however, I had to invent another, *new* method which was a combination of all three techniques and which was for music accompanying the *spoken word*. I wrote the music in advance, conducted—without orchestra—the actor on the stage in order to make him speak his lines in the required rhythm, and then, sometimes weeks later, guided by earphones, I recorded the orchestral part.

The playback system, which is used mostly for songs and dances in the so-called musicals, is without doubt the most satisfactory method for the composer. It not only enables him to create freely and independently but it also leaves him undisturbed by all kinds of noises such as cannon shots, ship sirens, rain and thunderstorms. No dialogue—the composer's most hated rival—not even the softest footsteps (let alone galloping horses, rattling automobiles, or roaring railroad trains!) interfere with his music. I myself have made only one such happy musical. Since *Captain Blood* I have been busy exclusively with the third and last technique—that of scoring. And I must confess that, despite the definite advantages offered the composer by the playback, I consider the task of composing and recording music for the completed picture the most interesting and, for the composer, the most stimulating. When, in the projection room or through the operator's little window, I am watching the picture unroll, when I am sitting at the piano improvising or inventing themes and tunes, when I am facing the orchestra conducting my music, I have the feeling that I am giving my own and my best: Symphonically dramatic music which fits the picture, its action and its psychology, and which, nevertheless, will be able to hold its own in the concert hall. And if the picture inspires me, I don't even have to measure or count the seconds or feet. If I am really inspired, I simply have luck. And my friend, the cutter, helps my luck along.

However, I am fully aware of the fact that I seem to be working under much more favorable conditions than my Hollywood colleagues, who quite often have to finish a score in a very short time and in conjunction with several other composers.

So far, I have successfully resisted the temptations of an all-year contract because, in my opinion, that would force me into factory-like mass production. I have refused to compose music for a picture in two or three weeks or in an even shorter period. I have limited myself to compositions for just two major pictures a year.

Further, I am told that my method of composing is entirely different from that employed by other Hollywood composers. I am not composing at a desk writing music mechanically, so to speak, for the lengths of film measured out by an assistant and accompanied with sketchy notes on the action of those sections, but I do my composing in the projection room *while the picture is unrolling before my eyes*. And I have it run off for me again and again, reel by reel, as often as I need to see it.

It is entirely up to me to decide where in the picture to put music. But I always consult thoroughly with the music-chief whose judgment, based on years of experience, I consider highly important. I also keep the producer well informed and always secure his consent for my musical intentions first. But in none of my assignments have I ever "played" my music first to either the music-chief, the director, or the producer. And the studio heads never make the acquaintance of my music until the day of the sneak preview. The executive producer always calls me in for the running of the picture's final cut and I am invited to voice my opinion for or against proposed changes, and I may make suggestions myself.

The actual composing of the music is not begun until the final cut of the picture is ready. But most of my leading themes and general mood motifs suggest themselves to me on reading the manuscript. Only when the picture has reached the stage of the final cut can I proceed to compose the exact lengths needed for the different music spots. Changes after the preview are often painful, although fortunately I have not suffered any particularly smarting musical losses.

I have often been asked whether, in composing film music, I have to consider the public's taste and present understanding of music. I can answer that question calmly in the negative. Never have I differentiated between my music for the films and that for the operas and concert pieces. Just as I do for the operatic stage, I try to invent for the motion picture dramatically melodious music with symphonic development and variation of the themes.

The toughest problem in film music production is and remains the *dupe* system, i.e. the combining of dialogue, sound and music. It is difficult from the beginning to strike the right balance between dialogue and music, but it is achieved fairly accurately in the small intimate dupe room which is acoustically ideal. However, when the film reaches the theatres which are large, noisy, acoustically uneven, often poorly equipped, this delicate balance is easily upset, and even distorted.

But I am convinced that in time better solutions will be found. Motion pictures are young and neither the public nor those who are making them have a right to be impatient or ungrateful for what has already been achieved.

NOTES

1. Korngold to Warner Bros. producer Hal Wallis, 11 February 1938; transcribed in Brendan G. Carroll, *The Last Prodigy: A Biography of Erich Wolfgang Korngold* (Portland, OR: Amadeus Press, 1997), 270–71.

2. This pivotal moment in Korngold's life is described in detail in a section of Luzi Korngold's biography of her husband included in "Farewell to Vienna," in this volume, as well as in the letter from Julius Korngold to his son dated 15 March 1938, reproduced in "Give Up Your Plans of Coming Home," also in this volume.

3. José Rodriguez, ed., *Music and Dance in California*, comp. William J. Perlman (Hollywood, CA: Bureau of Musical Research, 1940), 137–39.

4. Ibid., 5.

5. The "click track" is a metronomic device used during film scoring sessions to provide a regular beat for the musicians, but it can also be handy for composers as a guide when writing the music itself. Though it is an established part of the film composer's tool kit today, in 1940 the click track was still a relatively recent development, given that synchronized soundtracks (including music) had only just arrived in the late 1920s and had not been standardized when Korngold first came to Hollywood.

Faith in Music!

ERICH WOLFGANG KORNGOLD
INTRODUCED BY KEVIN C. KARNES

This short essay was Korngold's last published statement on music, and in it he made no mention of his own. Written in October 1955, less than half a year after what would turn out to be his final, dispirited return from Europe, "Faith in Music!" recapitulates a position he outlined in "Notes for an Interview," updating it for the postwar world, with its collective witness to what had recently been the unimaginable, technologized violence of the interceding years. Against the backdrop of his critical failures in Austria and West Germany, and recasting his apology for the untimeliness of all great works of music, he wrote: "The true creative artist does not wish to recreate for his fellow man the headlines screaming of atom bombs, murder, and sensationalism found in the daily paper."[1]

The occasion for his writing was an invitation from Ulric Devaré (also De Vaere), a young musician and author from Southern California who found inspiration in Korngold's music and at least a measure of emotional support in the Korngold home. A graduate of UCLA and an assistant to the émigré organist Edouard Nies-Berger, Minister of Music at the First Congregational Church in Los Angeles, Devaré credited his exchanges with Erich and Luzi Korngold as his foremost inspiration in writing his book, also called *Faith in Music*. He recounted "being with him and his brilliant wife, inspired by his wisdom, philosophy and great gift."[2] Devaré was devoutly Christian, but "faith" in his book is an ecumenical concept, potentially even a non-theological one. "I call my book *Faith in Music*," he wrote, "for I have found that throughout the centuries the majority of great masters and artists were people of faith." He continued: "It is with faith that we venture into music, music that brings faith, music that extols more than do words, feelings, inspirations, the patter of life itself. All of this can be expressed in music."[3] Korngold's first paragraph in the essay below, written as a foreword to Devaré's volume, could stand as a precis of the book as a whole.

Treating the topic of religious conviction only on occasion, Devaré penned a listener's guide to what he considered the great works of Western music, written for a musically literate yet generally unprofessional audience. He mostly considered classical music, but he included discussions of African-American spirituals (he admired Marian Anderson's performances in particular) and film music as well. Calling Max Steiner "the dean of American film composers," Devaré did not treat Korngold's film scores at length, but his admiration for his work is clear.[4] Possibly revealing something of his personal contact with the composer, he noted that Korngold's Second Symphony—left incomplete in manuscript at the time of his death in 1957—was "soon to be performed in the United States." He identified its key correctly as F major (only a handful of intimate acquaintances would have had access to its score), and he described it as "probably the greatest orchestral work since Strauss's *Also Sprach Zarathustra* and Mahler's *4th Symphony* [sic], for sheer tonal beauty and genius of orchestration."[5] One should note, however, that Korngold never got so far as orchestrating his manuscript score.

Korngold's biographer Brendan Carroll reports that Devaré delivered the eulogy at the composer's funeral service.[6] In 1957, Devaré dedicated a short collection of aphorisms to Korngold and his wife. Still later, in a dramatic poem narrating Christ's last words and death, Devaré acknowledged "Madame Erich Wolfgang Korngold" among those who had continued to provide him with support.[7] The proceeds he earned from publishing *Faith in Music*, Devaré reported, were donated to the African mission founded in 1913 by the musicologist, physician, missionary, and philanthropist Albert Schweitzer, who had mentored Devaré's own mentor in Los Angeles, the organist Nies-Berger.[8]

Faith in Music!

Could one not rightfully assume that the creative musician, who must surely believe in his own creativity in order to be able to transmit it to his audience convincingly, is bound to believe in the highest creator of all being, all life, all the mysterious forces of nature? And isn't music indebted to this faith, be it of a purely religious or a philosophical nature, for the most lofty and uplifting works of its literature?

We have been given the immortal passions of Johann Sebastian Bach, in his *High Mass in B Minor*, Beethoven's *Missa Solemnis*, Mozart's *Requiem*, Schubert's movingly beautiful *Mass in E-flat Major*, Brahms's chaste *German Requiem*, Mahler's *Resurrection Symphony*, Stravinsky's *Symphony of*

Figure 1. Late image of Korngold playing the piano.

Psalms. Nor should we forget the grandiose *Requiem* of Berlioz, and even less, the solemn *Te Deum* of Anton Bruckner, who with childish, charmingly naïve proof of his faith, dedicated his *Ninth Symphony* to His Lord ("Dem lieben Gott").

But even the purest operatic composers such as Verdi or Rossini, who dared not leave their field of opera in order to prove themselves in the sphere of the symphony, have given to the world perhaps their most noble creations in the area of religious creativity: Verdi's magnificent, song-filled *Requiem*, and Rossini's lovely, melodic *Stabat Mater*. As the supreme example of such a transformation, the last work of Richard Wagner, his *Bühnenweihfestspiel*, *Parsifal*, will uniquely preserve its enduring and culminating status.

As we bring to mind the immeasurable wealth of beauty which the prodigious, creative masters have left to us through their great works as their legacy, it is difficult to suppress serious regrets that in the musical arts, indeed in all arts, there exists a tendency away from beauty towards ugliness, away from the noble towards the revolting, ill-sounding and chilling. I, myself, do not believe in the mistaken thesis that art should mirror its time. The horrors of the Napoleonic war years are hardly recognizable in the compositions of Schubert or Beethoven; the beginning of the industrial-mechanical age, which surely had its roots in the invention of the steam driven locomotive, is mirrored in no way in the poetic works of Chopin, and still less in the music dramas of Richard Wagner, derived as they are from German legend. No, I am much more inclined to believe the opposite: the genuine artist creates at a distance from his own time, even for a time beyond. The true creative artist does not wish to re-create for his fellow man the headlines screaming of atom bombs, murder, and sensationalism found in the daily paper. Rather for his fellow men, he will know how to take and uplift him into the purer realm of phantasy.

May I be permitted then to offer a slight variation, another meaning to the title of this book. I have "Faith in Music." I have faith and I have confidence that the classic and romantic masterworks, the works of Bach, Haydn, Mozart and Beethoven, Schubert, Schumann and Mendelssohn, the symphonies of Brahms, Tchaikovsky, Bruckner and Mahler, as well as the charming French and Italian operas; and last, but not least, the operas of the German masters, Mozart, Wagner, and Richard Strauss, will continue to maintain their unbroken vigor and impact, and will bring to mankind today and in the future, pleasure and exaltation, dedication and happiness.

That this book may contribute to a genuine comprehension and enjoyment of the purest of all arts, "holy music," as it is called so beautifully in Strauss's *Ariadne*, is my sincere wish.

Erich Wolfgang Korngold

North Hollywood
October 1955

NOTES

1. Erich Wolfgang Korngold, "Faith in Music!," foreword to Ulric Devaré, *Faith in Music* (New York: Comet Press, 1958; orig. 1956), viii. Korngold's essay appears on pp. vii–ix of Devaré's book. Korngold's spellings of composers' names and titles of works are tacitly modernized in the present volume.

2. Devaré, *Faith in Music*, xi. Biographical information on Devaré is drawn from Ulric De Vaere, "Schweitzer's Reverence for Life," *Music Journal* 32/10 (December 1974): 22, and from the author's attendant biographical statement on page 5 of that issue of the journal.

3. Devaré, *Faith in Music*, xi, 3.

4. Ibid., 57. Devaré discusses Anderson's performances of spirituals on page 5.

5. Ibid., 59.

6. Brendan G. Carroll, *The Last Prodigy: A Biography of Erich Wolfgang Korngold* (Portland, OR: Amadeus Press, 1997), 395n12. I have been unable to locate documentary evidence in support of this claim, but Carroll's account matches the recollection of Korngold's granddaughter, Kathrin Hubbard, in an email to me, 22 October 2018.

7. Ulric Devaré, "The Woman of Light" (1956–57), in his *Journey into Harvest* (London: Villiers Publications, 1961); Ulric Devaré, *Pietà* (London: Villiers Poetry, 1959), 4.

8. Devaré, *Faith in Music*, vi.

Coda

Before and After Auschwitz: Korngold and the Art and Politics of the Twentieth Century

LEON BOTSTEIN

An unbroken record of condescension and disregard has shadowed the music of Erich Wolfgang Korngold since he first burst on the world scene as a prodigy of unparalleled gifts in 1908, at age eleven. The nadir of Korngold's reputation occurred in the decades that followed the end of World War II when leading critics, composers, and scholars either took no notice or denied Korngold the status of a major composer.

Times have changed. Since the early 1970s, spurred by popular modern recordings of Korngold's film music and the embrace of the Violin Concerto as a favored vehicle by a new generation of aspiring violinists, both Korngold's career as a composer and his output have gained in currency and respectability. Korngold's posthumous good fortune is the unanticipated consequence of the return to legitimacy, at the end of the twentieth century, of an aesthetic eclecticism regarding contemporary music. The belief in the exclusive legitimacy of an aesthetics of a radical modernism—justified by history, for the postwar world—has vanished. Minimalism, a new Romanticism, the integration with forms of popular music, and the blurring of genre distinctions all can be found in the music composed during the last forty years. These have turned Korngold from marginal figure into a prominent representative of the twentieth century, alongside other unjustly forgotten composers of a more "conservative" character.

Undeniable historical facts have also helped make the Korngold revival plausible. A striking eclecticism in compositional style flourished earlier in the twentieth century, both before and after World War II. Schoenberg and Stravinsky may have been the century's most prominent personalities, but they were part of a complex and varied musical culture that boasted many eminent protagonists of widely divergent approaches to the writing of new music (including the older but vigorous, productive, and combative Richard Strauss).

The barbarism and horror of World War II deepened the extent to which aesthetic claims on behalf of a break with the past assumed an irresistible significance. In the late 1940s and early 1950s, proponents of a radical departure from past practices, particularly those of late nineteenth-century Romanticism, believed that they were following an ethical imperative. How could one write music in the contemporary world that sounded like the music officially endorsed by fascism and the Nazi state? Modernism that had resisted fascist values and been declared "degenerate," such as the Second Viennese School, emerged from the war with unrivaled prestige.

But as the war and the Holocaust faded from memory, attitudes changed. The rediscovery of Mahler in the late 1950s and early 1960s, for example, was propelled at the start by a sense of Mahler as the Mahler of Theodor W. Adorno—the precursor of a modernist challenge to the conceits of late Romanticism. Mahler was understood as fighting to reclaim the autonomy of music as an art form from its subordination in post-Wagnerian aesthetics. Mahler was said to have shattered the complacency of musical practices in order to reassert music's inherent link to freedom and individuality. The success of the Mahler revival at the end of the twentieth century, however, was based on listening to Mahler quite differently: as the apogee of an expressive and progressive Romanticism rooted in the nineteenth century. This was the Mahler of Leonard Bernstein.

The sensibilities that ultimately propelled Mahler into the center of concert repertory in the 1980s and 1990s—Mahler as master of late Romanticism—also inspired efforts to look back and locate early twentieth-century composers who had been forgotten or neglected, especially those who were not central to the narrative of modernism's development but who were nonetheless victims of exclusion, exile, incarceration, and extermination during the 1930s and 1940s. Korngold came back into view, alongside Alexander Zemlinsky, Franz Schreker, Erwin Schulhoff, and Viktor Ullmann (to name just a few).

In Korngold's case, snobbery and envy of him retarded his acceptance as a "serious" composer. Stunning success in Hollywood gained him few friends and advocates. But now that a Korngold revival is underway on concert and opera stages (as well as in scholarly circles), the time has come to revisit, in a dispassionate manner, the doubts about Korngold's music that plagued the composer from the start of his career. Although there are now three recent biographies—in addition to the first Korngold monograph by R. S. Hoffmann and Luzi Korngold's book on her husband (completed after his death)—most current writing on Korngold is driven by a polemical, revisionist agenda.[1] Zealous enthusiasm has supplanted the pattern of neglect.

Though it is no longer necessary to make the case for Korngold against once powerful and persuasive detractors, the compensatory advocacy we now encounter suggests that Korngold fans may not yet be prepared to confront—without rancor—criticisms put forth by Korngold's contemporaries that may possess merit. The fact that Korngold was relegated to the margins as a serious voice in the world of concert music and opera may not have been only the result of Nazi persecution, anti-Semitism, the consequences of exile, or the tyranny of a cabal dedicated to promoting modernist aesthetics. Now that Korngold's chamber music, songs, orchestral works (including extracts from the film scores), and his music for the theater, both opera and operetta, have emerged from the shadows and been accorded the proper respect, what should be made of the controversy that surrounded his music?

None of the composers deemed "conservative" in their musical practices and unjustly neglected after 1945 (Zemlinsky and Schreker come to mind, as do Max Reger, Franz Schmidt, Joseph Marx, Othmar Schoeck, and Hans Pfitzner) ever achieved the international notoriety Korngold did, despite intense debates about their work. The impact of their music, whether admired or criticized, remained confined within distinct national and linguistic barriers. Korngold, in contrast, immediately captured the imagination of the wider international public and the press. His astonishing gifts as a prodigy and the refined maturity and distinctive craftsmanship he displayed from the start made him controversial. The stardom and potential role in music history that the eleven-year-old Korngold acquired as a composer came too early for comfort. Korngold's youthful prominence was reminiscent of Mozart, given that his father, Julius, was a powerful and feared figure, the chief music critic of Vienna's most respected and influential newspaper.[2]

The astonishing musical precocity of the young Korngold—his seemingly effortless but sophisticated and up-to-date command of harmony, sonority, and a subtle expressive rhetoric was unprecedented for a teenager, with the possible exceptions of Camille Saint-Saëns and Felix Mendelssohn. There is no way to sift out the awareness among Korngold's contemporaries of his youth from the other variables in their reactions to this creditable young composer. The price the young Korngold paid for writing works that betrayed no evident external hallmarks of immaturity was to become subject to the same sort of criticism directed at composers twice his age. Precocity inspired doubt and suspicion. In 1916, Hugo von Hofmannsthal, writing to Richard Strauss, reported that he had heard Korngold's one-act opera *Der Ring des Polykrates*. Hofmannsthal (who never revealed any personal antipathy to the composer) was dismayed.

The work seemed "ghastly." It was like the shadows cast by objects. It was a "bewitching mirror" of "unappealing" qualities characteristic of the present moment in history. Korngold's opera, taken as a whole, seemed pointless "because it lacked inner necessity."[3]

A similar concern ran through Paul Bekker's 1920 review of Korngold's greatest operatic triumph, *Die tote Stadt*. Bekker faulted the composer for failing to go beneath the surface. The music failed to generate a powerful sense of drama, despite its veneer of beauty, charm, grace, and variety. Korngold's music was refined, "sweet," and self-consciously "sentimental," but not truly deep or intimate. Korngold's talent seemed "derivative" and imitative. The music was consistently appealing but its effect static and tiring. Its shifts in style and mood never suggested a sufficient originality or instinct for dramatic development. A lingering sense of artificiality and superficiality hovered over a spectacular display of unequaled compositional virtuosity.[4]

Arthur Seidl echoed these opinions in his 1921 account of *Die tote Stadt*. The music lacked "inner unity" despite its resolute allegiance to a melodic beauty reminiscent of Puccini, and a series of fine lyric set pieces explicitly structured in opposition to the Wagnerian ideal of the music drama. There was something quite out of touch with contemporary sensibilities, Korngold's brilliant display of Strauss-like orchestral effects notwithstanding. Seidl thought Korngold failed to generate his own unique synthesis, and seemed content to string together disparate moments of music, each quite derivative, albeit masterfully executed. The work oscillated between Strauss-like sonorities, an "Offenbach-Bizet" world of dance and dreams, and a "Wagner-Pfitzner"-like approach to musical characterizations of fate and mysticism.[5]

These expressions of doubt and skepticism ought not be dismissed out of hand (as Korngold's advocates do) by ascribing their origins to a variety of personal prejudices and malicious motives, such as Bekker's strong advocacy of Schreker. The proper context is rather the fierce debate over what kind of music was adequate to the historical circumstances Europe faced in the years that immediately followed the end of World War I. The war had been brutal. It brought the nineteenth century to a chaotic end. Its consequences were catastrophic and transformative, beginning with the redrawing of the map of Europe and the dissolution of the Habsburg Empire.

An acute sense of a radical discontinuity with the past prevailed throughout the interwar years, fueled not only by the war's immediate effects on daily life—including poverty, migration, and the 1918 influenza epidemic—but also by technological changes (telephone, radio, gramophone, film) that signaled the emergence, on an unprecedented scale, of a popular and international mass culture. Europe was suddenly faced with the dramatic and powerful presence of America, the creation of the Soviet Union, the growing dominance of large-scale industrial production, and a pervasive economic and political instability.

A sense of modernity was inescapable. The two questions facing artists, writers, and musicians between 1914 and the outbreak of World War II were straightforward. How does one respond to the new realities, accompanied, as they were, by an overriding sense of an unprecedented distance from the remembered past? And in the changed landscape of life, how and for whom was one making music, and to what end? All attempts to answer these questions were inevitably forced to struggle with the allure of an assertion of the new and a competing urgency to preserve tradition.

Writing near the end of the interwar period, in 1937, Siegfried Kracauer framed the matter in terms of the need to confront a nineteenth-century notion that music, and perhaps all art, were instruments of "magic" that could transcend the mundane and the real. Faced with contemporary life, was it right to continue to hide behind the magic of the aesthetic and thereby deflect or deny the oppressive grip of the rational and mundane? Kracauer's answer was that music's "most important and now entirely undeniable function, in fact, lies in its capacity to practice white magic, and to strip the illusions that surround us of their magic power."[6]

Music needed to practice "white" magic—that is, criticism and resistance, the inverse of its traditional function. "Black" magic—music's unique power to offer the individual an exit from the quotidian—had to be abandoned. The experience of aesthetic beauty, construed in traditional terms, was an indirect affirmation of an otherwise intolerable, cruel, and unjust world. Contemporary music needed to provide neither an escape nor a distraction, but to do the opposite, and assume a truth-telling function. Composers had the obligation to confront the use of the aesthetic as camouflage or justification, to forswear its unwillingness to face the historical moment, and use music's unique power to shatter complacency.

The interwar years presented composers with a paradox. History could not be avoided. Those who sought to do something entirely new and those who sought to defend the inherited practices were both trapped in an intense dialogue with the past. The question was how to conduct that dialogue. In 1930 Ernst Krenek, Korngold's prolific contemporary who experimented with a wide range of approaches to writing music, all in search of an adequate response to the uniqueness of the present, acknowledged "the self-evident dependency" of any composer on the "process of history."[7] For those determined to stick to inherited and established materials and models in composition, the task was to find out how those materials might be given "new" meaning and serve "newer and freer ideas." Since the meaning of any already familiar musical practice implicitly changes with time, a radical change in the surface of music can actually imply the priority of the past by asserting, falsely, that the new has no past at all. Should a composer "decide to use outmoded musical means," the composer must realize that those means "would receive new historically determined meanings" due to "the extra-musical dependency of music on history."[8] By the same token, radicalism as a denial of the existence of tradition could easily and inadvertently legitimize it.

Such opinions expressed by the likes of Krenek and Adorno might seem a world apart from Korngold's concerns. However, Korngold had amazed his contemporaries before the war by how up to date and modern his music was whereas, after the war he appeared to resist the challenge of the historical moment by keeping a distance from most, if not all, modernist movements. He chose to assert a conservative faith in the canons of musical beauty and the arsenal of musical practices rooted in the fin de siècle he deemed normative. As Krenek suspected, the "outmoded" means Korngold held on to would gain new meanings; in Korngold's case that meaning was an association with the politics of reactionary conservatism.

In the interwar years, Korngold embraced the wit and grace associated with the Viennese operetta, and retained his admiration for the melodic gifts of Puccini. At the same time, he never lost a reverence for Richard Strauss. Korngold could play Strauss's entire *Elektra* from memory. One of the things he most looked forward to in the weeks before his death was listening to a live broadcast of *Elektra* from Salzburg, with score in hand.[9] Korngold dedicated his 1919 symphonic poem *Sursum Corda* to Strauss, whose orchestral writing it emulated. Korngold's postwar musical conservatism contrasted sharply with how young he still was in the 1920s. Strauss was sixty-four when World War I ended, Pfitzner fifty-nine, and Korngold only twenty-one. Korngold stood out within his generation as a formidable young voice for continuity and tradition.

The political and economic realities of the interwar years lent historical justification to the idea that modernism in the arts demanded a conscious confrontation with tradition, particularly the practices of aesthetic realism. Korngold may have stuck to what Krenek termed "outdated expressive means," but he did so, as his critics willingly admitted, with panache and incomparable finesse, while lending those expressive means a distinctive melodic and harmonic character. That allowed him to enjoy success with a public that resisted the assault on the legacy of late Romanticism in the 1920s.

The historical events in the years between 1933 and 1945, however, particularly the Holocaust, shattered any lingering legitimacy the nostalgia and complacency represented by the adherence to past musical practices still possessed. The need for self-examination about the nature, habits, and purposes of making art became unavoidable and imperative. Terrifying as the years of the Second World War were, postwar revelations about the death camps and the extent and barbarity of genocide made it impossible to deflect fundamental questions about the role art and culture might have played and what sort of art was adequate to the world after Auschwitz. Returning thoughtlessly to some semblance of normalcy seemed implausible. During the last twelve years of Korngold's life, the connection between past and present in the materials and methods of art, the interplay between art and ethics, and therefore the function and place of art music in a world after the Holocaust remained open questions for émigrés, exiles, and survivors, and particularly for composers within the European nations that had witnessed and participated in the barbarism and violence of the war.

Elisabeth Lenk, a student in West Germany in the early 1960s, remembered how Adorno, her teacher, put the matter: "After everything that has occurred, there is no longer anything harmless or neutral."[10] In 1962, writing in the magazine *Merkur*, Adorno observed, "The basis of art itself is shattered . . . an unbroken relationship to the aesthetic realm is no longer possible. The concept of a culture that has been resurrected after Auschwitz is illusory and nonsensical, and every artistic form that still manages to be created pays the bitter price for it. But because the world has survived its own destruction, it nevertheless needs art as its unconscious history writing. The authentic artists of the present are those in whose work the most extreme horror still resonates."[11]

For Adorno, art after Auschwitz had to possess "truth content" and could not rely on some sentimental or naïve sense of a "neutral" gift of inspiration or on timeless norms that bypass the need for a "self-understanding" rooted in confrontation with the historical moment. Art after Auschwitz, therefore, needed to "push away" from tradition. If in the "ruins" left behind by the war there indeed was still a basis for hope that might be conveyed through word, sound, and image, that glimmer of renewal could only be realized in art that "resolutely renounces" tradition. The artist must turn "away from the tradition" because the pursuit of tradition "misuses" the residual reason to hope and abuses our senses in order "to tell lies."[12]

The work of Samuel Beckett was, for Adorno, an exemplar of how the artist could respond authentically to this challenge.[13] If art was, in Kracauer's term, "white magic," and therefore something human that "transcended" the confines of subject matter (word and images), then the purest and highest medium of the aesthetic, for Adorno, was music.

Music, after Auschwitz, therefore possessed the moral obligation to convey "anxiety" and the suffering and "terror of men in the agonies of death, under total domination"[14] through a new form of magic, a means of expression that shattered the claim to validity of a past "magic," the aesthetic tradition that had failed to confront the stark historical realities and helped make the unthinkable—the barbarities of Auschwitz—real.

Yet using the suffering of victims as the direct substance of art was as fraught with danger as pursuing art that pretended the Holocaust had not happened. Despite the inherent danger of exploiting suffering and horror and using the aesthetic to render the unspeakable palatable through art, there was, for Adorno, at least one admirable musical model in Schoenberg's 1947 *A Survivor from Warsaw*. As Adorno wrote in the 1950s, "Horror has never rung as true in music, and by articulating it, music regains its redeeming power through negation."[15] The negation was audible in Schoenberg's renunciation of tradition in the shape and character of the music. He "combed" through its ruins and inserted them into the form of a fragment so tightly structured that the work was at one and the same time evocative of and distant from inherited traditions. Here was a musical work that, in being truthful in its referencing of the past and rejecting it, was also ethical.[16]

As Adorno's friend and survivor of Theresienstadt H. G. Adler wrote, achieving a truthful art in the wake of the Holocaust did not necessarily imply the priority of a certain type of astringent modernism. Adler had no use for Beckett; he did not categorically reject the possibility that familiar and older forms of lyricism and expression might escape the charge of either thoughtlessness about history or the unwitting collaboration with the culture and society that had made the Holocaust possible. As long as the individual artist maintained an authentic commitment to logic, truthfulness, and form, he or she could find the aesthetic means to convey the brutal facts and produce art without descending into the maudlin or the sentimental. One could avoid a nostalgia that ignored the Holocaust without relying on a style that explicitly confronted inherited criteria of comprehensibility, accessibility, and beauty. Therefore, although Adler shared Adorno's admiration of Schoenberg and *A Survivor from Warsaw* (for Adler, one of the few works that communicated horror with artistry by being "overwhelmingly emotional" through its disciplined use of musical materials and logic), he, like Krenek before him, left open the possibility that, in the right hands, inherited aesthetic practices might assume new and constructive humanistic meaning.[17]

Korngold, however, appeared to bypass the issue of this entire, intense post-Auschwitz debate about how art might be possible, and what sort of music was required in the contemporary world. His response to history, including his 1938 emigration and his ill-fated return to Europe in 1949, was to resist the notion of a need for any radical discontinuity in art parallel to the break with the past represented by Auschwitz. He seemed not to contemplate the changed ethical and political context. In 1952 he reasserted the necessity of adhering to a tradition of "inspiration, form, expression, melody, and beauty" against "atonality and ugly dissonance."[18] He acted as if normative aesthetic values were the only things at stake. His conscience as an artist required that he demonstrate the resilience and power of the inherited aesthetic principles he considered absolute and valid and fight for the renewal of a shared heritage of musical beauty and form in the face of horror, terror, anxiety, and suffering.

The irony of Korngold's position was that the character and qualities of music he celebrated and pursued were those advocated explicitly as part of the ideology of Nazism and Italian fascism. The prewar campaign against "degenerate" art and against the varieties of modernism that had emerged in the interwar years echoed the language and ideals Korngold reaffirmed after 1945. The contemporary European composers who shared his commitments were mostly sympathizers and collaborators. Korngold, a Viennese Jew in exile, whose family and friends suffered and died during the war and who was surrounded by other exiles, held firm to a pre–World War I construct of "inspiration, form, expression, melody, and beauty." These derived from three traditions: German, Viennese, and Italian. All three had been tainted and compromised by their protagonists between 1938 and 1945.

To understand Korngold's defense of tradition after World War I and again after World War II—his avoidance of any direct confrontation with the defining events of his time, and his rejection of radical formulations of modernism—a closer look at his ideals is required.

Korngold's Aesthetic Credo

In 1943 the film *The Constant Nymph* was released. Based on a novel and play by Margaret Kennedy, the score for the film was written by Korngold. But his role in making the film most likely extended to shaping the story and the dialogue, since at its core the film concerns the predicament facing the twentieth-century composer, and the screenplay deviates considerably from the novel. Improbable as it may seem from the vantage point of the early twenty-first century, the protagonist is indeed a composer of "classical" music, Lewis Dodd (played by Charles Boyer).

The film opens with a scene set in Brussels at some indeterminate time between the wars (the novel was first published in 1924).[19] Dodd has just received reviews from a concert in London at which a symphonic work of his had its premiere. The reviews are disastrous. The music is described as the work of a talented "mechanic." Dodd is accused of celebrating dissonance and making the listener "uncomfortable." Devastated and depressed, he decides to visit the family of his mentor, Albert Sanger, a composer who lives in the mountains of Switzerland.

Sanger has four daughters and a new Russian wife. Dodd is fond of the girls and brings with him some music he tossed off for their use, a mere present composed without pretense. Dodd arrives, predictably, from the modern city to its most cliché-ridden opposite, the high mountains of Switzerland, the ultimate European symbol of the power and beauty of nature unspoiled by man. He meets the Sanger "circus," a bustling household of women. They all adore him, particularly Tessa (played by Joan Fontaine), a young woman who suffers (no surprise) from a fatal heart condition. Dodd is strangely impervious to Tessa's fragility and her infatuation with him. In a private conversation with Sanger (seated at the piano), Dodd complains of the fiasco in London. Meanwhile the Sanger children begin to play the "trifle" he has written for them. Sanger hears Dodd's melody and is enchanted. Sanger begins to improvise on it and tries to persuade Dodd to write a symphonic poem based on the tune and abandon the modernist style he has pursued. Sanger advises Dodd to cease being "ashamed of melody."

Dodd leaves Sanger to help the daughters perform his little piece for them. Suddenly, Sanger dies. As Dodd and the daughters gather around the body, a piece of manuscript paper is found. On it is Dodd's melody with the beginnings of an elaboration and the title "Tomorrow, a Symphonic Poem," scrawled on it in Sanger's handwriting, along with the admonition to compose such a tone poem. The story line then develops around the wealthy family of Tessa's mother and one of her sisters. That family rescues two of the girls from poverty and Dodd marries the beautiful heiress of the family. He remains oblivious to Tessa's infatuation. Nevertheless, before leaving Switzerland for London, Dodd and Tessa commune together in nature, discussing poetry, love, and suffering, without which there is, the script argues, no true art. Nature and love emerge as the only genuine source of music, whose essence is, in turn, rooted in melody and tonality.

From that point on, the film centers on a new orchestral work Dodd is writing for a performance in London. When a piano version is performed at a house concert Tessa, now living with Dodd and his wife (in uncommon luxury), listens and remarks on how the music seems like "mathematics" and sounds like a "railway engine." The music is explicitly modern, without evident sentiment or heart. It possesses neither melody nor beauty. Dodd's wife endorses her husband's forward-looking composition, but Tessa rejects it. Dodd ultimately falls under the spell of the innocent and childlike devotion of the unschooled Tessa and her spontaneous spirit. He gradually realizes her love and reciprocates. He decides to follow her as his muse, and to return to the melody that had once enchanted Sanger and Tessa.

Dodd writes "Tomorrow," a symphonic poem for orchestra, women's choir, and mezzo-soprano solo. It is entirely tonal and lyrical. The film ends with its triumphant premiere, and the death of his muse, Tessa. With tears streaming down his face, Dodd hugs Tessa's lifeless body. The viewer realizes that Dodd has finally encountered love and suffering and that his loss will be translated into the writing of music from the heart, firmly rooted in melody and tonality—a natural music—that employs the full range of the practices of late Romanticism, including the harmonic and textural complexity of Richard Strauss, the melodic magnetism of Puccini, and the sweetness and lightness of Johann Strauss Jr.

The "modern" music Korngold wrote for the middle of the film that Tessa—the constant nymph—rejects is a curious hybrid parody of Hindemith, Schoenberg, and Stravinsky. It represents the "ugly" atonal alternative to the tonal melodiousness Korngold believed was rooted both in human nature and the natural world—and was therefore the only legitimate basis for the art of music. The work that closes the film and marks Dodd's conversion to Tessa's naïve and healthy instincts (heard by Tessa only over the radio), was subsequently extracted by Korngold as a concert piece.

Korngold would repeat this transfer of music from film to concert stage in the 1946 *Deception*, a film that also centers on a composer (this time a rich and successful one) who writes a cello concerto for a rival in an effort to win the affections of a protegé (Bette Davis). Korngold expanded the concerto as heard in the film into a self-standing, one-movement concert piece. In *Deception*, the composer (Claude Rains) is an egocentric and narcissistic character, a synthesis of the personalities of Richard Wagner and Arnold Schoenberg. In the film the composer-protagonist Hollenius is declared the greatest living composer and is placed between Richard Strauss (representing the past) and Stravinsky (the present). The aesthetic principles ascribed to Dodd and Hollenius in *The Constant Nymph* and *Deception* are unambiguous evocations of Korngold's commitments. Hollenius even suggests Korngold's sense of his own proper place in music history.

Deception has the virtue of explicitly referencing the war. Hollenius's rival, the cellist Karel Novak (Paul Henreid), is a European refugee, a hero of the resistance, and the survivor of a concentration camp. He wishes to return to the concert stage and pick up his career where he left off before the war. There are no comparable allusions to politics in *The Constant Nymph*. That film is centered entirely on the composer and his struggle to find his true voice, whereas in *Deception*, the love triangle dominates—involving the composer, the cellist, and Bette Davis as Christine Radcliffe, hardly an innocent creature or a child of nature immune to the blandishments of civilization (as Tessa is). *Deception* ends with Radcliffe shooting Hollenius at point-blank range because she fears he plans to humiliate the cellist. In contrast, death in *The Constant Nymph* is utterly natural: the fulfillment of a congenital destiny devoid of human intervention and triggered by pure and intense emotion.

Korngold wrote the music for *The Constant Nymph* in 1942. His decision to engage this subject and write the music at this historical moment (unlike his competitors in Hollywood, Korngold had his choice of films and limited the number he was required to write for) invites a comparison to Richard Strauss's last opera (and opus number) *Capriccio*, completed in 1941 and premiered in October 1942. What is remarkable about both works is that they were written during the darkest days of the war, at a time when Nazi Germany seemed headed for victory; the Battle of Stalingrad had just begun in the fall of 1942. Both works were already well underway in December 1941, when the "Final Solution" was being crafted at the Wannsee Conference.

But Strauss (at home on the side of the perpetrators) and Korngold (in exile, a victim) were both able to immerse themselves in and pursue aggressively historic aesthetic debates from the prewar era, one concerning the eighteenth-century quarrel about the priority of music over words, and the other the interwar dispute about whether post-Wagnerian materials and methods were appropriate in modern times. The eruption of a new world war seems to have inspired both composers to avail themselves of the opportunity to have the last word on a matter of aesthetics, since there seemed little chance that the world would return to a state of normalcy that might be hospitable to such musings.

The intensity of Korngold's clear identification with the argument of *The Constant Nymph* is mirrored by his own explicit ambition to vindicate the constancy of musical aesthetic values as true and linked to nature. Korngold rejected the Wagnerian notion that history should be understood as evolutionary and progressive. The ideological overlaps between Strauss's and Korngold's credo justify the comparison with *Capriccio*. At the same time, although Strauss may have been the composer Korngold admired most, even if he was aware (as he must have been) that Strauss was collaborating with the Nazi regime, there is no reason to think that Korngold knew of Strauss's new opera.

The Constant Nymph also needs to be understood in the context of two events that occurred during its genesis and release. Both involve fellow Viennese Jews who, like Korngold, were in exile. One was Schoenberg's composition of his twelve-tone but tonal setting of Byron, the *Ode to Napoleon*, a stunningly dramatic work defined by a fierce anti-Nazi sensibility bordering on despair, between March and June 1942. The other is the February 1942 suicide of Stefan Zweig. Zweig was convinced that German, the language of his literary vocation, had been irrevocably discredited and hijacked by Nazism and that he could never regain his reading public. In the darkest of times, ones that revealed the depth and extent of human evil, Korngold articulated his defense of tonality, melody, and musical beauty—pre–World War I hallmarks of culture that had already assumed status as reactionary values during the interwar years.

The Constant Nymph and *Deception* not only help clarify Korngold's understanding of the calling of composer and musician but they are also symptomatic of the extent to which Korngold had been insulated from politics throughout his career. That insulation suggests a nagging question that haunts Korngold's reputation and the reception of his music, particularly the music from his time in Hollywood, including the instrumental music that utilized material from the film scores. This question was posed for music in the aftermath of the war by Leo Schrade, the eminent musicologist and Monteverdi expert, in his Charles Eliot Norton Lectures from 1963. "Does tragedy no longer resound in music and musician[s] of today?" Schrade lamented, with a veiled allusion to contemporary mass culture. "Our sense of genuine greatness may be deadened by the noise that nowadays is made of trifles . . . we may have become callous to the reverberation of tragedy."[20] Nonetheless, for Schrade (and his generation), in music "the history of artists is, and must be by its nature, the history of tragedy."[21]

The way in which Thomas Mann, in 1945, chose to characterize the German character as fundamentally musical helps explain Korngold's insularity with respect to history and politics. For Mann, music was the essence of inwardness, a path to the interior of the soul. This synthesis of idealism and cultural pride lent legitimacy to the shielding of the musical from matters of politics and society. Mann cited Balzac, who observed that Germans were incapable of playing the "instruments of freedom" although they were adept at "playing the instruments of music."[22] World War II and Nazism had shown Mann the consequences of the German Faustian ambition regarding music as emblematic of interiority and the concomitant conceit about the well-earned German superiority in creating it. The tragedy was that "the musicality of the soul costs dear in another sphere—in the political sphere, that of human coexistence."[23]

Korngold's oft-quoted 1946 statement that "music is music," no matter its form or intended purpose, and that "the composer needs to make no concessions to whatever he conceives to be his own musical ideology" was more than a defense of the music he had written for films.[24] It was an assertion of his self-image as the defender of a specifically German tradition, mediated by its most distinct and persuasive realization, the musical culture of nineteenth-century Vienna. What made Korngold's chauvinism as poignant as it was astonishing was his stubborn refusal to acknowledge a century of anti-Semitic polemic in German culture that denied Jews the capacity to represent the special German gift of musicality, a line of argument that reached its apogee under the Nazis.

It comes as no surprise, then, that among the most telling enterprises Korngold undertook in the postwar era was his creation of the music for a 1955 movie on the life of Richard Wagner, *Magic Fire*. Korngold makes a cameo appearance as a conductor in the film, playing the part of Hans Richter at the opening of Bayreuth in 1876. *Magic Fire* is remarkable in two respects. First in the deft ingenuity displayed by Korngold in sewing together fragments from Wagner and turning them into a film score, in a manner somewhat reminiscent of his approach to adapting Mendelssohn's music for Max Reinhardt's *A Midsummer Night's Dream*. Second, and more significantly, was his willingness to write for a film that sanitized Wagner's personality and politics and avoided any focus on the exceptional place occupied by anti-Semitism in Wagner's ideology and career. Wagner had been a dominant voice in the successful dissemination of the anti-Semitic theory that Jews were inherently bereft of genuine aesthetic creativity, incapable of becoming truly German, and therefore incapable of serving as protagonists of the unique German gift for music. *Magic Fire*, a depiction of Wagner that downplayed a key aspect of Wagner's character and cultural and political influence, became yet another vehicle for Korngold's defense of his aesthetic credo and his own place in history.

The startling whitewashing of Wagner less than a decade after World War II can be explained by the unique roots of Korngold's self-image. Three factors were decisive: Korngold's career as a child prodigy composer, the outsized influence of his father, Julius Korngold, and the allegiance to Vienna's idea of itself as the city of music shared by father and son alike.[25] Each of these factors had a common corrosive undercurrent: a prevailing anti-Semitism articulated precisely in the terms of Richard Wagner's influential arguments and rhetoric.

The Jewish Question

There is no doubt that Erich Wolfgang Korngold, as a prodigy, was a phenomenon. His prodigious musical gifts were astonishing in that the music he wrote before reaching adulthood gave no hint that he was a child or adolescent. This led anxious observers to fear that this unprecedented talent would be deprived of access to a normal process of coming of age. Erich's father was warned not to exploit his son. The contradiction between a music that seemed to persuasively convey emotional depth with sophisticated musical means and the extreme youth of a composer who himself had no experience of love, pain, suffering, desire, and loss naturally fueled mistrust.[26] The only precedent for the young Korngold's accomplishment was not Mozart (despite the recurring comparisons to him) but Mendelssohn, whose early output (the string symphonies and the Octet, for example) also revealed few traces of his youth. The fact that Mendelssohn—along with Meyerbeer—was a central target of Wagner's anti-Semitic theory of Jewish creative impotence and, like Korngold, had been born a Jew, was not lost on critics of the young Korngold.

For that reason Rudolf Stephan Hoffmann felt compelled to devote a separate section in his 1922 biography of Korngold (then only twenty-five years old) designed to refute claims that there was something particularly "Jewish" about Korngold and his music. He defended Korngold's originality and significance against the claim that his compositions were nothing more than brilliant examples of specifically Jewish gifts of shrewd imitation and self-promotion.[27]

Hoffmann understood that there were four strands to the anti-Semitic critique of Jewish composers in German-speaking Europe, all derivative of Wagner. First was the idea that Jews, by virtue of their distinct history, were pariahs, fundamentally disconnected from German land, language, history, and society, and therefore cut off from the authentic sources of aesthetic creativity. Second, Jews were masters of abstract, rational calculation, adept at dissection and analysis and therefore imitation. Jews were skilled reproductive talents, and brilliant at copying, but incapable of true originality. Third, Jews, in the era following emancipation had come to dominate in modern urban culture and economic life, and consequently the commerce of the arts, particularly through their control of journalism and the press. Last, having shed their external garb of exoticism Jews assumed the characteristics of cosmopolitanism. They masqueraded as members of the majority, thereby becoming an insidious, nearly invisible threat to a healthy, genuine German national culture.

Hoffmann grasped that all these accusations could be readily leveled against Korngold. First, his exceptional talent could be ascribed to a special Jewish gift of mimicry and emulation. Second, the complexity of his musical language—his skills in realizing the logic of form, his handling of counterpoint, his harmonic sophistication—could all be contingent on the special Jewish gift of intellectual manipulation and abstraction and not on a true spiritual affinity. Above all, Korngold's worldwide fame was plausibly the consequence of a conspiracy that included his father, a powerful music critic, and the Jewish-controlled press, particularly Vienna's leading daily, the *Neue freie Presse* (for which Julius Korngold wrote), as well as several music journals and publishing houses, all in the hands of Jews.

Hoffmann's rebuttal did not dwell on the fact that some of Korngold's detractors were Jews—the critics Robert Hirschfeld and Paul Bekker among them. Rather, Hoffmann went after the premises of turn-of-the-century anti-Semitic cultural criticism. Hoffmann quoted generously from theorists who assumed the impossibility of acculturation and the indelibility of racial characteristics. But for Hoffmann, history refuted these ideas. Since the eighteenth century, a class of "European" composers had developed who commanded a "European" musical language. Korngold may have been descended from Jews, but he was no longer a Jew. An advanced "European" culture that transcended archaic national characteristics was a sign of modernity and was audible in the very accomplished cosmopolitan character of Korngold's music. Korngold's identity as a "European," Hoffmann argued, could be inferred from his music. If indeed any residual indelible "Jewish" inherited characteristics remained in the character of modern "European" composers who had descended from Jews, why was there such a marked disparity in the kind of music written by Schreker, Schoenberg, Mahler, and Korngold?[28] The suspicion that some shared but hidden "Jewish" element lurked in the music of all these composers, or in the artistry of performers such as Bruno Walter, Joseph Joachim, or Karl Tausig, was unwarranted.

Hoffmann drew on the popularity among German-speaking readers of sweeping theories of history. Hoffmann referred explicitly to Oswald Spengler's *The Decline of the West* (1918).[29] The achievement of Jews like Korngold—their capacity to emancipate themselves from the narrow determinants of place, belief, race, and language—were indications of a larger pattern of historical change. For better or worse, the acculturation and assimilation of the Jews of Europe were harbingers of the historical destiny facing all *Mitteleuropäer* (Central Europeans). A new "European" transnational identity had come into being. The time had come to ignore the racial and national heritage of all "creators" of art and focus on the shared ideals and substance reflected in the works they created. For Hoffmann, Mahler was the clearest example of the need to do so. Hoffmann compared the alleged Jewish exoticism in Mahler's music to an Orientalism equally audible in the music of Max Bruch and Karol Szymanowski. Korngold, like Mahler, was no Jew, because according to the logic of history, the "Jew has become a European."[30]

In terms of history Hoffmann's argument was more nostalgic than persuasive. In the sense of Hugo von Hofmannsthal's "bewitching mirror," Hoffmann's analysis actually vindicated the widespread fear, in both postwar Austria and Germany, of how precarious the future of a distinct German identity had become. His argument harked back to the prewar ideal of a supra-national Habsburg identity that sought to compete successfully against a political nationalism based on myths of racial homogeneity and shared history. As the writer Joseph Roth often quipped, the only true citizens of the Habsburg Empire seemed to have been the Jews. By the early 1920s, the vision of a multinational European culture and cosmopolitan identity had become an object of attack in the context of nationalist fervor in the new nations of postwar Central and Eastern Europe. The ultimate irony was that in the interwar years Korngold, the conservative, and Schoenberg, the radical modernist, both saw themselves not as cosmopolitans, but as the contemporary standard bearers of a unique cultural heritage: German, in Schoenberg's case, and in Korngold's case, the aesthetic culture of Vienna.[31]

Throughout the 1920s, particularly in the wake of the extraordinary success of *Die tote Stadt*, Korngold's music would be derided on the basis of the cornerstone claims of Wagner's anti-Semitism. Writing to Richard Strauss in November 1922, the composer Max von Schillings (who later became an ardent Nazi) complained at length about the difficult situation he faced in Berlin. He blamed the "Alberichs" (a transparent reference to Wagner's dwarfs in the *Ring*, long understood as representing Jews), who were now in control of cultural policy and the press in the Weimar Republic. Schillings' bête noir was Paul Bekker, who was, ironically, not enamored of Korngold, but favored the "Neutöner"—the word applied to assertive modernist composers, many of them Jews. "There is no society dedicated to fighting anti-Aryanism in the arts," Schillings lamented, "only one against anti-Semitism. You know that chapter."[32]

But what was most galling for Schillings, who hated "father and son" Korngold, was the fact that he had read "with some pleasure" (as he put it sarcastically) that in America, the newspapers reported that his own opera *Mona Lisa* had been "modeled" on Korngold's *Tote Stadt*.[33] As Strauss knew well, *Mona Lisa* had premiered in 1915, five years before

Die tote Stadt, and become a tremendous hit. Between 1915 and 1934, the opera would be performed over 1,500 times all over the world, including New York. Strauss was planning to stage it at the Vienna State Opera. Schillings' exasperation took the form of an explicit reference to Wagner's notorious major essay on Jews and music: "If ever 'Judaism in Music' was enriched by a new chapter, it has been through the talented Erich Wolfgang, a sweet boy."[34]

All the elements of post-Wagnerian anti-Semitic stereotyping were evident in Schillings' comments about Korngold: the Jewish control of the press, and the particularly Jewish talent for appropriation, and a Jewish gift for mimicry. *Die tote Stadt* was, if anything, imitative of his own *Mona Lisa* in terms of structure (a prologue and epilogue) and the use of a dream sequence. Julius Korngold's contemptuous and dismissive 1915 review of *Mona Lisa* had not disposed Schillings to a more generous view of Erich Wolfgang.[35] But even Schillings could not deny Korngold's talent, innocence, and youth.

Schillings' correspondent, Richard Strauss, has been characterized by Korngold's biographers and partisans as admiring and supportive of Korngold. Strauss was the contemporary composer to whom Erich Wolfgang looked up to most, and Strauss's influence is audible throughout Korngold's career. However, Strauss's attitude was far more complicated.

Egotism and a nearly obsessive focus on getting his own work performed defined Strauss. Little else seemed to matter—and certainly not politics. He had little time or sympathy for contemporaries who were composers, all of whom seemed more rivals than colleagues. During the 1920s he cultivated performers with an eye to getting his works on the stage. The closest interaction between Korngold and Strauss occurred between 1919 and 1924, when Strauss shared the directorship of the Vienna State Opera with Franz Schalk. Unfortunately, Julius Korngold opposed this administrative setup, and quickly became an unrelenting thorn in the side of the new management. Schalk was stridently anti-Semitic, and his correspondence with Strauss suggests that he suspected—as did Schillings—that Strauss might sympathize.[36] But Strauss's anti-Semitism was reflexive and marginal, dictated only by self-interest. In 1924, his only son married into a Jewish family. Much as he maintained some skepticism about Mahler's virtues as a composer, his regard was not compromised by anti-Semitism but by plausible doubts about the music. Strauss considered Schoenberg, whom he knew, a formidable talent who had simply gone off the rails (*wahnsinnig*). He refrained from criticizing Schoenberg's music as typical of Jewish calculation and abstract thinking.[37] Schoenberg's abandonment of inherited logic and expressive conventions of music was just errant nonsense and a passing fad.

If Strauss's vigorous advocacy of the young conductor George Szell during his tenure at the Vienna Opera is any indication, Korngold's status as a Jew played a minor role, if any, in Strauss's attitude toward him. Szell—who early on exhibited unmistakable brilliance as a composer and was published by Universal Edition, with whom he signed a ten-year contract at age fifteen—was equally a fabulous pianist.[38] Both Szell's parents were Hungarian Jews, and he was born Jewish in Budapest in 1897, the same year as Korngold. The family subsequently converted to Catholicism. Conversion was somewhat more common among elite assimilated Hungarian Jews in Budapest than among their counterparts in Vienna. Yet many Viennese musicians converted, often to Protestantism (as a compromise, as Schoenberg did) for career purposes and intermarriage. The Viennese list of Jewish converts includes Arnold Rose, the concertmaster of the Vienna Philharmonic, and several of his colleagues.

George Szell was exactly Erich Wolfgang Korngold's age. Szell's parents moved to Vienna when George was three. Szell made his debut when he was ten and a half: the Vienna Tonkünstler under Oskar Nedbal performed an original orchestral work by him in the Musikverein, and Szell played a Mozart piano concerto. As in the case of Korngold, the press made comparisons to Mozart. Even Julius Korngold was impressed. His archenemy, Hirschfeld, was entirely won over.[39]

Szell's parents, proud as they may have been, were somewhat better at shielding their son from overexposure, though as a young man he struggled to overcome the trauma of having been a prodigy. Szell made a tour of Europe in 1908 that included a successful debut in London. His early compositions—the 1918 orchestral *Variations on an Original Theme*, for example—reveal a level of maturity and refinement equal to that exhibited by Korngold (and it has been suggested that Szell wrote hundreds of works before turning twenty-one).[40] But in the end, Szell considered his own compositions too derivative and ceased composing. Strauss was so impressed with the nineteen-year-old's conducting that he waged a vociferous, byzantine, but ultimately unsuccessful struggle to hire Szell at the opera.

By then, Julius Korngold had come to see Szell as a rival to his son and was fiercely opposed to his having a post in Vienna. Szell went on to Berlin, only to be handed the 1924 Berlin premiere of *Die tote Stadt* because Erich Kleiber refused to conduct the work in view of a nasty review he had gotten in Vienna from Julius. The Berlin premiere's success was more muted than elsewhere, fueling Julius's anti-Berlin bias in favor of the German capital's rival, Vienna. Szell's role was passed over by both Korngolds. Szell's experience with *Die tote Stadt* did not lead to any later connection with Korngold's music: excerpts from the Berlin production would be the only recordings of Korngold's music Szell ever made. In all this intrigue, there was no hint of anti-Semitism on Strauss's part. And this was not on account of Szell's baptism; by the 1920s political and cultural anti-Semitism had everything to do with constructions of race, and nothing to do with religion.

Strauss derided all the "moderns" in the 1920s, Jewish or not, and he did not wish to be associated with them. He denigrated his rivals as all equally second-rate, from Pfitzner to Schreker and Korngold, and he made fun of their efforts. He was amazed at Hindemith's talent as performer and composer, but thought of him as a nutty, naughty wild young man.[41] Erich Wolfgang Korngold, contrary to the claims of his biographers, seems to have acted like a prima donna at the Vienna Opera, annoying Strauss and Schalk both.[42] Yet they were eager to please and backed the staging of Korngold's two one-act operas and *Die tote Stadt*.

Strauss was quite indifferent to Korngold's work. There was far worse around. In his April 1945 letter to Karl Böhm (an enthusiast of the Nazi regime), Strauss, always eager to anticipate the consequences brought to the visibility of his music by political change, included Korngold's *Polykrates* in a long list of the opera repertoire that would be essential in the postwar world.[43]

Strauss, in his short-lived role at the Vienna Opera, did not wish to strengthen the perception that he himself was a reactionary. He sensed that he was falling fast from prominence, and sought to counter the perception that his greatest and most innovative work lay behind him. The statistics of opera performances in Germany during the mid- and late 1920s bear out Strauss's anxieties. Far and away the largest number of performances between 1926 and 1931 were of Puccini operas. Next came Strauss, with about half that number.[44] Lagging far behind were performances of operas by Pfitzner, Weill, Schreker, and Korngold.

What worried Strauss was the fate of his new works, not that of *Salome*, *Elektra*, or *Der Rosenkavalier*. His most recent opera from the late 1920s was the 1927 *Die ägyptische Helena*, written with Hofmannsthal. Perhaps inspired by Korngold's successful 1923 adaptation of Johann Strauss Jr.'s *Eine Nacht in Venedig* and his own instinct to turn away from the monumental Wagnerian toward the operetta as a model for a successful new opera, Hofmannsthal proposed to Strauss an Offenbach-like treatment of the Helen of Troy story.[45] Ironically, Hofmannsthal and Strauss produced in this last of Strauss's so-called marriage operas a subtle and serious musical and literary deconstruction of romance. *Die ägyptische Helena* confronts the complexity of forgiveness in the wake of adultery and jealousy, and the difficulty couples face trying to reclaim their love.

To Strauss, Korngold was clearly a competitor. In 1921, before going on tour with the Vienna Philharmonic, Strauss remarked to Schalk that he was going to America in part to raise money for Vienna. But he also did not want to leave unchallenged the impression in America that "Erich Wolfgang Korngold alone represents music."[46] Strauss, however, remained respectful and performed Korngold on the 1923 Vienna Philharmonic tour of South America alongside Schmidt, Mahler, and Schillings.

Die ägyptische Helena premiered in the same season as Korngold's *Das Wunder der Heliane*. Strauss's new opera received 173 performances in German-speaking Europe, Korngold's 80. By the next season, Korngold's opera struggled. But so too did Strauss's. After *Das Wunder der Heliane* Korngold turned away from serious opera to pursue the operetta path, including adaptations of *Die Fledermaus* in 1929 and Offenbach's satirical 1864 *La belle Hélène* in 1931. In the two seasons between 1929 and 1931, there were only 35 performances of Strauss's new opera out of a total of 890 Strauss performances.[47] During the same period, there were only 31 performances of any Korngold opera. This contrast, however, did not reassure Strauss.

For Strauss no contemporary composer truly rivaled the quality and importance of his own music. He was intent to show how superficial all new music was—whether modernist or conservative, whether by Schreker, Krenek, or Korngold. When one compares the exploration of love, marriage, and mythic incarnations of the feminine in Strauss's and Korngold's operas from 1927, the contrast is striking. Korngold's opera is rooted in symbolism and stays at the level of a parable. The protagonists in *Heliane* seem hardly real and individual. Desire and love remain idealized constructs lavishly translated into music. In contrast, Strauss and Hofmannsthal transform myth. Helen and Menelaus become recognizable human personalities trapped in a marriage torn by crisis. Helen's decision to reject magic, forgetfulness, and illusions and face the hard task of forgiveness and reconciliation stands in contrast to the more impersonal and metaphysical representation of resurrection, miracle, salvation, and renewal in Korngold. Korngold's score is beautiful, but there is more nuance, drama, and intensity in Strauss.

Korngold's failure to match the success of *Die tote Stadt* with *Das Wunder der Heliane* may have provided him with the impetus to turn to intensive work in the operetta field. His facility, range, and ingenuity— and his life experience—were suited to the lighthearted, decorative, and entertaining fantasy world of the genre. Korngold's achievement in the operetta field prepared him brilliantly for his subsequent turn to composing for films.[48]

Both fields prized his talent and refinement, and his quick skill in writing for the theatrical moment. Korngold's intuitive affinity for the light and gracefully satirical theater are central to understanding his mature aesthetic. And that aspect of Korngold's aesthetic was in turn a reflection of the particular ways in which he came to construe and love his native city, Vienna.

Korngold's Vienna

Hermann Broch, the writer born in 1886 in Vienna to a well-to-do Jewish textile manufacturer, was nearly an exact contemporary of Korngold, and came from the same milieu. Broch died in 1951, like Korngold an exile in America. In *Hugo von Hofmannsthal and His Time*, Broch penned a trenchant and unsentimental analysis of the Vienna in which he and Korngold were born and came of age. Broch observed:

> Although Vienna felt itself . . . an art city par excellence. . . . It was far less a city of art than a city of decoration par excellence. Consonant with its decoration, Vienna was cheerful, often idiotically cheerful, but with little sense of indigenous humor or even sarcasm and self-directed irony . . . the decorative was legitimate in Vienna. . . . Vienna confused culture with "museumness" [*Museumshaftigkeit*] and became a museum to itself. . . . Because Haydn and Mozart, Beethoven, and Schubert had miraculously converged on this spot, had been badly treated and had nevertheless composed, Vienna set itself up as a musical institution. . . . The "museumish" [*das Museale*] was reserved for Vienna, indeed as a sign of its ruin, the sign of Austrian ruin. For in despondency decay leads to vegetating, but in wealth it leads to the museum. Museumishness [*Musealität*] is the vegetating of wealth, and Austria at the time was still a wealthy country. . . . And Austria, as a country that had partly lost, partly squandered its world-political mission, was utterly unfit to contain such a city. After 1848, the city . . . moved ever more deeply into the un-revolutionary, the hedonistic, the skeptic-courteous, courteous-skeptic. Vienna became an "un-worldly city," and,

without thereby becoming a small town, it sought small-town tranquility, small-town narrow-mindedness, small-town pleasures, the charm of "once upon a time.". . . The operetta form created by Strauss became a specific vacuum-product; yet as a vacuum decoration it proved itself all too durable, and its later worldwide success can be taken as a *mene-tekel* [the writing on the wall in the Book of Daniel] for the submergence of the whole world into a relentlessly widening value vacuum. Vienna, center of the European value-vacuum—surely a somewhat absurd honor and distinction, yet not so absurd when one takes into account the sociopolitical texture of the city, the social texture of Austria itself, unique in Europe.[49]

It was the peculiar destiny of Jews like Erich's parents—who moved to the city of Vienna after the constitutional reforms of 1867 that created the Austro-Hungarian Empire—not only to absorb this peculiar Viennese culture, but to become its most ardent protagonists. The highly visible allegiance to and outsized participation in the city's aesthetic culture of civic self-celebration by Viennese Jewry (who, by 1914, accounted for over 12 percent of the city's population) triggered a critical reaction, much of it drawn from within Vienna's Jewish community. Korngold made his spectacular entrance into Vienna's musical life at a time defined by a sharp and bitter struggle over the character and function of art, and above all music. And in Vienna in the early twentieth century, art was politics.

Julius Korngold was a visible and influential figure on the side of those who defended Vienna's "museum" self-image and its conceit as the city of art par excellence. Many Jews of his generation, particularly those who had migrated to the city from within the Empire (Julius was born in Brno), boasted of a cherished civic identity based on a special aesthetic sensibility centered on music. Insofar as the legitimacy of one's status as a citizen of Vienna was located in a culture of music, that sensibility was not a matter of birth but could be acquired by newcomers. Musical culture functioned as a surrogate for ordinary politics in Vienna and defined a public realm in which acculturation became a route to a significant measure of social equality with the potential of neutralizing if not vanquishing the city's pervasive anti-Semitism. For Julius, Vienna's historic preeminence in the arts had been sustained throughout the nineteenth century and continued into the early years of the twentieth.

Broch's sharp and sarcastic distinction between the aesthetic and the decorative and his stress on the apolitical construct of the vacuum of values that the ornamental within Viennese culture masked, served as the fault line separating defenders and critics in the pre–World War I years during which young Erich rose to fame. Broch's analysis echoed the views of two of the leading voices of criticism of Vienna's culture and civic self-image: Arnold Schoenberg and the writer Karl Kraus, both native sons of the city and both Jews.

They had ardent followers. Kraus's ally, the architect Adolf Loos, argued in 1910 for a fundamental distinction between surface and structure, particularly in architecture, charging that the ornament and facade associated with nineteenth-century historicism were "crimes."[50] The overarching assumption sustained by the self-appointed protectors of Vienna was that, like a museum, the city had become the arbiter of aesthetic greatness precisely as a "museum." In the eyes of the critics, this historicist premise, rooted in normative standards from the past, threatened to render Vienna provincial. Furthermore, supporting this civic cultural self-image as the guardian of timeless norms of the past was a mediocre and corrupt press that shaped public opinion.

Schoenberg became notorious in Vienna between 1906 and 1914 as a leading critic of Vienna's smug historicist sense of superiority by becoming mentor to a new generation of composers. He challenged the distinction between consonance and dissonance, and sought to emancipate musical values from the habits of Romanticism in order to restore the inherent autonomy of music. Schoenberg was inspired by eighteenth-century and early nineteenth-century models of musical logic, in which musical ideas and their development prevailed, in contrast to the late nineteenth-century's use of music as illustration or narrative.[51] Music needed to communicate meaning and aesthetic ideals through musical procedures, and not rely either on surface style or rhetorical associations with words and images. Like Kraus, Schoenberg challenged the authority of critics like Julius Korngold and their judgment, especially their self-appointed status as protectors of a hallowed past. Schoenberg followed Kraus in attacking the tastes of the public and their spokesmen, the critics, as not only philistine, ignorant, and hollow, but symptomatic of a pervasive, distorted, and corrosive sentimentality.

The essential underpinning of Kraus's and Schoenberg's critique of the norms of Viennese aesthetic taste and musical culture—shared by a younger generation of composers, artists, architects, and writers—was their belief in a link between art and ethics. The aesthetic represented more than an arena of enjoyment and entertainment. Art possessed truth value. It was a powerful means by which to combat deceit, hypocrisy, and complacency in the face of injustice, passivity, and self-deception. Mahler earned the admiration of the critics of the Viennese cultural establishment not so much on account of the specific qualities of the music he wrote, but on account of the courageous integrity he displayed as composer and conductor, his disregard for convention, his open confrontation with mediocrity masquerading as tradition, and his generosity to advocates of the new.

Julius Korngold, in contrast, saw his role as the defender of Vienna's musical heritage against the threat posed by its critics and a new generation. His Mahler (whom he and Erich idolized) was not Schoenberg's or Berg's Mahler. Korngold's Mahler was the last representative of the nineteenth century, not a prophet of a new era. He did not usher in a rebellion against Viennese cultural norms. Mahler's departure in 1907 did not diminish Vienna's standing as exemplary of the highest standard of musical culture and taste; it was merely the tragic consequence of unnecessary intrigue.

Indeed Julius (and Mahler as well) never challenged the idea that Vienna had earned its place as the defender of genuine musical values. In 1937, shortly before his forced exile to America (joining his son), Julius praised "musical Vienna" for resisting the pressure of "fanatical adherents, partisans, fellow traveling snobs" to embrace new music based on "principles of anarchy" that deviated from "the Viennese tradition." The Viennese possessed an "unerring sense for music." Julius delighted in recounting how the Viennese audience, one that was "particularly sophisticated, particularly capable of judgment and not at all reactionary," laughed, hissed, and whistled during a performance of a new work by Hindemith.[52]

In the interwar years, Julius feared the "false Americanization of European culture." His bête noir was jazz, and consequently Krenek's *Jonny spielt auf*, whose sensational success in Vienna threatened his son's new opera, *Das Wunder der Heliane*. Julius was proud that in Vienna, "where the greatest creative musicians consistently have chosen to work," the barbaric noises of the modern city and the kitsch of inferior peoples had only limited and fleeting success. As a result of "tradition and many years of music-loving taste and learning, bolstered by an elementary instinctive feeling for music," both the lay public and the professional community of Vienna could distinguish the "genuine from the fake" in new music. The Viennese would never fall for the destructive distortions of neoclassicism or the "non-melody and anti-song" character of modern opera, whether by Schreker, Hindemith, or Berg.[53]

In Julius's view, the entire oeuvre of Debussy "pales when confronted with the spirit and feeling of a theme from Beethoven that may suddenly appear, or when a heartfelt melody by Schubert is heard."[54] At the heart of Julius's allegiance to Vienna was the idea that its musical culture—including the music of Johann Strauss Jr.—was properly defined by the ideals of tonal melodic beauty and the conception of music as centered on "expression" (*Ausdruck*). The "spiritual" could not be communicated through music without an explicit commitment to expressiveness as defined by nineteenth-century Romanticism. The new music of Stravinsky, Schoenberg, Hindemith, and their followers was, in his view, an assault on music as a means of expression and consequently little more than a foray into raw sonorities and "motoric" rhythms. He posed the rhetorical question "Is it really possible to overcome the substance of feeling in, for example, the music of Bach, Mozart, Beethoven, Brahms, Strauss, and Mahler?"[55]

Not surprisingly, followers of Kraus and Schoenberg launched a counterattack on Julius Korngold as the quintessential representative of a complacent Viennese aesthetic tradition. In 1932, Willi Reich, Alban Berg's biographer, and Krenek, together with Rudolf von Ploderer, founded the magazine *23: Eine Wiener Musikzeitschrift*. It was explicitly modeled on Kraus's legendary *Die Fackel* (The Torch). Its purpose was to expose the corruption of Viennese music criticism, its ignorance, intolerance, and stupidity. The journal's name referred to paragraph 23 in Austrian law governing libel. Like *Die Fackel*, *23* was published irregularly and its format and print copied Kraus's publication exactly. Krenek distilled the mission of *23* by declaring that Kraus and Schoenberg had miraculously emerged from the "Viennese decadence" of the 1870s and "brought forth unrest that was truly healthy and decisive for European culture." For Krenek, their attack on the bankruptcy of Viennese culture represented the real and proper "Austrian destiny."[56]

In the very first issue, the editors took aim at Julius Korngold by exposing his hypocrisy regarding the conductor Franz Schalk. They accused Korngold of changing his views—expressed in his inflated, hyperbolic, judgmental, and pontificating prose—purely on the basis of whether Schalk (or any conductor) performed his son's works.[57] Korngold sued. The legal proceedings initially found against Reich, but ultimately acquitted him. *23* was relentless in its pursuit of Korngold and his colleagues, described as purveyors of a "judgmental emptiness, a pseudo-liberal philistine form of cultivation expressed in mere generalities and self-important banalities."[58] The magazine parodied Julius's theatrical display of disapproval while attending concerts, accused him of deceit and corruption (usually on behalf of his son), of ignoring important concerts of new music, promoting the second-rate, and of favoring a clique of conservative composers, Joseph Marx (a friend of Erich's) among them.

The parody, insult, and satire were unrelenting, so much so that Hans Heinsheimer, the publisher and a patron of new music, including that of

Berg (who supported and also contributed to *23*), challenged the purpose and tone of the magazine, claiming it was too mean-spirited, too obsessed with the trivial details of Viennese musical politics, and too eager to attack minor critical voices. The editors responded and published their exchange.[59] Their most persuasive defense of their mission came in 1932 when they described the reaction to a performance of *The Rite of Spring* in Vienna, when a significant part of the audience hissed and put their hands over their ears. This, the editors noted, was Vienna's reaction to a work that was twenty years old, acknowledged and embraced all over the world.[60]

The intensity of the divide between Korngold and the circle around *23* can be properly understood through the lens of the tense political context in which arguments about art took place. The smug self-satisfaction represented by Korngold and disseminated by Viennese journalism, which sought to insulate the artistic and intellectual community of the city from aesthetic "anarchy," was seen equally as a defense against the prospect of political and social reform and the fear of a corruption of morality and respectability. But Vienna's self-image as a cultural arbiter constituted a dangerous delusion. It condemned the city not only to provincialism, but its sentimental, illusory embrace of a dream-like "un-worldly" culture stripped the aesthetic realm of any chance to combat the evident rise of fascism and Nazism and a real threat to freedom.

For most of *23*'s short life (the last issue appeared in September 1937), the shadow of the Nazi seizure of power and the emergence of Austrofascism, particularly after the 1934 assassination of Dollfuss, was ever-present. Modernist music and composers and performers of Jewish descent, already banned in Germany, were in danger in Austria; an Anschluss was clearly in the making. The allure of fascism was strengthened not merely by politics, but by the entrenched cultural habits, the corruption of language, and the trivialization of the aesthetic dimension that dominated in the city.

But Julius Korngold remained undeterred in his allegiance to the myth of Vienna, even in exile during the darkest moments of World War II. In his memoirs, written in 1942 in Los Angeles, Korngold reflected on the legacy of his mentor Eduard Hanslick, the critic who dominated the Viennese scene during the second half of the nineteenth century and who chose Korngold to be his successor at Vienna's leading daily newspaper.[61] Korngold imagined how Hanslick might have reacted to the "chaos" of the day, the "destruction of the tonal order, the distortion of voice leading, sound and rhythm, to this mad passion for the ugly, against expression [*Ausdruck*], feeling, soul and all that is human—in other words all that is bound up with the beleaguered Romanticism."[62] How pleased Hanslick would have been to see how in Vienna the "monstrosity" of modern music "disappeared" like a "bad dream." Hanslick would have been proud to see how "Vienna withstood" the modern, protecting its character and reputation as the city of music and remaining "true to its great tradition, its healthy culture of music and its unique gift for music."[63]

Throughout his life, Erich followed his father's line in defense of Vienna's inherited aesthetic culture. In 1933 he wrote a satirical letter to the editors of *23*, complaining that he was receiving, without having asked, copies of the magazine. He assured the editors that not only had he no interest and had never subscribed, but the issues, unread, had been consigned to the trash, waiting to be collected.[64] A little more than a year before his death Erich wrote Joseph Marx to express his agreement that his father's unpublished 1937 book, Julius's attack on "the new un-music," deserved publication. Erich lamented how prevalent the "disgusting" in music and painting had become. His father's views were ever more pertinent in the "atomic age" when "atomic" musicians and painters prevailed and a "clique of terror" made up of powerful "sodomite art-snobs" conspired to suppress any criticism.[65] In tone and substance the son increasingly emulated his father.

In 1947 Erich, who anticipated a negative critical reaction to his recently completed Violin Concerto, wrote his own prefatory note to the concerto. "I have always remained true to my own beliefs; that music should be melodic, and as an old Viennese master used to preach and teach to me—'*wohllautend*' (well sounding)."[66] For Erich—and his father before him—the central question facing the world of music after 1945 was: "Is there still a place and a chance for music with expression and feeling, with long melodic themes, formed and developed on the principles of the classic masters—music conceived in the heart and not on paper?"[67]

Between 1923 and 1944, Erich produced nine separate theatrical scores based on the Viennese tradition of operetta and dance. Seven dealt with the music of the Strauss dynasty and two were based on music by a key figure in the so-called Silver Age of operetta, Leo Fall. In addition, Erich reworked Offenbach's *La belle Hélène*, first for the German-language stage and then in 1944 for New York. His revisions, rearrangements, and reorchestrations of Strauss and Offenbach did not sit well with the circle around Kraus and Schoenberg. Kraus venerated Offenbach; he became legendary for his one-person recitations of Offenbach (with piano accompaniment). In Kraus's view Erich had committed the cardinal sin of modernizing and sentimentalizing Offenbach and Strauss.[68]

Self-deception, misplaced nostalgia, and a taste for obscuring reality and therefore the truth through the celebration of an aesthetic defined by superficial norms of grace, a style of sweetness and maudlin sentiment flourished in Vienna. This was enabled and emboldened by the pleasing appearance of surface beauty and a Viennese penchant for the theatrical and decorative. The apolitical aesthetic civic culture that blossomed in the late nineteenth century after Austria's decisive defeat at the hands of the Prussians in 1866 concealed a gradual but ultimately terrifying descent into political irrelevance and powerlessness. Only the outward trappings of grandeur remained in Vienna. That discrepancy between surface and fact encouraged ethical thoughtlessness and emptiness. And this was all masked by aesthetic charm. Music's role in hiding and justifying the gap between appearance and reality may have begun with Johann Strauss Jr., but his works for the stage and his long-form waltz compositions—particularly "On the Beautiful Blue Danube," its evident nostalgia notwithstanding—nonetheless retained an integrity and charm evocative of an earlier time, the era before the economic crisis and nearly two-decades-long stagnation in Vienna that began in the 1870s. Beneath the illusion buttressed by art, in the years between 1873 and the late 1890s, Vienna witnessed harsh changes: rapid demographic growth, a housing shortage, and a growing enthusiasm for anti-Semitic politics. Korngold's new versions of Strauss were seen as violating whatever residual unspoiled, preindustrial innocence they once referenced.

As Erich discovered, painfully, in 1949, the Vienna he believed he knew—whose heritage he sought to validate and which he longed for throughout his exile in America—had vanished. The disappointment he and his wife, Luzi, experienced on their first trip back was overwhelming. Korngold had every intention of returning to Vienna permanently and picking up where he had left off in 1938, as a composer of opera and concert music. Luzi recalls how, on arriving in the city, Erich was overcome both with joy (seeing the places of his youth) and sadness (when he saw the bombed-out Vienna State Opera).[69]

Erich found out that not only had he been forgotten, but that a new generation thought his aesthetic outdated. Colleagues and neighbors who remained from the old days, owing to their compromised behavior during the Nazi period, were cool, resentful, or hypocritical. The Vienna he remembered came back to him not through people but through the landscape and memories. Luzi confessed to Joseph Marx in 1957 that given the traumatic shock of his 1949 return, Erich decided he would only visit Vienna again "incognito." He had no desire to relive the "vulgar enmity, hate, intrigues, failure to keep one's word, and humiliation" to which he had been subjected by his native city upon his return.[70]

Still, Korngold never relinquished his nostalgia and cherished his memory of the Vienna of the past. His image stemmed initially from the years before 1918, but its final shape was defined by the twenty years thereafter, when he was intensively engaged with the traditions of Viennese musical theater—the years of *23* and his struggle against an emergent and distinctive, albeit eclectic twentieth-century musical modernism.[71] The last two compositions Korngold wrote mirrored this lifelong deep association with his image of Vienna. His last completed work, *Straussiana for Orchestra*, one of two works for school orchestra, was based on three short Strauss pieces. And its immediate predecessor, Opus 41, is a song to words by the author whose book had been the inspiration for *Das Wunder der Heliane*, Hans Kaltneker. Titled "A Sonnet for Vienna (In Memoriam)," it was an explicit musical epitaph for an idealized city that was once "a Psalm" that had come from the "mouth of God," a city that had witnessed "the poetry and song from the tongue of the most blessed Angels."[72]

The startling fact is that the Vienna for which Korngold longed was, and always had been, an illusion. Before 1914, Korngold was shielded economically by his parental home and by his status as a prodigy. But the Vienna Erich witnessed in the 1920s and 1930s was marked by poverty, civil war, migrants from the East, virulent anti-Semitism, economic strain, and the arrival of fascism, first in the guise of Austrofascism and ultimately Nazism. The hijacking of the University of Vienna and other institutions of learning by the right wing during the 1920s, resulting in a decline in standards, had already become evident, as had increasing discrimination and violence against Jewish students and professors.[73] As the composer Karol Rathaus observed in 1923, after he returned to live in Vienna (he had studied there with Schreker before the war), the city was markedly changed and he immediately felt alienated from it. As an Eastern European Jew, he found it inhospitable. Rathaus confessed that "in these times" he often felt "ashamed" at his "superfluous" vocation as an artist, and that it seemed impossible to find a way to earn any sort of living. In the end, however, surrounded by catastrophic political and social realities, perhaps there was nothing left, Rathaus concluded, but to "embrace the romantic trick, and fly from the present, on the not altogether perfect wings of fantasy, into the world of art."[74]

In the 1930s, Erich indulged in just such a flight from the present through the music of Viennese operetta. The subsequent sojourn in Hollywood did not damage his love of his native city and therefore he believed that the Vienna that shunned him in the 1950s was a changed city. He never lost his faith in the reality of the Vienna he knew and remembered, a city he had learned to love and see, ironically, through the lens fashioned by his father. The attention and lavish praise Erich had experienced as a child only confirmed Julius's idealized picture of Vienna.

But as Kraus, Berg, Krenek, and Schoenberg realized, the post–World War I Vienna no longer fit the myth and illusions nurtured under the Habsburg monarchy to which father and son Korngold maintained their allegiance. The Vienna Erich encountered in the 1950s had already been visible beneath the surface during the interwar years. Hugo Bettauer, a writer and journalist who campaigned against pervasive anti-Semitism in Vienna, was targeted, successfully, for assassination in 1925. He was shot to death by an Austrian Nazi who was outraged by Bettauer's brilliant satirical depiction of a future Vienna without Jews, in the 1922 book *Die Stadt ohne Juden* and the film it inspired. The assassin was incarcerated in a psychiatric hospital for only eighteen months. The Vienna of the 1950s was Bettauer's dystopian vision come to life.[75]

Julius Korngold

Julius Korngold's influence on Erich extended well beyond shaping his son's perception of Vienna. Considerable ink has been spilled on the close, complex but symbiotic relationship between father and son. Remarkably, Julius continued to exercise a powerful artistic hold over his son until his death in 1945, despite his cruel behavior toward Erich's wife and fierce quarrels between father and son. The elder Korngold was a frequent presence in Erich's Hollywood studio. Erich never lost the desire to win his father's approval, even though Julius overtly expressed contempt and disappointment with his son's apparent retreat from concert music and opera and his success as a composer for film and theater.

Few relationships, including the one most often invoked as a point of comparison, the dynamic between Leopold Mozart and his son Wolfgang Amadeus, invite so readily a foray into psychobiography. However, given Julius's extensive body of written work, there is little reason to engage in speculation. Erich internalized with remarkable accuracy his father's well-known views on the aesthetics of music and on what sort of music a composer in the twentieth century should write.

The primary source for Julius's views is his unpublished 1937 *The Twilight of the Idols of Atonality: Critical Essays on the History of New Musicisms*. The Viennese publisher Doblinger intended to bring the book out and produced page proofs that Julius edited and sent back to Vienna. But in the wake of the Anschluss, publication was aborted. After the war, the page proofs were deposited in the Austrian National Library.[76]

The book is in four sections. The first covers "Impressionism," the leading composers of the early twentieth century from Debussy to Bartók, Szymanowski, Suk, Delius, Vaughn Williams, and Shostakovich, among others. Julius's furious condemnation of Krenek's *Jonny spielt auf* gets its own chapter. Korngold groups composers by nationality. Ernest Bloch is considered as the sole representative of America; only in the third section of the book are there passing and condescending mentions of Louis Gruenberg, Heitor Villa-Lobos, and Carl Ruggles. Most of the space in the first section of the book is devoted to Stravinsky.

The second section, "Atonalism," focuses on Schoenberg and the Second Viennese School, primarily Berg and Webern (although considerable attention is also given to Egon Wellesz). At the end is a discussion of composers viewed as responding to Schoenberg and Stravinsky, primarily Hindemith and Kurt Weill. The third of the book's four major sections contains Korngold's analysis of five festivals of contemporary music that took place in the interwar years. The fourth and last section is a "Coda": a miscellany made up mostly of previously published essays that cover Matthias Hauer, jazz, and Korngold's two-part summation, an imaginary dialogue between an old man and a young woman, and a final articulation of the author's judgment on the "idols" of atonality.

The book is repetitious. Much of the text stems from previously published criticism, so the same points, in the same language, are made over and over again. One can appreciate Karl Kraus's horror at the prose style. Korngold is relentlessly judgmental and given to rhetorical flourishes and hyperbole. Intent on impressing his reader with his familiarity with music theory and history as well as a detailed knowledge of the repertory, he pontificates, hurling accusations, expressing despair, and rendering final verdicts.

Julius's views closely match the beliefs of his son, as does the manner in which both characterized the challenge facing the contemporary composer. Julius's core belief is that the tonal system, defined by the triad and the system of major and minor and the pitch relationships located in the circle of fifths, is a matter of nature and the only true basis of music. Music that abandons the logic of tonality cannot be beautiful. It cannot express feeling or anything connected to the human heart. Music that distorts the essential harmoniousness of tonal music defies nature and is "unhealthy." Only tonality can lend music its capacity to create form, drama, and meaning, and therefore it is indispensable for the ultimate purpose of music—expression. Music properly rooted in tonality is organic in form. That which is not tonal is mechanical, materialistic, and machine-like.[77]

Given this premise, the essence of music is melody. Julius excoriates composers—Hindemith and Schoenberg among them—who are allegedly responsible for foregrounding counterpoint and the extension of the "linear," apparently in emulation of Bach and eighteenth-century music, at the expense of the priority of melody that calls for support from harmony. Korngold argues that the "horizontal" and the "vertical" were properly integrated in the age of the Viennese classical masters—Haydn, Mozart, and Beethoven—and that true melody, although linear, implies and requires the vertical: harmony. The two primary and unsuccessful surrogates for melody that Julius associates with new modern movements are the preference for abstract counterpoint that defies tonal logic, and a tendency to revel in novel machine-like sounds and sonorities. Verdi and Puccini are held up as models for the singing melody and a healthy harmonic sound world.[78]

Although Julius avoided an extensive discussion in the book of the music of Franz Schreker (a rival to Erich's prominence as a composer of operas), his earlier reviews of Schreker indicate that his primary objection was the apparent absence of melody and its elaboration, features indispensable to opera.[79] Schreker was clearly a talent to reckon with. But lush sonorities and uncommon harmonies without a melodic framework dominated. To Korngold, "rarefied" sounds too readily suggested a profundity (to which, Korngold observed, German audiences seemed hopelessly addicted) that was actually absent.

Everything about Schreker struck Julius Korngold as bordering on the decadent. Using a dense technical vocabulary, Korngold challenged musical expressionism's use of harmonic relationships and polytonality, its penchant for a dense sensual sound; Korngold associated these qualities with Schreker (and the music of his students, as Karol Rathaus's ill-fated 1923 Second Symphony demonstrates). In his 1920 review of *Die Gezeichneten*, the absence of melody and its development and a persuasive musical substance were singled out for criticism. The sharp and consistent denigration of Schreker, masked always by faint praise, even in the cameo appearance Schreker makes in the 1937 book (and therefore several years after Schreker's unexpected death in 1934), points to a hectoring moralism lurking beneath all of Julius's aesthetic judgments. Julius actually spent more time attacking Schreker's libretti than his music. But the key point was that Schreker's shortcomings were dangerous not merely as musical models for future composers; they exposed the potential of the musical theater to corrupt morality and decency. Schreker's talent was not strictly musical but manipulative on behalf of the "lust" and "dread" his operas provoked.[80] In 1937, Korngold directed similar moral objections vociferously against Hindemith's *Nusch-Nuschi*, the last of three controversial one-act operas Hindemith wrote in the 1920s.[81]

According to Julius, modern composers, with few exceptions, abandoned the central legacy of the nineteenth century, the traditions and practices of Romanticism in music. For Korngold, the Wagner of *Tristan* marked the apogee of musical progress; the best of what followed, including Richard Strauss, was commentary surrounding a main text. Romanticism, through the expansion of tonal practice into chromatic harmony, had developed the full arsenal of expressiveness. He dismissed the neoclassicism of the 1920s.

Given that beauty in music was by definition contingent on the logic of the tonal, its highest level of cultivation occurred in the late nineteenth century. Nonetheless, the eras before Romanticism, from the Renaissance on, taken as a whole, constituted the permanent foundation of "art music"; musicality therefore required knowledge of and respect for the past and the truth revealed in that past. Distortion or deviation was a deliberate promotion of the ugly and the artificial. At best they were acts of deracinated thought and intellect, detached from human emotion, the human spirit. Musical beauty was, for Korngold, derived from timeless and true principles of musical grammar and syntax. The corruption of beauty was a deception and a moral insult to the human. It was not only "degrading" but also dangerous as a potential influence on the development of a "healthy" collective "soul of the people."[82]

Korngold's sweeping denunciation of the leading trends in music around the world reflected two sociopolitical convictions. The first was about radical revolutions. His short foray into music under the Soviets led him to characterize much of it—primarily Prokofiev—as "Bolshevik." There are passing references to the radical phase of the French Revolution and the guillotine as metaphors for the modernist rejection of nineteenth-century aesthetic values. The second political inference was sociological. The appearance of modernism and its resonance within the public mirrored the dangerous realities of modern life: the power of mechanization and industrialization, the growth of cities, and the consequences of both the war and the peace.[83]

The apostles of the modern sought to evoke and mirror these deleterious phenomena. Julius believed music should do the very opposite and avoid a "pseudo art masquerading under the banner of contemporaneity." Music needed to resist contemporary threats to values that might be temporarily under siege but remained nonetheless true. These included a respect for nature as well as criteria of human "health" rooted in a fundamental organic logic, one that in turn justified a normative definition of harmony and form. Korngold cited Wagner, ironically, as exemplary of a composer who fought against the times he lived in. Wagner transformed myth through music and reasserted essential normative truths, and particularly the "purely human" in its role as an essential basis for human expression. "True art is timeless; music is always so," Korngold concluded.[84]

It is astonishing that Julius Korngold, writing in the mid-1930s, was oblivious to the political links between his aesthetic ideals and those of the composers he tolerated—Franz Schmidt, Joseph Marx, and Hans Pfitzner, as well as Richard Strauss—and conservative or fascist politics. Korngold was cool to Pfitzner's music; it was grim and heavy. But he admired Pfitzner's polemical writings, his attack on modernism, and his notion of the centrality of spontaneous and intuitive aesthetic inspiration. Given Korngold's 1937 book's focus on new trends in music, Strauss and Pfitzner are mentioned only in passing. More astonishing is the lack of place accorded Erich's former teacher Alexander Zemlinsky, even though some of his most important works were written in the 1920s.[85] Zemlinsky played a crucial role in Erich's development as a composer, and the father repaid the composer with gracious and supportive reviews in 1910 and 1917. Yet in 1937 Korngold used one of his most effective means of criticism against Zemlinsky: silence. The absence of any review in the major newspaper of Vienna had always been seen as an intentional kiss of death.[86]

Puccini and Strauss are presented as benchmarks and cast within a conventional canonic lineage that begins with Bach and ends with Wagner, Brahms, and Bruckner. Korngold's sense of an aesthetic and moral crisis is so intense that he reasserts his ideals on practically every page: Melody that implies a pleasing harmony is indispensable to beauty. Beauty in turn is understood as the provision of transparent harmonious sounds adequate to human expression. Music exists to inspire more than a visceral "physiological" response. It is the medium of "pathos," "feeling," and the "spiritual." "Without expression there is no art, and without the need for expression there is no cultivated human being, particularly now and forever," Korngold concluded.[87]

Although Korngold recognizes Janáček's talent, he systematically belittles his music as essentially undramatic, reliant on color and mere repetition. The "dramatic-psychological transformation of motives and the association of ideas" are absent in the score.[88] And Bartók might be "a true musician," but his tendency to avoid all expressiveness and concentrate on a constructed complexity of mere sound, colored by Hungarian exoticism, is unfortunate; Bartók is seen as veering toward the atonal.[89] Korngold recognizes the genius of Stravinsky but finds the neoclassical phase sterile and too anti-Romantic. Korngold's favorite work is *The Soldier's Tale*. In its ironic surface Korngold finds relief from the "primitive" ostinato rhythms and oppressively national character of *The Rite of Spring*.[90] Schoenberg, for whom Korngold also has respect, is guilty of deviating from the style of *Verklärte Nacht* and *Gurrelieder*, rejecting tonality and promoting an artificial system of composition reliant on the contrapuntal and "linear."[91] Korngold also recognizes Berg's gifts and concedes that *Wozzeck*, repugnant as it may be, is uniquely successful as a modern opera, though not susceptible of emulation.[92] Younger composers such as Honegger and Martinů are dismissed as mere builders of mechanical sound without beauty, drama, or soul. There is no mention at all of Sibelius.

At the end of this extended and unforgiving diatribe, Korngold holds out one hope against the nightmare of "decades" of destruction to the "tonal order" as well as the "reduction" of music to "noise" and the sounds of machines—not to speak of the catastrophic appropriation of the primitive in the form of the American jazz found in "art music." A "naïve" creative composer is needed to combat the war against expression, feeling, and "the swing of the soul," the war against naturalness, "grace," "higher" human values, and everything contained in the musical concept of the Romantic inherited from the nineteenth century. Korngold assures the reader that this new young talent—whom he knows but does not mention—will for certain, "today or tomorrow," compose according to the "linguistic foundations" of Brahms, Mahler, and Strauss. That savior is none other than his own son.[93]

The terrifying irony of Korngold's views is their more than passing resemblance to the aesthetic ideology of Nazism and its predecessors, the post-Wagnerian line of criticism rooted in anti-Semitism and German cultural chauvinism. Korngold's crusade was the one taken up by the campaign against "degenerate" art, and by the Reichsmusikkammer under Strauss and his successors. Much as Korngold would have liked to place Mahler between Brahms and Strauss, the Austrofascists would have none of it. As Rudolf von Ploderer observed shortly after the Nazi rise to power, Joseph Marx cast doubt on the quality of Mahler's work, including Mahler's command of symphonic form. In a review of a performance of Mahler's Symphony No. 1, its one virtue was its appeal to nature. This allowed Marx to make a pointed comparison between Mahler and Heinrich Heine. Marx closed his review with a "panegyric" to Wagner. The politics of this review were hardly latent or obscure.[94]

The ideological resemblance between Korngold's aesthetics and the aesthetics of fascism revealed the influence of Oswald Spengler. Spengler, owing to his unwillingness to defer to the Nazis, fell out of favor with the regime. But it is hard to overestimate the popularity and influence of

The Decline of the West on readers, including future Nazis, after the first part of Spengler's work came out in 1918. Spengler placed a characteristically German emphasis on the power of music. In modernity, only music retained the capacity to circumvent the rationalizing tyranny of the visual. Visual space and the "steely tyranny of light" and sight mirrored the domination of reason in modernity and diminished the intuitive. Music, however, broke the power of the visual, and through an immediacy, transmitted by hearing, could "reach the soul's final secret."[95]

Spengler's advocacy of music had a specific construct in mind. Art for Spengler was by definition an "expression-language." Its purest incarnation was music. Western art had "reached its highest point in chamber music," music that was exclusively instrumental. But that high point also revealed a "Faustian" turn.[96] "Faustian" was a code word for the unique aspect of Western culture that prizes "deep consciousness and introspection of the ego and a resolutely personal culture." For all its accomplishments, the Faustian turn led the twentieth century to overvalue technology and the idea of progress.

Spengler's brand of historical pessimism (to which Korngold referred explicitly in his 1937 book)[97] was rooted in a belief in an organic cycle in history comparable to the sequence of seasons. The West was in its "winter," a period of social conflict and decline. That was made evident by Spengler's claim that "the last of the Faustian arts died in '*Tristan*.' This work is the giant keystone of Western music."[98] Music from that point on would inevitably tend to the superficial and the meaningless. Spengler's belief in the inherent estrangement between races and their cultures, Thomas Mann noted with some irony, made it impossible for Spengler to imagine the emergence of a new work of Western music after *Tristan* that embodied with authenticity the experience of love. Mann countered with Mahler's *Das Lied von der Erde*, which he regarded as a true and organic synthesis of ancient Chinese culture with the most advanced Western music, an event deemed impossible by Spengler.[99]

Spengler's alluring philosophical framework lent a coherent worldview to the retrospective aesthetics advocated by Korngold, fascism, and its predecessors in the interwar era. Spengler's philosophy of history in turn justified the ideals of a restorative reactionary conservatism. It offered Broch's "museum" of art the historical justification for its moral critique of the social and economic achievements of modernity. Spengler's fear of a modern culture tied to science and technology, and therefore purely "instrumental reason" as opposed to action based on the individual, inward and intuitive, and his skepticism regarding democracy and a nationalism based on reductive notions of racial purity lent

Korngold's prejudices and ideals a new popular philosophical justification. Modernism constituted conformism and superficiality—the descent into uniformity and fashion.

Alban Berg, who periodically engaged in written polemics (most prominently against Pfitzner), gave a radio interview in 1930 on the subject of "atonality." Reich in 1936 decided to publish the interview in *23*. Berg used the ubiquity of the word *atonal* by critics to counter the prevailing Spengler-like view that the high point of musical culture had passed and that the new and modern lacked interiority, were impotent, and violated both nature and history. Berg challenged the validity of the meaning ascribed to "atonality" and highlighted its abuse as a word with which to undermine contemporary music, notably Schoenberg's twelve-tone method of composition. He argued that the criteria of musical form and logic as elaborated by the Classical masters from Haydn to Schubert were structural and not dependent on an exclusive system of pitch relationships, and therefore inevitably linked to a particular "luxurious sensuous Italian" tradition of melody (a pointed reference to Puccini, a figure of veneration for both Korngolds). After all, Berg argued, the melodic in Bach had been entirely different.[100]

Berg criticized Korngold's worldview. The only real meaning of the word *atonal* was its rhetorical utility in describing new music that did not sound like the music of late Romanticism and was "against the nature of music, ugly, without inspiration, wrong-sounding and destructive." The claims that a new era of musical anarchy had come into being, marking the end of true musical values, hid under this meaningless label. Such claims were little else than the demonstration of a "need for familiar combinations" that inspire no pushback in the listener. Korngold and his kind were apt to embrace bland and mediocre tonal music as pleasing even when it actually violated the "holy laws" of tonality as revealed by the procedures of Classicism.[101] Like Schoenberg, Berg challenged the claim, made by Korngold and critics associated with him, that they actually understood what made the instrumental music of Mozart, Haydn, Beethoven, Schubert, and Brahms great.

The Predicament of Erich Wolfgang Korngold

As the music and argument of *The Constant Nymph* and *Deception* suggest, Julius's son absorbed and internalized his father's point of view, even though he knew and valued Schoenberg's music and deeply admired Stravinsky. In only one respect did Erich assert his independence. His father had limited use for light music and the musical theater. Julius's encounter as a student with Bruckner left him with an abiding respect and admiration for the monumental, metaphysical, and melodramatic in music. For Julius the ideal synthesis was the reconciliation between the melodic allure of Verdi and Puccini and the German symphonic heritage with its overt spiritual ambitions.

Erich, however, took a particular pleasure in elegance, charm, and wit. After writing *Das Wunder der Heliane*, he devoted his efforts to fashioning his own alternative to ugliness and mechanical abstract music—music that projected love, happiness, humor, and optimism. Happy endings delighted him, as did the human capacity to overcome danger and suffering.[102] The intense engagement with modernizing the operetta and waltzes of Johann Strauss in the midst of the economic and political turmoil of the 1930s revealed a determination to sustain a magical world that would remind listeners of the best in human nature through a sentimental but non-trivial aesthetic of fantasy and hope uniquely characteristic of nineteenth-century Vienna. The best example was the 1930 singspiel pastiche arranged by Korngold, *Walzer aus Wien*.

Korngold's score for the 1935 Reinhardt film *A Midsummer Night's Dream* was the bridge between the lyricism and lightness of Johann Strauss and the symphonic music for Hollywood films that Korngold invented. Mendelssohn was well known among composers for his relative optimism and transparency, and for the affirmative sensibility in his music that also led him to be criticized as superficial when compared to Schumann and Chopin.[103] In Hollywood, however, Korngold went well beyond Johann Strauss and Mendelssohn and integrated the sound world of Richard Strauss and Gustav Mahler to create monumental, dramatic music and a musical fabric that matched, in terms of harmony and sonority, the modern technological possibilities inherent in sound film. In a direct refutation of the views expressed by Schoenberg, Adorno, and Schrade, the real tragedies of contemporary life—the horror and suffering before and after World War II—demanded avoidance and resistance, and not direct expression. Erich's resistance, in musical terms, was to create a modern version of Julius's musical principles for a distinctly modern medium.

Most of the Hollywood films Korngold composed for are bereft of despair and pessimism. Juarez triumphs, not only politically but ethically, given his remorse at the death of Maximilian. So too does Robin Hood. Tragic as the end of *The Private Lives of Elizabeth and Essex* may seem, the power of love remains undiminished and the danger of tyranny is made clear. As in *Robin Hood*, the message of *The Sea Hawk* is the resolve to fight successfully for freedom against tyranny.[104] Last but not least, *Kings Row* depicts the triumph of good over evil. In the two films Korngold had a hand in shaping plot and dialogue, *The Constant Nymph* and *Deception*, which center on a composer protagonist, there are hints of tragedy and suffering. *Deception* may contain the only direct reference to the war, but the cellist who survives is not a representative of the unique victims of the Holocaust, the mass of innocent civilians. He is a resistance fighter, a political opponent.

In Korngold's films, as in the operetta theater, the audience comes away with a sense of well-being, and a measure of hope that heroism is possible, that right can overcome wrong, that justice will prevail. Human beings—even Lewis Dodd in *The Constant Nymph*—can change. In the 1930s and 1940s, these seemingly naïve and simplistic hopes were radical assertions. They were fantastic objects, blind hopes, and illusions easily subject to criticism as a form of escapism and a thoughtless sentimentalizing of human nature and history.

In the last phase of his career, Korngold came face to face with the grim reality beneath the veneer of grace, lightness, and refinement he associated with Vienna. Korngold dreamed of a triumphant return there as a composer of chamber and orchestral music and of opera. He found himself alternatively excoriated as out of date and old-fashioned (by "communists"), unwelcome as a survivor (by Nazis), and as a reminder of societal guilt (by active and passive Nazi collaborators).[105]

Resentful and disappointed as he was, Korngold did not abandon the image he had fashioned of Vienna. Unlike Kurt Weill, who reinvented himself as an American composer and did not look back or suffer homesickness; or Schoenberg, who harbored a cynical resentment for Vienna and embraced the Revisionist Zionist movement; or even Hugo Burghauser, the bassoonist who wielded enormous power in the governance of the Vienna Philharmonic owing to his prominence in the 1930s as an Austrofascist, and who, despite many postwar honors from Vienna, never went back and reached retirement in the orchestra of the Metropolitan Opera (and never tired of lamenting the low level of American mores and culture),[106] Erich Korngold could not let go. He died hoping that Vienna would finally come to its senses and welcome him by mounting a new production of *Die tote Stadt*, thereby restoring him to his rightful place in the history of music in Vienna.

Erich's idealization of Vienna was consistent with a parallel ambition to realize the aesthetic principles he inherited from his father through his music for the stage and not the screen. The four most significant instrumental works to emerge from Erich's extraordinary run as a Hollywood composer were the Third String Quartet, the Cello Concerto, the Violin

Concerto (originally intended for Bronislaw Huberman but premiered and promoted by Heifetz), and the F-sharp Symphony, which received its first adequate performance under William Steinberg.[107] All four utilized material from the films. The string quartet has elements from *Between Two Worlds* and *The Sea Hawk*; the Cello Concerto from *Deception*; the Violin Concerto from *The Prince and the Pauper, Juarez, Another Dawn*, and *Anthony Adverse*; and the symphony from *Captain Blood, The Private Lives of Elizabeth and Essex, Kings Row*, and *Anthony Adverse*.

This pattern of borrowing is consistent with Korngold's notion that "music is music" and that it matters not for what medium music is written. The criteria of judgment are constant. The matter, however, may not be quite so simple. Writing for instruments without an explicit narrative, for example, certainly possesses a high degree of resemblance to narrative instrumental forms. In Richard Strauss's case, storytelling and the utilization of formal structures specific to musical logic became intertwined. The same sort of overlap between form and narrative is present in opera. Berg, in *Wozzeck*, and Puccini, in *Manon Lescaut*, used musical procedures to provide the underlying structure for a dramatic scene. And the use of leitmotifs in Wagner was an extension of procedures developed by Berlioz and Liszt in works for instrumental forces alone.

If one accepts Julius Korngold's version of music history, the film medium emerged after the end of the era of Classicism and Romanticism. Moving images were to some degree anticipated in musical forms that sought to evoke, over a finite time span, the sensation of sequences of images—a sort of pictorial realism suggested by sound. Examples of this include the "Ocean" Symphony of Anton Rubinstein and Strauss's *Don Quixote*. Erich Korngold's debt to Richard Strauss, and his lifelong admiration for his music, was based in part on Strauss's appropriation and invention of musical practice on behalf of a starkly illustrative and evocative realism. Strauss's ambition to pierce the illusion of music as metaphysical and spiritual, to bring it down to earth and link it to the quotidian and the human, earned him considerable opprobrium in the 1890s, including from Julius's mentor and protector Eduard Hanslick.

Not surprisingly, the use of instrumental and orchestral music during the "silent" film era only deepened the family resemblance between the experience of listening to sixty minutes of orchestral narration evocative of nature—or, in the case of Tchaikovsky, illustrative of personalities, events, emotions, and sensibilities—and watching a visualized story. The adaptability of much of nineteenth-century music to cartoon animation supports this observation. Dvořák, during his time in America, was approached to write music for a historical pageant shown with a new technology—rapidly moving still photographs projected onto a screen. He declined. But the entrepreneurs who approached him showed good judgment, as the storytelling power of the composer's final set of tone poems set to the poetry of Karel Erben make clear.[108]

But the sound film presented a radical departure. Unlike opera, where the theatrical argument is largely put to music and sung, or the musical theater, which alternates speaking with singing, the sound film integrated on a flat screen speech and image with an unmatched capacity to project the illusion of realism. The film could also record and transmit ambient noise.

Most remarkably, the artificiality of the audibility of dialogue opened the possibility of utilizing music in varying supportive roles. A soundtrack is something heard only by the viewer, not the characters on screen. Only when music is the subject of the narrative do the characters and audience share the aural experience. Most of the time something else is happening visually or dramatically, whether it be a shot of an empty landscape, a battle, or a verbal exchange. Music is used to frame the event, deepen its power, anticipate it, or assist the audience in recognition and reflection. The role of music in sound film was different from that in opera, chamber music, sacred choral music, or operetta. Its role was closest, however, to operetta, given operetta's variety and its constant interaction with speech and dance.

The challenge Korngold faced as he ventured out of Hollywood in the 1940s to reclaim his position as a preeminent composer of "high art" music in the grand tradition was whether the thematic material he had used in films—his appropriation of leitmotif technique to strengthen the coherence and flow of a story, or the use of dramatic gestural music to depict pomp and circumstance, violence, desire, or love—could be taken out of the film context, even as fragments, and reworked to function in compositions dependent on the musical procedures of development, elaboration, combination, and recapitulation that together render a large-scale instrumental work persuasive. Was his use of material from the movies any different from the use of folk tunes by Haydn, Bartók, or Copland?

Parts of an answer may lie in the reasons for Korngold's success in Hollywood, the reasons his invention of the symphonic sound track as a central component of the modern, mass-distributed sound film with star actors in plots that told stories from history, myth, and fiction was so influential. One explanation, and not an altogether flattering one, can be gleaned from the 1947 collaborative book on film music by Hanns Eisler (a composer with deep leftist political commitments who fled to America) and Adorno, *Composing for the Films (Komposition für den Film)*.[109]

There is little doubt that the model for what Eisler and Adorno called "bad habits" in writing for film was Korngold. To start with, they argued that the leitmotif, whose proper function in Wagner was symbolic and therefore intended to lift the visual into the "realm of metaphysical meaning," was reduced in the film medium to that of "servant" to the dominant task of representing reality.[110] Furthermore, in film there is no time for the development of leitmotifs, only repetition. The implication is that the sort of themes that work well in films tend to be the most mundane and clichéd since their function is routinely descriptive. They are not simple or neutral enough (like Diabelli's triple-meter dance tune that so absorbed Beethoven) to inspire extended transformation. They are so closely marked with regard to their non-musical significance as to defy successful transformation.

The criteria for good melodies in film are neither poetic (as in song and opera) nor self-referentially musical. Melodies for films are judged by their specific utility, not by their musical "soul." Eisler and Adorno viewed film as resembling prose, not poetry. The illusion of realism, on which the commercial film traded so well, required that the pace and speed of events should vary in duration, rendering strictly musical criteria of symmetry and structure incompatible with film. Julius and Erich's central commitment—to melody—was now driven not by poetic or musical values but the by use of cinematic time in the telling of a dramatized story.

As if that were not enough, Eisler and Adorno pointed out an obvious but radically new context, the unavoidable fact that much of film music was never intended to distract from the visual and dramatic. Film music was never in the foreground, or written to be heard on its own. Even the overtures accompanied credits. Film music also needed to be written to focus on the most important dimension of a scene—the impending kiss, the joy of an embrace, the shock of the recognition of danger. Furthermore, the film medium used music to suppress individualized responses by individuals and level their reactions to generate uniformity fit for commerce based on a mass audience. Music in films is written to help everyone rejoice, be frightened, or be sad at the same moment. The descent into sentimentality becomes a foregone conclusion. But in instrumental music, there is no telling how any individual might respond; music as a medium on its own, even in opera and song, offers a much wider range of individualized reflection and response than music tethered to a film.

The fact that much of film music was meant to add, discreetly, to what was happening on screen, and not be listened to independently but rather absorbed in the wake of action and image, required music that did not attract attention to itself as music. One basic task of film music, for example—that of illustration—was a key "bad habit." Music was no longer a medium that connected to ideas and to the spiritual. It became a medium of decoration and ornamentation. Eisler and Adorno understood that the necessity for music to illustrate meant exploiting existing rhetorical associations and resisting any sort of independent musical innovation tied to the expression of inwardness. This led to the creation of stock music, musical clichés, and the standardization of how music was understood—or rather translated into word and image—by the public.

The absorption of the spectrum of late-Romantic musical practice into the modern Hollywood sound film was nonetheless Korngold's singular achievement. He managed, despite Eisler and Adorno's skepticism, to make the soundtracks flow as if they possessed the coherence of a tone poem. However, the cherished language of art music was compelled to become routine and standardized. Furthermore, as Eisler and Adorno realized, the context of the sound film effectively brought the successful evolution of a new age of modern music to a halt; film music depended on inherited familiarity. The dominance of the film medium had the effect of turning art music to stone, like Lot's wife. The form that stone image of a living art took happened to be the vocabulary, aesthetics, and style of Korngold—a brilliant but utilitarian extension of the world of Mahler and Strauss.

The price paid by this marriage between the musical world of late Romanticism and twentieth-century film was the end of individualized hearing, and therefore music as a human avenue of freedom from the tyranny of linguistic meaning and visual knowledge. Eisler and Adorno were not far from Spengler in regarding "Faustian" music as a last remaining exit and refuge from standardization, conformity, and uniformity. Through film, music lost its essential character as having meaning independent of any visual or linguistic construct of subject matter.

There may be more truth to this line of criticism than Korngold partisans may acknowledge. The fecundity, ingenuity, and astonishing beauty of Korngold's melodies, harmonies, and dramatic scenes in the Hollywood scores have never been equaled. But their impact may inevitably be tied to their context. Eisler and Adorno were wrong that the music in Korngold's films was not meant to be heard. The music actually was heard, but as an integral part of the film experience. But that does not mean that its character, which was determined by its use in film, easily lent itself to adaption in freestanding musical forms. For all the popularity of the Violin Concerto, its beauty and the consummate craft it displays, try placing it alongside the Berg or Sibelius Concertos. Can it be denied, as Hofmannsthal observed in 1916, that beneath the brilliance of Korngold's concerto there may be some lack of "inner necessity," on account of the character of the musical material? The Cello Concerto could easily fall under a comparable cloud of doubt. The F-sharp Symphony, however, suggests a much more complex sensibility, an ambition that permits it to escape successfully the limits of film music.

The tragedy was, in twentieth-century terms, that Erich Wolfgang Korngold died young. The F-sharp Symphony most directly mirrors his ambition to fulfill his father's hope that he would return to the opera stage and concert hall and play a crucial role in the future of music. Assuming a counterfactually speculative context of his having lived for an additional quarter-century, the proper comparisons might then be to the postwar music of Martinů, Shostakovich, Karl Amadaeus Hartmann, György Ligeti, and Luigi Dallapicolla. As more Korngold is performed, as it should be, it will have to compete with Mahler, Bruckner, Suk (whom Julius admired), Berg, Bartók, Sibelius, Zemlinsky, Schmidt, and Schreker. The last three, despite Julius's best efforts, might emerge as stronger rivals for our attention. Might Erich's critics have been onto some fundamental shortcoming in the astonishingly well-made, sophisticated, and original music by this phenomenal and precocious talent?

Given the exceptional circumstances of Erich Wolfgang Korngold's life, the legitimate sources of critical hesitation are not hard to conjure. As a prodigy with domineering parents, Erich may never have actually grown up. He certainly lived a charmed life, shielded from the grim historical context of the 1920s and 1930s. He mistook the Vienna of Johann Strauss Jr. and his successors in the Silver Age of Viennese operetta for reality. His prodigious gifts revealed an uncanny capacity to emulate with empathy, which is why he was adept, his entire life, at writing and arranging music that sounded authentically like Mendelssohn or Johann Strauss. His distorted childhood and failure to break free from his father or a sentimental image of Vienna may have limited his sense of the human condition and led him not only to be kindly, but also distant from the presence of evil and suffering. Erich's allegiance to musical beauty and the language of musical Romanticism was much like the defiance of a child against the corruption and conceits of adulthood. There was no reason to stop dreaming and turn toward the actual horror.

Korngold's transition from a sheltered, idealized Vienna, understood as a magical world of beauty and grace rooted in the nineteenth century, to Hollywood, the twentieth-century capital of the fabrication of illusions and dreams about life and the world, was seamless, for it matched his talent and sensibilities. By comparison to other exiles, his life in America was charmed. Korngold's capacity to share his gift of forgetfulness with the world that witnessed Auschwitz and Hiroshima took the form of a spellbinding music of love, fantasy, and adventure. He wrote music that sought to encourage hope. His achievement was unique; and perhaps, now that his music has returned to favor, Korngold's special place in history will be to inspire, against all odds, through optimism and transparent musical beauty, the best in human nature.

NOTES

I would like to thank Christopher H. Gibbs, Daniel Goldmark, Kevin C. Karnes, Irene Zedlacher, and Peter Filkins for their advice and help.

1. The first two biographies were Rudolf St. Hoffmann, *Erich Wolfgang Korngold* (Vienna: Verlag Stein, 1922); and Luzi Korngold, *Erich Wolfgang Korngold: Ein Lebensbild* (Vienna: Verlag Elisabeth Lafite, and Österreichischer Bundesverlag für Unterricht, Wissenschaft und Kunst, 1967). The pathbreaking appreciation of Korngold was Brendan G. Carroll's *The Last Prodigy: A Biography of Erich Wolfgang Korngold* (Portland, OR: Amadeus Press, 1997). His advocacy has been indispensable to the Korngold revival. Other recent books include Jessica Duchen, *Erich Wolfgang Korngold* (London: Phaidon, 1996); and Guy Wagner, *Korngold: Musik ist Musik* (Berlin: Matthes & Seitz, 2002). This latter volume contains the most accurate biographical information, particularly on the matter of Erich's older brother. Of importance is also the catalogue from the Vienna Jewish Museum's 2007 exhibition on the Korngolds; see Michaela Feuerstein-Presser and Michael Haas, *Die Korngolds: Klischee, Kritik und Komposition* (Vienna: Jüdisches Museum der Stadt Wien, 2007). On the early Korngold, see Ute Jung-Kaiser and Annette Simonis, eds., *Erich Wolfgang Korngold, "der kleine Mozart": Das Frühwerk eines Genies zwischen Tradition und Fortschritt* (Hildesheim: Georg Olms, 2017). Biographical information is drawn from these volumes.

2. The best sources for understanding Julius Korngold's views and status in Vienna are Julius Korngold, *Deutsches Opernschaffen der Gegenwart: Kritische Aufsätze* (Vienna: Nikola Verlag, 1922), his *Die romanische Oper der Gegenwart* (Vienna: Nikola Verlag, 1922), and his memoir *Die Korngolds in Wien* (Zurich: M&T Verlag, 1991). See also David Brodbeck's essay on Korngold father and son in this volume.

3. Richard Strauss and Hugo von Hofmannsthal, *Briefwechsel* (Zurich: Atlantis, 1978), 337.

4. The review is excerpted in part in Luzi Korngold, *Erich Wolfgang Korngold*, 104–6. On Bekker, see Christopher Hailey, *Franz Schreker (1878–1934): Eine kulturhistorische Biographie*, trans. Caroline Schneider-Kliemt and Volkmar Putz (Vienna: Böhlau, 2018); and Julius Korngold's hostile remarks in his memoir *Die Korngolds in Wien*.

5. Arthur Seidl, *Neuzeitliche Tondichter und zeitgenössische Tonkünstler: Gesammelte Aufsätze, Studien und Skizzen* (Regensburg: Gustave Bosse, 1926), 245–46.

6. Siegfried Kracauer, "Über neue Musik," *23: Eine Wiener Musikzeitschrift* 31–33 (September 15, 1937): 31–35.

7. Theodor Adorno and Ernst Krenek, *Briefwechsel* (Frankfurt: Suhrkamp, 1974), 188.

8. Ibid.

9. Wagner, *Korngold: Musik ist Musik*, 435–36.

10. Susan Gillespie, ed. and trans., *The Challenge of Surrealism: The Correspondence of Theodor W. Adorno and Elisabeth Lenk* (Minneapolis: University of Minnesota Press, 2015), 56.

11. Theodor W. Adorno, "Jene Zwanziger Jahre" (Those Twenties), in *Gesammelte Schriften*, vol. 10/2, ed. Rolf Tiedemann (Frankfurt: Suhrkamp, 2003), 506.

12. Theodor W. Adorno, "Ohne Leitbild: Über Tradition" (Without a Model: On Tradition), in *Gesammelte Schriften*, vol. 10/1, 320. See also Theodor W. Adorno, *"Ob nach Auschwitz noch sich leben lasse": Ein philosophisches Lesebuch*, ed. Rolf Tiedemann (Leipzig: Suhrkamp, 1997).

13. See the discussion in Stefan Müller-Doohm, *Adorno* (Malden, MA: Polity Press, 2009), 356–60.

14. T. W. Adorno, *Prismen: Kulturkritik und Gesellschaft* (Frankfurt: Suhrkamp, 1976), 214.

15. Ibid., 183–84.

16. Ibid., 181. On these issues, see Robert W. Witkin, *Adorno on Music* (New York: Routledge, 1999), 129–43; Max Paddison, *Adorno's Aesthetics of Music* (Cambridge: Cambridge

University Press, 1993), 266–76; Lucia Sziborsky, *Adornos Musikphilosophie: Genese, Konstitution, pädagogische Perspektiven* (Munich: Wilhelm Fink, 1979), 172–75 and 196–97; and Martin Shuster, *Autonomy after Auschwitz: Adorno, German Idealism, and Modernity* (Chicago: University of Chicago Press, 2014), 99–123.

17. See H. G. Adler, "Arnold Schönberg: Eine Botschaft an die Nachwelt," *Literatur und Kritik* 103 (1976): 129–39. About Adler and Adorno, see Peter Filkins, *H. G. Adler: A Life in Many Worlds* (New York: Oxford University Press, 2019), 245–52 and 326–28.

18. Quoted in Carroll, *The Last Prodigy*, 348.

19. Margaret Kennedy, *The Constant Nymph* (New York: Doubleday 1924). There were two previous film adaptations, in 1928 and 1933.

20. Leo Schrade, *Tragedy in the Art of Music* (Cambridge, MA: Harvard University Press, 1964), 17.

21. Ibid., 129.

22. Thomas Mann, "Germany and the Germans (1945)," in Roger Allen, *Wilhelm Furtwängler: Art and the Politics of the Unpolitical* (Woodbridge: Boydell 2018), 240–41. The full text of the essay is reprinted as an appendix.

23. Ibid.

24. Korngold, quoted in Duchen, *Erich Wolfgang Korngold*, 179.

25. See, for example, Martina Nussbaumer's discussion of the construct in her *Musikstadt Wien: Die Konstruktion eines Images* (Freiburg: Rombach, 2007).

26. See Wagner, *Korngold: Musik ist Musik*, 39–56; and Ute Jung-Kaiser, "Korngolds Ballettpantomine *Der Schneemann* (1908)—Das vielverschprechende Werk eines 'Wunderkindes,'" in Jung–Kaiser and Simonis, *Erich Wolfgang Korngold, "der kleine Mozart,"* 73–80.

27. Hoffmann, *Erich Wolfgang Korngold*, 121–25.

28. Ibid., 124.

29. Oswald Spengler, *The Decline of the West*, trans. Charles Francis Atkinson, 2 vols. (London: George Allen & Unwin Ltd., 1918). See 183–294, vol. 1, particularly 191, 231–31, 291–94. The original German version was published as *Der Untergang des Abendlandes: Umrisse einer Morphologie der Weltgeschichte*. See Thomas Mann's 1922 "Über die Lehre Spenglers," in *Essays*, vol. 3: *Musik und Philosophie*, ed. Hermann Kurzke (Frankfurt: Fischer, 1978), 148–49; and Schoenberg, "Spengler nach dem Untergang," in *Prismen*, 74–81.

30. Hoffmann, *Erich Wolfgang Korngold*, 122. See also the excellent analysis in Arne Stollberg, "'Wirkung ohne Ursache' oder 'Opera pur'? Erich Wolfgang Korngolds *Die tote Stadt* hinter den Klischees ihrer Rezeption," in Jung–Kaiser and Simonis, *Erich Wolfgang Korngold, "der kleine Mozart,"* 173–78; also Giselher Schubert, "Zur Einschätzung und Deutung des musikalischen Fortschrittsdenken in der Musikkultur der Weimarer Republik," in *Musikkultur in der Weimarer Republik*, ed. Wolfgang Rathert and Giselher Schubert (Mainz: Schott, 2001), 54–65.

31. On Schoenberg, in this regard, see Klara Moricz, *Jewish Identities: Nationalism, Racism, and Utopianism in Twentieth-Century Music* (Berkeley: University of California Press, 2008), 201–21.

32. Roswitha Schlötterer, ed., *Richard Strauss–Max von Schillings: Ein Briefwechsel* (Pfaffenhofen: Ludwig, 1987), 204

33. Ibid., 204–5.

34. Ibid., 205.

35. "Mona Lisa," in Julius Korngold, *Deutsches Opernschaffen*, 356–67.

36. See Günter Brosche, ed., *Richard Strauss–Franz Schalk: Ein Briefwechsel* (Tutzing: Schneider, 1983), 63, 72, 174, 282–83. Strauss certainly resented the treatment he received from Julius Korngold, as he confessed to Stefan Zweig in August of 1932. In *Strauss–Zweig: Briefwechsel* (Frankfurt: Fischer, 1957), 33.

37. Ibid., 164.

38. Ibid., 66–83. See also Michael Charry, *George Szell: A Life of Music* (Urbana: University of Illinois Press, 2011), esp. chap. 1, "The New Mozart," 3–22.

39. Ibid., 7. See also Marcia Hansen Kraus, *George Szell's Reign* (Urbana: University of Illinois Press, 2017), 1–5.

40. For a recording, see *Szell, Heger, Bülow, Weingartner: Original Music by Legendary Conductors*, National Philharmonic of Lithuania, cond. Leon Botstein, CD, Arabesque (2004).

41. *Strauss–Schalk: Ein Briefwechsel*, 224–25.

42. Ibid., 282–83.

43. In Richard Strauss, *Betrachtungen und Erinnerungen* (Zurich: Atlantis, 1981), 72–74.

44. See Michael Walter, *Richard Strauss und seine Zeit* (Laaber: Laaber Verlag, 2000), 351–52, see also 78–83.

45. Strauss and Hofmannsthal, *Briefwechsel*, 343–48, 358–60, and throughout their discussions on the opera, 519–56.

46. *Strauss–Schalk: Ein Briefwechsel*, 208, 342.

47. Walter, *Richard Strauss und seine Zeit*, 351–52. See also *Strauss–Schalk: Ein Briefwechsel*, 104; and Walter Werbeck, "Revolution und Musik: Richard Strauss und die Weimarer Republik," in Rathert and Schubert, eds., *Musikkultur in der Weimarer Republik*, 66–81.

48. As has been observed, in Korngold's 1938 *Robin Hood* score, evocations of the operetta are audible, including a borrowing from Leo Fall, and a sequence that earned the nickname "Robin Hood in the Vienna Woods."

49. Hermann Broch, *Hugo von Hofmannsthal and His Time: The European Imagination, 1860–1920*, ed., trans., and introduced by Michael P. Steinberg (Chicago: University of Chicago Press, 1984), 60–61.

50. Adolf Loos "Ornament und Verbrechen," in *Sämtliche Schriften*, vol. 1 (Vienna: Herold, 1962), 276–87; see also Ernst Krenek "Erinnerung an Karl Kraus," *23: Eine Wiener Musikzeitschrift* 28–29 (November 10, 1936): 1–14.

51. See Schoenberg's published and unpublished essays and aphorisms from before 1918 in Arnold Schönberg, *"Stile herrschen, Gedanken siegen,"* in *Ausgewählte Schriften*, ed. Anna Maria Morazzoni (Mainz: Schott, 2007).

52. Julius Korngold, *Atonale Götzendämmerung: Kritische Beiträge zur Geschichte der Neumusikisms*, unpublished proofs in the Österreichische Nationalbibliothek (Austrian National Library) (Vienna: Doblinger), 114, 150–52, 166.

53. Ibid., 75–83.

54. Ibid., 10.

55. Ibid., 45.

56. Ernst Krenek, "Karl Kraus und Arnold Schoenberg," *23: Eine Wiener Musikzeitschrift* 15–16 (October 25, 1934): 3–4.

57. *23: Eine Wiener Musikzeitschrift*: Nr. 1 (January 1932): 4–5; Nr. 3 (March 23, 1932): 16; Nr. 13 (November 1, 1933): 19–23.

58. Ibid., Nr. 4 (May 1, 1932): 11.

59. Ibid., Nr. 7 (December 23, 1932): 10–16.

60. Ibid., 24.

61. Julius Korngold, *Die Korngolds in Wien*, 93–95.

62. Julius Korngold, *Atonale Götzendämmerung*, 248–49.

63. Julius Korngold, *Die Korngolds in Wien*, 95.

64. Letter of 1 April 1933, published in *23: Eine Wiener Musikzeitschrift* 11–12 (1933): 22.

65. Erich Korngold to Joseph Marx, 15 October 1956, in Lis Malina, ed., *Dear Papa, How Is You? Das Leben Erich Wolfgang Korngolds in Briefen* (Vienna: Mandelbaum Verlag, 2017), 275.

66. Quoted in Carroll, *The Last Prodigy*, 329.

67. Ibid.

68. See Georg Knepler, *Karl Kraus liest Offenbach: Erinnerungen, Kommentare, Dokumentation* (Vienna: Löcker, 1984).
69. Luzi Korngold, *Erich Wolfgang Korngold*, 90.
70. Luzi Korngold to Marx, in Malina, *Dear Papa: How Is You?*, 278.
71. For an account of the political and social context of the Vienna operetta world in the late 1920s and 1930s, see Gerhard Oberkofler and Manfred Mugrauer, *Georg Knepler: Musikwissenschaftler und marxistische Denker aus Wien* (Innsbruck: Studien Verlag, 2014), 31–44.
72. Erich Wolfgang Korngold, "Sonett für Wien," Op. 41 (Mainz: Schott, 1957) 1–3.
73. See Klaus Taschwer, *Hochburg des Antisemitismus: Der Niedergang der Universität Wien im 20. Jahrhundert* (Vienna: Czernin, 2015), esp. chap. 2.
74. Quoted in Martin Schüssler, *Karol Rathaus* (Frankfurt: Peter Lang, 2000), 49. See also Susanne Rode-Breymann, "'Alte' und 'Neue' Musikmetropolen: Wien und Berlin vor und nach 1918," in Rathert and Schubert, eds., *Musikkultur in der Weimarer Republik*, 42–53.
75. Hugo Bettauer, *Die Stadt ohne Juden: Ein Roman von Übermorgen* (Vienna: Gloriette, 1922).
76. My thanks to Bernhard Steiner for providing copies of the proofs for Julius Korngold's *Atonale Götzendämmerung*.
77. See, for example, 75–82 and 265–270 in ibid. There are bizarre errors in the page proofs; the most egregious, the wrong first name for Josef Suk, whom Korngold calls Franz Suk.
78. Ibid., 24–25, 35, 200. For Julius Korngold's praise of Puccini, see his reviews from 1907 to 1920 in *Die romanische Oper der Gegenwart*, 56–97.
79. See Julius Korngold's review of *Das Spielwerk und die Prinzessin* from 1913 in *Deutsches Opernschaffen*, 308–31; and *Die Korngolds in Wien*, 169 and 262.
80. Julius Korngold, "Die Gezeichneten" (1920), in *Deutsches Opernschaffen*, 318–30.
81. On Hindemith's *Nusch-Nuschi*, see Julius Korngold, *Atonale Götzendämmerung*, 149.
82. Ibid., 277–81.
83. Ibid., 57–60 and 190–91.
84. Ibid., 200–201 and 268–71.
85. Ibid., 177 and 224.
86. See Marc D. Moskovitz, *Alexander Zemlinsky: A Lyric Symphony* (Woodbridge, UK: Boydell Press, 2010), 197–98.
87. Julius Korngold, *Atonale Götzendämmerung*, 35–36 and 237–41.
88. Ibid., 74–75.
89. Ibid., 86–91.
90. Ibid., 43–57.
91. Ibid., 104–13.
92. Ibid., 122–33.
93. Ibid., 276.
94. Rudolf Ploderer, "Marx und Mahler," *23: Eine Wiener Musikzeitschrift* 11–12 (June 30, 1933): 13–18.
95. Spengler, *The Decline of the West*, 2:8.
96. Ibid., 1:191.
97. Julius Korngold, *Atonale Götzendämmerung*, 133.
98. Spengler, *The Decline of the West*, 1:291.
99. Thomas Mann "Über die Lehre Spenglers," in *Essays*, 3:148–49.
100. Alban Berg, "Was ist atonal?," *23: Eine Wiener Musikzeitschrift* 26–27 (1936): 1–11.
101. Ibid., 11.
102. See Wagner, *Korngold: Musik ist Musik*, 203–22.
103. See for example the treatment of Mendelssohn in Charles Rosen, *The Romantic Generation* (Cambridge MA: Harvard University Press, 1995).

104. See Ben Winters, *Erich Wolfgang Korngold's "The Adventures of Robin Hood"* (Lanham, MD: Scarecrow Press, 2007), 65–67.

105. Erich did, however, refer to Carl Orff's *Antigone* as a "Nazi" opera in a 1949 letter to his mother. Malina, *Dear Papa: How Is You?*, 256.

106. See Bernadette Mayrhofer and Fritz Trümpi, *Orchestrierte Vertreibung: Unerwünschte Wiener Philharmoniker—Verfolgung, Ermordung und Exil* (Vienna: Mandelbaum Verlag, 2014), for information on Burghauser and the Vienna Philharmonic under fascism. See an alternative view of Korngold's exile in Bryan Gilliam, "A Viennese Opera Composer in Hollywood: Korngold's Double Exile in America," in *Driven into Exile: The Musical Migration from Nazi Germany to the United States*, ed. Reinhold Brinkmann and Christoph Wolff (Berkeley: University of California Press, 1999), 223–42.

107. On the F-sharp Symphony, see Amy Wlodarski's essay in this volume.

108. See Leon Botstein, "Reversing the Tradition: Innovation, Modernity and Ideology in the Work and Career of Antonín Dvořák," in *Dvořák and His World*, ed. Michael Beckermann (Princeton: Princeton University Press, 1993), 44–46.

109. Theodor W. Adorno and Hanns Eisler, *Komposition für den Film* (1969), in Adorno, *Gesammelte Werke*, vol. 15 (Frankfurt: Suhrkamp, 1976), 7–146. This discussion refers to chaps. 1 and 2 in particular.

110. Ibid., 16.

Index

Note: page numbers followed by "n" indicate chapter endnotes. Page numbers in italics refer to figures and musical excerpts. Throughout the index, EWK refers to Erich Wolfgang Korngold; "Julius" and "Luzi" refer to his father and wife, respectively.

Index of Korngold's Works

Adventures of Robin Hood, The, 104, 116–17, 122–27, *123*, 207, 216–18, 247, 301, 311n48
Another Dawn, 104, 114–17, 120, 122, 247, 303
Anthony Adverse, 104, 111, 116, 121–26, 175, 207, 213, 223, 227, 303
Between Two Worlds, 116–17, 119–22, 125, 129n17, 303
Captain Blood, 104, 116, 123–26, 128n5, 175, 207, 211–12, 223, 227–28, 250, 303
Cello Concerto in C Major, 164n39, 167, 302–3, 307
Constant Nymph, The, 105, 113, 116, 126, 128n5, 128n8, 271–75, 300, 302
Danton, 227
Deception, 111, 113, 116, 121, 123, 126, 128n2, 164n39, 167, 273–75, 300–303
Devotion, 105, 111, 114, 116–20, *118*, 124, 125
Don Quixote pieces, 4, 26
Dramatic Overture, 196
Escape Me Never, 111, 113, 114, 117, 120, 122, 126, 128n5
Give Us This Night, 104, 112, 207–11, 223, 231n1
Gold cantata, 3–4, 29, 34n61, 98
Green Pastures, The, 125, 213–14, 247
Hearts Divided, 247
Juarez, 104, 111, 114, 122–23, 128n8, 128n11, 176, 247, 301, 303
Die Kathrin, 63n7; EWK's focus on, 202; Julius on, 237, 239, 240; New Opera Co. and, 103, 105; orchestral tone color in, 120; postwar Vienna and, 168; premiere of, 185n11, 207, 214–16, 236; scheduled premiere and anti-Semitic reviews, 92–93; work on, 207, 208, 210, 213, 227
Kings Row: atonality and, 148–50, *149*; Bellamann and, 134–39; cues number, titles, and orchestrators, 159–61; disability, representation of, 144–45, 155–57; in letters, 105; masculinity in, 157–58; in *The Masterson Inheritance* (radio), 111; meaning of title, 131; melodrama and horror genres and, 143–44; Menzies as production designer, 145; overview, 131–34; Parris-Drake motive, 150–55, *151–57*; peculiar moments and deep focus, 145–48, *146–48*; plot of novel and of film, 140–43; Randy motive, *152*, 153; scoring and thematic technique, 122, 125; sound world of, 116, 117, 120; *Star Wars* and, 129n27, 132, *133*, 162n5, 162nn2–3; Symphony in F and, 303; triumph of good over evil, 301–2
Lieder: Opus 18, 49–50, 117; Opp. 29 and 31, 99, 105; work on, 237
"Love for Love," 117, 129n18
Mad Empress, The, 114, 128n11
Magic Fire, 112, 276
Midsummer Night's Dream, A, 93, 104, 123, 208, 223, 249, 276, 301
Much Ado about Nothing suite, 95–96
Of Human Bondage, 111, 116, 117, 120–21, *124*, 124–26

• 315 •

operetta arrangements/adaptations: *Die Fledermaus/Rosalinda*, 223, 234, 283; *Die geschiedene Frau*, 92; *Die schoene Helena (La belle Hélène)*, 104, 283
Passacaglia in C Minor, 33n57
Passover Psalm, A, 90, 91, 95, 105
Piano Sonata No. 1 in D Minor, 4, 7, 26–27, 194, 198n5
Piano Sonata No. 2 in E Major, 22, 196
Piano Sonata No. 3 in C Major, 216
Piano Trio in D Major, 13–16, 196
"Pierrot Lied," 82–83
Prayer, 90, 91, 95
Prince and the Pauper, The, 104, 116, 125, 126, 129n27, 247, 303
Private Lives of Elizabeth and Essex, The, 104, 111, 113, 116–17, 121–22, 125, 128n8, 175, 247, 301, 303
Der Ring des Polykrates, 117, 233, 265–66
Rose of the Rancho, The, 112
Rübezahl, 229
Schauspiel-Ouvertüre, 22
Der Schneemann (The Snowman), 4, 21, 26–29, 33n58, 194, 196, 203, 225
Sea Hawk, The, 104, 111–16, *115*, 121, 125–27, 128n2, 301, 303
Sea Wolf, The, 104, 117, 120, 125
Sieben Märchenbilder (Seven Fairy-Tale Images), 196
Sinfonietta in B Major, 22–25, 75
Sonata in G Major for Piano and Violin, 22
songs. *See* Lieder
"Sonnet for Vienna (In Memoriam), A," 292
Straussiana for Orchestra, 292
String Quartet No. 1 in A Major, 51
String Quartet No. 3 in D Major, 237, 302–3
Sursum corda, 123, 218, 268; Strauss and, 45
Symphonic Serenade in B-flat Major, 175
Symphony in F-sharp: Adagio, 175, 177–79; ambition of, 307; borrowing from film music, 303; dedication to Roosevelt, 168, 169; EWK's commentary about, 99; film material integrated into, 175; Finale, 179–83, *180*, *181*; modernism and, 184, 189n93; neo-Romanticism, postwar European musical culture, and, 169; overview, 174–75; postwar Vienna, EWK's return, and, 172–74; premiere of, 25; Scherzo, 175–76, *177*, 179; Viennese premiere, 168–69; work on, 237

Symphony No. 2 in F Major (incomplete), 256
Die tote Stadt, 117, 203; Arvey on, 225; Bekker and Seidl on, 266; Bruges and acoustic space in, 70, 75–83; *Heliane* and, 49; interwar popularity of, 72; Landau on, 104; libretto for, 77, 86n35; mentioned in Gmunden, 188n54; modern tensions in, 70; operetta work and, 283–84; orchestration, 80–81; postwar Vienna revival (cancelled), 168; premieres, 233, 281–82; revival hopes, 302; Rodenbach's *Bruges-la-morte*, 72–77, *76*; Schillings on, 279–80; stage design, 77, *78*; Strauss and, 45
variations on a theme by Zemlinsky, 26, 194
Vier kleine Karikaturen für Kinder, 39, 117
Violanta, 49, 203, 225, 233
Violin Concerto in D Major, 99, 167, 175, 179, 184, 237, 290, 302–3, 306–7
Walzer aus Wien, 301
Das Wunder der Heliane, 43, 44, 48–54, 117, 203; acoustic space in, 83; anti-Semitism in reviews of, 93; compared to Strauss, 283; decision to compose, 41; influences and reception, 43–52; *Jonny spielt auf* compared to, 37–38, 60–61, 287; Kaltneker and, 292; Nazis and, 92; opera genre in 1920s and, 37–38; plot and themes, 41–43; premiere, 233; tonality, atonality, and, 47, 150

Index of Names and Subjects

Academy Award, 247
acoustic space: Brno vs. Vienna and, 67; interiority, exteriority, and, 71–72, 79; in *Jonny spielt auf*, 83; orchestration and, 80–81; politicization of sound in culture, 84; Rodenbach's portraits of Bruges and, 72–75, *78*; Simmel on urban modernity, psychology, and, 70–71; in *Die tote Stadt*, 70, 75–83; urban soundscape of modernity in Vienna, 67–70; in *Das Wunder der Heliane*, 83
Adler, H. G., 270

Index

Adorno, Theodor, 121, 186n29, 264, 268–70; *Komposition für den Film*, 304–6
Anderson, Marian, 256
Anschluss, 236, 241–43, 245n19, 289, 293
Anthony, Elizabeth, 171
anti-Semitism: Austrian national identity and, 91; bans on EWK's music, 168, 185n10, 234; elements of critique of Jewish composers, 277–78; EWK's early reception and, 11–13; in German culture, EWK's refusal to acknowledge, 276; Hoffman's defense of EWK, 277–79; Julius on, 239, 242–43; responses to EWK, 92–93; Schillings, Strauss, and, 279–81; Schuschnigg and, 235; of Wagner, 276, 277, 279–80. *See also* Jewish identity and Jewishness
Arnaud, Leo, 129n17
Arvey, Verna, 223–30
atonality. *See* tonality and atonality
Auschwitz, art after, 269–71
Austrofascists, 289, 292, 298, 302

Bach, David Josef, 15–16, 23
Bach, Johann Sebastian, 193, 226, 295, 297; *High Mass in B Minor*, 256
Bahr, Hermann, 13
Balzac, Honoré de, 275
Bartók, Béla, 294, 297, 304, 307; *Concerto for Orchestra*, 164n39; *Vier kleine Karikaturen für Kinder* and, 39
Batka, Richard, 18–19, 21–22
Beckett, Samuel, 269, 270
Beer, August, 6
Beethoven, Ludwig van, 193, 196, 226, 258, 288, 295, 300, 305; *Eroica*, 202; *Missa Solemnis*, 256; Vienna and, 284
Bekker, Paul, 59–60, 63n3, 266, 278, 279
Bellamann, Henry, 131, 135–39, *136*, 163n12, 163n25
bells and acoustic space, 81–82
Berg, Alban, 57–58, 139, 287, 289, 293–94, 300, 306–7; Violin Concerto, 186n29; *Wozzeck*, 202–3, 298, 303
Berg, Christian, 73
Berlioz, Hector, 303; *Requiem*, 257
Bernstein, Leonard, 264
Bettauer, Hugo, 293
Bienerth, Baroness Anka von, 7
Bizet, Georges, 266

Blanke, Henry, 128n11
Blitzstein, Marc, 104, 105
Bloch, Ernst, 97, 98, 99, 103, 294
Bohlman, Philip V., 171, 187n35
Böhm, Karl, 282
Bordwell, David, 145
Botstein, Leon, 90
Bradford, James, 128n11
Brahms, Johannes, 258, 288, 297, 298, 300; *German Requiem*, 256–57
Brecht, Bertholt, 95
Brett-Smith, Richard, 187n33
Brno (Brünn), Moravia, 31n26, 67
Broadway Melodies Pop Concert (1945), 97
Broch, Hermann, 284–86
Brown, Joe E., 223
Brown, Royal, 128n2
Bruch, Max, 226, 279
Bruckner, Anton, 178, 258, 297, 307; Ninth Symphony, 257; *Te Deum*, 257
Bruges: Rodenbach's portraits of, 72–75, *76*, *77*; in *Die tote Stadt*, 75–83; tourism in, 73
Brunner, Fritz, 7
Brunner, Karl Heinrich, 172, 187n41
Bucharoff, Simon, 114
Burghauser, Hugo, 302
Busoni, Ferruccio, 60
Byrns, Harold, 168
Byron, Lord, 275

Cage, John, 25
Cagney, James, 103, 105, 179, 223
Cairol, Eduard, 74–75
Calico, Joy, 177
Carbonara, Gerard, 248
Carroll, Brendan G., 32n36, 63n10, 150, 162n3, 162n5, 164n39, 169, 185n10, 185n13, 188n56, 188n67, 256
Castelnuovo-Tedesco, Mario, 97, 101; "Dances of King David," 102
Castiglioni, Iphi, 217
Chagall, Marc, 97
Cheng, William, 69
Chopin, Frédéric, 258, 301
Chua, Daniel, 174
Churain, Jaro, 113
Clare, George, 67
click tracks, 249, 252n5
close synchronization, 124

INDEX

Cohan, George, 179
Composing for the Films (*Komposition für den Film*) (Eisler and Adorno), 304–6
"Composing for the Pictures" (Arvey), 223–30
Conlon, James, 102
Copland, Aaron, 104, 105, 145, 304; *Appalachian Spring*, 182
correspondence of EWK: Alfred Roller, 77, *78*; Alma Mahler, 99; Anneliese Landau, 93, 98, 99, 103–6; Jacob Sonderling, 91; Joseph Marx, 175; Julius Korngold, 100, 233–43; Ludwig Strecker, 92; Luzi Korngold, 97; maternal grandparents, 75; seized by Nazis, 30n9; unaddressed, on ruins, 175
Craig, Siobhan, 187n40
Crist, Elizabeth Bergman, 182–83

Dallapicolla, Luigi, 307
Debussy, Claude, 6, 47–49, 287, 294; *Pelléas et Mélisande*, 202–3
Decsey, Ernst, 6, 26–29, 33n54, 213
deep focus, photographic, *146*, 148
de Havilland, Olivia, 223
Dehmel, Richard, 188n66
Delius, Frederick, 47, 294
Dessau, Paul, 97
Devaré, Ulric (or De Vaere), 202, 255–56
Diabelli, Anton, 305
Diefendorf, Jeffrey, 170, 172
Dieterle, William, 223
Dollfuss, Engelbert, 235, 289
Dos Passos, John, 170
Downes, Olin, 167–68, 185n9
Downes, Stephen, 169
Duchen, Jessica, 91, 94, 95, 135
dupe system, 251
Dvořák, Antonín, 303–4

Easter Accords (April 1938), 244n7
Ebensee camp, 173, 187n48
Eckmann, Alfred, 216, 220n12
Eisler, Hanns, 121; *Komposition für den Film*, 304–6
electronic music, 120
emigration to United States, 83–84, 207, 210–11
"Entartete Musik" exhibition (Düsseldorf, 1938), 92

Erben, Karel, 304
Eshel, Amir, 183
European transnational identity, 278–79
Evans, Jane, 98
exile vs. émigré, 94–95
expressionism, 61, 145, 148, 153, 295
exteriority and interiority, 71–72, 79

Faith in Music (Devaré), 202, 255–58
Fall, Leo, 290, 311n48; *Die geschiedne Frau*, 92
fascism, aesthetics of, 298–99
"Faustian" music, 299, 306
Feld, Leo, 198n6
film scores. *See* Warner Bros. film scores; *Index of Works*
Finston, Nathaniel, 248
Fitelberg, Jerzy, 101–2
Flesch, Carl, 22
Flynn, Errol, 211, 217
Foley, Matt, 184
Forbstein, Leo, 115, 128n11, 129n13, 212, 217–18, *248*
Fraenkel, Alfred von, 239, 244n9
Fraenkel-Ehrenstein, Luise von, 244n9
Franchetti, Aldo, 123
Franklin, Peter, 87n40
Franz Joseph I, Kaiser, 196, 198n7
Freud, Sigmund, 141, 155
Friedhofer, Hugo, 113–15, 129n13, 159–61
Fuchs, Robert, 3, 29, 194, 198n4, 225
Furtwängler, Wilhelm, 92, 185n10

Gerhardt, Charles, 111–12, 134, 162n5
Gerigk, Herbert: *Lexikon der Juden in der Musik*, 92
Giger, Andreas, 185n11
Gilliam, Bryan, 93, 132–33, 149–50, 162n3, 169
Ginsburg, Robert, 180
Gleber, Anke, 85n18
Goehr, Lydia, 174–75
Goldmark, Carl, 3, 13, *14*
Goldoni, Carlo: *The Servant of Two Masters*, 105
Graf, Max, 10–11, 15, 23
Graham, Martha, 182
Gruenberg, Louis, 97, 294

Index

Haas, Michael, 89–90, 91, 94, 168–69
HaCohen, Ruth, 90
Hammerstein, Oscar II, 211, 223
Hammond, Laurens, 129n20
Handel, George Frideric, 208
Hanslick, Eduard, 3, 4, 67–68, 89, 233, 289–90, 303
Hartmann, Karl Amadaeus, 307
Hauer, Matthias, 294
Haydn, Josef, 258, 284, 295, 300, 304
Heifetz, Jascha, 99, 303
Heindorf, Ray, 114, 160, 248
Heine, Heinrich, 298
Heinsheimer, Hans, 288–89
Henry, Walter, 60
Hermand, Jost, 94–95
Herrmann, Bernard, 148
Hertzka, Emil, 7
Hindemith, Paul, 39, 139, 236, 273, 282, 287–88, 294–95; *Nusch-Nuschi*, 296
Hinton, Stephen, 236
Hirschfeld, Robert, 278, 281
Hitler, Adolf: Austria and, 209, 216, 218, 220n13, 234–36; EWK on, 99, 167; Julius on, 237–38; Landau on, 98, 103; rise to power, 92, 95, 234; Schoenberg on, 97
Hoffmann, Rudolf Stephen, 225, 264, 277–79
Hofmannsthal, Hugo von, 265–66, 279, 282–83, 284, 306–7
Holloway, Robin, 38
Holocaust, 89–90, 171–72, 268–71
Holocaust remembrance concerts, 89–90
Honegger, Arthur, 298
Hornbostel, Erich von, 6
horror film genre, 143–44
Höselberg, Schloss (Gmunden, Austria), 173, 207, 210, 213–15, 247
Howe, James Wong, 145, 151
Hubbard, Kathrin, 97, 99
Huberman, Bronislaw, 303
humor, musical, 117–18
Humperdinck, Engelbert, 6, 28
Huysmans, J. K., 72
Huyssen, Andreas, 169

Ingram, Rex, 214
interiority and exteriority, 71–72, 79

International Composers concert (Jewish Centers Association of Los Angeles, 1945), 95–97, *96*, 100
International Society for New Music, 51
interviews: "Composing for the Pictures" (Arvey), 223–30; "Notes for an Interview," 201–3
irony, comic and Romantic, 56–57
Ives, Charles, 137, 139

Janáček, Leoš, 297
jazz and jazz opera, 37, 55–60, 92, 108n25, 117, 298
Jelusich, Mirko, 245n19
Jerger, Alfred, *57*
Jewish identity and Jewishness: assimilated Jewish Community in Vienna, 13; conversion to Christianity, 281; correspondence between EWK and Anneliese Landau, 103–6; European transnational identity and, 278–79; EWK's attitudes toward, 94–101; EWK's relation to, 91–92; Holocaust remembrance concerts and "re-ghettoization of Jewish composers," 89–90; "Jewish character" vs. "Jewish in a biographical way," 101–2; Luzi and EWK's childhoods in secular Jewish households, 220n7; Viennese aesthetic culture and, 285. *See also* anti-Semitism
Joachim, Joseph, 278
Johnson, Hall, 214
Johnson, Julian, 70

Kahn, Alexander, 100
Kalbeck, Max, 8–10, 13–15, 23–25
Kallina, Anna ("Aunt Anna"), 241–42, 244n14
Kaltneker, Hans, 46, 291; *Die Heilige*, 41
Karr, Jay Miles, 138–39
Kaun, Bernhard, 114, 159
Keller, Gottfried, 198n6
Kennedy, Margaret, 271
Kerber, Erwin, 237, 238, 239, 244n4
Kern, Jerome, 104, 105–6
Keysar, Ariala, 90
Kiepura, Jan, 211, 215
Kings Row (Bellamann), 131, 140–43, 163n25

• 319 •

Kings Row (film). See *Index of Works*
"kitsch," 93
Kleiber, Carlos, 92
Kleiber, Erich, 281
Klob, Karl M., 19–22
Knöpfelmacher, Prof., 213, 216
Kohner, Robert, 220n12
Kolisch, Rudolf, 211
Kornau (Eduard Korngold), 241, 245n15
Korngold, Erich Wolfgang: aesthetic credo of, 271–76; birth of, 31n26; cartoon of, as *The Snowman*, *195*; as child prodigy, and Viennese reception, 3–29, 69, 208, 233, 265, 277; citizenship, U.S., 104, 241–42; death and funeral of, 256, 307; education, 4, 6–7, 29, 98, 225; emigration to Los Angeles, 83–84, 207, 210–11; excluded from 20th-century music histories, 132–33; as exile, 94–95, 183, 184; in film *Magic Fire*, 276; interviews, 201–3, 223–30; Jesus, comparison to, 17; last career phase of, 302–8; Luzi's biography of, 45, 75, 207–19, 264; Mendelssohn, comparison to, 277; modern urban environments and, 69; Mozart, comparison to, 3, 6, 12, 18–19, 21, 89, 208, 265, 277; "music is music," 236, 276, 303; photographs of, *5*, *40*, *43*, *224*, *235*, *248*, *257*; posthumous reputation and revival, 263–64; as prima donna at Vienna Opera, 282; "Recollections of Zemlinsky from My Years of Study," 193–97; secular Jewish childhood, 220n7; "Some Experiences in Film Music," 247–51; Vienna, idealization of, 290–93, 307; Vienna, return to, 84, 172–74, 291, 302; wedding, 208, *209*; wit of, 135. *See also* correspondence of EWK; interviews
Korngold, Ernst (son of EWK), 211, 215–19, 236–42, 247
Korngold, George "Schurli" (son of EWK), 134, 149, 162n5, 211, 213, 216–19, 239
Korngold, Hans (or Hanns) Robert (brother of EWK), 241–42, 244n14
Korngold, Josephine Witrofsky (mother of EWK), *20*, 91, *235*, 236, 244n14

Korngold, Julius (father of EWK), *20*, *235*; Arvey on, 229; in Brno/Brünn, 31n26; on Bruges, 75; death of, 25, 237; EWK as boy prodigy and, 3–4, 7–18, 21–24, 233, 265, 277; EWK's aesthetics taken from, 293; EWK's postwar career and, 169; *Heliane* and, 41, 56; in Hollywood, 236–37; Hollywood work, disapproval of, 139, 301; Jewishness and, 94, 100; *Jonny spielt auf* and, 58; Judaism and, 91; letters to EWK, 233–43; Mahler obituary, 37; marriage of EWK, reaction to, 233–34; modernism and, 51; on "new un-music," 290; parallels with Leopold Mozart, 18–19; on Schillings' *Mona Lisa*, 280; Schoenberg and, 148–49; Strauss and, 23, 45, 233–34, 280; Szell and, 281–82; *Die tote Stadt* libretto, 77, 86n35; *The Twilight of the Idols of Atonality*, 293–300; Vienna and Romanticism, defense of, 285, 287–89; Vienna soundscape and, 68–69
Korngold, Luzi (wife of EWK; born Luise von Sonnenthal): Arvey on, 223; on Bruges, 75; correspondence, 101; Devaré and, 255, 256; *Erich Wolfgang Korngold: Picture of a Life*, 45, 75, 207–19, 264; *Heliane* and, 41; Jewishness and, 97; Julius's reaction to, 233–34; in Los Angeles, 94; recollections and observations of, 92, 95, 187n54, 188n56, 202; return to Austria, 173–74, 291; secular Jewish childhood, 220n7; wedding, 208, *209*
Kosmin, Barry, 90
Koussevitzky, Serge, 213, 220n11
Kracauer, Siegfried, 267, 269
Kralik, Heinrich, 168
Kraus, Karl, 17–18, 288, 290, 293, 294
Krauthammer, Charles, 101
Krenek, Ernst, *39*, 99, 108n25, 139, 267–68, 283, 293; *Der goldene Bock*, 61; *Jonny spielt auf*, 37–38, 42, 52–61, 63n9, 83, 287, 294; *Karl V*, 61; *Leben des Orest*, 58, 61; *Pallas Athene weint*, 61
Kretzschmar, Hermann, 6, 28

Landau, Anneliese, 91, 93, 95–106
Lehar, Franz, 226

Index

Lehmann, Lotte, 203; in *Heliane*, 41
Leichtentritt, Hugo, 6
leitmotifs, 303, 305
Lenk, Elisabeth, 269
Lenya, Lotte, 186n19
Leoffler, James, 90
Leopoldskron, Austria, 215
Lessing, Gotthold Ephraim, 22, 32n45
letters. *See* correspondence of EWK
Levant, Oscar, 103, 105
Lexikon der Juden in der Musik (Stengel and Gerigk), 92
Ligeti, György, 307
Liszt, Franz, 303; *Mazeppa*, 123; *Prometheus*, 123
Loos, Adolf, 71, 286
Louise, Anita, 223
Lucas, George, 162n5

Mahler, Alma, 13, 91, 99, 193
Mahler, Gustav: Arvey on, 226; Eighth Symphony, 105; as "European" composer, 278, 279; EWK on, 258; EWK's film music and, 301; on EWK's *Gold*, 3–4; EWK's remembrance of, 98, 105, 194; EWK's Symphony in F-sharp and, 178; Fuchs and, 198n4; Jewishness and, 92, 98, 105; Julius and, 37, 233, 288, 298; Landau on, 103; *Das Lied von der Erde*, 299; noise-aversion of, 68; obituary, 37; as posthumous competition, 307; *Resurrection Symphony*, 257; revival of, 264; Strauss on, 280; Symphony No. 1, 298; "Urlicht," 98–99; Viennese aesthetic culture and, 286–87; Weingartner and, 7–8
Mann, Thomas, 275–76, 299
Mansell, James G., 72
Marsop, Paul, 6, 28
Martinů, Bohuslav, 298, 307
Marx, Joseph, 175, 265, 288, 290, 291, 297, 298
Masterson Inheritance, The (radio), 111–12, 127, 128n2
McClary, Susan, 129n21
melodrama genre, 143
Mendelssohn, Felix, 89, 99, 223, 258, 265, 277, 307; *A Midsummer Night's Dream*, 93, 123, 234, 249, 276

Menghin, Oswald, 245n19
Menzies, William Cameron, 145, 151
Meyerbeer, Giacomo, 277; *Robert le diable*, 82
Milhaud, Darius, 97
Mitropoulous, Dimitri, 184
modernism: acoustic space and, 67–68; EWK on, 202–3; EWK's sonic relationship with, 69–70; exclusion of EWK from historical narratives, 132–33; film scores and, 117, 120; *Heliane* and, 50–51; interwar period and, 266–68; Julius's Romanticism and, 288–89; melody as missing from, 203; Richard Strauss on, 201–2, 282; Symphony in F-sharp and, 184; Zemlinsky's teaching and, 194
Monteux, Pierre, 248
Mozart, Leopold, 18–19, 293
Mozart, Wolfgang Amadeus: *Bastien und Bastienne*, 18; EWK compared to, 3, 6, 12, 18–19, 21, 89, 208, 265, 277; EWK on, 105, 258; "Mozart Evening" at the Urania, 17–18; *Requiem*, 256; Vienna and, 284
Müller, Hans, *43*
Murphy, Scott, 150, 162n3, 164n40
Music and Dance in California (Rodriguez), 247–51
music spotting notes, 113, 128n5

Napoleon, 202
narrative instrumental forms, 303–4
Nazi ban on EWK's music, 168, 185n10, 234
Nedbal, Oskar, 13, 281
neoclassicism, 57–58, 62, 70
neurasthenia, 72
Nies-Berger, Edouard, 255, 256
Nikisch, Artur, 6, 28, 105
Novachord, 120–21
Novotná, Jarmila, 215, 216

Offenbach, Jacques, 266; *La belle Hélène*, 104, 283, 290
orchestration: acoustic space and, 80–81; *Dramatic Overture*, 196; EWK's instruction in, 196; of film scores, 113–14; *Kings Row*, 159–61; *Märchenbilder*, 196; *Der Schneemann* (Zemlinsky), 6–7

• 321 •

Orientalism, 125
"Over There" (Cohan), 179–83
Pachter, Henry, 184
Pahlen, Richard, 7
Parmenter, Ross, 167
pastness, 69, 74, 125
Pataky, Koloman von, 57
Patteson, Thomas, 129n21
Payer, Peter, 67
Pfefferman, Naomi, 93
Pfitzner, Hans, 266, 268, 282, 297, 300
Pfohl, Ferdinand, 6, 28, 46–48
Pick, Robert, 171
playbacks, 249–50
Ploderer, Rudolf von, 298
Pollack, Howard, 90, 101
Pollak, Egon, *43*
Powell, Dick, 223
Preminger, Otto, 239, 242, 244n9
Prokofiev, Sergei, 168, 296
Pro Musica Hebraica, 101
Proust, Marcel, 72
Puccini, Giaocomo, 105, 203, 266, 273, 295, 297, 300, 301; *Manon Lescaut*, 303; *Turandot*, 47

Raab, Leonid, 114
Rathaus, Karol, 292; Second Symphony, 295
Ravel, Maurice, 97
Reagan, Ronald, 131, 145, 164n31
"Recollections of Zemlinsky from My Years of Study" (EWK), 193–97
Reed, Carol, 170
Reger, Max, 6, 265
Reiner, Fritz, 168
Reinhardt, Max, *224*; *Danton* and, 227; death and memorial service of, 98–99; *Die Fledermaus* and, 234; Goldoni's *The Servant of Two Masters*, 105; Julius on, 240; Luzi and, 217; *Midsummer Night's Dream* and, 93, 208, 223, 249, 276, 301; on way to U.S., 215
Reinhardt Workshop for Stage, Screen and Radio, 239, 244n8
Respighi, Ottorino, 139
Réti, Rudolph, 51
Riefenstahl, Leni, 187n40
Ritter, Alexander, 45
Röbbeling, Hermann, 243, 245n19
Robert, Richard, 15–16, 23–25, 32n36

Rodenbach, Georges: *Bruges-la-morte*, 72–77, 76, 82; *Le Carilloneur*, 73–74; "Du silence," 74; *Le Règne du silence*, 74
Roder, Milan, 114, 159–61
Rodziński, Artur, 213, 220n11
Roller, Alfred, 77
Romanticism: Berg's Violin Concerto and, 186n29; Hollywood sound film and, 306; irony in *Heliane*, 56–57; Julius on, 296; Julius vs. modernists and, 288–89; Krenek and, 58, 61; postwar departure from, 264; Schoenberg on, 286. *See also* ruins
Romberg, Sigmund, 248
Rooney, Mickey, 223
Roosevelt, Franklin Delano, 168–69
Rose, Arnold, 281
Rossini, Gioachino: *Stabat Mater*, 257
Roth, Joseph, 279
Rothstein, Edward, 101
Royle, Nicholas, 73
Rózsa, Miklós, 129n27
Rubinstein, Anton: "Ocean" Symphony, 303
Ruggles, Carl, 294
ruins: Eshel on, 183; postwar Vienna and, 170–74; rubble aesthetic vs. ruin aesthetic, 186n26; Symphony in F-sharp and, 175–84; as traumatic mode of modernism, 169–70, 184

Sabatini, Rafael, 211
Sachse, Leopold, *43*
Said, Edward, 183
Saint-Saëns, Camille, 265
Salten, Felix, 13
Salzburg Festival (1938), 236, 238, 239
Schalk, Franz, 8, 11, 233–34, 280, 283, 289
Schillings, Max von, 279–80; *Mona Lisa*, 279–80
Schipa, Tito, 248
Schmidt, Franz, 198n4, 265, 297, 307
Schnabel, Artur, 22
Schnitzler, Arthur, 13
Schoeck, Othmar, 265
Schoenberg, Arnold: atonality and, 150; in Berlin and emigration to U.S., 177; "Brahms and the Progressive," 51; in California, 148–49, 211; *Deception* as reference to, 273; essay in *Music and Dance in California*, 248; as "European" composer, 278;

EWK contrasted with, 236; EWK's *Constant Nymph* and, 273; EWK's operetta arrangements and, 290; EWK's Symphony in F-sharp and, 175; EWK's *Vier kleine Karikaturen für Kinder* and, 39; formalism and, 203; German cultural heritage and, 279; *Gurrelieder*, 203, 298; Jewishness and, 91, 97, 100; Julius vs., 288, 294, 295, 298; Nazi ban on music of, 177; new vs. old sound and, 69; *Ode to Napoleon*, 275; prominence of, 263; Revisionist Zionism and, 302; on Romanticism, 286; school of, 38, 58; Society for Private Musical Performances, 51; sonic space and, 71; on Strauss, 39–40; Strauss on, 280–81; *A Survivor from Warsaw*, 99, 270; twelve-tone method, 275, 300; valued by EWK, 300; *Verklärte Nacht*, 176–77, *178*, 188n66, 203, 298; Viennese culture, criticism of, 286; Zemlinsky and, 148, 193, 194–95
Schoenberg, Gertrud, 211
Schoenberg, Nuria, 211
"Schott, Paul" (nonexistent librettist), 86n35
Schrade, Leo, 275
Schreder, Karl, 11–12
Schreker, Franz, 47, 80, 198n4, 264–66, 278, 282–83, 287, 295, 307; *Die Gezeichneten*, 295
Schubert, Franz, 196, 202, 258, 284, 287, 300; *Mass in E-flat Major*, 256; "Unfinished" Symphony, 123
Schubert, Giselher, 189n78, 189n93
Schulhoff, Erwin, 264
Schumann, Robert, 258, 301
Schuschnigg, Kurt von, 217, 220n13, 235–38, 244n6
Schwarz, Vera, *57*
Schweitzer, Albert, 256
Second Viennese School, 57–58
Seidl, Arthur, 266
Shostakovich, Dmitry, 168, 307
Shuk, Lajos, 248
Sibelius, Jean, 198n4, 298, 306, 307
Simmel, Georg: "The Metropolis and Modern Life," 70–71
Slatkin, Eleanor, 167
Society for Private Musical Performances, 51

"Some Experiences in Film Music" (EWK), 247–51
Sonderling, Jacob, 91–92, 97, 99–100
Sonnenthal, Adele, 241, 243, 245n20
Sonnenthal, Adolf Ritter von, 210
Sonnenthal, Helene "Nene" von, 215, 218, 243, 245n20
sound worlds of EWK's film scores, 116–21
Speer, Albert, 172
Spengler, Owald, 278, 298–300, 306
Spielberg, Stephen, 162n5
Sprecht, Richard, 6
Springer, Max, 42
Staatsoper (Vienna State Opera): *Die Kathrin* scheduled premiere, 207
Star Wars, 129n27, 132, 162n5, 162nn2–3
Steinberg, William (Hans Wilhelm), 100, 168, 303
Steiner, Max, 114, 132, 234, *248*, 256
Stengel, Theo: *Lexikon der Juden in der Musik*, 92
Sterne, Jonathan, 69
Sternwartestrasse house, 234, 236
Stone, Will, 73
Straus, Oscar, 13, 106
Strauss, Johann, Jr., 92, 203, 258, 288, 291–92, 301; *Eine Nacht in Venedig*, 282; *Die Fledermaus*, 223, 234, 283
Strauss, Richard: *Die ägyptische Helena*, 282–83; anti-Semitism and, 279–81; *Ariadne*, 40, 258; *Capriccio*, 274–75; *Don Quixote*, 303; *Elektra*, 40, 61, 268, 282; on EWK, 28, 280–83; EWK on, 203, 258; EWK's *Constant Nymph* and, 273–75; on EWK's *Der Schneemann*, 6; EWK's *Die tote Stadt* and, 233, 266; EWK's *Heliane* and, 43–47; on EWK's Piano Trio in D Major, 13; EWK's reverence for, 268; *Die Frau ohne Schatten*, 45, 60; *Guntram*, 46–47, 62; Hofmannsthal's letter to, 265–66; *Intermezzo*, 40, 58, 60; Jewishness and, 94; Julius and, 23, 45, 233–34, 280, 296, 297; *melodischen Einfall*, 50; on modernism, 201–2; narrative instrumental forms and, 303; Reichsmusikkammer under, 298; relationship with EWK, 44–45; *Der Rosenkavalier*, 40, 56, 117, 282; *Salome*, 40, 43–45, 150, 282; Schillings letter to, 279–80; Schoenberg on, 39–40

Stravinsky, Igor: EWK on, as ballet composer, 229; EWK's *Constant Nymph* and, 273; EWK's *Heliane* and, 47, 49; EWK's *Vier kleine Karikaturen für Kinder* and, 39; Julius on, 294, 297–98; neoclassicism and, 70; *Petrushka*, 203, 213; prominence of, 263; *The Rite of Spring*, 289, 298; on ship with Korngolds, 213; *The Soldier's Tale*, 298; *Symphony of Psalms*, 257; valued by EWK, 300
Strecker, Ludwig, 92, 174
Strecker, Willy, 174
Stumpf, Carl, 6
Suk, Josef, 294, 307
Swarthout, Gladys, 211
Swithinbank, Mick, 175, 179
Szell, George, 281–82; *Variations on an Original Theme*, 281
Szymanowski, Karol, 279, 294

Taplinger, Robert, 134–35, 139
Taruskin, Richard, 38, 60
Tauber, Richard, 203, 216
Tausig, Karl, 278
Tchaikovsky, Pyotr, 258, 303
Temianka, Henri, 96
Thimig, Helene, 101, 215, 217, 240, 244n8, 244n11
Third Man, The (Reed), 170–71
Toch, Ernst, 97, 100, 114, 248; *Der Fächer* (The Fan), 100; *The Princess and the Pea*, 100
Toluca Lake home, California, 94, 217, 236, 245n20
tonality and atonality: art after Auschwitz and, 271; Berg on, 300; *Constant Nymph* and, 273; *Heliane* and, 47, 150; Julius's *The Twilight of the Idols of Atonality*, 293–300; *Kings Row* and, 150; Schoenberg and, 150; Songs (Opus 18) and, 49–50
Toscanini, Arturo, 236, 238
23: Eine Wiener Musikzeitschrift, 288–89

Ullmann, Viktor, 264

van der Lek, Robbert, 175, 179
Vaughn Williams, Ralph, 294
Verdi, Giuseppe, 202, 295, 301; Requiem, 99, 105

Vereinigung Wiener Musikreferenten (Association of Viennese Music Critics), 16
vibraphone, 120
Vidler, Anthony, 71
Vienna: aesthetic culture, criticism and defense of, 284–90; American bombing campaigns and ruins of, 170–74, 186n19; anti-Semitic press in, 11–13; appearance-reality gap, 291; Brno vs., 67; EWK as child prodigy and, 3–13; EWK's idealization of, 290–93, 302–3, 307; EWK's temporary return to (1949), 84, 172–74, 291, 302; Hitler's invasion of, 218; Jewish circles in, 13, 94; Luzi on, 210, 214–16; reconstruction (*Neugestaltung*), 172; return to, 173–74; Symphony in F-sharp and, 176–79; urban soundscape of modernity in, 67–70
Vienna Boys' Choir, 170
Viertel, Salka, 105
Villa-Lobos, Heitor, 294

Wagner, Richard: anti-Semitism of, 276, 277, 279–80; *Deception* as reference to, 273; EWK on, 202; EWK's *Heliane* and, 47, 56; EWK's *Vier kleine Karikaturen für Kinder* and, 39; film *Magic Fire* about, 276; *Das Judenthum in der Musik*, 11; Julius on, 297; leitmotifs in, 303, 305; *Die Meistersinger von Nürnberg*, 179; neoclassicism and, 62; *Parsifal*, 258; *Ring* cycle, 179, 203, 279; Strauss and, 46; *Tristan und Isolde*, 179, 296, 299
Wallis, Hal, 115, 212, 217
Walter, Bruno, 45, 92, 168, 207, 214, 216, 238, 243, 278
Ward, Stephen Victor, 73
Warner, Jack, 115, 212, 223
Warner Brothers film scores: EWK on, in Arvey interview, 226–28; *Heliane* and, 61; in *The Masterson Inheritance* (radio), 111–12, 127, 128n2; positivity of, 301–2; reception history, 111–12; reuse of film music in EWK's postwar concert music, 175; role of music in sound film, 304; scoring and thematic technique,

121–27; significance of, 127; "Some Experiences in Film Music" (EWK), 247–51; sound world and orchestral colors, 116–21; working practices, 112–15. See also *Index of Works*
Watkins, Holly, 71
Webern, Anton von, 294
Weigl, Karl, 13
Weill, Kurt, 60, 97, 108n25, 236, 294, 302
Weingartner, Felix, 4, 7–8, 11, 22–23, 24
Wellesz, Egon, 51, 294
Werfel, Franz, 91
Wetzelsberger, Bertil, 92
Williams, John, 111, 127; *Star Wars*, 129n27, 132, 162n5, 162nn2–3; *Superman: The Movie*, 132
Willson, Meredith, 248
Winter, Ludwig, 7
Winters, Ben, 79, 94
Wiskocil, Barbara "Betti," 240, 244n12
Wittgenstein, Paul, 3
Wolf, Emil, 242, 245n14
Wolf, Hugo, 17, 19, 198n4
Wolf-Ferrari, Ermanno: *Susannens Geheimnis* (*Il secreto di Susanna*), 8
Wood, Sam, 145
Worland, Gayle, 89
World War I, 69
World War II, 264

Zeisl, Erich, 91, 95, 100
Zemlinsky, Alexander von, 9; analytical methods of, 45; EWK instructed by, 4, 6–7, 29, 98, 225; Fuchs and, 198n4; Julius's silence on, 297; as Kapellmeister, Vienna Volksoper, 198n9; *Kleider machen Leute*, 195, 198n6; music of, in EWK's Dec. 1910 performance, 13; as posthumous competition, 307; postwar neglect of, 265; Prague, departure for, 4, 196; "Recollections of Zemlinsky from My Years of Study" (EWK), 193–97; reputation as teacher, 193; revival of, 264; Schoenberg and, 148, 193, 194–95; variations on theme by, 26
Zweig, Stefan, 67, 275

Notes on the Contributors

Leon Botstein is president and Leon Levy Professor in the Arts of Bard College, author of several books, and editor of *The Compleat Brahms* (Norton, 1999) and *The Musical Quarterly*. The music director of the American Symphony Orchestra and The Orchestra Now and conductor laureate of the Jerusalem Symphony Orchestra, he has recorded works by, among others, Szymanowski, Hartmann, Bruch, Dukas, Foulds, Toch, Dohnányi, Bruckner, Chausson, Richard Strauss, Mendelssohn, Popov, Shostakovich, and Liszt. In 2018 he assumed the position of artistic director of the Grafenegg Academy in Austria.

Bryan Gilliam has been on the musicology faculty at Duke University since 1986 and, in 2004, was appointed to the Bass Society of Fellows. He serves as associate editor for *The Musical Quarterly* and on the board of advisors of the Kurt Weill Edition, and has published articles in *JAMS*, *19th-Century Music*, *Cambridge Opera Journal*, among others, and several books. His areas of research include Richard Strauss, Anton Bruckner, fin-de-siècle Vienna, music and film of the Weimar era, music and National Socialist politics, and Hollywood film music, including Korngold.

Daniel Goldmark is professor of music and director of the Center for Popular Music Studies at Case Western Reserve University. He is the series editor of the Oxford Music/Media Series, and is the author and/or editor of books on animation, film, and music, including *Tunes for 'Toons: Music and the Hollywood Cartoon* (University of California Press, 2005) and *Sounds for the Silents: Photoplay Music from the Days of Early Cinema* (Dover, 2013).

Lily E. Hirsch is visiting scholar at California State University, Bakersfield. She is the author of *A Jewish Orchestra in Nazi Germany: Musical Politics and the Berlin Jewish Culture League* (University of Michigan Press, 2010), *Music in American Crime Prevention and Punishment* (University of Michigan Press, 2012), *Anneliese's Life in Music: Nazi Germany to Émigré California* (Eastman Studies in Music, 2019), and, as co-editor, *Dislocated Memories: Jews, Music, and Postwar German Culture* (Oxford University Press, 2014), winner of the American Musicological Society's Ruth A. Solie Award.

NOTES ON THE CONTRIBUTORS

Kevin C. Karnes is professor and chair of the department of music at Emory University. His work includes the books *A Kingdom Not of This World: Wagner, the Arts, and Utopian Visions in Fin-de-Siècle Vienna* (Oxford University Press, 2013) and *Arvo Pärt's Tabula Rasa* (Oxford University Press, 2017). He also co-edited the Bard Festival volume *Brahms and His World* (rev. ed., 2009). He serves as editor of the Oxford Keynotes Series published by Oxford University Press, and as editor-in-chief of *JAMS* (the *Journal of the American Musicological Society*).

Sherry Lee is associate professor of musicology and associate dean of research at the University of Toronto Faculty of Music. A specialist in music and modernist cultures, nineteenth- and twentieth-century opera, philosophical aesthetics, and sound studies, her work appears in *JAMS*, *Cambridge Opera Journal*, *Music and Letters*, *19th-Century Music*, the *Germanic Review*, and various collected volumes including the *Oxford Handbook of Music and Disability Studies* (2016), *Music, Modern Culture, and the Critical Ear* (Routledge, 2018), and *A Companion to Adorno* (Blackwell, 2019). Her monograph *Adorno at the Opera* is forthcoming from Cambridge University Press, and with Daniel Grimley she is preparing *The Cambridge Companion to Music and Modernism*.

Neil Lerner has written widely on topics involving film music and music for other screen media including television and video games. His work appears in numerous essay collections, journals, and encyclopedias, and he has edited or co-edited four books: *Sounding Off: Theorizing Disability in Music* (Routledge, 2006), *Music in the Horror Film: Listening to Fear* (2010), *Music in Video Games: Studying Play* (2014), and *The Oxford Handbook of Music and Disability Studies* (2016). Besides editing the Routledge Music and Screen Media Series, he also served as editor of the journal *American Music*.

Sadie Menicanin is a PhD student in historical musicology at the University of Toronto. Specializing in late nineteenth- and twentieth-century music and visual culture, her research interests include musical constructions of space, Austro-German modernisms, opera staging and dramaturgy, and film music. Her dissertation examines the aesthetics and politics of gardens in Viennese music for the stage around World War I.

Ben Winters is senior lecturer in music at The Open University, UK, and has research interests in Korngold and film music. He is the author of *Erich Wolfgang Korngold's "The Adventures of Robin Hood": A Film Score*

Guide (Scarecrow Press, 2007) and *Music, Performance, and the Realities of Film* (Routledge, 2014). His recent essays on Korngold appear in *Music, Modern Culture, and the Critical Ear* (Routledge, 2018), which he co-edited; *The Cambridge Companion to Film Music* (Cambridge University Press, 2016); and *The Impact of Nazism on Twentieth-Century Music* (Böhlau Verlag, 2014). He co-edits the Ashgate Screen Music Series for Taylor & Francis.

Amy Lynn Wlodarski is the author of *George Rochberg, American Composer: Personal Trauma and Artistic Creativity* (Boydell & Brewer, 2019) and *Musical Witness and Holocaust Representation* (Cambridge University Press, 2015). Her research on postwar Jewish music and trauma, which has received national recognition from the American Musicological Society (2016) and the Society for American Music (2012), has been supported by institutions including Harvard University, the Fulbright Commission, and the National Endowment for the Humanities. She is currently associate professor of music at Dickinson College.

Charles Youmans, professor of musicology at Penn State University (University Park), works primarily on Richard Strauss and Gustav Mahler. His recent publications include *Mahler and Strauss: In Dialogue* (Indiana University Press, 2016) and nine chapters on Strauss's tone poems in the *Richard Strauss Handbuch* (Metzler/Bärenreiter, 2014). He is the editor of the forthcoming *Mahler in Context* (Cambridge University Press).

OTHER PRINCETON UNIVERSITY PRESS
VOLUMES PUBLISHED IN CONJUNCTION WITH
THE BARD MUSIC FESTIVAL

Brahms and His World
edited by Walter Frisch (1990)

Mendelssohn and His World
edited by R. Larry Todd (1991)

Richard Strauss and His World
edited by Bryan Gilliam (1992)

Dvořák and His World
edited by Michael Beckerman (1993)

Schumann and His World
edited by R. Larry Todd (1994)

Bartók and His World
edited by Peter Laki (1995)

Charles Ives and His World
edited by J. Peter Burkholder (1996)

Haydn and His World
edited by Elaine R. Sisman (1997)

Tchaikovsky and His World
edited by Leslie Kearney (1998)

Schoenberg and His World
edited by Walter Frisch (1999)

Beethoven and His World
edited by Scott Burnham and Michael P. Steinberg (2000)

Debussy and His World
edited by Jane F. Fulcher (2001)

Mahler and His World
edited by Karen Painter (2002)

Janáček and His World
edited by Michael Beckerman (2003)

Shostakovich and His World
edited by Laurel E. Fay (2004)

Aaron Copland and His World
edited by Carol J. Oja and Judith Tick (2005)

Franz Liszt and His World
edited by Christopher H. Gibbs and Dana Gooley (2006)

Edward Elgar and His World
edited by Byron Adams (2007)

Sergey Prokofiev and His World
edited by Simon Morrison (2008)

Brahms and His World (revised edition)
edited by Walter Frisch and Kevin C. Karnes (2009)

Richard Wagner and His World
edited by Thomas S. Grey (2009)

Alban Berg and His World
edited by Christopher Hailey (2010)

Jean Sibelius and His World
edited by Daniel M. Grimley (2011)

Camille Saint-Saëns and His World
edited by Jann Pasler (2012)

Stravinsky and His World
edited by Tamara Levitz (2013)

Franz Schubert and His World
edited by Christopher H. Gibbs and Morten Solvik (2014)

Carlos Chávez and His World
edited by Leonora Saavedra (2015)

Giacomo Puccini and His World
edited by Arman Schwartz and Emanuele Senici (2016)

Chopin and His World
edited by Jonathan D. Bellman and Halina Goldberg (2017)

Rimsky-Korsakov and His World
edited by Marina Frolova-Walker (2018)

GPSR Authorized Representative: Easy Access System Europe - Mustamäe tee
50, 10621 Tallinn, Estonia, gpsr.requests@easproject.com

www.ingramcontent.com/pod-product-compliance
Lightning Source LLC
Chambersburg PA
CBHW030432300426
44112CB00009B/960